ANALYZING CULTURES

Advances in Semiotics

Thomas A. Sebeok, General Editor

Analyzing Cultures

An Introduction and Handbook

MARCEL DANESI
AND
PAUL PERRON

INDIANA UNIVERSITY PRESS
Bloomington and Indianapolis

This book is a publication of

Indiana University Press
601 North Morton Street
Bloomington, Indiana 47404-3797 USA

http://www.indiana.edu/~iupress

Telephone orders   800-842-6796
Fax orders   812-855-7931
E-mail orders   iuporder@indiana.edu

The paper used in this publication meets the
minimum requirements of American National
Standard for Information Sciences—Permanence
of Paper for Printed Library Materials,
ANSI Z39.48-1984.

Manufactured in the United States of America

Library of Congress Cataloging-in-Publication Data

Danesi, Marcel, date
    Analyzing cultures : an introduction and handbook /
by Marcel Danesi and Paul Perron.
        p.   cm. — (Advances in semiotics)
    Includes bibliographical references and index.
    ISBN 0-253-33567-1 (cl : alk. paper). —
ISBN 0-253-21298-7 (pa : alk. paper)
    1. Semiotics. 2. Culture—Semiotic models.
I. Perron, Paul.   II. Title.   III. Series.
P99.D358   1999
302.2—dc21   99-28479

    3   4   5   04

Contents

PART II
THE SEMIOTIC STUDY OF CULTURE

PART III
A PRACTICAL SYNTHESIS

Introductory Remarks

Human beings the world over share one fundamental reality—they are born into, reared in, and probably cannot survive without, a *culture*. Even individuals who have decided at some point in their lives to live a hermetic existence, far removed from any society, are nonetheless bearers of skills and knowledge that they have acquired as a consequence of simply being born in a cultural ambiance. Culture sets *Homo sapiens* apart from all other species. For this reason, it is perhaps more accurate to use the term *Homo culturalis* to characterize the human species. *Homo culturalis* is above all else a meaning-seeking species, whose hunger and search for *meaning* to its existence has led it to invent myths, art, ritual, language, science, and all the other cultural phenomena that guide its search. The study of how humans search for and make meaning comes under the rubric of *semiotics*. This science studies what is perhaps the most fundamental condition of this search—the capacity for creating and using *signs* for representing the world. If there is one trait that distinguishes the human species from all others, it is precisely the role that signs play in human consciousness. These provide humans with powerful mental tools for asking questions about who they are, where they fit into the scheme of things, and why they are here.

The purpose of this book is to paint a semiotic portrait of *Homo culturalis* for students taking beginning courses in semiotics, communications, media, or culture studies. Its layout of topics is based on the organization of the first-year course in semiotics and communication theory one of the authors has been teaching at Victoria College of the University of Toronto since 1987. Together, we have composed it so that a broad audience can appreciate the fascinating and vital work going on in this relatively unknown area of inquiry, most of which is often too technical for general consumption. For this reason, both the expository style and the contents of this book are intended for beginning students, and interested readers generally, who want, or need, an overview of semiotic theory and practice. Prior technical knowledge is not necessary. We have made every attempt possible to build upon what the reader already knows intuitively about signs and culture. Nevertheless, the writing is not so diluted as to make it a popular "all-you-wanted-to-know-about-semiotics-but-were-afraid-to-ask" book. Some effort to understand the contents of each chapter on the part of the reader will be required. The more technical parts might even entail re-reading.

Since the focus of the book is practical, it can also be used as a reference volume to complement or supplement courses that deal with culture from their own perspectives, such as psychology, anthropology, sociology, and history. It is therefore designed to be both an introduction to, and/or a handbook for, the semiotic study of culture.

The plan and contents of this book have been shaped by an amalgam of suggestions and insights that we have picked up from our students. It is divided into three parts: (1) *Basic Notions and Views*, (2) *The Semiotic Study of Culture*, (3) *A Practical Synthesis*.

Part I: Basic Notions and Views (Chapters 1–3)

The three chapters in this opening part are designed to lay the theoretical groundwork for the semiotic study of culture. In chapter 1, we commence by sketching a brief historical outline of the various approaches that have characterized the study of culture inside and outside the field of semiotics proper. Then, we cast a brief glance at the theories that have been put forward to explain why and how culture may have originated, with a view towards defining culture in semiotic terms and differentiating it from such cognate notions as *society, race, ethnicity*, and a few others that are often confused with *culture*. After that, we introduce the reader to the spheres—kinship, religious, political, legal, economic, and educational—that compose the institutional orb of culture.

In chapter 2, we discuss and illustrate in a general way what a semiotic approach to culture entails. We start off by taking the reader on a rapid historical journey through the semiotic landscape, ending up with a brief consideration of the contributions made by the Swiss linguist Ferdinand de Saussure and the American logician Charles S. Peirce to the establishment of the modern-day science of signs. In the process, we will differentiate semiotics both from *communication science* and from the contemporary approach to the study of human mental functioning known as *cognitive science.* We also identify the various interdisciplinary dimensions that a modern semiotic approach to culture would enlist, for semiotic analysis is, above all else, an interdisciplinary mode of scientific inquiry. We end the chapter by discussing briefly the guiding principles of semiotic analysis.

In chapter 3, we introduce the reader to the "basics" of semiotic analysis, synthesizing for the reader what is known in this field about (1) the various ways in which *semiosis*, the innate capacity to produce and understand signs, manifests itself in human representational activities and systems; (2) the kinds of signs that characterize human semiosis; (3) the properties that signs have; (4) the ways in which signs cohere into structural systems; (5) the effects of signs on perception and thinking.

Part II: The Semiotic Study of Culture (Chapters 4–11)

Chapters 4 to 11 are designed to show the reader in practical ways how semioticians would go about identifying, documenting, and explaining the various *meaning-based* aspects of culture and human behavior.

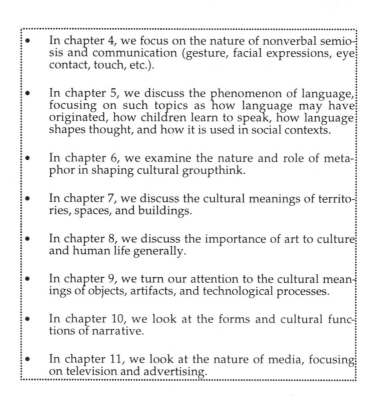

- In chapter 4, we focus on the nature of nonverbal semiosis and communication (gesture, facial expressions, eye contact, touch, etc.).

- In chapter 5, we discuss the phenomenon of language, focusing on such topics as how language may have originated, how children learn to speak, how language shapes thought, and how it is used in social contexts.

- In chapter 6, we examine the nature and role of metaphor in shaping cultural groupthink.

- In chapter 7, we discuss the cultural meanings of territories, spaces, and buildings.

- In chapter 8, we discuss the importance of art to culture and human life generally.

- In chapter 9, we turn our attention to the cultural meanings of objects, artifacts, and technological processes.

- In chapter 10, we look at the forms and cultural functions of narrative.

- In chapter 11, we look at the nature of media, focusing on television and advertising.

Part III: A Practical Synthesis (Chapter 12)

The final part consists of one chapter containing a synthesis of the main points covered on semiotic method and on the nature of culture. We start by dividing the task of semiotic analysis into *macrosemiotic* and *microsemiotic* components—illustrating practically how to carry out each type of investigation. The former is concerned, in essence, with examining the relation of the parts to the whole, i.e. of signs and texts to the constitution of a culture; the latter is concerned instead with examining how the parts glean their meanings from the whole, i.e. how the meanings of texts created or used in specific contexts are governed by embedded cultural meanings.

We warn the reader that the topics chosen for treatment, and the specific contents of each chapter, reflect our own interests and our own particular approach to semiotics. Nevertheless, since it has been used in various manuscript forms in actual classes, and has therefore been subjected to the critiques of students, we believe that this text will induce in our readers a nonpartisan, discriminating view of culture that they might not have had before reading it (as we believe it has in our own students). That alone will make the writing of this book worthwhile.

In our opinion, the value of semiotics lies in providing a discriminating screen for filtering the unconscious meanings conveyed by the culturally forged signs and images that assail us on a daily basis—images that surreptitiously, but gradually, shape our thoughts and lifestyle behaviors, as well as covertly suggesting how we can, as a species, best satisfy our innermost urges and aspirations. The semiotic "filtration process" allows us to uncover the implicit messages in those images. But we emphasize from the very outset that this is not a critical book about "the modern world." There are many works currently on the market that look at modern-day consumerist cultures trenchantly that the reader can consult, if he/she so desires. Rather, the aim of this book is to put the reader himself/herself in a better position to decipher the hidden meanings woven into the images that are produced by such cultures.

Pedagogical Features

To render this introductory survey even more useful as a classroom text or as a self-study manual, we have used a cross-reference system throughout it so as to direct the reader's attention to previous or subsequent sections that also deal with the subject matter at hand. At the end of the book, we have included a series of activities and questions for discussion for each chapter that can be taken up in class, or else used as guidelines for self-study to review a chapter's main ideas and contents.

Finally, we have included at the back:

- brief biographical sketches of some of the scholars whose ideas are discussed in the text, summarizing their relevance to the study of signs and/or culture;

- a glossary of technical terms;

- an extensive bibliography that can be scanned by anyone wishing to fill in the gaps left by our treatment.

The reader should note that we have abandoned the convention of using "he/she," "his/her," "him/her," and "himself/herself," using instead the following abbreviations:

- *s/he* for "he/she";
- *h/er* for both "his/her" and "him/her";
- *h/erself* for "himself/herself."

Acknowledgments

We would like to thank, above anyone else, our students. Their critical responses to our lectures, along with the many enthusiastic classroom discussions we have had with them over the years, have encouraged us to write this manual for a broader audience. We would like to thank our friend and colleague Pascal Michelucci who technically produced this book. A special thanks goes out to those university administrators under whom we have worked and from whom we have always received enthusiastic support. They are: Drs. Eva Kushner, Roseanne Runte, Alexandra Johnston, Brian Merrilees, and William Callahan. Finally, a special debt of gratitude is owed to Professor Thomas A. Sebeok, Professor at Indiana University and Honorary Fellow of Victoria College (University of Toronto), for the unwavering support he has always given to the study and development of the Program in Semiotics and Communication Theory at the University of Toronto. It is his intellectual influence that has shaped the study of semiotics in classrooms throughout this continent, and particularly in our own classrooms.

Marcel Danesi and Paul Perron
University of Toronto, 1999

Part I

Basic Notions and Views

A science that studies the life of signs within society is conceivable. It would be part of social psychology and consequently of general psychology; I shall call it semiology (from Greek semeion "sign"). Semiology would show what constitutes signs, what laws govern them.

Ferdinand de Saussure (1857–1913)

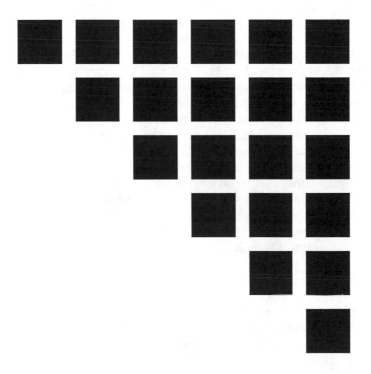

1

WHAT IS CULTURE?

Our history is written in our genes and in our actions. We can do little about the former, but virtually everything about the latter, if we are a free people.

Cavalli-Sforza and Cavalli-Sforza
(1995: xi)

1.0 PRELIMINARY REMARKS

The emergence of *Homo culturalis* onto the evolutionary scene can be traced originally to the development within the human species of an extremely large brain, averaging 1400 cc/85.4 cu. in., more than 2 million years ago. Humankind's ability and disposition to think and plan consciously, to transmit learned skills to subsequent generations knowingly, to establish social relationships in response to need, and to modify the environment creatively are the felicitous consequences of that momentous evolutionary event. The brain's great size, complexity, and slow rate of maturation, with connections among its nerve cells being added through the pre-pubescent years of life, has made it possible for *Homo culturalis*, in effect, to step outside the slow forces of biological evolution and to meet new environmental demands by means of conscious rapid adjustments, rather than by force of genetic adaptation: i.e. it has bestowed upon the human species the ability to survive through intelligent activities in a wide range of habitats and in extreme environmental conditions without further species differentiation. However, in balance, the prolonged juvenile stage of brain and skull development in relation to the time required to reach sexual maturity has exposed neonatal human beings to unparalleled risks among primates. Each new infant is born with relatively few innate traits yet with a vast number of potential behaviors, and therefore must be reared in a cultural setting so that it can achieve its biological potential. In a phrase, Culture has taken over from Nature in guaranteeing the survival of the human species and in charting its future evolution.

Evidence from the field of *paleontology*, the science of fossil interpretation, suggests that cultures have ancient origins. The fashioning of tools, the earmark of early cultures, was accomplished at least 2.5 million years ago, as was the use of gesture for communication. Gradually, planned hunting, fire-making, the weaving of cloth, and the ritualized burial of the dead became well-established characteristics of hominid groups. By about 100,000 years ago, the making of art, communication by means of language, and communally-established systems of ethics became the distinctive attributes of the first human *tribes*. Since then *culture*, in the sense of individuals living together, thinking and planning consciously, transmitting skills and systems of social relationships to each other through language, and working together to modify the environment, has become the defining attribute of the human species.

So, the question of what is culture is hardly a trivial one. To understand human nature is to unravel the *raison d'être* of culture. Although interest in culture is as old as human history, the first *scientific* definition of culture had to await the nineteenth century, when the British anthropologist Edward B. Tylor defined it in his 1871 book *Primitive Culture* as "a complex whole including knowledge, belief, art, morals, law, custom, and any other capability or habit acquired by human beings as members of society." Tylor's definition was also one of the first ever to differentiate qualitatively between *culture* and *society*. Although these terms continue to be used commonly as synonyms in many languages, in actual fact they refer to different things. Within a social collectivity, there can, and frequently does, exist more than one culture. In an opposite manner, several societies can be thought of as belonging to the same general culture—e.g. European culture, Asian culture, African culture, etc. Societies are simultaneously the geographical and historical "reifications" (manifestations) of cultures: i.e. they have existence in time and space, enfolding the *signifying* processes that shape and regulate the lives of the people who live within them.

Like other species, *Homo culturalis* has always lived in groups for protection and refuge, thus enhancing its survivability. But, as Tylor's definition implies, human societies involve much more than instinctive group behavior. The primary purpose of this text is, as a matter of fact, to highlight those aspects of human gregarious life that transcend the survival functions of other animal groupings.

The amount and diversity of scientific research that has been conducted on cultural systems since the publication of Tylor's book in 1871 have reached mind-boggling proportions. And yet, the reason culture came about in the first place remains largely an enigma to this day, even though various intriguing hypotheses about its origins and *raison d'être* have been formulated on the basis of a veritable stockpile of paleontological and archeological information. In this opening chapter, we will start our excursion into culture with a panoramic survey of those hypotheses. Needless to say, we cannot possibly go into any depth or detail here. In one chapter, all we can really do is scratch the surface of the historical record. We will therefore be selective, highlighting those ideas that we consider to be relevant to the focus of this text, even if this entails leaving out many others whose influence on the development of culture theory is hardly negligible. After a brief historical foray, we will move on to a succinct consideration of some rudimentary matters, casting a glance at what is most prominent in discussions about the origins of culture with an eye towards putting forth a working *semiotic* definition of this phenomenon that reflects the paleontological record. Finally, we will describe the principal *spheres* —kinship, religious, political, legal, economic, and educational—that constitute the institutional systems that have emerged to regulate social interaction in the human species.

As the reader may have surmised by now, we have coined the term *Homo culturalis* simply as a stylistic device. There is no evidence to suggest the existence of a species identifiable as *Homo culturalis*, separable or differentiable in evolutionary lineage from the other species of *Homo*. The term is a rhetorical figure, meant to highlight the fact that in the evolutionary heritage of human beings, culture stands out as a truly remarkable attainment.

1.1 THEORIES AND VIEWS OF CULTURE

Scientific research on all facets of culture is less than 150 years old. As mentioned, the first step to make discussions of culture more scientifically objective, rather than based on philosophical or theological opinions, was taken in the nineteenth century by the British scholar Edward B. Tylor (1832–1917), after he became interested in how other people lived while accompanying his colleague Henry Christy on a scientific journey through Mexico in 1856. As a result of this trip, Tylor wrote the first true *anthropological* study of culture in 1871, in which he examined the rituals and symbol systems of the indigenous peoples of Mexico. He then proceeded to establish the first chair in anthropology at the University of Oxford in 1884, which he himself held from 1896 to 1909. Shortly thereafter, in 1888, similar chairs and departments were founded at Harvard and Clark Universities in the United States. Their purpose was to give the scientific study of cultures academic status and autonomy.

General philosophical interest in the phenomenon of culture, however, is as old as civilization itself. It can be seen, for instance, in the written descriptions of the first travelers of the ancient world who were captivated by the behavioral diversity that they saw among the peoples they visited. From the first observations of the Greek historian Herodotus to the most recent documentations of modern-day anthropologists, those who have made it their objective to study culture have tended to do so by means of an essentially descriptive, or so-called *ethnographic*, method, i.e. by the technique of chronicling first-hand the characteristics of each culture's language, artifacts, modes of dress, rites of passage, religious and mythological systems of belief, rituals, ceremonies, and indigenous art forms.

The starting point for a historiography of culture is the work of the Greek historian Herodotus (c. 484–425 BC), who spent a large part of his life traveling through Asia, Babylon, Egypt, and Greece, noting and recording for posterity the differences he perceived (with respect to Athenian culture) in the language, dress, food, etiquette, legends, history, and rituals of the people he came across. The comparative annotations he made in his great work *History*—the Greek word for "inquiry"—constitute the first significant accounts of the cultures of virtually the entire ancient Middle East, including those of the Scythians, Medes, Persians, Assyrians, and Egyptians. Inspired by the *History*, other ancient historians, like the Roman Tacitus (c. 55–117 AD), also made it a point to describe the languages, character, manners, and geographical distribution of the peoples they visited. Their writings constitute valuable addenda to Herodotus' ethnographic commentaries.

In the medieval era, the Italian adventurer Marco Polo (c. 1254–1324) became fascinated by the customs of the people he met on his travels through China and other parts of Asia. Fortunately, he also decided to chronicle his voyages. To this day, his account—called the *Travels*—remains perhaps the most famous and influential travel book in history. With a wealth of vivid detail, Marco Polo gave medieval Europe its first glimpse into the cultures of China and other Asian countries, including Siam (Thailand), Japan, Java, Cochin, Ceylon (Sri Lanka), Tibet, India, and Burma. His book also became the source for some of the first maps of Asia made in Europe. And it helped to arouse in Christopher Columbus (1451–1506) an interest in the Orient that culminated in his exploration of America in 1492, while attempting to reach the Far East by sailing due west from Europe, as Polo had suggested. Incidentally, the all-sea route from Europe to the Far East around Africa outlined in the *Travels* was verified by the Portuguese navigator Vasco da Gama (1460?–1524) in 1497–1498.

In the fourteenth century, the Algerian scholar Ibn Khaldun (1332–1406) wrote a truly fascinating treatise on the subtle behavioral differences that existed between nomadic and city-dwelling Bedouins, in which he noted that the environment where the two groups lived was responsible for their dissimilar personalities. His work, therefore, is not only a valuable guide to the history of fourteenth-century North African cultures, but also an early blueprint for relativistic theories of culture, which hold that culture and habitat mold the individual's character and worldview. A society, he observed, was held together by the unifying force of religion, and it arose and fell according to "cultural laws" that could be empirically discovered by an observer since they reflected both a group's pattern of adaptation to habitat and the kinds of representational systems (language, rituals, etc.) it had developed over time.

After the voyages of discovery and conquest of the Americas in the late fifteenth century, there arose a heated philosophical debate in Europe on the indigenous peoples of the so-called "New World." The world was, of course, "new" to those who lived on the eastern shores of the Atlantic; it certainly was not to those who were already living there in flourishing and technologically advanced societies. Late in the sixteenth century, the French essayist Michel de Montaigne (1533–1592) tried to dispel the pejorative popular view that had arisen in Europe vis-à-vis the indigenous peoples of the Americas, arguing that it was crucial above all else to understand their cultural systems on their own terms, not in terms of European systems of ethics. But Montaigne's reasonable viewpoint had to await the eighteenth century to gain acceptance and currency. In that century, the philosopher Jean-Jacques Rousseau (1712–1778) even went so far as to call for the elimination of the vitiating influences of Western civilization. He expounded the view that European science, art, and social institutions had corrupted humankind and that the "natural" form of communal life was morally superior to the "civilized" one.

Rousseau's radical perspective was a consequence of, and a reaction to, the emerging intellectual climate of eighteenth-century Europe —characterized appropriately as the Age of Enlightenment. Impressed by Isaac Newton's (1642–1727) scientific discoveries in physics and mathematics, the thinkers of the age believed that they could also unlock the laws of thinking by the use of scientific reason. Although Enlightenment philosophers saw religion—especially Roman Catholicism —as the principal force that had enslaved the human mind in the past, most did not renounce it altogether, accepting the existence of God and of a spiritual hereafter, but rejecting most of the intricacies and rituals of Christian theology. Human aspirations, they believed, should be centered not on the next life, but rather on the means of improving earthly life. Enlightenment intellectuals reexamined and questioned all received ideas and values, exploring new ways of thinking in many different domains of knowledge. The Enlightenment marked a pivotal stage in the decline of Church influence on Western society at large and the growth of modern secularism.

Evolutionism

The Enlightenment opened the doors to the founding of the social sciences. Extremely influential in shaping the early scientific theories of cultural origins was the notion of *cultural evolutionism.* The catalyst was Charles Darwin's (1809–1882) theory of *natural selection* that he explicated in his 1858 masterpiece, *On the Origin of Species.* On one of his trips to the Galápagos Islands, a Pacific island group six hundred miles west of Ecuador, to collect data on different species, it dawned upon Darwin that the young born to any species intensely competed for survival and that those surviving to produce the next generation tended to embody favorable natural variations (however slight the advantages might be), passing these on by heredity. Therefore, he posited that each generation would improve adaptively over preceding generations, and that this gradual and continuous process was the source of the evolution of the species as a whole. Natural selection was only part of Darwin's radical theory; he also introduced the idea that all related organisms are descended from common ancestors.

The most publicized and scathing attacks on Darwin's ideas came at first not from academia but, understandably, from the religious community. The very thought that human beings could have evolved through natural processes denied, to the shocked minds of the religious people of the era, the special creation of humankind by God, placing people on the level of brute animals. Simply put, Darwin's ideas posed a serious challenge to orthodox theological doctrine. But the potency of the early religious opposition to evolutionary theory was weakened by a discovery made, ironically, by an Augustinian monk, Gregor Johann Mendel (1822–1884). Between 1856 and 1863 Mendel cultivated and tested more than 28,000 pea plants, carefully analyzing seven pairs of seed and plant characteristics. His tedious experiments showed, for instance, that if tall and dwarf peas were crossed, hybrid offspring would result that resembled the tall parent rather than being a medium-height blend. To explain this he conceived of hereditary units, now called genes, which he claimed were responsible for passing on dominant or recessive characteristics.

The final damaging blow to any religiously-motivated opposition to Darwin's theory came in 1953, nearly a century after the publication of *On the Origin of Species,* when biologists James Watson (1928–) and Francis Crick (1916–) demonstrated that the genetic fabric of all organisms is composed of two nucleic acids, deoxyribonucleic acid (DNA) and ribonucleic acid (RNA). Nucleic acid molecules contain genetic codes that dictate the manufacture of proteins, and the latter direct the biochemical pathways of development and metabolism in an organism. Watson and Crick's work showed that mutations in the position of a gene, or in the information coded in the gene, can affect the function of the protein for which the gene is responsible. Natural selection operates by favoring or suppressing a particular gene according to how strongly its protein product contributes to the reproductive success of the organism. In a phrase, the discovery of DNA and RNA verified, conclusively, that physical evolution is a matter of genetic reorganization.

While the purely biological aspects of Darwin's theory now seem unlikely to be challenged by any substantive counter-proposals or alternatives, the extension of Darwinian evolutionary theory to explain human nature and culture has, on the other hand, always been fraught with difficulties. Soon after the publication of *On the Origin of Species*, a number of intellectuals came to see culture ultimately as an extension of biological forces, a collective adaptive phenomenon that emerged, so they claimed, to enhance the survivability and progress of the human species in nonbiological ways. The British philosopher Herbert Spencer (1820–1903), for instance, described cultural institutions as outcomes of natural selection, as explainable and as classifiable as living things. The idea that gained a foothold in early theories, therefore, was that all cultures, no matter how diverse they may seem, developed according to a regular series of predictable stages reflecting a predetermined pattern built into the genetic blueprint of the human species. The American anthropologist Lewis Henry Morgan (1818–1881) epitomized this view by arguing eruditely in his 1877 book *Ancient Society* that humanity had progressed by force of physical impulse from savagery, to barbarism, to civilization.

Relativism

An early attack on cultural evolutionism was made by the German social theorist Karl Marx (1818–1883). Marx argued that new forms of culture emerged not as adaptations to genetic tendencies, but as consequences of individuals struggling to gain control over their personal and social lives. But as the nineteenth century came to a close considerable dissension developed even within the ranks of the cultural evolutionists themselves. Some reasoned that culture might have certainly enhanced human survivability and reproductive success in some ways, but in many others it had, curiously and incomprehensibly, put humankind's survival at risk—humans must be nurtured for a prolonged period of time prior to sexual maturity (known as the stage of *neoteny*), they cannot run as fast on average as other primates, they commit suicide for emotional and social reasons, and they do many other such things that would seem indeed to put in jeopardy their very survival. And yet, without culture modern human beings would have great difficulty surviving. Anthropologist Clifford Geertz (1973: 23) has perhaps best expressed the paradox of the human condition by stating wryly that without culture human beings would be "unworkable monstrosities, with few useful instincts, few recognizable sentiments, and no intellect."

At the turn of the twentieth century, attacks on cultural evolutionism from anthropological quarters were mounting steadily. The American Franz Boas (1858–1942) saw the notion that cultures resulted from natural selection as not only oblivious of human history, but also as highly fanciful, without any empirical foundations. He argued his counter-case on the basis of a large body of information that he had amassed from his extensive fieldwork on the indigenous cultures of North America. The many differences he found among aboriginal peoples led him to argue against a universal biological paradigm for culture. If anything, he retorted, the reverse was true—culture, the distinguishing trait of the human species, had become the primary "reshaper" of the biological paradigm. The view espoused by Boas came to be known as *cultural relativism*. While evolutionists saw humans as "adaptations" to the forces of natural selection, Boas saw them as "makers" of their own worlds and of themselves.

Among Boas' students at Columbia University in the 1920s and 1930s, Edward Sapir (1884–1939), Margaret Mead (1901–1978), and Ruth Benedict (1887–1948) became well-known cultural relativists in their own right. Sapir (1921) devoted his career to determining the extent to which the language of a culture shaped the thought patterns of its users. Mead (1939, 1950) sought to unravel how child-rearing practices influenced the behavior and temperament of the maturing individual. Benedict (1934) was fascinated by the fact that every culture developed its own particular canons of morality and lifestyle that largely determined the choices individuals made throughout their life cycle. From the moment of birth the customs into which an individual is born shape h/er behavior and worldview. By the time s/he can talk, s/he has become a creature of h/er culture—its habits are h/er habits, its beliefs h/er beliefs, its challenges h/er challenges.

The relativistic perspective put forward and defended by anthropologists during the first decades of the twentieth century continues, to this day, to constitute a primary approach to culture theory in American anthropology generally. But the reaction against the evolutionism of the previous century was not limited to North America. It came from European quarters as well. The Polish-born British anthropologist Bronislaw Malinowski (1884–1942) also argued with great conviction that cultures came about so that the human species could solve similar basic physical and moral problems the world over. Malinowski claimed that the signs, symbols, codes, rituals, and institutions that humans created, no matter how strange they might at first seem, had universal structural properties that allowed people everywhere to solve similar life problems. Marriage, for instance, was instituted to regulate sexual urges that could otherwise lead to overpopulation; economic institutions were founded to ensure the provision of sustenance; and so on. So, for Malinowski, culture was created by humans themselves as an external regulatory system.

The British anthropologist Alfred Radcliffe-Brown (1881–1955) similarly downplayed the evolutionist explanations of culture. He noted, for instance, that in a specific cultural context even a physical response like weeping could hardly be explained in purely biological terms. Among the Andaman Islanders, in the east Bay of Bengal, he found that it was not primarily an expression of joy or sorrow, but rather a response to social situations characterizing such meaningful events as peace-making, marriage, and the reunion of long-separated intimates. In crying together, the people renewed their ties of solidarity.

Sociobiology

Twentieth-century theories of culture, such as those put forward by Boas and Malinowski, were formulated in part as reactions against unfounded nineteenth-century evolutionist views. But evolutionism was never toppled within academia as an alternative to the relativist study of culture. On the contrary, discoveries in genetics, especially in the area of cloning, have come forward to bolster the evolutionist perspective more than ever before, as evolutionists themselves have become at the same time much more sophisticated and clever in arguing their case persuasively. Although they might appear to an outsider to be merely a matter of academic quibbling, the differences between evolutionists and relativists actually reflect a profound chasm in worldview that exists in Western society at large, and the outcome of the debate between these two camps will have a lasting effect on how future societies will develop and rationalize their ethical and moral systems. So, it is hardly a moot academic disputation.

The modern-day version of evolutionism goes under the rubric of *sociobiology*. Sociobiology combines information from the social and physical sciences to study and explain the biological and cultural bases of human behavior. The sociobiological story of evolution starts with the origin of life, defined in terms of a tiny simple organism with the capacity to reproduce itself. Next comes a more complex cell—the basis of all higher life forms including human body tissues. The next evolutionary step leads to larger multicellular organisms (flatworms, crustaceans, etc.) with the capacity to develop more complex organs like eyes and brains. The last, giant step is the emergence of the human mind.

Sociobiologists attempt to describe what caused the change from largely genetically programmed behavior to reflective thought in the human species in terms of a gene-culture *coevolution* process. This process was purportedly triggered in *Homo habilis* after this species of hominid had learned how to use the hands to make tools—*Homo habilis* was a species of human beings that existed between 1.5 and 2.0 million years ago, considered to be an ancestor of modern human beings and the earliest hominid to make tools. *Homo habilis* beings were small creatures with a human body and a brain similar to that of an ape. They lived in groups as hunter-gatherers on the savanna plains of Africa. Threatened by larger mammals, but desperately needing to catch game in order to survive, they had to learn how to act cooperatively, to think logically, and to communicate among themselves in some fashion. So, they developed social rules for hunting, food sharing, the division of labor, mating, etc. Theirs was the earliest human culture.

In this scenario, cognitive states were purportedly generated by genetic processes as humans responded to new cultural demands. As cultures became more complex, so did the human mind. Humans were forced to make choices that conferred upon them greater survival and reproductive abilities. Gene evolution gradually gave way to cultural evolution. The body's survival mechanisms were eventually replaced by the survival formats provided by culture.

The sociobiological perspective has gained widespread popularity beyond academia in part as a result of the publication of accessibly written books such as those by the contemporary British biologist Richard Dawkins—e.g. *The Selfish Gene* (1976), *The Blind Watchmaker* (1987), *River Out of Eden* (1995). With great rhetorical deftness and aplomb, Dawkins portrays cultures as collective adaptive systems that emerged in the human species to enhance its survivability and future progress by replacing the functions of genes with those of mental units that he calls *memes*—a word he coined in direct imitation of the word *genes*. Dawkins defines *memes* as replicating patterns of information (ideas, laws, clothing fashions, art works, etc.) and of behavior (marriage rites, love rituals, religious ceremonies, etc.) that people inherit directly from their cultures. Like genes, memes involve no intentionality on the part of the receiving human organism. Being part of culture, the human being takes them in unreflectively from birth, and then becomes part of a collective system that passes them on just as unreflectively to subsequent generations, allowing them to improve adaptively over preceding generations. The *memetic code* is thus responsible for cultural progress, advancement, and betterment, having become the primary agent in the human species' evolutionary thrust forward. Dawkins' clever proposal poses an obvious challenge to virtually everything that has been written in traditional philosophy, theology, and the social sciences on human nature. If Dawkins is correct, then the search for meaning to existence beyond physical survival is essentially over. Any attempt to seek metaphysical meaning to life would be explained as one of the intellectual effects of culturally inherited memes such as *soul*, *God*, and *afterlife*. To sociobiologists, these memes have evolved simply to help human beings cope with their particular form of consciousness, thus enhancing their collective survivability as a species—no more, no less.

In our opinion, Dawkins' case is, at its core, a deceptive metaphorical one. Genes can be identified and separated from organisms, and then studied, altered, and even cloned physically. That is a scientific fact. The theory of *memes*, on the other hand, is no more than Dawkins' own idea of how cultures influence behavior. He has simply cast his theory in persuasive analogical form. Only in a technological society that is being constantly exposed to the convincing discourse of evolutionary biology, to advancements in cloning and genetic engineering, is the portrayal of human ideas, information, and behavioral patterns as if they were genes a believable one. Indeed, even before Dawkins put forward his meme theory, the parallelism between ideas and genes was already firmly entrenched in the Western worldview, as can be gleaned from samples of common discourse such as the following:

- Where did you *get* that idea from?
- That idea has *spread* quickly throughout society.
- This idea has been *inherited* from previous generations.
- Many of his ideas have been *passed on* fruitfully.
- Those ideas have to be *adapted* to meet new conditions.

But in actual fact there is no empirical way to verify the reality of memes, as defined by Dawkins; they can only be talked about as if they existed. In effect, Dawkins' books have made it obvious how gullible to evolutionary discourse have modern-day views of human nature and culture become. Sociobiologists claim to investigate the biological bases of the social behaviors of animals, such as aggression, territoriality, social systems, and mate selection, seeking to understand how natural selection underlies the development of these behaviors in animals, including humans. Their view of human nature has, understandably, aroused a great deal of controversy. Opponents consider sociobiology no more than a sophisticated modern-day purveyor of nineteenth-century biological determinism and, in effect, a supporter of existing inequitable social systems. Sociobiologists dispute such charges, using their studies of diverse animal species to argue in favor of innate biological control of all animal behaviors, including human ones, such as mate choice, gestural communication, incest avoidance, personality, and cognitive traits.

The key figure behind sociobiological theory and research is the American biologist E. O. Wilson (1929–), known for his work tracing the effects of natural selection on biological communities, especially on populations of insects, and for extending the idea of natural selection to human cultures. Since the mid-1950s, Wilson has constantly maintained that the psychological capacities and social behaviors that humans manifest are genetically based and that evolutionary processes favor those that enhance reproductive success and survival. Thus, characteristics such as heroism, altruism, aggressiveness, and male dominance, for instance, should be understood as evolutionary outcomes, not in terms of historical, social, or psychic processes. Moreover, he sees the creative capacities undergirding language, art, scientific thinking, etc. as originating in the same pool of genetic responses that help the human organism solve physical problems of survival and species continuity. As he has stated rather bluntly, "no matter how far culture may take us, the genes have culture on a leash" (in Wilson and Harris 1981: 464).

But so far, all sociobiology has produced is a theory, i.e. a particular type of discourse based on analogical thinking and parallelism among species. It has not produced any empirical evidence to link the human mind and culture to natural selection. Moreover, if there is any substance to Wilson's claim that language, art, science, etc. are reflexes of the same genetic responses that have helped the human species solve physical problems of survival and continuity, then one can legitimately ask: What do such things as paintings, music compositions, marriage rites, burial rites have to do with survival or reproductive success? As Sperber (1996) cogently argues, cultural representations, unlike genes, are not just replicators that mutate randomly and survive according to their adaptiveness—the crux of meme theory. These are always transformed in their interaction with the human minds that produce and sustain them. Nadeau (1991: 194), a vociferous critic of sociobiologists, has characterized their entire theoretical apparatus as no more than a "human product of world-constructing minds." Their claims have become so credible to the modern scientific imagination, says Nadeau, because it is susceptible to any new form of persuasive pseudoscientific discourse.

Obviously captivated by the iconoclastic rhetoric of sociobiological theory, many social theorists have come under its spell. Daniel Dennett (1991, 1995), for instance, has even gone so far as to explain the Self from a purely biological perspective. For Dennett, an organism comes to grips with its particular form of consciousness through the specific neural processes that filter and structure its intake of experience. This, he suggests, allows it to organize its own particular life demands and needs in such a way as to become cognizant of its role in the surrounding world. In the human being, traditional philosophies and religions have referred to this state of mind as Selfhood. However, as Dennett maintains, what we have traditionally called the Self is really no more than a convenient or fanciful notion that aims to assign great social or religious value to what really is a result of neural functioning. But, Dennett's critics counter, how would a purely physicalist definition of Self explain the expressions of Self that are found in art works and social relations, for instance? Moreover, what kinds of evidence would need to be collected to show a causal link between Selfhood and neural processes? As many critics complain, these questions are too often skirted by sociobiological theorists, or else dismissed by them as overly sentimental.

Sociobiology is really no more than a late twentieth-century version of radical cultural evolutionism. But upon closer examination, there really is no reason to believe that sociobiologists have explained human nature. To paraphrase the French philosopher and semiotician Michel Foucault (1926–1984), human beings have, since their origins, sought to understand and define their identities and their states of consciousness. They have done so by ascribing them to Nature, human effort, or God. As others have done in the past, the sociobiologists have simply placed most of their bets on Nature.

1.2 THE SEMIOTIC PERSPECTIVE

A large segment of contemporary semiotic work on culture can be characterized as essentially relativistic in its overall perspective. This will become clear as the reader works through the remainder of this book. Suffice it to say here that culture is seen by semioticians generally as a communal system of meanings that provides the means for human beings to translate their instincts, urges, needs, and other propensities into *representational* and *communicative* structures. The primary goal of semiotic analysis is to document and investigate these structures.

In effect, the study of representation and communication is a study in how the basic metaphysical questions that haunt humans everywhere—Why are we here? Who or what put us here? What, if anything, can be done about it? Who am I?—have been formulated across the world. As Johan Huizinga (1924: 202) has eloquently put it, these questions constitute the psychic foundations of cultural systems: "In God, nothing is empty of sense…so, the conviction of a transcendental meaning in all things seeks to formulate itself." The languages, myths, narratives, rituals, art works, etc. that human beings have invented guide their search to discover answers to the above questions.

Semiotics does not attempt to answer why these questions are intrinsic to human consciousness, because it knows that such an answer is unlikely. Rather, it limits itself to a less grandiose scheme —describing the representational activities that these questions animate everywhere around the globe. The semiotic agenda is thus shaped by a search for the "representational system" behind human forms of expression. Meaning is contained in these forms (known technically as *signs*). The coherence of these forms into an over-arching system of meaning produces what we call culture.

Semiotics draws on any discipline that has a similar or parallel objective. Particularly useful to the semiotic study of culture over the last century has been the field of *psychoanalysis*, the clinical approach to human mental pathologies founded by the psychologist Sigmund Freud (1856–1939). Freud's main contribution to the study of the human mind is, arguably, his notion that human *consciousness* is only the "tip of the psychic iceberg," so to speak. Below the "tip" is the *unconscious*, the region of the human mind that he claimed contained our hidden wishes, memories, fears, feelings, and ideas that are prevented from gaining expression by the conscious part of the mind. So, they manifest themselves instead by their influence on conscious processes and, most strikingly, through dreams, works of art, and language forms. Like evolutionists, however, Freud suggested that the unconscious had a strictly biological origin and that culture was essentially a collective system that emerged to regulate and constrain unconscious sexual urges.

For this reason, the brilliant Swiss psychologist Carl Jung (1875–1961) saw Freud's interpretation of the unconscious as too narrow. Jung accepted Freud's basic idea, but he divided the unconscious instead into two regions: a *personal unconscious*, containing the feelings and thoughts developed by an individual that are directive of h/er particular life schemes, and a *collective unconscious*, containing the feelings and thoughts developed cumulatively by the species that are directive of its overall life pattern. Jung described the latter as a "receptacle" of primordial images shared by all humanity that have become such an intrinsic part of the unconscious as to be beyond reflection. So, they gain expression instead in the symbols and forms that constitute the myths, tales, tunes, rituals, and the like that are found in cultures across the world. He called these universal images *archetypes*. For instance, the phallic symbols that cultures incorporate typically into their rites of passage, that surface commonly in works of art, and that find their way into the tales that are told throughout the world, are recognized instinctively in approximately the same ways by all humans, virtually irrespective of age, because they constitute an *archetype* of male sexuality buried deeply in the collective unconscious of the species.

Jung used the example of the "trickster" as indicative of what an archetype is and how it exerts a constant influence in instinctive human thinking and acting. In every person there exists a predilection for puerile mischief. This may manifest itself, Jung argued, as a desire for frivolity, as playing devil's advocate in a discussion, as a sly craving to mock someone's success, as an urge to steal something for the sheer thrill of it, and so on. Jung also pointed to the crystallization of the trickster in dreams, fairy-tales, myths, legends, poetry, and paintings across cultures. In Western culture, for instance, the trickster surfaces as Dickens' *Artful Dodger*, as the fabled character known as *Rumpelstiltsken*, as Shakespeare's Puck in *A Midsummer Night's Dream*, and in the character assumed by many modern-day comedians. The image that the trickster evokes in all of us is a perfect example of what an archetype is.

1.3 THE ORIGINS OF CULTURE

Finding hard scientific evidence to explain why culture emerged from the course of human evolution has proved to be a monumental challenge. So, scholars have understandably resorted to speculating or reasoning inferentially about what would happen if modern human beings were somehow forced to survive without culture. The best examples of this form of inferential thinking have, actually, come not from scientists or philosophers, but from writers of fiction—Daniel Defoe's novel *Robinson Crusoe* (1719) and William Golding's *Lord of the Flies* (1954), for instance, deal with intriguing fictional "test cases" of people forced to live outside of a cultural ambiance, inferring what would happen to them because of it and how they would respond to it.

Astonishingly, two real test cases turned up unexpectedly in the 1970s, stimulating great interest on the part of scientists worldwide. In 1970, a thirteen-year-old child named Genie was found in a room where she had been living alone since the age of fourteen months (Curtiss 1977). The child could not speak, and appeared to be puzzled by some cultural forms of expression, especially by artistic and narrative forms. It took a considerable amount of instruction to get her to speak and to understand such forms. Genie made considerable progress in a relatively short period of time, but she remained incapable of reaching the levels of ability achieved effortlessly by children who have enjoyed the benefits of a normal cultural upbringing. Then, in 1976 an adolescent boy was found in the forests of Burundi in central Africa. He had been living with monkeys; he walked on his hands and feet;

and he climbed trees like an ape (Classen 1991, Candland 1993). The Burundi child, too, was without language, and like Genie experienced great difficulty in learning to speak at high levels of proficiency.

What can be inferred from such cases of so-called "feral" children? The inability of Genie and the Burundi boy to develop a full command of language has been viewed by many linguists as convincing evidence to support Eric Lenneberg's 1967 claim of a *critical period* for the acquisition of language, i.e. of a biologically-determined timetable for language acquisition that starts at birth and is completed at puberty. On the basis of a large body of clinical studies, Lenneberg had noticed that most *aphasias*—the partial or total loss of speech due to a disorder in any one of the brain's language centers—were permanent if they occurred after the age of puberty. This suggested to him that the brain lost its capacity to transfer the language functions from the left hemisphere—the seat of language—to the nonverbal right hemisphere after puberty, which it was able to do, to varying degrees, during childhood. Lenneberg concluded that there must be a biologically fixed period for the lateralization of the language functions to the verbal left hemisphere and, more importantly, that such a process was innate and activated by simple exposure to language during childhood. The Genie and Burundi boy cases seem to support this hypothesis, showing that without such exposure during the critical period, the language faculty does not develop as it normally does.

In our view, however, enlisting such abnormal cases of "noncultural development" to support one theory or the other is far too speculative. In actual fact, they have further clouded the picture. If language is indeed a special type of innate faculty that develops automatically in humans within a critical period of time by simple exposure to it during childhood, then why did Genie and the Burundi child learn to speak nonetheless after that period, albeit in a rudimentary way? Moreover, a close reading of the research findings on the two feral children indicates that their main area of difficulty was chiefly psychomotor and syntactical in nature—i.e. they had difficulty pronouncing words and putting them together into well-formed sentences. But this did not hamper their ability to understand and get across even complicated ideas through the structures and categories of language that they could use. Another polemical question these cases have raised is the following one: If culture is indeed an external (nonbiological) survival and evolutionary system that has taken over the functions of physical evolution, as sociobiologists would claim, then why did both Genie and the Burundi boy survive without a normal cultural upbringing? Any coevolution theory would have to explain such anomalies much more explicitly.

Although ascertaining *why* culture came about in the first place remains difficult, determining *when* it appeared in the human chronicle poses much less of a conundrum. Human evolution probably began with the genus *Australopithecus*, whose fossils have been discovered at a number of sites in eastern and southern Africa. Dating from more than 4 million years ago (with fragmentary remains tentatively identified from as far back as 5 million years ago), the genus seems to have become extinct about 1.5 million years ago. All the australopithecines were efficiently bipedal and therefore indisputable hominids. But their brain size was only a little larger than that of chimpanzees (about 400 to 500 cc).

By about 1.5 to 2 million years ago, the fossil evidence suggests an evolutionary split in the australopithecine line, with one variety evolving towards the genus *Homo*, and finally to modern humans, and the other developing into species that eventually became extinct. A number of skulls and jaws from this period, found in Tanzania and Kenya in eastern Africa, have been placed in the category *Homo habilis*, meaning "handy human." *Homo habilis* possessed many traits that linked it both with the earlier australopithecines and with later members of the genus *Homo*—it made tools and it had the ability to communicate in nonverbal ways, especially through gesture (Cartmill, Pilbeam, and Isaac 1986). It seems likely that this species represented the evolutionary transition between the australopithecines and later hominids.

Fossil evidence of a large-brained, small-toothed hominid, known earliest from north Kenya and dating from 1.5 to 1.6 million years ago, has been placed under the rubric of *Homo erectus*, literally, "erect human." The first part of the time span of *Homo erectus*, like that of earlier hominids, is limited to southern and eastern Africa. Later—between 700,000 and 1 million years ago—*Homo erectus* seems to have migrated into the tropical areas of the Old World, and finally, at the close of its evolution, into the temperate parts of Asia. Archeological sites dating from the time of *Homo erectus* reveal a greater sophistication in toolmaking than was found at earlier hominid sites; they also provide suggestive evidence that this species knew how to make fire, that it had developed a sophisticated mode of gestural communication, and that it planned its social activities. The brain sizes of early *Homo erectus* fossils have been measured to be not much larger than those of previous hominids, ranging from 750 to 800 cc. Later *Homo erectus* skulls, however, possess brain sizes in the range of 1100 to 1300 cc, which fall within the size variation of *Homo sapiens*.

Between 200,000 and 300,000 years ago, *Homo erectus* evolved into *Homo sapiens*. Although placed in the same genus, the early *Homo sapiens* beings were not identical in mental abilities and physical appearance to modern humans. The latter, called *Homo sapiens sapiens*, first appeared around 100,000 years ago. There is some disagreement among paleontologists as to whether the hominid fossil record shows a continuous evolutionary development from *Homo sapiens* to *Homo sapiens sapiens*. Suffice it to say here that *Homo sapiens* groups shared many similar abilities and engaged in very similar social activities —they were highly efficient at adapting to the sometimes harsh climates of Ice Age Europe, they buried their dead deliberately, with the bodies sometimes being accompanied by stone tools, animal bones, and even flowers, and they communicated with both gesture and vocal language. By 30,000 to 40,000 years ago, *Homo sapiens* had evolved into *Homo sapiens sapiens* and had developed full language and symbolic abilities.

The most likely estimate, therefore, is that the first true cultures came into existence around 100,000 years ago—a period from which the plaster casts of skulls reveal that both Neanderthal and Cro-Magnon hominids had brains of similar size to ours (Lieberman 1972, 1991). The Cro-Magnons were representatives of the species *Homo sapiens sapiens*. They lived in western and southern Europe during the last glacial age. The name "Cro-Magnon" is derived from a rock shelter of that name in the Dordogne Department in southwestern France, where skeletal remains were discovered in 1868. The physical characteristics that distinguished the Cro-Magnons from the Neanderthals were a high forehead and a well-defined chin. Artifacts attributed to the earliest period of Cro-Magnon culture demonstrate clearly that they had mastered the art of fashioning many useful instruments from stone, bone, and ivory. They made fitted clothes and decorated their bodies with ornaments of shell and bone. A number of colored paintings left on the walls of caves near their habitats provide clear evidence that their form of social life was indeed based on culture. About 10,000 years ago, they started to domesticate plants and animals, initiating an agricultural revolution that set the stage for the events in human history that eventually led to the founding of the first civilizations.

As the scientific evidence suggests, the emergence of *Homo culturalis* is a consequence of four critical evolutionary events —bipedalism, a brain enlargement unparalleled among species, an extraordinary capacity for tool-making, and the advent of the *tribe* as the main form of human collective life. But before proceeding with this "evolutionary story," we must express a caveat about portrayals of this very kind. We have drafted our evolutionary narrative on the basis of the relevant scientific facts available. We are however aware that ours is one such story among many other possible ones. We are also aware that our account of the evolutionary antecedents to culture is by far an incomplete one because it lacks any consideration of the transition from bipedalism and brain growth to tribal culture; i.e. our story does not encompass the question of why bipedal apes with large brains felt impelled at a certain point in their evolution to fashion a social order characterized by rituals, a system of ethics, language, art, and so on. Evolutionary events in themselves tell us very little about that remarkable transition. Nevertheless, any coherent discussion of cultural origins cannot ignore the evolutionary findings, even though they must be taken with the proverbial grain of salt.

Bipedalism

One of the earliest of the major hominid characteristics to have evolved, distinguishing the species *Homo* from its nearest primate relatives—the gorilla, chimpanzee, and orangutan—was *bipedalism,* an adaptation to a completely erect posture and a two-footed striding walk. Almost all other mammals stand, walk, and/or run on four limbs. Those that stand on two have quite different postures and gaits from humans—kangaroos hop on their two feet; some monkeys only on occasion walk bipedally, especially when carrying food; chimpanzees are capable of brief bipedal walks, but their usual means of locomotion is knuckle-walking, standing on their hind legs but stooping forward, resting their hands on the knuckles rather than on the palms or fingers.

So, even though forms of bipedalism are observable in other primates, they are unlike the human type: all other forms of bipedal walking involve straight or bowed spines, bent knees, grasping (prehensile) feet, and some use of the hands to bear part of the body weight during locomotion. The uniquely S-shaped spinal column of humans places the center of gravity of the body directly over the area of support provided by the feet, thus giving stability and balance in the upright position.

Tools

Fossils discovered in Africa provide evidence that hominids walked erect and had a bipedal stride even before the great increase in their brain size. Complete bipedalism freed the human hand, allowing it to become a supremely sensitive limb for precise manipulation and grasping. The most important structural detail in this refinement was the elongated human thumb, which could rotate freely for the first time and, thus, be fully opposable to the other fingers. No doubt, this development made tool making and tool use possible. Moreover, some linguists claim that the erect posture gave rise to the subsequent evolution of the physiological apparatus for speech, since it brought about the lowering and positioning of the larynx for controlled breathing. In a phrase, bipedalism, tool-making, and language were probably inter-twined in their origins (Wilson 1998).

Although other species, including some non-primate ones, are ca-pable of tool use, only in the human species did complete bipedalism free the hand sufficiently to allow it to become a supremely sensitive and precise manipulator and grasper, thus permitting proficient tool making and tool use in the species. The earliest stone tools date back to about 2.5 million years ago. By 1.5 million years ago, sites in various parts of eastern Africa contain not only many stone tools, but also ani-mal bones with scratch marks that research has shown could only have been left by human-like cutting actions. One thing is certain—only in the human species does one find the capacity to fashion a great diver-sity of tools from the raw materials found in the environment to meet virtually any need that may arise (Montagu 1983, Noble and Davidson 1996: 22-56).

Brain Growth

Shortly after becoming bipedal, the evidence suggests, the human spe-cies underwent rapid brain expansion. In the course of human evolu-tion the size of the brain has more than tripled. Modern humans have a braincase volume of between 1300 and 1500 cc. The human brain has also developed three major structural components that undergird the unique mental capacities of the species—the large dome-shaped cere-brum, the smaller somewhat spherical cerebellum, and the brainstem. The size of the brain does not determine the degree of intelligence of the individual; this appears to be determined instead by the number and type of functioning *neurons* (nerve cells) and how they are struc-turally connected with one another. And since neuronal connections are conditioned by environmental input, the most likely hypothesis is that any form of intelligence, however it is defined, is most likely a con-sequence of upbringing. Unlike the early hominid adult skulls, with their sloping foreheads and prominent jaws, the modern human skull —with biologically insignificant variations—retains a proportionately large size, in relation to the rest of the body.

The large brain of modern-day *Homo culturalis* is more than double that of early tool-makers. This great increase in brain size was achieved by the process of *neoteny*, i.e. by the prolongation of the juvenile stage of brain and skull development in neonates (newborns). As a result, human infants must go through an extended period of dependency on, and stimulation by, adults. In the absence of this close external bond in the early years of life, the development of the infant's brain would re-main incomplete.

The Tribe

Like most other species, humans have always lived in groups. Group
life enhances survivability by providing a collective form of protection
and shelter against enemies and abrupt changes in the surroundings.
But at some point in their evolutionary history—probably around
100,000 years ago—bipedal hominids had become so adept at tool-
making, communicating, and thinking in symbols that they became
consciously aware of the advantages of a group life based on a common system of representational activities. By around 30,000 to 40,000
years ago, the archeological evidence suggests, in fact, that hominid
groups became increasingly characterized by communal customs, language, and the transmission of technological knowledge to subsequent
generations. Anthropologists have designated this form of group life
tribal.

    The tribal form of social life has not disappeared from the human
story. It has left its "archetypal" influence in the human psyche. In our
view, this is the reason why the *tribe* remains the type of collectivity to
which human beings instinctively relate even in modern times. In complex city-societies, where various cultures, subcultures, countercul-
tures, and parallel cultures exist in constant competition with each
other, where the shared territory is so large that it constitutes a mere
abstraction, the tendency for individuals to relate to tribal-type groupings that exist within the larger societal context manifests itself regularly. People continue to perceive their membership in smaller groups
as more directly meaningful to their lives than allegiance to the larger
society and/or nation. This inclination towards tribalism, as Marshall
McLuhan (1911–1980) emphasized, reverberates constantly within
modern-day humans, and may be the source of the angst and sense of
alienation that many modern-day city-dwelling individuals feel, living
as they do in large, impersonal social systems.

1.4 DEFINING CULTURE

In their classic study of culture several decades ago, the anthropologists
Kroeber and Kluckholn (1963) found 150 qualitatively distinct definitions of this term scattered throughout the scientific literature. Interestingly, they found broad consensus on two points: (1) that culture is a
way of life based on some system of shared meanings; and (2) that it is
passed on from generation to generation through this very system. In
this book we will refer henceforward to this system as the *signifying
order*. For the present purposes, suffice it to say that the *signifying order*
is the aggregate of the *signs* (words, gestures, visual symbols, etc.),

codes (language, art, etc.), and *texts* (conversations, compositions, etc.) that a social group creates and utilizes in order to carry out its daily life routines and to plan its activities for the future. Each culture, no matter how technologically advanced it may be, traces its origins to an early tribal signifying order. Human *culture* can thus be defined as *a way of life based on a signifying order developed originally in a tribal context that is passed along through the signifying order from one generation to the next.*

The signifying order is what the philosopher Karl Popper (1902–1994) called a "World 3" state of knowing. Popper classified human knowing into three states, which he called "Worlds." "World 1" is a state of *sensory knowing*. This inheres in the sensory, unreflective experiences humans have of physical objects and activities, as governed by neuronal signals—electrical impulses between brain cells— transmitting messages along nerve paths that cause muscles to contract or limbs to move, and sensory systems to respond to perceptual input. "World 2" is a state of *subjective knowing*. This inheres in the subjective responses humans have to perceptual input. This is the level at which a "sense of Self" endows an individual with the ability to differentiate h/erself from the beings, objects, and events present in the world. "World 3" is a state of *communal knowing*. This inheres in the systematic form of knowing with which culture equips human beings for coping with daily life and for living together in groups.

The most crucial difference between human knowing and that of all other species can be discerned in World 3 states. There is no evidence to suggest that other species are capable of these states to the extent that humans are, if at all; i.e. it is unlikely that animals are capable of producing and understanding art, language, science, or any other World 3 form of knowing and communicating. Its capacity for and reliance upon World 3 states for daily life make *Homo culturalis* unique among species.

1.5 SOCIETY, RACE, CIVILIZATION, NATION

As mentioned, the first signifying orders were forged in tribal settings. These came about, arguably, to help tribal people regulate and safeguard the ways in which they lived, planned, and communicated. The early tribal orders thus probably emerged to satisfy the apparent need the first sentient and reflective human beings felt to preserve and transmit to subsequent generations any experiences they perceived were meaningful, any communal forms of expression they thought were useful, and any knowledge or skill they felt served some beneficial function. Archeological evidence suggests that as the members of the early tribes became more culturally sophisticated around 10,000

years ago—i.e. as their signifying orders grew in complexity to meet
increasing technological and agricultural needs—they sought larger
territories with more natural resources within which to live. This
brought about a breakdown of some of the early tribal cultures. As they
expanded, the tribes came to accept and accommodate, by necessity or
coercion, members of other tribes within their broadening habitats.
This led to what the anthropologist Desmond Morris (1969) calls the
formation of super-tribes—expanded groupings of people that came
about as a consequence of tribal expansion and tribal admixture. The
evidence suggests that the first super-tribal arrangements were established on the basis of a dominant signifying order—typically that of the
founding or conquering tribe—so that social interaction and shared
activities could unfold efficiently and routinely. The first super-tribes
date back only 5,000–6,000 years, when the first cities came onto the
scene. Given their larger territorial extension and their acceptance of
competing tribal signifying orders, these constituted true societies in
the modern sense of the word.

Society

A *society* can thus be defined as a *super-tribe*, a collectivity of individuals who, although they may not all have the same tribal origins, nevertheless participate, by and large, in the signifying order of the founding
or conquering tribe (or tribes). The establishment of a dominant signifying order makes it possible for individuals to interact practically and
habitually with each other. Unlike tribes, super-tribes can enfold more
than one signifying order. As a consequence, individuals may, and
typically do, choose to live apart—totally or partially—from the main
signifying order.

     As a concrete example, consider what people living in the modern
society known as the United States call loosely "American culture." The
signifying order that defines this culture traces its origins primarily to
the signifying order of the British people who settled in the United
States a few centuries ago. Since then, American society has also ac-
commodated and sanctioned aboriginal and other parallel cultural systems, each one entailing a different way of life, a different language, a
different system of rituals, etc. Moreover, within the dominant signifying order, diversification has come about as a consequence of the tendency of splinter groups—known as *subcultures*—to emerge within
large and impersonal societies. Thus, it is possible for an individual
living in the United States to remain apart from the dominant signifying order by espousing a parallel one or becoming a participant in a
subcultural one. But very much like tribal people, a city-dwelling individual living in America today who chooses to live apart from the

dominant signifying order will typically face social risks, such as exposure to various forms of ridicule or censure and perhaps even exclusion from participation in various institutional systems or communal activities.

Race

Human beings the world over typically classify and think of themselves as members of *races* and/or *ethnic* groups, i.e. as belonging to a group of people with whom they have a common genetic link. But racial or ethnic classifications are often ambiguous and misleading. No two human beings, not even twins, are identical. The proportions of traits, and even the kinds of traits, are distributed differently from one part of the world to another. But, as it turns out, these proportions are quantitatively negligible. Geneticists have yet to turn up a single group of people who can be distinguished from outsiders by their chromosomes. There is no genetic test or criterion that can be used to determine if one is racially or ethnically, say, Caucasian, Slavic, or Hopi. Populations are constantly in genetic contact with another. The many varieties of modern *Homo sapiens sapiens* belong to one interbreeding species, with surprisingly little genetic difference among individuals. In fact, it has been established that 99.9% of DNA sequences are common to all humans (Sagan and Druyan 1992: 415).

So, from a purely biological standpoint, human beings defy classification into types. Nevertheless, the historical record shows that from ancient times people have, for some reason or other (perhaps tribalistic in origin), always felt it necessary to classify themselves in terms of racial or ethnic categories. The Egyptians, the ancient Greeks of Homer's time, and the Greeks and Romans of classical times, for instance, left paintings and sculptures showing human beings with perceived racial differences. And most languages of the world have words referring to people in terms of physiological, anatomical, and social differences.

In the Western world, the systematic study and classification of races was a consequence of the worldwide explorations of the sixteenth and seventeenth centuries, which piqued the interest of Europeans in the peoples of other lands. A century later, the Swedish botanist Carolus Linnaeus (1707–1778) was among the first to consider categorizing the apparent varieties of human beings. But it was the German scholar Johann Friedrich Blumenbach (1752–1840) who gave the Western world its first racial typology. After examining the skulls and comparing the physical characteristics of the different peoples of the world, Blumenbach concluded that humanity had five races: Caucasians (West Asians, north Africans, and Europeans except the Finns and the Saami), Mongolians (other Asian peoples, the Finns and the Saami, and the

Inuit of America), Ethiopians (the people of Africa except those of the north), Americans (all aboriginal New World peoples except the Inuit), and Malayans (peoples of the Pacific islands).

These five divisions remained the basis of most racial classifications well into the twentieth century and continue to be commonly accepted in popular thinking even today. But population scientists now recognize the indefiniteness and arbitrariness of any such demarcations. Indeed, many individuals can be classified into more than one race or into none. All that can be said here is that the concept of *race* makes sense, if at all, only in terms of lineage: i.e. people can be said to belong to the same race if they share the same pool of ancestors. But, as it turns out, even this seemingly simple criterion is insufficient for rationalizing a truly scientific classification of humans into discrete biological groups in such a way that everybody belongs to one and only one because, except for brothers and sisters, no individuals have precisely the same array of ancestors. This is why, rather than using genetic, anatomical, or physiological traits to study human variability, anthropologists today prefer to study groups in terms of geographic or social criteria. *Race* and *ethnicity* are now viewed by social scientists fundamentally as historical or cultural notions.

Civilization

The term *civilization* implies essentially a modern society, or group of societies, with a distinctive recorded history and with common institutions (religious, political, legal, economic, educational, etc.). A civilization is, more specifically, a complex social system encompassing a mixture of tribal and super-tribal signifying orders, but marked by its own civil (city-based), rather than just tribal or religious, history. The first civilizations in the current-day Middle East, for example, came onto the scene between 5000 and 3000 BC. Sumer, Babylon, and Egypt were among the first large social groupings to encompass not only a mainstream form of culture, but also a complex diversity of peoples and languages, and to distinguish between civil and religious institutions.

Europeans became interested in the civilizations of other lands during the Enlightenment, when scholars started searching for universal patterns in the history of humanity. But their efforts were somewhat skewed by their tendency to ignore customs that they saw as irrational. In the nineteenth century, on the other hand, philosophers like Johann von Herder (1744–1803) and G. W. F. Hegel (1770–1831) viewed all cultural systems as intrinsically valid, equal, and rational in their own terms, springing from a universal propensity of human groups to make sense of the habitats in which they lived. Writing a "rational" history of any civilization, they claimed, would therefore be a futile task, given the lack of universal criteria for defining rationality.

Nation

Like other terms discussed above, *nation* is a problematic one to define. People experience national sentiments only in relation to some specific situation that they feel unites them in an abstract way—e.g. Americans tend to become *nationalistic* when American teams or soldiers are in combat in the sports arena or the military one as the case may be. But people tend typically to feel allegiance more to the city, town, or region in which they were reared or in which they reside. This is why they are quick to show loyalty to the sports teams, individual athletes, performers, etc. representing their local area (city, town, etc.) in competitions. In a very real sense, these areas are felt to be communal extensions of personal identity—in semiotic terms, they can be said to be perceived as spatial *representations* of the collective *persona*.

A remarkable case-in-point of this tendency is an event that takes place twice a year in the city of Siena. In this Tuscan city, the popular Palio horse race traces its history right back to Siena's origins as a city-state. The city is divided into *contradas*—streets within the city. A person belonging by reason of birth and/or ancestry to a *contrada* is expected to have allegiance to its totemic symbol (the caterpillar, the duck, etc.) for life. The week preceding the Palio is characterized by elaborate ceremonies and rituals within each *contrada*, ending with the blessing of the horse. Feelings of loyalty become intense, to the point that spouses belonging to different *contradas* are expected to leave their immediate family and return to their original folds for the entire week. Emotions run high during the actual horse race in the central Piazza del Campo. The winning jockey is celebrated and glorified; losing jockeys are often denigrated and, not infrequently, even attacked physically. Winning or losing the Palio is a matter of collective *contrada* pride.

Clearly, the Sienese perceive themselves, first and foremost, as belonging to a local space, the *contrada*, which is concretely understandable in terms of their life experiences, rather than to the city as a whole, let alone the Italian nation. The *contrada* is felt by the Sienese to be the critical component of identity.

Nationalism is, so to speak, an abstract extension of this type of collective persona. As such, it reflects the desire felt by people living in large and complex social systems to share values, speak a common language, and occupy a clearly bounded piece of real estate with each other. The *nation* concept can be traced to the rise in importance of the ancient city-states. This led, in turn, to the establishment of military and civil systems designed to protect them. The battles fought by armies in

the name of Egypt, Rome, and other ancient civilizations stirred the
first inklings of nationalistic patriotism.

During the Middle Ages, the cultural life of feudal Europe was
based on a common inheritance of ideas, social practices, and belief
systems transmitted through Latin, the language of the educated
classes, and a common religion, Catholic Christianity. However, with
the breakup of feudalism other communities and dynasties arose, fos-
tering new feelings of *nationality* (literally, "birth right") in order to win
support for their rule. These feelings were strengthened in various
countries during the Reformation of the sixteenth century, when the
adoption of either Catholicism or Protestantism as a national religion
became an added impetus for social cohesion on a broader scale.

The turning point in the rise of nationalism in Europe was the
French Revolution of 1789. National feeling in France until then was
centered in the monarchy. As a result of the Revolution, loyalty to the
monarch was replaced by loyalty to the *patrie* ("fatherland"). This is
why the *Marseillaise*, the anthem of the French Revolution that later
became the national anthem, begins with the words *Allons, enfants de la
patrie* ("March on, children of the fatherland"). In 1789 the medieval
French Estates-General, consisting of separate bodies representing the
clergy, the aristocracy, and the common people, was transformed into a
National Assembly. Regional divisions, with their separate traditions
and rights, were abolished, and France became a uniform and united
territory, with common laws and institutions.

The ascent of nationalism throughout Europe coincided generally
with the spread of the Industrial Revolution, which promoted unified
economic development, a working middle class, and parallel forms of
representative government. As a consequence, national literatures and
artistic forms (in music and the visual arts) arose to express common
traditions. New emphasis was given to historical symbols. New holi-
days were introduced to commemorate various events in social history.
The drafting of national constitutions and the struggle for political
rights gave people after the Industrial Revolution the sense of helping
to determine their fate as large communities and of sharing responsibility for the future well-being of all nations. At the same time, the growth
of trade and industry led to the rise of economic units larger than the
traditional cities.

In the period after World War II, successful nationalist movements
sprang up throughout the world, particularly in Africa and the Middle
East. By 1958 newly established nation-states in those regions included
Israel, Morocco, Tunisia, Libya, the Sudan, Ghana, the United Arab Republic (Egypt and Syria), and Iraq. In the 1960s and 1970s Algeria,
Libya, and many British, French, and Belgian colonies in Africa became
independent. In Eastern Europe in the 1990s, where nationalist pas-

sions had largely been held in check since World War II, the decline of Communist rule unleashed separatist forces that contributed to the dissolution of the Soviet Union, Yugoslavia, and Czechoslovakia.

1.6 THE SPHERES OF CULTURE

Signifying orders manifest themselves temporally and spatially in institutional structures that we will call *spheres* in this text. Cultural spheres are, in a certain sense, "domesticating" systems. Living no longer principally in the wilderness, where their hominid ancestors had to rely primarily on instinct for survival, tribal humans came to depend primarily upon communal spheres for the bare necessities of life.

Anthropologists divide the main spheres into *primary*—kinship and religious—and *secondary*—political, legal, economic, and educational. Primary spheres are characterized by face-to-face modes of communication and interaction and by a feeling of solidarity. Secondary spheres, on the other hand, are based on more conventionalized and impersonal forms of communication and interaction. The latter took on greater importance in the first super-tribal collectivities, where consensual patterns of interaction would have been impossible on the basis of the primary spheres alone.

The word *consensus* requires further elaboration here. It means, literally, "sense-making together." In a collectivity of any kind, consensus implies adherence to the norms of behavior and communication that are deemed appropriate by the collectivity as a whole. These are established and enforced primarily by those who are centrally located within the most dominant sphere in a collectivity at a specific point in time. If that sphere is the religious one, for instance, then the leader or leaders of that sphere will dictate what the norms are; if it is the political sphere, then those located in a central position within that sphere will determine them. Those who do not comply with such norms risk censure, punishment, and/or marginalization. Indeed, those who reject them outright must show the validity of why they are doing so publicly. Otherwise, in all kinds of societies they risk facing some form of rebuke, chastisement, or castigation.

The Kinship Sphere

In his monumental study of social organization, Charles H. Cooley (1909) defined *kinship* as the primary sphere of culture *par excellence*, giving stability and perpetuity to the activities of the tribe. However defined, membership in a kinship unit provides every human being with a primary identity and a vital sense of belonging. This is why people tend to feel a "kinship bond" when they meet a stranger of the same lineal descent, and why, at some point or other in their lives, many (if not most) individuals tend to become interested in where the "roots" of their "family tree" lead. As the great sociologist Max Weber (1864–1920) remarked, leadership in early tribal cultures tended to emerge typically from within kinship units, because their communal activities revolved around the family with the most power and ability to withstand opposition from within the tribe.

The central feature of the kinship sphere is the primary mother-child bond, to which diverse cultures have added different familial relations by the principle of descent, which connects one generation to the other in a systematic way and which determines certain rights and obligations across generations. Descent groups are traced typically through both sexes, i.e. *bilaterally*, or through only the male or the female link, i.e. *unilaterally*. In unilateral systems the descent is known as *patrilineal* if the derivation is through the male line, or *matrilineal* if it is through the female line. Anthropological surveys of kinship systems have shown in recent years that half of the world's cultures are patrilineal, one-third bilateral, and the remainder matrilineal. Bilateral kinship systems are characteristic of modern-day hunting-gathering tribes, such as the !Kung of the Kalahari Desert in southern Africa and the Inuit in northern Canada; and they are becoming increasingly characteristic of modern Western societies as well. Less frequent ways for tracing descent are the *parallel* system, in which males and females each trace their ancestry through their own sex, and the *cognatic* method, in which the relatives of both sexes are considered, with little formal distinction between them.

Kin members are everywhere categorized in ways that assign specific roles and expected behaviors to each individual. The categories are represented by the *names* given to individuals. These may also indicate how a kinship sphere assigns the inheritance of goods and property. The Iatmul of New Guinea, for instance, assign five different names to the first, second, third, fourth, and fifth child in such a way that in any quarrels over inheritance, the first and third children are expected to join forces against the second and the fourth.

The Religious Sphere

The idea that there is life beyond death is an ancient one, as borne out by the discovery that the ritualized burial of the dead is at least 350,000 years old. This is a truly extraordinary idea that has dictated the course of cultural evolution since ancient times; but why it became an intrinsic feature of human consciousness constitutes a mystifying enigma. Suffice it to say for the present purposes that the notion of a spiritual afterlife is the motivation behind the emergence of religion in human cultures.

The *religious sphere* can be defined as a communal system of interaction and complex rituals designed to reflect the will of the gods or of the powers and forces that are believed to reside in the world of the afterlife. As such, this system ties people together, allowing them to express a common sense of purpose beyond immediate life. The term *religion* stems from the Latin word *religio* "to bind, fasten," an etymology that reflects how in early cultures an individual was perceived to be bound by certain mystical or metaphysical (literally "beyond the physical") rites and symbols to the tribe in which s/he was reared. To live "unreligiously" would have implied rejecting the tribe's signifying order that bound the tribal members together. The salient feature of early religious belief systems was the absence of any sharp boundary line between the spiritual and the natural worlds, a characteristic that is still found in some modern-day religious practices such as *Shinto*, a religion practiced in Japan. The Japanese term *Shinto* (from *shin* "spirit") means both "the way of the gods" and "the way of the spirit." The term is also used in common Japanese discourse as an exclamation similar to "Wonderful!" In Shinto, every human being, rock, tree, animal, stream is perceived as having its own wonder. There is no doctrine, creed, or formulated canonical system; Shinto is fundamentally concerned with expressing wonder, respect, and awe for everything that exists. This concern involves treating everything as if it were a person, not in the sense of being inhabited by some human-like ghost or spirit, but in the sense of having a mysterious and independent life of its own that should not be taken for granted.

Tribal metaphysical beliefs led to the establishment of astrology as one of the first sciences. Its widespread popularity in today's secular cultures bears concrete witness to the persistence of the tribal concept that human character and destiny are intertwined with natural processes. The Chaldeans, who lived in Babylon, developed one of the original forms of astrology as early as 3000 BC. The Chinese started practicing astrology around 2000 BC. Other varieties emerged in ancient India and among the Maya of Central America. Astrology grew out of observations that certain astronomical bodies, particularly the sun, affected the change of seasons and the success of crops. From such observations, ancient tribal peoples developed a system of metaphysics by which the movements of other bodies such as the planets affected or represented all aspects of life. By around 500 BC, astrology had spread to Greece, where such philosophers as Pythagoras and Plato incorporated it into their study of religion and the cosmos. Astrology was widely practiced in Europe through the Middle Ages, despite its condemnation by the Church. Many scholars of the era viewed astrolog' and astronomy as complementary sciences until about the 1500s. Only then did the discoveries made by astronomers undermine astrology as a science.

The importance of the religious sphere to the constitution of culture can be seen in the fact that wizards, priests, and shamans have always tended to be the leaders of a tribe as a whole (or to share the leadership with a powerful clan). These were thought to have direct contact with supernatural beings and forces, and thus to be endowed with magical powers that allowed them to cure diseases and to influence the course of events in the world. Early ritualistic practices were invariably organized and supervised by such leaders. In the super-tribal arrangements of the ancient world, however, religious leaders retained only a part of their authority, having to share power increasingly with leaders coming out of the emerging political sphere. With the rise of complex social systems and civilizations these two spheres developed increasingly autonomous, but complementary, functions.

The idea of religious feeling as a personal, cosmological view of the world, reflecting a profound spiritual need to know oneself, came out of the ancient civilizations, when the binding function of religious rites could no longer be maintained intact given the presence of competing religious systems and ideas within the new super-tribal cities. Hence, individuals started to experiment with religious feelings independently of tribal practices, developing a broader and more personal view of spirituality separate from, albeit originally derived from, the tribal version.

Religions with a strong theistic system of belief arose in the ancient civilizations, which provided the social conditions for people to develop a marked sense of demarcation between subjective consciousness and the natural world. This led to a view of the universe as having a pattern to it that humans did not invent, but that they discovered by reasoning about it. The more people appreciated the complexity of the pattern, the more they tended to formulate a conception of a Supreme Intelligence (monotheism) or Intelligences (polytheism), immeasurably greater than a mere mortal, who must know it in its entirety.

The religious sphere continues to be a part even of modern-day secular societies, where religious rituals and symbols continue to form the fabric of modern cultures, even if people are no longer aware of their religious derivations. As the Canadian literary critic Northrop Frye (1912–1991) argued, in his book *The Great Code* (1981), religious symbols remain as residues in the artistic practices and in the everyday discourse patterns of even those societies that define themselves as largely secular. Frye showed how the Bible, for example, is the implicit code sustaining and informing Western literature, art, and social institutions. Anyone who has not had access to this code, Frye suggested, will simply not understand the Western world. The stories of Adam and Eve, of the Tower of Babel, of Paradise lost and regained, of the Flood and Noah's Ark have supplied not only the themes for the great art and literary works of Western civilization, but also the symbols shaping the daily thought and discourse patterns of Western peoples, even if most have never read the Bible. The signifying order is built from this code, diffusing its meanings throughout the entire social system. In the English language, for instance, life is commonly referred to as a journey through the waters (the Ark story), human beings as fallen creatures (the Adam and Eve story), and so on. So, too, cultures with different religious traditions have their own codes that must be accessed through their signifying orders in order to interpret the deeper strata of meanings that are expressed in their arts, literatures, and languages.

The Political Sphere

The need for stability and social cohesiveness in the emerging supertribal systems of the ancient world led to a rise in the prominence and influence of secondary cultural spheres. Awareness of the growing role of the *political sphere* in human affairs, for instance, can already be seen in Plato (c. 428–347 BC), who attempted to reconcile the religious and political spheres by proposing a model of a community that would be governed by an aristocracy of "philosopher-kings." But it was Aristotle (384–322 BC) who recognized the ever-increasing power of the *political*, *legal*, and *economic spheres* in city-state cultures. In his *Politics*, he suggested that these were often in conflict with the religious sphere because of the tension created by their overlapping moral jurisdictions.

This tension extended well into the Middle Ages, an era in Western history characterized by a protracted struggle for supremacy between the Roman Catholic Church and the Holy Roman Empire. This conflict was reflected in the scholarly writing of the era. The philosopher St. Thomas Aquinas (1225–1274), for instance, defended the traditional role of the Church in his *Summa Theologica* (1265–1273), while the great Italian poet Dante Alighieri (1265–1321) argued, in his *De Monarchia* (c. 1313), for a united Christendom under one emperor and pope, each supreme in his appropriate sphere. By the time of the Renaissance, intellectuals like Niccolò Machiavelli (1459–1527) transcended the traditional church-state debate by evaluating the problems and possibilities of governments seeking to maintain power in non-religious, nonmoralistic ways. Some years later, the English philosopher Thomas Hobbes (1588–1679) argued that the power of the political sphere in regulating the affairs of a culture should be unlimited, since he believed culture to be primarily a "social contract" which individuals living in a society agreed to accept so that they could protect themselves from their own brutish instincts and make possible the satisfaction of desires.

Political and legal systems probably started out in the shadow of human needs, urges, and fears, as Hobbes maintained. But the fact that they overlapped with religious spheres in early societies suggests that there was more to the emergence of politics in human affairs than just the regulation of brutish instincts. The rise of the political sphere in human cultures probably reflected the reorientation of the "communal gaze" away from looking "up" or "beyond" to the gods for guidance, as it was accustomed to doing in tribal contexts, to looking "down" towards the more immediate, secular world of human leaders. As the philosopher John Locke (1632–1704) observed, this is why political and legal systems, unlike religious ones, can be legitimately overthrown if they fail to discharge their functions to the people since, unlike religious systems, these are perceived as being totally the brainchildren of human minds.

The Legal Sphere

Rudimentary types of legal systems existed in early tribal cultures. They were a blend of custom, religion, and magic grounded in consensus about what was appropriate and right for the tribe as a whole. The visible authority was the powerful clan member and/or the religious ruler; the ultimate authorities were the gods, whose will was thought to be revealed in the forces of Nature and in the revelations of the religious leader. Wrongs against the tribe, such as acts of sacrilege or breaches of custom, were met with group sanctions, ridicule, and hostility. The wrath of the gods, on the other hand, was appeased typically through ritualistic ceremonies ending in sacrifice or in the expulsion of the wrongdoer. Wrongs against individuals, such as murder, theft, adultery, or failure to repay a debt, were avenged by the family of the victim, often in the form of actions against the family of the wrongdoer.

In the early super-tribal collectivities, secondary legal spheres grew in tandem with political systems. Courts and written laws were established to replace religious principles or rules and the advice-giving practices of tribal chieftains, elders, or shamans. One of the first set of written laws dates from Hammurabi (died 1750 BC), King of Babylon, who united the diverse tribes in Mesopotamia by strategically conquering territories in the region from approximately 1792 to 1750 BC.

The first significant example of a written legal code is the ancient Roman one—a code that has influenced most of the legal systems of the modern world. In the eighth century BC the legal sphere of Rome was characterized largely by a blend of custom and interpretation by magistrates of the will of the gods. But the magistrates eventually lost their legitimacy as the plebeian classes threatened to revolt against their discriminatory practices. This led to one of the most consequential developments in the history of law—the Twelve Tables of Rome, which consisted of laws engraved on bronze tablets in the fifth century BC. Concerned with matters of property, payment of debts, and appropriate compensation for damage to persons, these tables are the source for the widespread modern belief that fairness in human affairs demands that laws regulating human conduct be expressed in writing.

The common-law system of England is another well-known historical example of a legal code that was devised to replace previous systems. Before the Norman Conquest (1066), England was a loose confederation of societies, whose laws were largely tribal in origin. The Anglo-Norman rulers then created a system of centralized courts that operated under a single set of laws that superseded the rules laid down by earlier societies. The resulting legal system, known as the Common Law of England, began with laws for common customs, but over time involved the courts in constantly revising laws.

The Economic Sphere

Economic activities in tribal societies were based on hunting, gathering, and the exchange of manufactured goods. As such activities expanded in new super-tribal collectivities, the *economic sphere* gained more and more autonomy, taking on a greater role in the development of technology and in shaping signifying orders.

The importance and legitimacy of the economic sphere in the Western world were discussed by Adam Smith (1723–1790) and John Stuart Mill (1806–1873). Although the two had many differences of opinion, they shared the view that private property and free markets were the cornerstones of all successful modern economic systems. Opposition to the Smith-Mill view came primarily from social theorists like Karl Marx (1818–1883), for whom the very principle of private property and free markets was the key to the inequities and exploitation that characterize modern societies. Marx believed that this principle was certain to falter because it reflected the inequitable practice of concentrating income and wealth in ever fewer hands, thus creating increasingly severe crises of unemployment and social unrest.

The Educational Sphere

In tribal cultures, the vital function of transmitting the signifying order to subsequent generations was, and continues to be, carried out within the primary spheres. In ancient Egypt, for instance, the priests of the society also taught writing, science, mathematics, and architecture in temple schools. To this day, these spheres are still perceived as critical in guaranteeing the preservation and perpetuation of the signifying order—i.e. they are felt to be fundamental in imparting to young children what they should know first about the world, what language they should learn to speak, and what values they should acquire. But in modern cultures today the function of educating the young after the neonatal and early infancy periods of development is expected to take place through a secondary sphere—known more commonly as the *school system*—which provides professionally-trained individuals for this task.

It was the ancient Greeks who dislodged schooling from the religious sphere. In the Greece of classical times the practice of assigning the teaching of the liberal arts, mathematics, philosophy, aesthetics, and gymnastic training to secular teachers trained in each of these areas grew out of the notion of a "well-rounded" education. After an initial period of intense loyalty to the old religious traditions, Roman society approved the appointment of Greek teachers, but eventually developed its own highly-trained secular educators. According to the first-century educator Quintilian (c. 35–95 AD), the proper training of the child was to be organized around the study of language, literature, philosophy, and the sciences, with particular attention to be paid to the development of character. As the Roman Empire declined, Christianity became a potent cultural force in the countries of the Mediterranean region and in several other areas of Europe. Since then the history of education in Western society has been marked by a struggle between religious and secular forces for control of this vital sphere. The early Fathers of the Church, especially St. Augustine (354–430 AD), emphasized the development of educational methods and curricula that reflected Christian ideas. Two revivals of learning took place in the ninth century, one on the Continent, under Charlemagne (742–814 AD), and one in England, under King Alfred the Great (849–899 AD). Between the eighth and the eleventh centuries the Moorish conquerors of Spain revived the secular idea of the Roman university in the capital city of Córdoba, which became a center for the study of philosophy, ancient civilizations, science, and mathematics in the eleventh and twelfth centuries.

In the same centuries, education came under the influence of the ideas and doctrines of the Scholastic theologians, who reconciled Christian theology with the pre-Christian philosophical ideas of Aristotle and Plato. The theologian Peter Abelard (1079–1142?), pupil of St. Thomas Aquinas, and other renowned Scholastic teachers attracted many students, laying the intellectual foundations for the establishment of universities in the north of Europe in the twelfth century.

Of significance to the development of schooling systems during the Middle Ages were the views of Muslim and Jewish scholars. Not only did they promote advanced forms of education within their own societies, but they also served as translators of ancient Greek writings, thus bringing the ideas of the classical world to the attention of European scholars. Many excellent teachers of the Greek language and literature who had migrated from Constantinople to Italy influenced the work of European educators such as the Dutch humanist Desiderius Erasmus (1466–1536?) and the French essayist Michel de Montaigne (1533–1592). The major emphasis of this period was, therefore, on the classical subjects taught in the Latin grammar school, which remained as the chief secondary school of Europe until the early twentieth century.

During the seventeenth century, the emphasis shifted towards scientific disciplines. Influenced by the writings of Francis Bacon (1561–1626), Christ's Hospital in London was probably the first secondary school to introduce a curriculum based on scientific subjects. That was also the century in which the French philosopher and mathematician Réné Descartes (1596–1650) emphasized the use of logical reasoning as a fundamental skill to be honed by educational curricula, while John Locke (1632–1704), like Bacon before him, recommended a curriculum and method of education based on the empirical examination of demonstrable facts before reaching conclusions. But the greatest educator of the century was Jan Komensky, the Protestant bishop of Moravia, better known by his Latin name, Comenius (1592–1670). Comenius emphasized stimulating the pupil's interest and teaching with reference to concrete things rather than to verbal or logical descriptions of them. He clearly foreshadowed modern-day educational techniques.

The foremost educational theorist of the eighteenth century was Jean-Jacques Rousseau (1712–1778), who insisted that educators should treat children as children, not as miniature adults, cultivating the personality of the individual child with great care and devotion. Motivated by Rousseau's persuasive arguments, governments in England, France, Germany, Italy, and other European countries established obligatory national school systems designed to actualize Rousseau's idea that true education was to be based on the needs and potentials of the child, rather than on the needs of society or the precepts of religion. This "child-centered" view of education was entrenched further in the Western mindset by the work of the American philosopher and educator John Dewey (1859–1952). Dewey's ideas continue to inform the major methods of instruction in elementary schools of the United States and other Western countries to the present day.

In the twentieth century secular educational systems became prevalent throughout industrialized societies. But even in such cultures, certain groups of people continue to prefer the strictly religious form of education. Private or separate schools, as they are commonly called, exist typically for this reason. Thus, the age-old tug between the religious and secular spheres for control of the minds of children continues to characterize education in societies throughout the world.

2

THE FIELD OF CULTURAL SEMIOTICS

Semiotics never tells you what to think, only how to think and how to probe beneath the surface.

Solomon (1988: 13)

2.0 PRELIMINARY REMARKS

The theoretical tools that semiotics makes available for probing cultural systems do not serve primarily to produce quantitative data or general models of human group behavior. Rather, they are useful for sketching a detailed and revealing portrait of *Homo culturalis* as a meaning-seeking creature. These tools are particularly effective for unraveling the tribal roots of modern-day signifying orders. Indeed, the two terms, *tribe* and *culture*, are essentially synonymous from a semiotic perspective. As anthropologist Desmond Morris (1969: 5) has aptly put it, even in modern-day complex societies, the human being refuses "to lose its tribe." A major focus of semiotics is thus to sift out the tribal residues from signifying orders, distilling from them their universal properties. To the semiotician, the foods people eat, the facial decorations they put on, the words they invent, the objects they make and use, the myths they tell, the rites they perform, the sexual practices they engage in, the arts they appreciate, the stories they tell are all rooted in basic properties of signification.

Homo culturalis is a direct descendant of *Homo signans*, "the signer." The Stone Age sketches on cave walls of jumping and dying animals give unequivocal testimony to how truly advanced and sophisticated *Homo signans* was as a "representer" or "modeler" of the world. Indeed, the distinguishing characteristic of the human species has always been its remarkable ability to represent the world in the form of pictures, vocal sounds, hand gestures, and the like. This ability is the reason why, over time, our species has come to be regulated not by force of natural selection, but by "force of history," i.e. by force of the accumu-

lated *meanings* that previous generations have captured and passed on
in the form of signs. As opposed to Nature, culture is everywhere
meaningful, everywhere the result of the innate human need to seek
meaning and order in existence.

General or *theoretical semiotics* is the science that studies signs and
how they produce meanings. It seeks to unravel the nature, origin, and
evolution of signs. If there is any one finding of semiotic research that
stands out from all others it is that, despite great diversity in the
world's sign systems, the difference is more one of detail than of substance. All sign systems continue to serve the original functions for
which they were designed—to allow humans to *represent* the world in
some *meaningful* way—revealing strikingly similar properties across
cultures. *Cultural semiotics* is the science that applies sign theory to the
investigation of signifying orders. Since the middle part of the twentieth century, it has grown into a truly enormous field of study. It now
includes, among other things, the study of bodily communication, aesthetics, rhetoric, visual communication, media, myths, narratives, art
forms, language, artifacts, gesture, eye contact, clothing, advertising,
cuisine, animal communication, rituals—in a phrase, anything that has
been invented by human beings to produce *meaning*.

The purpose of this chapter is to sketch a general picture of what
cultural semiotics is and purports to do. We will start by tracing a historical outline of the study of signs, as a background to current practices in theoretical semiotics, taking a digression to assess the goals and
methodology of the so-called *cognitive science* enterprise. We have decided to do this because since the mid-1980s this science has become
highly influential in shaping views about human nature and culture;
consequently, it cannot be ignored in a text like this one. We will then
outline the main disciplinary sources that cultural semiotics draws
upon in order to carry out its particular mode of investigation. Finally,
we will discuss basic principles of cultural semiotic analysis.

2.1 THEORETICAL SEMIOTICS

The modern-day practice of semiotics traces its origins to the writings
of the Swiss linguist Ferdinand de Saussure and the American philosopher Charles S. Peirce. But interest in signs reaches back several millennia. The first definition of *sign* as a physical *symptom* came from
Hippocrates (460–377 BC), the founder of Western medical science,
who established *semeiotics* (from *semeion* "mark, sign") as a branch of
medicine. The physician Galen of Pergamum (139–199 AD) further entrenched semeiotics into medical practice more than a century after
Hippocrates, a tradition that continues to this day in various European

countries: e.g. in Italy the study of symptoms within medicine is still called *semeiotica*.

The physician's primary task, Hippocrates claimed, was to unravel what a *symptom* stands for—a *symptom* being, in effect, a *semeion* that stands for something other than itself. For example, a dark bruise, a rash, or a sore throat might stand respectively for a broken finger, a skin allergy, a cold. The medical problem is, of course, to infer what that *something* is:

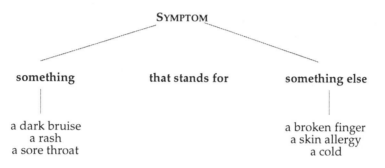

SYMPTOM

something   that stands for   something else

a dark bruise   a broken finger
a rash   a skin allergy
a sore throat   a cold

Medical diagnosis is, in effect, basic semiotic science, since it is grounded on the principle that a physical *symptom* stands not for itself but for an anomalous state or condition. Substituting [A] for the *something* in the above illustration and [B] for the *something else*, a *symptom* can be defined formally as the relation [A *stands for* B]. In the remainder of this manual, this formula will be abbreviated to [A ≡ B].

Ancient Views

The study of how "things stand for other things" became the prerogative of philosophers around the time of Plato (c. 428–c. 347 BC), who suggested that words, for example, were deceptive "things" because they "stood for" reality not directly, but as idealized mental approximations of it. As an example of what Plato meant, consider the concept to which the word *circle* calls attention. Circles do not really exist in Nature. They are ideal forms: i.e. when geometers define a circle as a series of points equidistant from a given point, they are using idealized logical thinking. They are not referring to actual physical points. So, Plato argued, an object existing in the physical world is called a circle insofar as it resembles the ideal form as defined by geometers. The circles that people claim to see in Nature are approximations of this form. Thus, the meaning implied by the word *circle* is unlikely to have been pried out of Nature directly.

Plato's illustrious pupil Aristotle (384–322 BC) accepted his mentor's notion of ideal forms, but he also argued that these were discoverable from observing the actual things that exemplified or "contained" them in the world. Together with the Stoic philosophers (Stoicism was a Greek school of philosophy founded by Zeno around 308 BC), Aristotle took it upon himself to investigate the "stands for" phenomenon in human representation more closely, laying down a theory of the sign that has remained basic to this day. He defined the *sign* as consisting of three dimensions: (1) the physical part of the sign itself (e.g. the sounds that make up a word such as *red*); (2) the *referent* to which it calls attention (a certain category of color), (3) its evocation of a *meaning* (what the referent entails psychologically and socially). Aristotle added that these three dimensions were simultaneous in the sign. And, as Aristotle correctly claimed, it is indeed impossible to think of a word like *red* (a vocal sign made up of the sounds *r-e-d*), without thinking at the same time of the color category to which it refers (the referent), and without experiencing the personal and social meaning(s) that such a referent entails. In philosophical theories of the sign ever since Aristotle, this simultaneity has been modeled as a triangular relation:

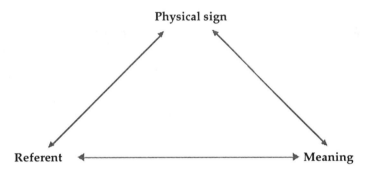

The next major step forward in the study of signs was the one taken by St. Augustine (354–430 AD), the philosopher and religious thinker who was among the first to distinguish clearly between *natural* (nonarbitrary) and *conventional* (arbitrary) signs, and to espouse the view that there was an inbuilt *interpretive* component to the whole "stands for" process. A *natural sign* is one that was created originally by someone to simulate some perceivable property of its referent (e.g. the word *chirp* was fashioned obviously to imitate the sound made by a bird); a *conventional sign*, on the other hand, is one that makes no apparent allusion to any perceivable sensory feature of its referent. St. Augustine's notion of an *interpretive* component was consistent with the *hermeneutic* tradition established by Clement of Alexandria (150?–215? AD), the Greek theologian and early Father of the Church. *Hermeneutics* is the study of how to interpret ancient texts, especially those of a religious or mythical nature. Clement established the method of ascertaining, as far as possible, the meaning that a Biblical writer intended on the basis of linguistic considerations and relevant sources. Clement also maintained that the interpreter should not ignore the fact that the original meaning of the text developed in the course of history, and that the act of interpretation was bound to be influenced by cultural factors.

Medieval Views

St. Augustine's views lay largely forgotten until the eleventh century, when interest in the nature of human representation was rekindled by Arab scholars who translated the works of Plato, Aristotle, and other Greek thinkers. The result was the movement known as Scholasticism. Using Greek classical ideas as their intellectual framework, the Scholastics wanted to show that the truth of religious beliefs existed independently of the signs used to represent them. But within this movement there were some—the nominalists—who argued that "truth" was a matter of subjective opinion and that signs captured, at best, only illusory and highly variable human versions of truth. The French theologian Peter Abelard (1079–c. 1142) proposed an interesting compromise to the debate, suggesting that the "truth" that a sign purportedly captured existed in a particular object as an observable property of the object itself, and outside it as an ideal concept within the mind. The "truth" of the matter, therefore, was somewhere in between.

No doubt the greatest intellectual figure of the medieval era was St. Thomas Aquinas (1225–1274), who combined Aristotelian logic with the Augustinian theory of representation in a comprehensive system of thought that became the most acclaimed theory of knowledge in Roman Catholicism. Aquinas argued that signs allowed humans to reason about scientific and philosophical truths rather effectively, since they were derived from sense impressions, but that the tenets of religion were beyond sensory and rational comprehension and, therefore, had to be accepted on faith. Medieval perspectives on signs culminated with the iconoclastic ideas of John Duns Scotus (c. 1266–1308) and William of Ockham (c. 1285–c. 1349), both of whom stressed that the Platonic ideal forms were merely the result of signs referring to other signs, rather than to actual things.

Renaissance and Post-Renaissance Views

After the Florentine intellectual Marsilio Ficino (1433–1499) translated Plato's writings into Latin in the fifteenth century, a new freer mood of debate emerged in Western academies and in society at large. Shortly thereafter, the discovery of heliocentricity by the Polish astronomer

Nicolaus Copernicus (1473–1543)—the theory that the sun is at rest near the center of the universe, and that the earth, spinning on its axis once daily, revolves annually around the sun—along with the scientific work of the English philosopher and statesman Francis Bacon (1561–1626) and the Italian physicist and astronomer Galileo Galilei (1564–1642), established reason and science, not religious faith, as the primary standards of knowledge-making. By the seventeenth and eighteenth centuries philosophers like Thomas Hobbes (1588–1679), René Descartes (1596–1650), Benedict Spinoza (1632–1677), Gottfried Wilhelm Leibniz (1646–1716), and David Hume (1711–1776) argued that even the properties of the human mind could, and should, be studied as objectively and as rationally as physical phenomena, foreshadowing the birth of scientific psychology in the nineteenth century. The eccentric Italian philosopher Giambattista Vico (1688–1744) was among the few who went against this grain, proposing instead a method for unraveling the nature of mind which, even today, would be considered unorthodox at best and pseudo-scientific at worst. But Vico's method is very much in line with current semiotic thinking, since it entailed exploring the underlying meanings of ancient myths and symbols, and studying the signifying properties of metaphor as the basis for understanding human cognitive processes (Danesi 1993).

Like Vico, the British philosopher John Locke (1632–1704) also attacked the prevailing belief of his times that mental states could be studied on their own, independent of sensory experience. For Locke, all information about the physical world came through the senses and all thoughts could be traced to the sensory information on which they were based. A little later, the Irish philosopher George Berkeley (1685–1753) even cast doubts on the human mind's ability to know the world at all as it really is, while the German philosopher Immanuel Kant (1724–1804) speculated that the mind was predisposed by its nature to impose form and order on all its experiences, thus creating, *ipso facto*, its own particular brand of sense-based knowledge. Kant's views laid the groundwork for Romantic philosophers like Georg Wilhelm Friedrich Hegel (1770–1831), Friedrich Nietzsche (1844–1900), Edmund Husserl (1859–1938), and, later, Martin Heidegger (1889–1976) to put forward the view that *reality* itself was a figment of the human imagination, created by the mind to help it cope with the impulses of human instincts, passions, and desires.

Modern Views

It was John Locke who introduced the formal study of signs into philosophy in his *Essay Concerning Human Understanding* (1690), anticipating that it would allow philosophers to understand the interconnection between representation and knowledge. But the task he laid out, of discovering the properties of the sign, remained virtually unnoticed until the Swiss linguist Ferdinand de Saussure (1857–1913) and the American philosopher Charles S. Peirce (1839–1914) took it upon themselves to provide a scientific framework that made it possible to envision even more than what Locke had hoped for—namely, an autonomous field of inquiry centered on the sign. The subsequent development of semiotics as a distinct scientific domain, with its own methodology, theoretical apparatus, and corpus of findings, is due to the efforts of such twentieth-century scholars as Charles Morris (1901–1979), Roman Jakobson (1896–1982), Roland Barthes (1915–1980), A. J. Greimas (1917–1992), Thomas A. Sebeok (1920–), and Umberto Eco (1932–).

A large part of the increase in the popularity of semiotics in the late twentieth century can be traced back to the publication of several highly popularized critiques of Western culture by the social critic Roland Barthes (1915–1980) in the 1950s and 1960s. These put on display the power of semiotics to demystify the persuasive consumerist rhetoric that came forward at mid-century to uphold and glorify the ascent onto the world stage of a global pop culture. The popularity of semiotics increased even more so with the publication in 1983 of a bestselling medieval detective novel, *The Name of the Rose*, written by one of the most distinguished practitioners of semiotics, Umberto Eco (1932–). Incidentally, Eco (1976: 7) has defined *semiotics* as "the discipline studying everything which can be used in order to lie," because if "something cannot be used to tell a lie, conversely it cannot be used to tell the truth; it cannot, in fact, be used to tell at all." This is, despite its apparent facetiousness, a rather insightful characterization of semiotics, since it implies that we have the capacity to represent the world in any way we desire through signs, even in misleading and deceitful ways. This capacity for artifice is a powerful one indeed. It allows us to conjure up nonexistent referents, or refer to the world without any back-up empirical proof that what we are saying is true. As the linguist Aitchison (1996: 21) aptly puts it, the amazing thing about language is not that it allows us to represent reality as it is, but rather that it affords us "the ability to talk convincingly about something entirely fictitious, with no back-up circumstantial evidence." Arguably, culture itself is one "big lie," given that it constitutes a radical break from our biological heritage—a break that has forced us to live mainly by our wits. As Prometheus predicted in Aeschylus' (525?–456 BC) great ancient drama *Prometheus Bound,* the capacity for lying has ensured that "rulers would conquer and control not by strength, nor by violence, but by cunning."

The primary goal of *theoretical semiotics* is to document and theorize about a remarkable capacity of the human brain—the capacity to produce, understand, and make use of *signs*. The [**A** ≡ **B**] formula we used above to represent how a *symptom* is deciphered is, in effect, the general formula for the sign. The **[B]** part is known technically as the *referent*. There are two kinds of referents that signs capture, *concrete* and *abstract*: (1) a *concrete* referent, like the physical color designated by the word *red*, is something existing in reality or in real experience and is, normally, perceptible to the senses; (2) an *abstract* referent, like the notion represented by the word *democracy*, is something that is conceptual, i.e. something formed within the mind. Now, as the semiotician Charles Morris (1938, 1946) suggested, signs are powerful mental tools precisely because they allow human beings to "carry the world around in their heads," so to speak. This is known psychologically as *displacement*, the ability of the human mind to conjure up the things to which signs refer even though these might not be physically present for the senses to perceive and identify. The displacement property of signs has endowed the human species with the ability to reflect upon referents at any time and in any situation whatsoever within "mind-space."

A *sign* can be defined formally as anything—a word, a gesture, etc.—that stands for something other than itself (the referent). The word *dog*, for instance, is a sign because it does not stand for the sounds *d-o-g* that compose it, but rather for a domesticated carnivorous mammal (*Canis familiaris*) related to the foxes and wolves and raised in a wide variety of breeds:

Sign		**Referent**
↓		↓
d-o-g	stands for	🐕

The ability to make and use signs makes it possible to know and to remember what is known. As the great Russian L. S. Vygotsky (1978: 51) aptly remarked, the "very essence of human memory is that human beings actively remember with the help of signs." The overall goal of theoretical semiotics is, arguably, to unravel how signs allow human beings to *know*. The *meanings* of signs are the data that semioticians collect, and *meanings* are what they attempt to understand. Indeed, the three basic questions that guide all semiotic investigation are (1) *What* does something mean? (2) *How* does it mean what it means? (3) *Why* does it mean what it means?

To get a firmer grasp of how theoretical semiotic method unfolds, consider the word *red*. This is easily recognizable as a sign because it does not stand for itself, the sounds *r-e-d* that compose it, but rather for a color gradation of approximately 630 to 750 nanometers on the long-wave end of the visible spectrum. This is the sign's *referent*, namely, a category of color that is distinct from other categories that are labeled *yellow, red, green,* etc. Together, all such referents compose a particular domain of reference that allows speakers of English to talk and think about the physical phenomenon of color.

Knowledge of color entails knowledge of this domain. Clearly, this kind of knowledge is culture-specific. The very same color category to which the word *red* calls attention could have been represented differently in another culture: e.g. two words could have been used which, together, would cover the category to which *red* calls attention; or the referent captured by *red* could have been included within a larger category of color. Now, not only does the sign *red* make it convenient to refer to a specific color category in a displaced way, but it also conditions its users to anticipate its presence in other domains of reference. In effect, it becomes a productive resource for further meaning-making activities: i.e. it can be used to create new referents, as can be seen in expressions such as *the red light district, red flag,* etc.

This cursory "semiotic analysis" of *red* illustrates, in microcosm, how semiotic method is conducted. It also shows, again in microcosm, that *Homo culturalis* is by nature a sign-maker and a sign-user, and because of this, for at least a hundred thousand years h/er evolution has not been regulated by force of natural selection alone, but by "force of cultural history," i.e. by force of the accumulated *meanings* that previous generations have captured in the form of signs and passed on in cultural contexts. Signs are the result of the need that human beings the world over have to understand the world around them in conceptual ways. That is the central characteristic of the human species, which is called, not uncoincidentally, the "sapient" species *(Homo sapiens)*.

2.2 SAUSSURE AND PEIRCE

As mentioned, the establishment of semiotics as an autonomous science was made possible by the theories of the sign put forward by Saussure and Peirce at the threshold of the twentieth century. Semiotics was fashioned by these two thinkers as a *structuralist* science, i.e. as a mode of inquiry aiming to understand the sensory, emotional, and intellectual *structures* that undergird both the production and the interpretation of signs. The premise that guides structuralist semiotics is, in fact, that the recurring patterns that characterize sign systems are reflective of innate structures in the sensory, emotional, and intellectual composition of the human body and the human psyche. This would explain why the forms of expression that humans create and to which they respond instinctively the world over are so meaningful and so easily understandable across cultures.

Saussure

The linguist Ferdinand de Saussure (1857–1913) was born in Geneva. He attended science classes for a year at the University of Geneva before turning to language studies at the University of Leipzig in 1876. Specializing in *philology*, the study of language history, he published his only book when he was still a student, *Mémoire sur le système primitif des voyelles dans les langues indo-européennes* (1879), an important work on the vowel system of Proto-Indo-European, considered the parent language from which the modern Indo-European languages have descended. Saussure taught at the École des Hautes Études in Paris from 1881 to 1891. A while later he became a professor of Sanskrit and comparative grammar at the University of Geneva.

Although Saussure never wrote another book, his teaching proved highly influential. After his death, two of his students compiled his lecture notes and other materials into a seminal work, *Cours de linguistique générale* (1916), translated into English in 1959 as *Course in General Linguistics*. The book established a series of theoretical distinctions and notions that have become basic to the scientific study of language. And, as will be discussed in the next chapter (§3.3), his definition of the *sign* in that book has become a basic methodological blueprint for the investigation of signs, communication systems, and culture. Incidentally, Saussure used the term *semiology*, rather than *semiotics*, to refer to the scientific study of signs. He coined this term in obvious analogy to other scientific disciplines with names ending in the suffix -*logy*, which derives from the Greek term for "word," *logos*. Saussure's term reflected, in fact, his belief in the supremacy of language among representational systems. Nowadays, Hippocrates' original term, *semeiotics*, more commonly spelled *semiotics*, revived by the philosopher John Locke and adopted by Charles Peirce and Charles Morris, is the preferred one.

Saussure also remarked in the *Cours* that any true science of signs should include both *synchronic* and *diachronic* branches of investigation. The former would study signs at a given point in time, normally the present, and the latter how they change, in form and meaning, across time. As a simple case-in-point of what diachronic analysis entails, consider the word *person*. Recall from above that one of the questions that semioticians ask in carrying out their research is *why* a sign means what it means. Looking for an answer to the question of *why* this word means what it means today involves probing its origin and history. In ancient Greece, the word *persona* signified a "mask" worn by an actor on stage. Subsequently, it came to have the meaning of "the character of the mask-wearer." This meaning still exists in the theater term *dramatis personae* "cast of characters" (literally "the persons of the drama"). Eventually, the word came to have its present meaning of "human being." This diachronic analysis of *person* also provides insight into why we continue to this day to use theatrical expressions such as *to play a role in life, to interact, to act out feelings, to put on a proper face* [mask], and so on to describe the activities and behaviors of "persons."

Peirce

The American philosopher Charles Sanders Peirce (1839–1914) was born in Cambridge, Massachusetts, and educated at Harvard University. Between 1864 and 1884 he lectured intermittently on logic and philosophy at Johns Hopkins and Harvard Universities. In 1867 he turned his attention to the system of logic created by the British mathematician George Boole (1815–1864), and he worked on extending Boolean logic until 1885. Peirce became known during his lifetime primarily for his philosophical system, called pragmatism, according to which no object or concept possesses inherent validity or importance. The significance of something, he claimed, lies only in the practical effects resulting from its use or application. The "truth" of an idea, therefore, can be measured by the empirical investigation of its usefulness. Peirce's pragmatism was incorporated by William James (1842–1910) into psychology and by John Dewey (1859–1952) into education, profoundly influencing modern-day psychological theories and educational practices. As we shall see in the next chapter (§3.3), Peirce provided a fundamental typology of signs that, as will become evident throughout this book, can be applied profitably to the study of signifying orders.

2.3 SEMIOTICS VS. COMMUNICATION SCIENCE

Semiotics is often confused with the study of communication systems, a domain that falls instead under the rubric of *communication science.* Although the two share much of the same theoretical and methodological territory, communication science focuses more on the technical study of how messages are transmitted (vocally, electronically, etc.), whereas semiotics pays more attention to what messages mean and to how they are put together.

Among the first to study the technical features of communication systems was the American electrical engineer Claude E. Shannon (1948), who became famous for developing the mathematical laws governing the transmission, reception, and processing of information.

Shannon also introduced the following key terms into the study of communication: *sender, receiver, encoding, decoding, medium, information content, channel, noise, redundancy,* and *feedback.*

In Shannon's model of communication, message transmission occurs between a *sender* (such as a person speaking) who *encodes* a message—i.e. uses a *code* such as *language* to construct it—and a *receiver* who has the capacity to *decode* the message—i.e. to use the same code to understand what the message means. To get the message across to the receiver, the sender must use some means or device to convert it into a physical form in some *medium*—the voice, books, letters, telephones, computers, etc. A verbal message, for instance, can involve *natural* transmission, if it is articulated with the vocal organs; or else it can be transmitted by means of markings on a piece of paper through the *artifactual* medium of writing; and it can also be converted into radio or television signals for *mechanical* (electromagnetic) transmission.

Shannon also introduced the key notion of *information content* (**I**) as a measurable mathematical quantity. With this term he did not intend to refer to the meaning of the transmitted message, but rather to the probability that it will be received from a set of possible messages. The highest value of **I** = 1 is assigned to the message that is the least probable. On the other hand, if a message is expected with 100% certainty, its information content is **I** = 0. For example, if a coin is tossed, its information content is **I** = 0, because we already know its result 100% of the time—i.e. we know that it has a 100% probability of ending up as either heads or tails. There is no other possible outcome. So, the information carried by a coin toss is nil. However, the two separate outcomes "heads" and "tails" are equally probable. In order to relate information content in this case to probability, Shannon devised a simple formula, $\mathbf{I} = \log_2 1/\mathbf{p}$, in which **p** is the probability of a message being received and $\log_2 1/\mathbf{p}$ is the logarithm of $1/\mathbf{p}$ to the base 2. Log_2 of a given number is the exponent that must be assigned to the number 2 in order to obtain the given number: e.g. $\log_2$ of 8 = 3, because 2^3 = 8; $\log_2$ of 16 = 4, because 2^4 = 16; and so on. Using Shannon's formula to calculate the information content of the message "single coin toss" will, as expected, yield the value of 0, because 2^0 = 1. Shannon used binary digits, 0 and 1, to carry out his calculations because the mechanical communications systems he was concerned with worked in binary ways—e.g. *open* vs. *closed* or *on* vs. *off* circuits. So, if "heads" is represented by 0 and "tails" by 1, the outcome of a coin flip can be represented as either 0 or 1. For example, if a coin is tossed three times in a row, the eight equally possible outcomes (= messages) that could ensue can be represented with binary digits as follows:

- 000 (= three heads)
- 001 (= two heads in a row, a tail)
- 010 (= a head, a tail, a head)
- 011 (= a head, two tails)
- 100 (= a tail, two heads)
- 101 (= a tail, a head, a tail)
- 110 (= two tails in a row, a head)
- 111 (= three tails)

Information content is measured in terms of binary digits, or bits for short. Any outcome with a probability of 1/2 carries one bit of information; any outcome with a probability of 1/4 carries two bits of information; and so on. In the above list of outcomes, the probability of one outcome, say 000 or 111, is 1/8 and thus carries three bits of information.

Shannon defined *channel* as the physical system or phenomenon carrying the transmitted signal: e.g. vocally-produced sound waves are transmitted through air or through an electronic channel (e.g. radio). The term *noise* refers to some interfering element (physical or psychological) in the channel that distorts or partially effaces a message. In radio and telephone transmissions, *noise* is electronic static; in voice transmissions, it can vary from any interfering exterior sound (physical noise) to the speaker's lapses of memory (psychological noise). However, as Shannon demonstrated, communication systems have the feature of *redundancy* built into them for counteracting *noise*. This is the predictability that certain units or features of information will occur in a given type of message. For instance, in verbal communication the high predictability of certain words in many sentences ("Roses are red, violets are..."), the patterned repetition of elements ("Yes, yes, I'll do it; yes, I will") are all redundant features of language which increase the likelihood that a verbal message will get decoded successfully. Finally, Shannon used the term *feedback* to refer to the fact that senders have the capacity to monitor the messages they transmit and modify them to enhance their decodability. *Feedback* in human verbal communication includes, for instance, detecting reactions (facial expressions, bodily movements, etc.) in the receiver that indicate the effect of the message on h/er.

Developed originally as a theoretical framework for improving the efficiency of telecommunication systems, Shannon's model has come to be known as the "bull's-eye" model of communication, because it essentially depicts a sender aiming a message at a receiver as if at a bull's-eye target. Because this model came forward to provide a comprehensive framework for representing *information*, independently of its specific content or meaning and of the devices that carried it, it was appropriated in the 1950s and 1960s by linguists and psychologists as a general framework for investigating human communication systems. Although many semioticians have been openly critical of the view that human communication works according to the same basic mathematical laws as mechanical information systems, the general outline and notions (*encoding, decoding,* etc.) of the bull's-eye model have proved to be highly convenient for relating how communication unfolds between human beings.

2.4 SEMIOTICS VS. COGNITIVE SCIENCE

In the mid-1970s, a movement known as *cognitive science* came to the forefront in North American academies as a promising and exciting new field for studying human consciousness, fashioned primarily from insights and research techniques derived from the domain of *artificial intelligence* (AI) research. Since it appears to have many of the same methodological features as semiotics, it merits discussion here.

Despite its AI orientation, the roots of the cognitive science enterprise lie, actually, in the field of psychology as a scientific mode of inquiry. When Wilhelm Wundt (1832–1920) founded the first laboratory of experimental psychology in 1879 in Leipzig, he laid the groundwork for establishing a new scientific discipline of the mind, separate from philosophy, which he claimed would have the capacity to discover the "laws of mind" through a method of controlled experimentation with human subjects. This became the epistemological rationale for most of the experimental work in psychology conducted throughout the first five decades of the twentieth century. By the late 1960s, however, a new cadre of psychologists abandoned the experimental approach, seeking instead parallels between the functions of the human brain and those of computer programs. Computer terms like "storage," "retrieval," "processing," etc. became part of the emerging new lexicon of what came to be known as the *cognitive* movement in psychology, remaining, to this day, basic expressions for describing mental functions within psychology proper. Not unexpectedly, this led to the idea that conscious intelligence worked according to computational procedures; and this, in turn, led to a full-blown *cognitive science* movement by the mid-1970s. As Howard Gardner (1985: 6) has aptly pointed out, from its very outset this new enterprise was shaped by the view that there exists a level of mind wholly separate from the biological or neurological, on the one hand, and the social or cultural, on the other, that works like an electronic computer. Even though not all cognitive scientists think in this way, this "AI bias" remains, as Gardner (1985: 6) phrases it, "symptomatic" of the cognitive science enterprise to this day. By modeling mental processes in the form of computer programs, cognitive scientists insist, everything from emotions to problem-solving can be understood better.

The basis for this view is the mathematical concept of a *Turing machine* developed by Alan Turing (1912–1954). Turing showed that four simple operations on a tape—*move to the right, move to the left, erase the slash, print the slash*—allowed a computer to execute any kind of program that could be expressed in a binary code (as for example a code of blanks and slashes). So long as one could specify the steps involved in carrying out a task and translating them into the binary code, the Turing machine—now called a computer program—would be able to scan the tape containing the code and carry out the instructions successfully. In 1950, shortly before his untimely death in his early forties, Turing went one step further by suggesting that one could program a computer in such a way that it would have to be declared "intelligent." This notion has become immortalized in the *Turing test*, which goes somewhat as follows. Suppose an observer is in a room that hides behind one of its walls a programmed computer and, behind another one of its walls, a human being. The computer and the human being are allowed to respond to the observer's questions only in writing—say, on pieces of paper which both pass on to the observer through slits in the wall—so that the observer cannot tell directly who is the computer and who the human being. Now, if the observer cannot identify, on the basis of the written responses, who is the computer and who the human being, then s/he must conclude that the machine is "intelligent." It has therefore passed the *Turing test*.

Although Turing himself was well aware of the shortcomings of his test for establishing truly "intelligent activities" in the human sense, openly admitting that it would be impossible to program a computer to understand the more spiritual aspects of human consciousness, to some cognitive scientists his clever test suggested not only that humans were, in effect, special kinds of protoplasmic Turing machines, whose cognitive states, emotions, and social behaviors were therefore not only representable in the form of computer-like programs, but also that mechanical machines themselves could eventually be built to think, feel, and socialize like human beings. As Minsky (1986), Konner (1991), and other radical cognitive scientists have insisted, even the concept of the soul is really no more than a fanciful notion produced by the intelligence of the most advanced Turing machine so far produced by evolutionary forces, and consciousness itself is really no more than an operation of this machine designed to allow individuals to express and modify their emotions and their impulses.

An ingenious rebuttal to the Turing test, and thus to the entire cognitive science paradigm, was put forward in the early 1980s by the American philosopher John Searle (1984). Known as the Chinese Room counter-argument, Searle's rebuttal goes somewhat as follows. When it processes symbols during the Turing test, a computer does not know what it is doing. Just like an English-speaking person who translates Chinese symbols handed to h/er on little pieces of paper by using a set of rules, also provided for h/er, for matching them with other symbols, while knowing nothing about the story contained in the Chinese symbols, a computer has no sense whatsoever of the story contained in human symbols and communication. It is beyond the capacities of a Turing machine to understand human stories, because their meanings lie in psychic, historical, and cultural realities that lie beyond the computational functions of an electronic machine.

The cognitive science movement is really no more than a contemporary rendition of the "Cartesian project" that ushered in the modern era of rationalistic science. In their insightful book *Descartes' Dream*, Davis and Hersh (1986: 7) describe this project as "the dream of a universal method whereby all human problems, whether of science, law, or politics, could be worked out rationally, systematically, by logical computation." This project seemed realizable when the engineer Claude Shannon demonstrated that information of any kind, in both animal and mechanical systems of communication, could be described in terms of binary choices between equally probable alternatives (above, §2.3). By the 1950s, enthusiasm was growing over the possibility that computers could eventually carry out human thinking processes, since the brain was thought increasingly to be really no more than a special kind of Turing machine operating on the basis of a binary code as yet unknown. By the 1960s, phenomenal advances in computer technology seemed to make Descartes' dream a highly realizable one.

In our view, the Cartesian project will never be realized because it is beyond the nature of a machine to seek *meaning* to its existence. This is a need that is peculiar to the human condition and is beyond reproduction in mechanical form. It is also the basis for representational activities such as art works, scientific theories, and the like. AI theories and models of consciousness can perhaps give us precise information about how some forms of thinking unfold, especially those that involve deduction; but they tell us nothing about why consciousness came about in the first place. Moreover, there is no such thing as a true "theory of consciousness," because it is impossible for a human mind to come up with a set of objective axioms for capturing all the truths about itself. In 1931, when the logician Kurt Gödel (1906–1978) demonstrated rather matter-of-factly that there never can be a consistent system of axioms that will capture all the truths of arithmetic, he showed, in effect, that the *makers* of the axioms could never extricate themselves from the *making* of their own axioms. Gödel made it obvious that mathematics was made by people, and that the exploration of "mathematical truth" would thus go on forever so long as humans were around. Like other products of the human imagination, the world of numbers lies within the minds of humans. So too does the world of AI theories of human consciousness.

2.5 CULTURAL SEMIOTICS

Like cognitive scientists, semioticians too are interested in how the mind works, and especially in how it produces and understands signs. The main difference between the two disciplines, as they are currently practiced, lies in the fact that the cognitive science agenda is shaped by a search for a pattern of similarity between natural and artificial intelligence systems, whereas the semiotic agenda is shaped, by and large, by a search for the biological, psychic, and social roots of the human need for *meaning*, or as Searle put it (above, §2.4), for the story behind human symbols and forms of expression.

As an applied interdisciplinary science, *cultural semiotics* enlists not only the notions of theoretical semiotics in its investigation of cultural forms of expression, but also the insights coming out of the cognate fields of psychoanalysis (as already discussed in the previous chapter, §1.2), psychology, anthropology, archeology, linguistics, and neuroscience. The interweaving and blending of ideas, findings, and scientific discourses from these disciplinary domains is the distinguishing feature of the semiotic approach to culture analysis.

Psychology

Cultural semiotics is interested, for instance, in any finding or insight coming out of the field of psychology that is relevant to how signs are produced and understood. Particularly relevant to its objectives are the findings of the *Gestalt* school (German for "configuration"). Gestalt psychology traces its roots to the early work on the relationship between form and content in representational processes by Max Wertheimer (1880–1943), Wolfgang Köhler (1887–1967), and Kurt Koffka (1886–1941), as well as to the work on metaphor conducted by Karl Bühler (1934, 1951), the Wurzburg psychologists (e.g. Staehlin 1914), and Ogden and Richards (1923). The two primary objectives of Gestalt psychology are (1) to unravel how the perception of forms is shaped by the specific contexts in which the forms occur; and (2) to investigate how forms interrelate with meanings. One of the more widely-used techniques in semiotics, known as the *semantic differential*, was actually developed by the Gestalt psychologists Osgood, Suci, and Tannenbaum (1957). This will be discussed in the next chapter (§3.5).

Since its emergence in the previous century, scientific psychology has been caught in a tug of war between two radically different views of human mental functioning, *environmentalism* and *innatism*. From the former point of view, humans are seen as being born with their minds a *tabula rasa,* assuming their nature in response to the stimuli they encounter in their social environments. From the latter perspective, humans are also seen as malleable organisms, but they are not viewed as being born with an empty slate. Rather, in the terminology of cognitive science, they are seen as being "hard-wired" from birth to learn and behave in certain biologically-programmed ways. The acquisition of language, for instance, is said to occur through the operation of an innate *language acquisition device* (LAD) which is governed by the rules of a *universal grammar* (UG). Humans have no more control over their LADs than they do over their breathing. Of course, they can set up obstacles to block the functioning of their LADs, just as they can prevent themselves from breathing: i.e. they can refuse to process input by shutting themselves off from what is being said around them.

Recently, a new school has emerged, known as *evolutionary psychology*, that has been attempting to reconcile these two opposing perspectives (e.g. Pinker 1997). Taking their impetus from sociobiology, evolutionary psychologists attempt to explain human behaviors in terms of evolutionary patterns and by comparison with primate behaviors. According to this perspective, widely popularized by the zoologists Robert Ardrey (1966) and Desmond Morris (1969), human rituals such as kissing and flirting, for instance, are explained as modern-day reflexes of primate and early hominid behaviors. Aggression in males is viewed as a residue of animal territoriality, one of several mechanisms by which animals control access to critical resources. Males are described as competing for territories, either fighting actual battles or performing ritual combats as tests of their strength. Weaker males are portrayed as incapable of holding a territory or as being forced to occupy less desirable locations. Accordingly, aggression in modern human males is seen as a reflex of this mechanism. This kind of reasoning is extended to explaining all our feelings, thoughts, urges, artistic creations, and the like. All these are construed to result from the evolutionary processes started by our hunter-gatherer ancestors. Using population statistics, and making correlations between selected sets of facts, evolutionary psychologists aim to show that human traits of all kinds are inherited through the genetic code, not formed by individual experiences in cultural contexts.

The claim that there is a biological basis to psychic and social behaviors is, of course, partially true; but it is not totally true. By associating cultural forms of expression with primate behaviors, evolutionary psychologists are in effect engaging in unfounded extrapolations about human nature on the basis of simple observations of animal activities. There is of course no counter-argument against this form of reasoning. On the other hand, there is no concrete evidence to support it *a priori* either. Ultimately, that is the most serious flaw of evolutionary psychology—it is only speculation based on Darwinian-type reasoning.

Anthropology

The data coming out of the field of cultural anthropology, too, are relevant to cultural semiotics, because they constitute a vast array of cross-cultural "facts-on-file." Anthropologists obtain their information mainly by interviewing key informants, cross-checking their findings among several informants, and finally piecing the separate informant observations together with their own field notes. In describing a particular tribe, for example, they gather information about its location, passage and initiation rites, religious ideas, arts, myths, language, and then compare their findings to their own perceptions, so as to differentiate between responses peculiar to the society they are studying and those that can be surmised to be general to humankind. This method of investigation, known technically as *ethnographic*, is intended to clarify the roles of learned and innate behavior in the development of cultures.

Archeology

Because they provide an important glimpse into a culture's past, the findings and insights of archeologists are also useful to the goals of cultural semioticians. The artifacts recovered from the excavation of sites of past human habitations allow the semiotician to trace the origin and evolution of certain features of the culture's signifying order. The archeological perspective, therefore, constitutes a diachronic dimension in semiotic analysis—one that is vital for understanding how and why certain signs and signifying orders might have originated.

Archaeologists use various techniques to establish the time sequences of activities that have left physical remains. Of modern methods for dating such remains, the radio-carbon technique is perhaps still the most widely used. The basis of this method is that living plants and animals contain fixed ratios of a radioactive form of carbon, known as carbon-14. This deteriorates at a constant rate after death, leaving ordinary carbon. Measuring the traces of carbon in pieces of charcoal, remains of plants, cotton fibers, wood, and so forth permits the objects to be dated as far back as 50,000 years, although the method is sometimes extended to 70,000 years. Uncertainty in measurement increases with the age of the sample. Archeologists establish chronology also through stratigraphic analysis—i.e. through an analysis of the time-ordered deposits of soil, organic materials, and remains of human activity. Deposits at human sites gradually build up and cover each preceding phase. The task of stratigraphic analysts lies in piecing together the remains of floors, storage pits, and other constructions in a way that is consistent logically with the deposit sequences or layers found at the site.

Linguistics

The modern science of linguistics is the twin sister of modern semiotics, since both trace their parentage to Saussure's *Cours de linguistique générale*. Linguistics proper focuses on studying the forms and functions of sounds, words, and grammatical categories of specific languages, as well as the formal relationships that exist among different languages. Linguists divide language into various levels, of which the following three are the ones that have received the most scientific attention so far:

Phonology:

- This level is composed of the meaningful sounds of a language, known as its *phonemes*. Linguists distinguish *phonological analysis* from *phonetic analysis*, or the cataloguing and description of the raw sounds that humans are capable of making.

Morphology:

- This level is composed of the units, called *morphemes*, that carry meaning in a language. These may be word roots (as the *blue-* in *blueberry*), individual words (*boy, play, need*), word endings (as the *-s* in the plural form *boys, -ed* in the past tense form *played*), prefixes and suffixes (as the *pre-* in *preview* or the *-ness* in *awareness*), or internal alterations (*sing-sang, man-men,* etc.).

Syntax:

- This is the level where words and phrases are organized into sentences. The word order of most declarative sentences in English, for instance, reveals the underlying form **[S-V-0]** (= Subject-Verb-Object): e.g. *Alexander* (**S**) *loves* (**V**) *school* (**O**). The sequence **[V-0-S]** (*Loves school Alexander*), on the other hand, is normally not an acceptable one in English.

Among the first to use linguistic method as an investigative tool for studying culture in the 1920s were Franz Boas and his student Edward Sapir (chapter 1, §1.1). Challenging conventional analyses of language based on written traditions, these two anthropologists devised practical field techniques for identifying the phonemes and morphemes of unwritten languages. These techniques were synthesized, systematized, and elaborated by the American linguist Leonard Bloomfield in his 1933 book titled *Language*, which became a point-of-reference for detailed investigations of specific languages throughout the 1930s, 1940s, and 1950s.

In his *Cours de linguistique générale* (1916), Saussure distinguished between *langue* (French for "language"), the knowledge that speakers of a language share about what is acceptable in that language, and *parole* ("word"), the actual use of a language in speech. Saussure made an analogy to the game of chess to clarify the crucial difference between the two. The ability to play chess, he claimed, is dependent upon knowledge of its *langue*, i.e. of the rules of movement of the pieces—no matter how brilliantly or poorly someone plays, what the chess board or pieces are made of, what the color and size of the pieces are. *Langue* is a mental code that is independent of such variables. Now, the actual ways in which a person plays a specific game—why s/he made the moves that s/he did, how s/he used h/er past knowledge of the game to plan h/er strategy, etc.—are dependent instead on the person's particular execution abilities, i.e. on h/er control of *parole*. In an analogous fashion, Saussure suggested, the ability to speak and understand a language is dependent upon knowing the rules of the language game *(langue)*, whereas the actual use of the rules in certain situations is dependent instead upon execution factors *(parole)*, which may be psychological, social, and communicative.

In 1957 the American linguist Noam Chomsky (1928–) adopted Saussure's basic distinction, referring to *langue* as *competence* and *parole* as *performance*. Chomsky also entrenched Saussure's belief that the aim of linguistics proper was the study of *langue*. Chomsky defined his version of *langue* (*competence*) as the innate knowledge that people employ unconsciously to produce and understand grammatically well-formed sentences, most of which they have never heard before. He then proposed a system of analysis, which he called *transformational-generative grammar*, that would purportedly allow the linguist to identify and describe the general properties of this innate knowledge, sifting them out from those that apply only to particular languages. In acquiring a language, both general grammatical processes and language-specific rule-setting mechanisms are activated in the child; the former, called *universal principles* in recent versions of Chomskyan theory, are part of a species-specific language faculty that has genetic information built into it about what languages in general must be like; the latter, known as *parameters*, constrain the universal principles to produce the specific language grammar to which the child is exposed. Although Chomsky assigns some role to cultural and experiential factors, he has always maintained that the primary role of linguistics must be to understand the universal principles that make up the speech faculty. Chomsky's intractability in maintaining this position, in spite of research that has cast serious doubts upon it, understandably made him a target of bitter criticism throughout the 1980s and 1990s.

While linguistics proper has largely focused on studying *langue* since Saussure's time, two main branches of linguistics have sprung up since the late 1950s that now deal directly with *parole—sociolinguistics* and *psycholinguistics*. The field of *sociolinguistics* aims to describe the kinds of performance behaviors that correlate with the use of language in different situations. For example, sociolinguistic research has found that pronunciation is linked typically to social class in many cultures. People aspiring to move from a lower class to an upper one attach prestige to pronouncing certain sounds in specific ways, even overcorrecting their speech to pronounce words in ways that those they wish to emulate may not. *Psycholinguistics* is concerned with such issues as language acquisition by children, the nature of speech perception, the localization of language in the brain, and the relation between language and thought. The term *psycholinguistics* was coined in 1946 by the psychologist Proncko in an article he wrote for the *Psychological Bulletin*. In 1951, the psychologist George Miller provided the fledgling interdisciplinary field of inquiry with its first research agenda, which was expanded a few years later by those who participated in the Indiana University conference on psycholinguistics (Osgood and Sebeok 1954). Today it is one of the more productive and fascinating branches of the language sciences.

Of special relevance to the semiotic analysis of culture is the hypothesis put forward in the mid-1930s by Edward Sapir's famous student Benjamin Lee Whorf (1897–1941) that language shapes the specific ways in which people think and act. The question of whether or not the *Whorfian hypothesis* is a tenable one continues to be debated to this day. If the categories of a particular language constitute a set of strategies for classifying, abstracting, and storing information in culture-specific ways, do these categories predispose its users to attend to certain specific perceptual events and ignore others? If so, do speakers of different languages perceive the world in different ways? These are the kinds of intriguing questions that the Whorfian hypothesis invites.

This hypothesis has many antecedents. The two most important ones are the views of the philosopher Johann von Herder (chapter 1, §1.5), who saw an intimate connection between language and ethnic character, and the philologist Wilhelm von Humboldt (1767–1835), who gave Herder's hypothesis a more testable formulation by positing that the categories of a specific language were formative of the thought and behavior of the people using it for routine daily communication. A contemporary descendant of the Herder-Humboldt-Sapir-Whorf approach to language is the school of linguistics championed by Ronald Langacker (1987, 1990) and George Lakoff (1987), known as *cognitive linguistics*. The main claim made by cognitive linguists is that language categories reflect *cultural models* of the world which, in turn, influence how the speakers of a language come to think, act, and behave. This claim will be examined more closely in chapters 5 and 6.

Neuroscience

One other disciplinary domain from which cultural semiotics gleans many insights is *neuroscience*. As discussed in the opening chapter (§1.3), shortly after the advent of bipedalism, the brain of *Homo culturalis* started to expand rapidly, developing three major structural components—the large dome-shaped cerebrum, the smaller somewhat spherical cerebellum, and the brainstem. Information and theories about how the brain processes input and transforms it into representational structures are of obvious relevance to semiotics.

In humans, the brain is composed of about 10 billion nerve cells (*neurons*), which are together responsible for the control of all mental functions. In addition to neurons, the brain contains glial cells (supporting cells), blood vessels, and secretor organs. The cerebrum is the largest part of the human brain, making up approximately 85 percent of the brain's weight; its large surface area and intricate development account for the superior intelligence of humans, compared with other animals. It is divided by a longitudinal fissure (indentation) into right and left, mirror-image hemispheres. The left hemisphere controls most of the body's right side, whereas the right hemisphere controls most of the left side. The corpus callosum is the cable of white nerve fibers that connects these two cerebral hemispheres and transfers information from one to the other. Each cerebral hemisphere has an outer layer of gray matter called the cerebral cortex, about 3 to 4 mm. thick, and each is divided by fissures into five lobes. The two hemispheres are normally integrated in function, but each hemisphere is highly specialized.

The study of the brain goes back to ancient times, but the rise of an autonomous *neuroscience* traces its roots to the discovery in the previous century that the left hemisphere (LH) was the primary biological locus for language. It was the French anthropologist and surgeon Pierre Paul Broca (1824–1880) who made this discovery in 1861, when he noticed a destructive lesion in the left frontal lobe of the LH at the autopsy of a patient who had lost the ability to articulate words during his lifetime, even though he had not suffered any paralysis of his speech organs. Broca concluded that the capacity to articulate speech was traceable to that specific cerebral site—which shortly thereafter came to bear his name (*Broca's area*). This discovery established a direct connection between a semiosic capacity and a specific area of the brain. Broca was also responsible for suggesting that there existed an asymmetry between the brain and the body by showing that right-handed persons were more likely to have language located in the LH. Today, neuroscience has confirmed both that mental functions originate in one or the other of the two hemispheres and that the motor control system and sensory pathways between the brain and the body are crossed—i.e. that they are controlled by the contralateral (opposite-side) hemisphere.

In 1874 the work of the German neurologist Carl Wernicke brought to the attention of the medical community further evidence linking the LH with language. Wernicke documented cases in which damage to another area of the LH—which came to bear his name (*Wernicke's area*)—consistently produced a recognizable pattern of impairment to the faculty of speech comprehension. Then, in 1892 Jules Déjerine showed that problems in reading and writing resulted primarily from damage to the LH alone. So, by the end of the nineteenth century the research evidence that was accumulating provided an empirical base to the emerging consensus in neuroscience that the LH was the cerebral locus of language. Unfortunately, it also contributed to the unfounded idea that the RH (right hemisphere) was without special functions and subject to the control of the so-called "dominant" LH.

Following Wernicke's observations, the notion of *cerebral dominance*, or the idea that the LH is the dominant one in the higher forms of cognition, came to be widely held in neuroscience. Although the origin of this term is obscure, it grew no doubt out of the research connecting language to the LH and out of the cultural link in Western society between language and the higher mental functions. It took the research in neuroscience most of the first half of the twentieth century to dispel the notion that only the verbal part of the brain was crucial for the higher forms of cognition, and to establish the fact that the brain is structured anatomically and physiologically in such a way as to provide for two modes of thinking, the verbal and the visual.

It was during the 1950s and 1960s that the widely-publicized studies conducted by the American psychologist Roger Sperry (1913–1994) and his associates on epilepsy patients who had had their two hemispheres separated by surgical section showed that both hemispheres, not just a dominant one, were needed in a neurologically-cooperative way to produce complex thinking. Then, in 1967, a century after Broca's ground-breaking discovery, the linguist Eric Lenneberg established that the LH was indeed the seat of language, adding that the "critical period" for language to "settle into" that hemisphere was from birth to about puberty (chapter 1, §1.3).

In the 1970s research in neuroscience brought seriously into question the idea that the LH alone was responsible for language. The research suggested, in fact, that for any new verbal input to be comprehensible, it must occur in real-world contexts that allow the synthetic functions of the RH to do their interpretive work. In effect, it showed that the brain is prepared to interpret new information primarily in terms of its contextual characteristics. Today, neuroscientists have at their disposal a host of truly remarkable technologies for mapping and collecting data on brain functioning. Positron emission tomography (PET brain scanning), for instance, has become a particularly powerful investigative tool for neuroscientists, since it provides images of mental activities such as language.

It should be mentioned, for the sake of completeness, that the new technology has given us a glimpse into how the cortex is involved in producing various psychological functions, psychomotor movements, etc. However, there are other areas of the brain of which very little is known—such as the areas below the cortex, which are involved in the emotions. In evolutionary terms, these areas are older, tying us to our primate heritage. So, although much has been learned about the cortex since 1861, the brain in its totality still remains a largely mysterious organ.

2.6 THE SEMIOTIC INVESTIGATION OF CULTURE

To define semiotics as a *science* requires some justification. The question of whether or not the human mind and human cultures can be studied with the same objectivity as physical matter has always been a problematic one. Indeed, many semioticians refuse to call their field a *science*, since they believe that the study of signifying orders can never be totally objective. This is why many prefer to define it with terms like "activity," "tool," "doctrine," "theory," "movement," "approach" (Nöth 1990: 4, Sebeok 1990). However, we are in agreement with Umberto Eco (1978), who sees semiotics as a *science* in the traditional sense of the word for five fundamental reasons (Figure 2.1).

We are, of course, aware that any claim to "scientific objectivity" is to be tempered with caution and wariness. This is not unique to semiotics, however. It has, in fact, become characteristic of all the physical sciences in the twentieth century ever since Werner Heisenberg (1901–1976), the German physicist and Nobel laureate, put forward his now famous *indeterminacy principle* during the first part of the century, which debunked the notion of an objective reality independent of culture and of the scientist's personal perspective once and for all. Heisenberg claimed that reality was indeterminable outside of the individual observer's participation in it.

Figure 2.1

1.   it is an autonomous discipline;
2.   it has a set of standardized methodological tools;
3.   it has the capability of producing hypotheses;
4.   it affords the possibility of making predictions;
5.   its findings may lead to a modification of the actual state of the objective world.

To understand Heisenberg's principle, consider a practical example. Let's suppose that a scientist reared and trained in North America sees a physical event that she has never seen before. Curious about what it is, she takes out a notebook and writes down her observations in English. At the instant that our North American scientist observes the event, another scientist, reared and trained in the Philippines and speaking only the indigenous Tagalog language, also sees the same event. He similarly takes out a notebook and writes down his observations in Tagalog. Now, to what extent will the contents of the observations, as written in the two notebooks, coincide? The answer of course is that the two will not be identical. The reason for this discrepancy is not, clearly, due to the nature of the event, but rather to the fact that the observers were different, psychologically and culturally. So, as Heisenberg would have suggested, the true nature of the event is indeterminable, although it can be investigated further, paradoxically, on the basis of the notes taken by the two scientists. The semiotic analysis of culture, too, implies the "Heisenbergian" participation of the analyst in the act of analysis.

Axioms

Every scientific enterprise is constructed on the basis of *axioms*, the primary criteria for distinguishing a scientific enterprise from a nonscientific one established by the ancient Greeks, most probably during the fifth century BC. The axioms of any science must be consistent with one another and few in number. The axioms that in our view have guided the semiotician's exploration of culture in the last decade can be summarized as follows:

1. Signifying orders the world over are constructed with the same core of *signifying properties*.

2. This implies that there are universal structures of sense-making in the human species.

3. Signifying orders are specific instantiations of these structures.

4. Differences in signifying orders result from differences in such instantiations, as caused by human variability and fluctuating contextual-historical factors.

5. Signifying orders entail culture-specific classifications of the world.

6. These classifications influence the way people think, behave, and act.

7. Perceptions of "naturalness" are tied to cultural classifications.

The first six axioms will constitute the subject matter of the remainder of this manual. But the last axiom requires some commentary here. As an example of what this axiom implies consider, for instance, the perception shared by people living in Western society today that the wearing of high-heel shoes is a "natural" thing for women but an "unnatural" one for men. In reality, the classification of a clothing item in terms of gender is a matter of historically-based convention, not of naturalness or lack thereof. As a matter of fact, in the Baroque seventeenth century, high heels were the fashion craze for noblemen and male aristocrats generally, who obviously considered it quite "natural" to wear them.

Cultural classifications are so deeply rooted in human beings that they can even subtly *mediate* how we experience the world. A sign selects what is to be known and memorized from the infinite variety of things that are in the world. Although we create new signs to help us gain new knowledge and modify previous knowledge—this is what artists, scientists, writers, for instance, are always doing—by and large, we literally let our culture "do the understanding" for us. We are born into an already-fixed signifying order that will largely determine how we view the world around us. Only if, hypothetically, all our knowledge (which is maintained in the form of codes) were somehow erased from the face of the earth would we need to rely once again on our instinctive meaning-making tendencies to represent the world all over again.

As another example of the seventh axiom, consider the concept of health. Although this might at first appear to capture a universally-shared meaning, in actual fact what is considered to be "naturally healthy" in one culture may not coincide with views of health in another. Health cannot be defined ahistorically, aculturally or in purely absolute terms. This does not deny the existence of events and states in the body that will lead to disease or illness. All organisms have a species-specific bodily warning system that alerts them to dangerous changes in bodily states. But in the human species bodily states are also representable and thus interpretable in culture-specific ways. This is why in American culture today a "healthy body" is considered to be one that is lean and muscular. Conversely, in others it is one that Americans would consider too plump and rotund. A "healthy lifestyle" might be seen by some cultures to inhere in rigorous physical activity, while in others it might be envisaged as inhering in a more leisurely and sedentary lifestyle.

Moreover, as the writer Susan Sontag cogently argued in her compelling 1978 book *Illness as Metaphor*, the signifying order predisposes people to think of specific illnesses in certain ways. Using the example of cancer, Sontag pointed out that in the not-too-distant past the very word *cancer* was said to have killed some patients who would not have necessarily succumbed to the malignancy from which they suffered: "As long as a particular disease is treated as an evil, invincible predator, not just a disease, most people with cancer will indeed be demoralized by learning what disease they have" (Sontag 1978: 7). Sontag's point that people suffer more from interpreting their disease in cultural terms than from the disease itself is, indeed, a well-taken and instructive one.

Medical practitioners too are not immune from the influence of cultural symbolism. The body, as we shall see in chapter 4, is as much a source of symbolism as it is organic substance. Several decades ago, Hudson (1972) showed how this affects medical practices. He found that medical specialists trained in private British schools were more likely to achieve distinction and prominence by working on the head as opposed to the lower part of the body, on the surface as opposed to the inside of the body, and on the male as opposed to the female body. Hudson suggested that the only way to interpret such behaviors was in cultural terms: i.e. parts of the body, evidently, possessed a symbolic significance which influenced the decisions taken by medical students: "students from an upper-middle-class background are more likely than those from a lower-middle-class background to find their way into specialties that are seen for symbolic reasons as desirable" (Hudson 1972: 25).

3

The Signifying Order

3.0 PRELIMINARY REMARKS

Human beings are restless seekers of *meaning*—in life, in the universe, in their experiences. They seek it in the same way that they search instinctively for the necessities of physical survival and comfort. In their unquenchable search, they are guided by the remarkable ability to produce, understand, and use *signs*. Signs have helped human beings fill with *meanings* the immense void that would otherwise exist between their peculiar states of consciousness and the world. From time immemorial, these have given reassurance that there is continuity, purpose, *meaning* to life. The capacity for sign-making and sign-use has thus bestowed upon the human species the ability to cope effectively with the crucial aspects of human existence—knowing, behaving purposefully, planning, socializing, and communicating. Culture is a direct outcome of this capacity.

Culture is the system of shared meanings that is based on a *signifying order*, a complex system of different types of signs that cohere in predictable ways into patterns of representation which individuals and groups can utilize to make or exchange messages. The goal of this chapter is a technical one—to present and discuss the theoretical notions that permit a scientific analysis of this order. These allow the analyst to look systematically at a specific culture as a "container" of signs and their meanings. The goal of theoretical semiotics is to study the origins, nature, and properties of signs, that of cultural semiotics to examine their functions and uses within their "cultural containers."

3.1 SEMIOSIS AND REPRESENTATION

The primary objective of semiotics is to understand both the brain's capacity to make and understand signs, and the knowledge-making activity this capacity allows all human beings to carry out. The capacity is known as *semiosis*, the activity as *representation*. Semiosis is the neurobiological capacity itself that underlies the production and comprehension of signs, from simple physiological signals to those that reveal a highly complex symbolism; representation is a deliberate use of signs to probe, classify, and hence know the world.

The difference, but intrinsic interconnection, between semiosis and representation can be seen in early childhood behaviors. When an infant comes into contact with an object, h/er first reaction is to explore it with the senses, i.e. to handle it, taste it, smell it, listen to any sounds it makes, and visually observe its features. This exploratory phase of knowing, or *cognizing*, an object can therefore be called *sensory cognizing*, because the child is using the sensory apparatus s/he was born with to cognize the object in terms of how it feels, tastes, smells, etc. The resulting sensory units of knowing apparently allow the child to *recognize* the same object subsequently without having to examine it over again with h/er sensory system. Now, as the infant grows, s/he starts to engage more and more in *semiosic* behavior that clearly transcends this sensory cognizing phase; i.e. s/he starts to imitate the sounds an object makes with the vocal cords and to indicate its presence with the index finger. At that point in the child's development, the object starts to assume a new semiosic form of existence; it has, in effect, been transferred to the physical strategy used by the child to imitate its sound features or indicate its presence. This strategy produces the most basic type of sign, which, as Charles Morris (1938, 1946) suggested, allows the child from that point on to substitute the sign for the object. As mentioned in the previous chapter (§2.1), this is known as *displacement*. As the child grows, s/he becomes increasingly more adept at using signs to represent the world in a displaced manner. Incidentally, note that the word *represent* means, literally, "to present again," i.e. to present some referent again in the sign.

The instant children start to represent the world with signs, they make a vital psychosocial connection between their sensory states to their conscious thoughts about the world. To put it figuratively, signs constitute the "representational glue" that interconnects their bodies, their minds, and the world around them in a holistic fashion. Moreover, once the child discovers that signs are effective tools for thinking, planning, and negotiating meaning with others in certain situations, s/he gains access to the knowledge domain of h/er culture. At first, the child will compare h/er own attempts at representation to the signs to which s/he is exposed in specific contexts. But through protracted exposure and usage, the signs acquired in such contexts will become cognitively dominant in the child, and eventually mediate and regulate h/er thoughts, actions, and behaviors.

The interconnection among the body, the mind, and culture can be shown graphically as follows:

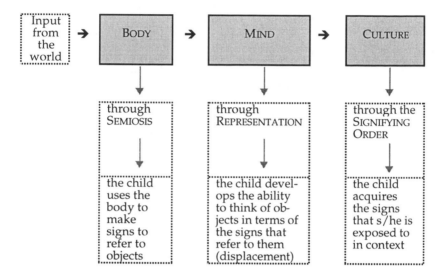

The signifying order thus provides the means for the developing human being to organize the raw information that is processed by h/er senses into meaningful wholes. But as a consequence, the understanding of the world is not a direct one. It is *mediated* by signs and, thus, by the referential domains that they elicit within mind-space.

Carl Jung, the great Swiss psychoanalyst (chapter 1, §1.2), was fond of recounting how signifying orders had the power to affect even what one sees. During a visit to an island tribal culture that had never been exposed to illustrated magazines, he found that the people of that culture were unable to recognize the photographs in the magazines as visual representations of human beings. To his amazement, he discovered that they perceived them, rather, as smudges on a surface. Jung understood perfectly well, however, that their erroneous interpretation of the photographs was not due to defects of intelligence or eyesight; on the contrary, the tribal members were clear-sighted and highly intelligent. Jung perceptively understood that their primary assumptions were different from his own and from those of individuals living in Western culture, because they had acquired a different signifying order that blocked them from perceiving the pictures as visual signs.

The signifying order can be compared to the default mode of computer software. A computer is formatted in a way that is known as its default mode. This format can, of course, be changed intentionally by a human programmer. But if there are no changes made, the computer will automatically operate according to its original format. Analogously, the signifying order is the human being's default mode for knowing the world. But in the same way that a human programmer can always choose to change a computer's format, so too, the individual human being can always decide to alter h/er own "format" at any time. Indeed, therein lies the paradox of the human condition —throughout the life cycle, there is an unexplainable need within each person to transcend the categories of knowing provided by the signifying order. When the categories of the latter fail a human being in h/er search for new or more profound meanings, then s/he can resort to h/er innate capacity for semiosis to alter the default mode. Changes to the signifying order's format, in fact, are what lead cumulatively to cultural change and evolution. Signifying orders are the products of human beings and, therefore, subject to being changed constantly by them to suit any new need or demand.

The interrelationship among *semiosis*, *representation*, and the *signifying order* can be summarized graphically as follows:

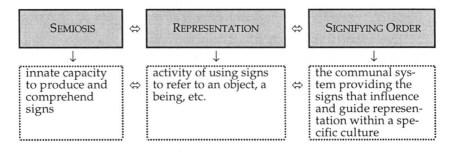

3.2 MODELING SYSTEMS

As mentioned, the human infant's first attempts to know things constitute an instinctive cognizing strategy based on the *sensible* properties of things (i.e. properties that can be sensed). This clearly serves to enhance recognition of the same things without any further processing of sensory input. But the extraordinary feature of human development can be discerned in the child's capacity to transcend sensory knowing and to engage in rudimentary representational activities (pointing and making imitative sounds). What feature of the brain endows human beings with this capacity? In our view, the most plausible answer to this question has been formulated by the American semiotician Thomas A. Sebeok, who argues that this capacity is the outcome of the presence of three types of semiosic systems in the human brain that allow for the *modeling* of experience:

- *Primary Modeling System* (PMS) = this is the neural system that predisposes the human infant to engage in simulative forms of semiosis.

- *Secondary Modeling System* (SMS) = this is the more complex neural system that predisposes the human infant to engage in verbal forms of semiosis as s/he develops.

- *Tertiary Modeling System* (TMS) = this is the highly complex neural system that allows the maturing child to engage in highly abstract forms of semiosis. As Sebeok (1994: 127) remarks, the TMS is "the most creative modeling that Nature has thus far evolved."

Modeling systems theory is a powerful analytical framework for explaining the etiology of representational systems, behaviors, and activities. The PMS is an innate neural system that endows the human infant who has passed through the sensory cognizing phase with the capacity to represent objects through imitative semiosis. Now, as the child develops cognitively and socially, h/er representational activities become more and more abstract, i.e. progressively more reflective of displacement. This secondary mode of knowing and representing is a concomitant of the brain's *secondary modeling system* (SMS). The SMS is a functionally more complex neural system that endows the child who has passed through the PMS phase with the capacity to represent objects primarily through verbal semiosis. Finally, at around 15–20 months the child starts manifesting increasingly the ability to engage in abstract symbolic representation. This is a concomitant of the maturing brain's *tertiary modeling system* (TMS). The TMS is a highly complex neural system involving all areas of the cortex, endowing the verbal child with the capacity to know and represent the world in abstract ways.

The two crucial insights of modeling systems theory can be summarized as follows: (1) representation is tied to three semiosic phases; and (2) these phases are evolutionary—i.e. the development of complex symbolic activity (= a TMS endowment) is dependent upon a prior emergence of verbal representational activities (= a SMS endowment) which is itself in turn dependent upon the development of early imitative semiosis (= a PMS endowment).

3.3 THE SIGN

As discussed in the previous chapter (§2.2), Ferdinand de Saussure and Charles S. Peirce were the two founders of contemporary semiotic science. Saussure's definition of the sign, in particular, laid down the course that semiotic inquiry was to take in the first half of the twentieth century.

The Saussurean Perspective

In the *Cours de linguistique*, Saussure defined the *sign* as something perceivable (i.e. made up of sounds, letters, etc.), which he termed the *signifier* (= [A] part of the sign), that is used to encode a concept, which he called the *signified* (= [B] part of the sign). He named the relation that holds between the two *signification* (= [A ≡ B]).

Saussure considered the connection between the signifier and the signified an arbitrary one. To make his point, he argued that there was no evident reason for using, say, *tree* or *arbre* (French) to designate "an arboreal plant." Indeed, any well-formed signifier could have been used in either language. A well-formed verbal signifier is one that is consistent with the phonological structure of the language in which it is coined (*tree* is well-formed in English; *tbky* is not). Saussure did admit, however, that there were some signifiers in a language that were obviously fashioned in imitation of signifieds. *Onomatopoeic* words (*drip, plop, whack*, etc.), he granted, did indeed attempt to reflect the sound properties that their signifieds are perceived to have. But Saussure maintained that onomatopoeia was a relatively isolated and infrequent phenomenon. Moreover, its highly variable nature across languages demonstrated to him that even this phenomenon was subject to arbitrary cultural perceptions. For instance, the word used to refer to the sounds made by a rooster is *cock-a-doodle-do* in English, but *chicchirichí* (pronounced "keekkeereekee") in Italian; the word referring to the barking of a dog is *bow-wow* in English, but *ouaoua* (pronounced *wawa*) in French. Saussure suggested that such onomatopoeic creations were only approximate and more or less conventional imitations of perceived sounds.

Many semioticians have differed with this specific part of Saussurean theory. What Saussure seems to have ignored is that even those who do not speak English, Italian, or French will detect an attempt in all the above signifiers to imitate rooster or canine sounds—an attempt constrained by the respective phonological systems of the languages that are, in part, responsible for the different phonic outcomes. Such attempts, in fact, probably went into the making of most words in a language, even though people no longer consciously experience words as physical simulations of their referents. This is because time and constant usage have made people forget the simulative connection between signifier and signified. Consider the word *duck*. This signifier is indeed one of an infinite number of permissible phonic creations that can be envisioned to encode the signified in English. But it is implausible that *duck* was created arbitrarily. More than likely, whoever originated that signifier did so in an attempt to simulate the sound s/he perceived ducks to emit. Now, whether or not this is what actually happened is beside the point. The interesting thing to note here is that once people are told about this hypothetical scenario, they start typically to experience the signifier consciously as onomatopoeic, rejecting alternative candidates that could in theory have been chosen to refer to a duck (e.g. *glop, jurp, flim*, etc.) as somehow "unnatural." Many semioticians argue that this kind of anecdotal evidence is rather extensive, and therefore that it strongly suggests that sign-creation is hardly an arbitrary, discretionary process, but rather one that is born of simulative primary modeling behavior.

The Peircean Perspective

Peirce called the perceivable part of the sign a *representamen* (literally "something that does the representing") and the concept that it encodes the *object* (literally "something cast outside for observation"). He termed the meaning that someone gets from the sign the *interpretant*. This is itself a sign (or more accurately a *signified* in Saussurean terms) in that it entails knowing what a sign means (stands for) in personal, social, and context-specific ways.

Peirce then subdivided the *representamina* of human representational systems into *qualisigns, sinsigns,* and *legisigns* (Figure 3.1). A *qualisign* is a representamen that draws attention to, or singles out, some *quality* of its referent. In language, an adjective is a qualisign since it draws attention to the qualities (color, shape, size, etc.) of referents. In other codes, qualisigns include the colors used by painters, the harmonies and tones used by composers, etc. A *sinsign* is a representamen that draws attention to, or singles out, a particular object in time-space: e.g. a pointing finger, the words *here* and *there*, etc. A *legisign* is a representamen that designates something by convention: e.g. words referring to abstract concepts, symbols, etc.

Peirce then identified three kinds of ways in which *objects* can be represented (Figure 3.2): (1) through some form of replication, simulation, or resemblance, called *iconic* representation (e.g. a photo resembles its object visually, a word such as *bang* resembles its object phonically, and so on); (2) through some form of indication, termed *indexical* representation (e.g. a pointing index finger is an indication of where an object is in space); (3) by convention, called *symbolic* representation (e.g. a *rose* is a symbol of love in some cultures).

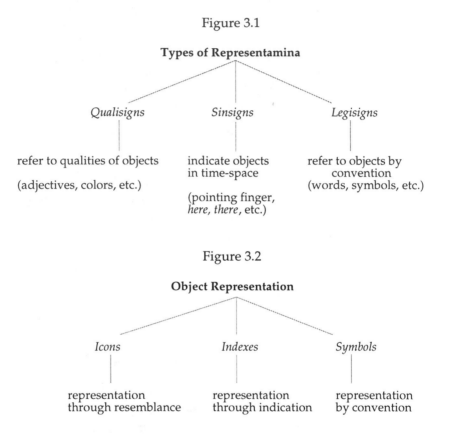

Figure 3.1

Types of Representamina

Qualisigns	*Sinsigns*	*Legisigns*
refer to qualities of objects	indicate objects in time-space	refer to objects by convention
(adjectives, colors, etc.)	(pointing finger, *here, there*, etc.)	(words, symbols, etc.)

Figure 3.2

Object Representation

Icons	*Indexes*	*Symbols*
representation through resemblance	representation through indication	representation by convention

Peirce viewed icons as the most basic type of signs, because they are tied to sense-based representation. Hence, he called them *firstness* signs, being physical substitutes for the referents themselves. But since icons are fashioned in cultural contexts, their manifestations across cultures are not exactly alike. Peirce used the term *hypoicon* to acknowledge this fact. A hypoicon is an icon that is constrained by the signifying order of a culture. But it can nevertheless be figured out by those who are not a part of the culture, if they are told what the referent is. Peirce defined *indexes* as *secondness* signs, because unlike icons they are not substitutes for their referents. Finally, he defined *symbols* as *thirdness* forms of representation, because in this case the sign, the sign-user, and the referent are linked to each other by the forces of historical and social convention, not by any sensory, temporal, or spatial phenomenon, situation, or circumstance.

Peirce suggested, moreover, that there were three types of *interpretants* (what the sign-user or sign-interpreter understands through the sign): (1) a *rheme* is an interpretant of a qualisign; (2) a *dicisign* is an interpretant of a sinsign; and (3) an *argument* is an interpretant of a legisign:

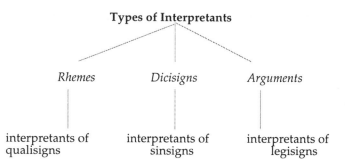

Like St. Augustine before him (chapter 2, §2.1), Peirce did not see the sign as independent of human variability—i.e. he did not consider it to be a purely conceptual means of knowing. The sign, for Peirce, is only a means of ascertaining the meaning intended on the basis of personal and social considerations, relevant sources, and historical factors.

The basic Peircean typology of signs can be summarized in chart form as follows:

MODE OF REPRESENTATION	TYPE OF REPRESENTAMEN	RELATION OF THE SIGN TO ITS REFERENT	TYPE OF INTERPRETANT THE SIGN EVOKES
firstness	qualisign	iconic	rheme
secondness	sinsign	indexical	dicisign
thirdness	legisign	symbolic	argument

3.4 MEANING

As mentioned in the previous chapter (§2.1), semioticians seek answers to the *what*, the *how*, and the *why* of meaning. But what is *meaning*? And indeed what happens when we define the *meaning* of a sign?

Take the dictionary definition of *cat* as "a small carnivorous mammal domesticated since early times as a catcher of rats and mice and as a pet and existing in several distinctive breeds and varieties." The first problem that emerges with this definition is the use of *mammal* to define *cat*—i.e. it makes the assumption that one is familiar with this term. But, then, what is a *mammal*? Once again, the dictionary definition is of little use because it defines *mammal* as "any of various warm-blooded vertebrate animals of the class Mammalia." And this leads to the question: What is an *animal*? The dictionary defines an *animal* as an *organism*, which it defines as an individual form of *life*, which it defines as the property that distinguishes living *organisms*. At this point the dictionary has gone into a loop—i.e. it has started to employ an already-used word, *organism*, to define *life*! This inbuilt circularity in dictionaries is even more apparent when the referent is abstract, as the following vignette devised by Hayakawa (1991) illustrates:

- What do you mean by *democracy*?

- Democracy means the preservation of human *rights*.

- What do you mean by *rights*?

- I mean those privileges God grants all of us—I mean man's inherent *privileges*.

- Such as?

- *Liberty*, for example.

- What do you mean by liberty?

- Religious and political *freedom*.

- And what does that mean?

- Religious and political freedom is what we enjoy under a *democracy*.

Not only does it seem that pinning down the *meaning* of words is probably a futile enterprise but, as the psychologist C. K. Ogden and the philosopher and literary critic I. A. Richards showed in their classic 1923 work, titled appropriately *The Meaning of Meaning*, the word *meaning* itself has many *meanings*. Here are some of them:

- She *means* to watch that show = "intends"

- A red light *means* stop = "indicates"

- Happiness *means* everything = "has the importance of"

- His look was full of *meaning* = "special import"

- Does life have a *meaning*? = "purpose"

- What does love *mean* to you? = "convey"

So, like the axioms of arithmetic or geometry, the notion of *meaning* is best left undefined in semiotic theory. It is something of which everyone has an intuitive understanding, but which virtually no one can really explain. It is a given. On the other hand, the term *signification*, as used in semiotics, is much easier to define, even though *meaning* and *signification* are used interchangeably by many semioticians. Essentially, *signification* designates what is inferable from the relation [**A** ≡ **B**]. Signification is not an open-ended process; it is constrained by a series of factors, including conventional agreements as to what [**B**] entails in specific contexts, the nature of the *code* to which the sign belongs, and so on. Without such inbuilt constraints, determining what a sign means would be virtually impossible.

Signification is a relational process—i.e. signs acquire their meanings not in isolation but in relation to other signs. Some of the more common relations are as follows:

- *Synonymy*: The relation by which the meanings of different signs intersect *(hide-conceal, big-large, etc.)*. The intersection is normally of the partial overlapping variety. The meanings are rarely completely coincidental.

- *Homonymy*: The relation by which two or more meanings are associated with the same sign *(play* as in *Shakespeare's play* vs. *play* as in *He likes to play)*.

- *Antonymy*: The relation by which different signs stand in a discernible "oppositeness" of meaning to each other *(love-hate, hot-cold, etc.)*. But antonymy is a matter of degree, rather than of categorical difference.

- *Hyponymy*: The process by which the meaning of one sign is included in that of another: e.g. the meaning of *scarlet* is included in the meaning of *red, tulip* in that of *flower*.

- *Proportionality*: The process by which distinctions among certain subsets of signs are maintained by the *components* that make up their meanings. These components are isolatable through *proportions* that can be set up among signs that are similar to those used in logic and mathematics *(man:woman:child :: bull:cow:calf)*.

Whereas the first four relational processes need little comment here, the last one requires further elucidation. In the proportion *man:woman:child :: bull:cow:calf* six components of meaning can be factored out. These are: [male], [female], [adult], [nonadult], [human], and [bovine]. These now allow us to understand at what level the proportion holds:

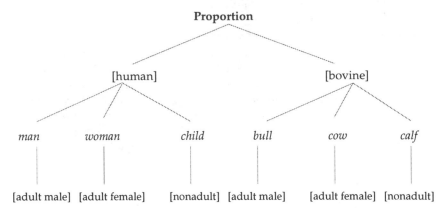

From this graph we can see that the proportion holds at its lowest, or *subordinate* level, where the components (also known as *features*) manifest an isomorphic pattern: [adult male]:[adult female]:[nonadult]: :[adult male]:[adult female]:[nonadult]. It is at the *superordinate* level that the main categorical distinction between the two sets of triplets is established by the features [human] *vs.* [bovine]. Like factors in arithmetical and algebraic expressions, these features allow the human mind to keep certain signs distinct by virtue of the fact that they enter with certain other signs into proportional relations. By virtue of these relations a manageable set of signs allows members of a society to represent economically an illimitable array of meanings, in the same way that an infinite set of numbers can be represented in normal decimal notation by different patterns among ten digits.

Concepts

The foregoing discussion raises the question of what a *concept* is. In semiotics, philosophy, and psychology the term *concept* is limited to designating a general strategy for classifying things that are perceived to subsume some general pattern. *Concept-formation* can thus be characterized as a "pattern-extracting" or "pattern-making" process that appears to serve some survival function in the human species. Distinguishing, for instance, between living and nonliving things is a conceptual pattern that, obviously, serves a useful purpose for people everywhere.

The psychological work on the nature of concepts is laden with controversy. But when looked at cumulatively and impartially, the research seems to support the following general distinction between concrete and abstract concepts—a *concrete concept* is one that is empirically demonstrable and an *abstract concept* is one that is not. A concrete concept is, therefore, one that encodes a pattern that can be seen, heard, smelled, touched, tasted, or observed in some direct way, while an abstract concept is one that encodes a pattern that is not so readily demonstrable. So, for example, the word *cat* refers to a concrete concept because one can always demonstrate or observe the existence of a cat in the physical world. The word *love*, on the other hand, refers to an abstract concept because, although love exists as an emotional phenomenon, it cannot be demonstrated empirically (i.e. the emotion itself cannot be observed apart from the behaviors, states of mind, etc. it produces).

The relevant psychological research shows that all concepts are formed in one of three general ways. The first is by *induction*—i.e. by extracting the pattern from specific facts or instances. For example, if one were to measure the three angles of, say, 100 specific triangles (of varying shapes and sizes), one would get the same total (180°) each time. This would then lead one to *induce* that the sum of the three angles of any triangle is the same. Induction reveals a type of conceptualization process designed to tease out a general pattern from specific occurrences. The second way in which humans form concepts is through *deduction*—i.e. by reaching a conclusion, or *deduction*, on the basis of certain observable facts or premises. It is the opposite of induction in that it entails inference of a pattern by reasoning from the general to the specific. For instance, if one were told that **A** is greater than **B**, and that **B** is greater than **C**, then one would *deduce* that **A** is (much) greater than **C**. Finally, there is a third type of concept-formation process that has, until recently, been largely neglected by mainstream philosophy and psychology, but which is, in effect, the crucial one that is involved in a large portion of abstract concept-formation. This was called, appropriately, *abduction* by Peirce. It is a blend of analogical, associative, and iconic pattern-inferencing. It can be defined simply as the derivation of an abstract pattern on the model of an existing concrete, or already known, pattern. A classic example of abductive reasoning can be seen in the theory of atomic structure proposed by the English physicist Ernest Rutherford (1871–1937). Rutherford conceptualized the inside of an atom as having the structure of the solar system, with electrons behaving like little planets orbiting around an atomic nucleus. His planetary model of atomic structure was, in effect, an abduction of solar-system structure.

The distinction between concrete and abstract concept-formation is, needless to say, a general one. In actual fact, there are many degrees and layers of concreteness and abstraction in conceptualization that are influenced by social, affective, and other kinds of factors. Suffice it to say here that concept-formation serves the basic purpose of organizing most of the raw, unorganized sensory information that comes from seeing, hearing, and the other senses into meaningful forms. Moreover, the type of conceptualization process enlisted depends on the type of pattern that the human mind seeks from a specific situation. Often, all three processes—induction, deduction, abduction—are involved in a complementary fashion.

In the early 1970s, the psychologist Rosch (1973) came to the conclusion that concrete concepts such as the colors display a three-tiered hierarchical organization that varies from language to language, from person to person. At the highest level, which she called the *superordinate* level, concepts have a highly general classificatory function. So, in the domain of color, the concept encoded by the word *color* itself would be a superordinate concept, because it refers to the general phenomenon of chromatism itself. Then there is the *basic* level, which is where a word such as *blue* would fit in. This is a "typological" level—i.e. the level at which "types" of color exist. The third level, which Rosch called the *subordinate* level, is where more detailed ways of classifying something occur. There are, in fact, many shades of *blue—dark blue, navy blue, sky blue, turquoise*, etc.—which we might need for specialized purposes.

3.5 DENOTATION, CONNOTATION, ANNOTATION

In semiotics, concepts are further classified according to the meaning patterns they exemplify. There are three general kinds of patterns: *denotative, connotative*, and *annotative*.

Denotation

Denotation is the initial conceptual meaning that is established between a signifier and a signified. But the *denoted signified* or *referent*, [B], is not something specific in the world, but rather a prototypical category of something. For instance, the word *cat* does not refer to a specific cat, although it can in a specific usage of the term, but to the category of animals that we recognize as having the quality "catness." The denotative meaning of *cat* is, therefore, really *catness*, a prototypical mental picture marked by specific *distinctive features* such as [mammal], [retractile claws], [long tail], etc. This composite mental image allows us to determine if a specific real or imaginary animal under consideration is an exemplar of [B]. Similarly, the word *square* does not denote a specific square, but rather a figure consisting of four equal straight lines that meet at right angles. It is irrelevant if the lines are thick, dotted, 2 meters long, 80 feet long, or whatever. So long as the figure can be seen to

have the distinctive features [four equal straight lines] and [meeting at right angles], it is identifiable denotatively as a *square*.
Connotation

A remarkable feature of human semiosis is that any sign can be *extended* freely to encompass other kinds of referents that appear, by association or analogy, to have something in common with [B]. This *extensional* process is known as *connotation*. As an example of how *connotation* works, consider again the word *square*. Its extended uses can be seen in utterances such as:

> • She's so *square* ("old fashioned")
>
> • He has a *square* disposition ("forthright," "honorable")
>
> • Put it *squarely* on the table ("evenly," "precisely")

Note, however, that the distinctive features of [B] are implicit in such extensional uses; i.e. an old-fashioned person, an honorable individual, and the action of laying something down evenly imply these features—a *square* is an ancient idea and known by everyone (hence "old-fashioned"); it is also a figure with every part equal (hence "forthright"); and it certainly is an even-sided figure (hence "evenly"). Any connotative extension of the word *square* is thus constrained by the original [B]. More formally, connotation can be defined as the mapping of [A ≡ B] onto a new referent, [C], ("old-fashioned," "forthright," "evenly," etc.), if [C] can be seen to entail [B] by association or analogy. This can be shown formally as follows:

$$[A \equiv B] \equiv [C] \Leftrightarrow [C \supseteq B]$$

This formula states that any sign [A ≡ B] can be applied to any other referent [C] by extension, if [C] entails the distinctive features of [B] ([C ⊇ B]). To use the above example of *square* connoting *evenly* as a concrete case-in-point, the above formula would be filled in as follows:

[*square* ≡ [four-sided plane figure of equal sides]] ≡ [evenly] ⇔ [evenly a four-sided plane figure of equal sides]

Connotation is the operative signifying mode in the production and decipherment of creative texts such as poems, novels, musical compositions, art works—in effect, of most of the non-mathematical and non-scientific texts that a culture produces. But this does not mean that meaning in science is necessarily encoded denotatively. On the contrary, many of the theories and models of scientists, as the philosopher Max Black (1962) argued, are born of connotative and/or metaphorical thinking, even though they end up being interpreted denotatively over time. The theory of atomic structure, for instance, was fashioned through analogical extension. It was presented as a tiny solar system by physicist Ernest Rutherford (above, §3.4), with a sun (nucleus) and orbiting planets (electrons, protons, etc.). The end result was a theory that extended a model that at the time it was devised was already familiar to scientists.

Annotation

There is another type of connotation that semioticians generally call *emotive*, but which we will call *annotation* instead. The word *yes*, for example, can have various emotive meanings, depending on the tone of voice with which it is uttered. If one says it with a normal tone of voice, it will be understood as a sign of affirmation. If, however, one says it with a raised tone, as in a question, *Yes?*, then it would imply doubt or incredulity. Such "added meanings" to the word *yes* are examples of *annotation*. This can be defined simply as the interpolation or assignment of subjective meanings to a sign or text.

In 1957, Osgood, Suci, and Tannenbaum invented an interesting technique for fleshing out the annotations that concepts entail, known as the *semantic differential*. This consisted in posing a series of questions to subjects about a specific concept—*Is it good or bad? weak or strong?* etc.—as seven-point scales, with the opposing adjectives at each end. The answers were then analyzed statistically in order to sift out any general pattern from them. Consider a hypothetical example. Suppose that various subjects are asked to evaluate the concept *President* in terms of seven-point scales such as the following:

young								*old*
	1	2	3	4	5	6	7	

practical								*idealistic*
	1	2	3	4	5	6	7	

modern								*tradi-tional*
	1	2	3	4	5	6	7	

attractive								*bland*
	1	2	3	4	5	6	7	

friendly   *stern*

$$\overline{1} \quad \overline{2} \quad \overline{3} \quad \overline{4} \quad \overline{5} \quad \overline{6} \quad \overline{7}$$

An informant who feels that a *President* should be modern would place a mark towards the *modern* end of the *modern-traditional* scale. One who feels that a *President* should not be too young or old would place a mark near the middle of the *young-old* scale; an informant who feels that a *President* should be bland would place a mark towards the *bland* end of the *attractive-bland* scale; and so on. If a large number of informants were asked to rate the term *President* in this way, then it would be possible to draw an ideal profile of the *presidency* in terms of the statistically significant variations in annotation that the term evokes.

Interestingly, research utilizing the semantic differential has shown that, while the meanings of most concepts are subject to personal interpretation and subjective feelings, the range of variation in annotation is not simply a matter of randomness, but forms a socially based pattern. In other words, the experiments have shown that the annotations of signs are constrained by culture: e.g. the word *noise* turns out to be a highly emotional concept for the Japanese, who rate it consistently at the ends of the scales presented to them; whereas it is a fairly neutral concept for Americans, who place it in the mid-range of the scales.

In effect, the signs that make up signifying orders refer to those aspects of reality or experience that specific cultures deem important, relevant, or useful. Therefore, what signs detect or capture in the world is always but a portion of what is around. But, as we have seen in the foregoing discussion, through the phenomena of connotation and annotation even the limited set of signs that a culture makes available to its members can be used to cover a very large domain of meaning. Moreover, as we shall see in chapter 6, new meanings and new forms of reference can always be created through *metaphor*.

3.6 PROPERTIES OF SIGNIFICATION

The semiotic investigation of *how* signs refer to the world (*signification*) has uncovered that signs have specific properties. It has shown, for instance, that signs can be classified as *witting* and *unwitting* (Sebeok 1994). *Unwitting* signs are those that are generated by bodily processes and are, ordinarily, beyond the conscious control of the individual. Most *signals* fall into this category. *Witting* signs are those that humans make and use intentionally to represent the world. The signifiers of unwitting signs are provided by biology; those of witting signs are created by individuals and cultures for specific purposes.

Signaling

The bodies of all animals produce signals to convey certain needs, to
respond to stimuli, etc., but what they mean will depend on the species.
As the biologist Jakob von Uexküll (1909) argued, the signaling system
is a derivative of anatomical structure. Animals with widely divergent
anatomies will manifest virtually no signaling patterns in common.

All animals are endowed with the capacity to use and respond to
species-specific signals for survival. Birds, for instance, are born prepared to produce a particular type of coo, and no amount of exposure
to the songs of other species, or the absence of their own, has any effect
on their cooing. A bird reared in isolation, in fact, will sing a very simple outline of the sort of song that would develop naturally in that bird
born in the wild. This does not mean, however, that animal signaling is
not subject to environmental or adaptational factors. Many bird species
have also developed regional cooing "dialects," apparently by imitat-
ing each other. Vervet monkeys, too, have the usual set of signals to
express emotional states and social needs, but they also have developed a particular predator signaling system—a specific call alerting the
group to eagles, one to four-legged predators such as leopards, another
to snakes, and one to other primates. The calls seem innate, but in actual fact the young of the species learn them only by observing older
monkeys and by trial and error. An infant vervet may at first deliver an
aerial alarm to signal a vulture, a stork, or even a falling leaf, but eventually comes to ignore everything airborne except the eagle.

Most signals are emitted unwittingly in response to specific types
of stimuli, urges, needs, and affective states. Because manifestations of
animal signaling are truly remarkable, it is little wonder that they often
trick people into seeing much more in them than is actually there. A
well-known example of how easily people are duped by animal signaling is the case of Clever Hans. Clever Hans was heralded the world
over as a German "talking horse" in 1904 who appeared to understand
human language and communicate answers to questions by tapping
the alphabet with his front hoof—one tap for *A*, two taps for *B*, three
taps for *C*, and so on. A panel of scientists ruled out deception by the
horse's owner. The horse, it was claimed, could talk! Clever Hans was
awarded honors and proclaimed an important scientific discovery.
Eventually, however, an astute member of the scientific committee that
had examined the horse, the Dutch psychologist Oskar Pfungst, came
to suspect that Clever Hans would probably not tap his hoof without
observing his questioner, since the horse had probably figured out—as
most horses can—what the *signals* that his owner was unwittingly
transmitting meant. The horse, Pfungst asserted, tapped his hoof only

in response to inadvertent cues from his human handler, who would visibly relax when the horse had tapped the proper number of times. To show this, Pfungst simply blindfolded Clever Hans, who, as a consequence, ceased to be so clever. The "Clever Hans phenomenon," as it has come to be known in the annals of psychology, has been demonstrated over and over with other animals as well (e.g. a dog will bark in lieu of the horse's taps in response to certain signals unwittingly emitted by people).

A large portion of communication among humans also unfolds in the form of unwitting signals. It has been shown, for example, that men are sexually attracted to women with large pupils, which signal unconsciously a strong and sexually tinged interest, as well as making females look younger (Sebeok 1994). This would explain the fashion vogue in central Europe during the 1920s and 1930s of a crystalline alkaloid eye-drop liquid derived from *belladonna* ("beautiful woman" in Italian). The women of the day used this drug because they believed —and correctly so, it would appear—that it would enhance facial appearance and sexual attractiveness by dilating the pupils.

But humans are capable as well of deploying witting signals for some intentional purpose—e.g. nodding, winking, glancing, looking, nudging, kicking, head tilting. As the linguist Karl Bühler (1934: 28) aptly observed, such signals act like regulators, eliciting or inhibiting some action or reaction. Signaling systems can also be created for conventional social purposes. The list of such systems is extensive, and includes railway signals, smoke signals, semaphores, telegraph signals, Morse code signals, warning lights, flares, beacons, balefires, red flags, warning lights, traffic lights, alarms, distress signals, danger signals, whistles, sirens, bleepers, buzzers, knocking, gongs, bells, drums.

Iconicity

An *icon* is a sign made to reflect some perceivable property of a referent so that it can be figured out in the signifier. Photographs, drawings, Roman numerals such as I, II, and III are visual iconic signs because they are created to reflect their referents visually; onomatopoeic words are vocal iconic signs because they are created to reflect sound properties of their referents; perfumes are olfactory iconic signs because they are meant to be suggestive of certain natural scents; a block of wood with a letter of the alphabet carved into it is a tactile icon because the letter's shape can be felt and figured out by touch.

Iconicity is seen by most semioticians as a primary strategy in representation—a view, incidentally, that has philosophical antecedents in John Locke (1632–1704), Giambattista Vico (1688–1744), Ernst Cassirer (1874–1945), and Suzanne Langer (1895–1985), among others. The English philosopher Locke argued, in fact, that words refer to sensible properties, with meaning being the internal operation of consciously *recognizing* these properties. The Italian philosopher Vico emphasized that the human mind "does not understand anything of which it has had no previous impression from the senses" (in Bergin and Fisch 1984: 123), because it is "naturally inclined by the senses to see itself externally in the body; and only with great difficulty does it come to understand itself by means of reflection" (Bergin and Fisch 1984: 95). The German philosopher Cassirer linked abstract forms of expression to an unconscious "grammar of experience" whose categories are not those of logical thought, but rather of an archaic mode of sensorial thinking that continues to gain expression through iconicity. The American philosopher Langer saw all efforts to know and understand through representation as essentially sensory-aesthetic reactions to the world.

The presence of *iconicity* in representational systems across cultures is strong evidence that human consciousness is attentive to the recurrent patterns of color, shape, dimension, movement, sound, taste, etc. detected by the human perceptual system. Archeological evidence attests to the ancientness of visual iconicity. The first inscriptions, cave drawings, small sculptures, and relief carvings of animals and female figures found in caves throughout Europe, such as those at Lascaux in France and Altamira in Spain, were created some 30,000 to 40,000 years ago. But even in the verbal domain iconicity was probably the primordial semiosic force in word creation (see chapter 5, §5.2). As Peirce so often remarked, the verbal symbols and abstractions that seem so remote from the sensorial realm were nonetheless born of iconic semiosis.

Indexicality

Indexes are signs created to identify something or someone in terms of its existence or location in time or space, or else in relation to something or someone else. Indexes do not resemble their referents, as icons do; they indicate or show where they are. The most typical manifestation of indexicality is the pointing index finger, which humans the world over use instinctively to point out and locate things, people, and events in the world. Many words, too, are indexes: e.g. *here, there, up, down* refer to the relative location of things when speaking about them.

Indexicality is known more technically as *deixis*. There are three types of deixis:

- *Spatial Deixis* is a form of reference by which the spatial locations of objects, beings, and events are either indicated or correlated by a manual sign like the pointing index finger, a demonstrative word like *this* or *that*, an adverb like *here* or *there*, etc.

- *Temporal Deixis* is a form of reference by which the temporal relations among things and events are either indicated or correlated by an adverb like *before*, *after*, *now*, or *then*, a timeline graph showing points in time as located to the left and right, or on top and below, of each other, etc.

- *Personal Deixis* is a form of reference by which the relations among participants taking part in a situation are either indicated or correlated by a personal pronoun like *I*, *you*, *he*, *she*, an indefinite pronoun like *the one*, *the other*, etc.

The presence of *indexicality* in representational systems across the world is evidence that human consciousness is attentive not only to patterns of color, shape, etc., resulting in iconic semiosis, but also to the recurrent cause and effect patterns that are contingent on time and space relations, resulting in indexical semiosis.

Symbolicity

Symbols are signs created by conventional means. Most semioticians agree that the emergence of symbolicity in humankind is what has endowed it with the capacity to reflect upon the world in purely conceptual ways. Words in general are symbolic signs. But any object, sound, figure, etc. can be fashioned and/or employed symbolically. A cross figure can stand for the concept "Christianity"; a V-sign made with the index and middle fingers can stand for the concept "peace"; white can be symbolic of "cleanliness," "purity," "innocence." These signifieds are established by convention.

The presence of *symbolicity* in representational systems across the world is evidence that human consciousness is not only attentive to physical and cause-and-effect patterns (resulting in icons and indexes respectively), but also to pattern in itself. The view of some semioticians—and it is ours as well—is that iconicity, indexicality, and symbolicity are interconnected in evolutionary terms. The anecdotal evidence to support this view is substantial: e.g. the child first learns to represent something by pointing to it (indexicality) and then naming it (symbolicity) later; people instinctively resort to iconicity (gesturing, making imitative sounds, etc.) and indexicality (pointing) when communicating with someone who does not speak the same language; iconic, indexical, and symbolic modes of representation often converge in the creation of a single sign; and so on. As an example of the latter, consider the common traffic sign for a crossroads:

The signifier of this sign consists of two straight lines, one with an arrowhead, intersecting at right angles. This cross figure is both an icon and a symbol—it is iconic because its shape visually resembles a cross-roads, but since the figure could easily be used in our society to represent other signifieds in other situations, it is also symbolic insofar as we need to know that it has been chosen, by convention, to refer to a cross-roads. Finally, the sign is also an index because when it is placed near an actual crossroads it indicates that one is about to reach it physically.

Symbolicity is the operative mode of representation in all convention-based systems. Consider, for instance, a typical high school problem in algebra:

> Mary has a number of dimes and nickels worth $2.00. If she has twice as many nickels as dimes, how many of each does she have?

This is solved, of course, by setting up an equation. First, a letter from the alphabet is selected, say x, to stand for the number of dimes. This is, of course, an arbitrary choice. Any other letter, or symbol (a dot, a line, etc.) for that matter, could have been chosen to represent the number of dimes. Incidentally, a letter symbol in algebra can stand for any number of things: a number of dimes, of boxes, of shoes, etc. *What* it stands for is irrelevant. The connection between x and a quantitative referent is purely arbitrary. Remarkably, this is precisely what allows people to solve such problems effortlessly. The rest of the reasoning process involved in solving the problem is tangential to this main point. It goes like this. One dime is worth $0.10, so x dimes are worth $0.10x$; there are twice as many nickels as dimes, or $2x$ nickels in total. One nickel is worth $0.05, so $2x$ nickels are worth $2(\$0.05x) = \$0.10x$. The two values add up to $2.00. So, the appropriate equation is $0.10x + \$0.10x = \$2.00$. Solving for x, we get $x = 10$. Thus, Mary has 10 dimes and 20 nickels.

Nowhere has symbolicity borne more remarkable fruits, in fact, than in the development of mathematics and science. An early impressive example of what it has permitted humans to do is found in the annals of geometric history. Standing during the summer solstice at Alexandria, and knowing that it was due north of the city of Syene, with the distance between the two cities being 500 miles, the Greek geometer Eratosthenes (275–194 BC) used simple geometric reasoning to calculate the earth's circumference—without having to do it physically. At the summer solstice, he reasoned, the noon sun is shining directly down into a well at Syene, since the sun is directly overhead at that time of day:

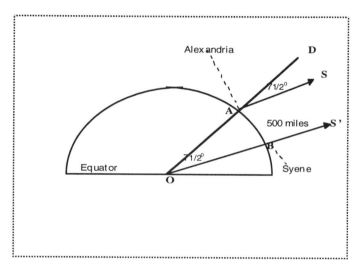

Eratosthenes, therefore, represented the direction of the sun with the straight line **OBS'** (in the illustration). At the same instant in Alexandria, he reasoned further, the actual direction of the sun was representable with **AS**, and the overhead direction with **OAD**. **AS** stood, in effect, for the direction of a ray of sun, and since all rays are parallel, then Eratosthenes knew that ray **AS** was parallel to ray **BS'** at Syene. From a theorem of Euclidean geometry, he was then able to conclude that the angles **DAS** and **AOB** are equal. On the basis of this knowledge, Eratosthenes proceeded to measure **DAS**, which he found to be 71/2°. This then was the size of angle **AOB** at Syene. But, Eratosthenes reasoned further, this angle is 71/2/360° (since the earth is virtually a sphere and therefore almost a 360° angle), or 1/48 of the entire angle at O. It followed from another fact of geometry that the arc **AB**, the distance between Alexandria and Syene, was 1/48 of the entire angle, which was, of course, the circumference of the earth. Therefore, Eratosthenes concluded, the circumference was 48 times the length of the arc: 48 x 500 = 24,000 miles. This is in close agreement with the actual known value today of 24,844 miles.

This story shows clearly how symbolic representation allows people to model the world in abstract ways, in accordance with established conventions (in this case of Euclidean geometry), and then discover facts about the real world through them. It has permitted people, in other words, to let go physically of their environment in order to grasp it in abstract ways. But symbolic methods of representation are not born symbolically. The early geometers of ancient Egypt, Sumer, and Babylon were concerned with such practical problems as measuring the size of fields and laying out accurate right angles for the corners of buildings. Their empirical discoveries, their meticulous diagrams, and their visual observations produced early iconic models that were refined and systematized later by the Greeks. By the sixth century BC the Greek mathematician Pythagoras (582?–500? BC) laid the cornerstone of symbolic geometry by showing that the various observations and iconic diagrams of the empirical geometers could be synthesized into a theorem. Other Greek geometers subsequently synthesized other observations into other theorems. The further synthesizing of theorems led to the establishment of geometry as a science. Only then could someone like Eratosthenes use its techniques to determine the earth's circumference.

3.7 STRUCTURAL RELATIONS

Recall from above (§3.3) that a legitimate verbal signifier in a language is one that shows consistency with the phonological structure of the language. The signifier *duck*, for instance, is an acceptable signifier to English-speaking ears because it conforms to English sound and word structure. The formation of any signifier, verbal or nonverbal, is constrained in fact by the *structural* requirements of the *code* (language, music, etc.) within which it is formed.

Paradigmatic Structure

There are three structural relations that characterize all codes. One is called *paradigmatic structure*. Consider the following words:

> - pin *vs.* bin
> - fun *vs.* pun
> - duck *vs.* luck

The different meanings of the words are detected, first, by virtue of the fact that they have different initial sounds that signal the differences. This differentiation feature of signs is known as *paradigmatic* structure. It is the relation whereby some minimal feature in a signifier is sufficient to keep it differentiated from all other signifiers of the same kind. Paradigmatic structure is found in all human systems. In music, for instance, a major and minor chord of the same key are perceivable as distinct on account of a half tone difference in the middle note of the chord; the left and right shoes of a pair of shoes are identifiable as different on account of their different orientations; and so on.

Syntagmatic Structure

Paradigmatic relations do not operate in isolation; they interact with combinatory and organizational relations. These are known as *syntagmatic*. Paradigmatic structure involves distinctiveness and selectability; syntagmatic structure involves combination and organization. The words *pin, bin, fun, run, duck, luck* are legitimate signifiers because the combination of sounds with which they are made is consistent with English syllable structure. The latter is an example of *syntagmatic* structure. On the other hand, *mpin, mbin, mfun, mrun, mduck, mluck* would not qualify as legitimate verbal signifiers in English because they violate its syllable structure. Syntagmatic structure too is found in all human systems. In music, for instance, a melody is recognizable as such only if the notes follow each other in a certain way (e.g. according to the rules of classical harmony); two shoes (with different orientation) are considered to form a pair if they are of the same size, style, and color; and so on.

In essence, something is a sign if it has a discernible (repeatable and predictable) form and is constructed in a definable (patterned) way. Signs are like pieces of a jigsaw puzzle. These have visual features on their "faces" that keep them distinct from each other, as well as differently-shaped "edges" that make it possible to join them together in specific ways to complete the overall picture.

Analogical Structure

The third structural relation is called *analogy*. This is a replacement relation, by which one type of sign can replace another in a specific way. Thus, for example, European cards can replace American cards for playing solitaire if an analogy is made between European and American suits. The model of planets orbiting around the sun can be used by analogy to represent the structure of an atom, whereby the sun is replaced by the nucleus, the orbiting planets by electrons, and so on.

Analogy is a force of change in sign systems. Words are often reformed or created on the model of existing grammatical patterns in a language. For example, in Old English the plural of *name* was *naman*. This was changed over time to *names* on the model of nouns like *stone—stones*. Analogy is the operative force when children utter a form like *goed*, rather than *went*. This is created in analogy with forms like *played, stayed*, etc.

3.8 CODES AND TEXTS

A *code* is a *structural system*, i.e. a system in which signs reveal a specific paradigmatic, syntagmatic, and analogical architecture. A simple example of a code is the game of solitaire. The cards in this code are legitimate signs if they have been constructed with distinctive features (in terms of suit and number value); if they can be organized in vertical columns to complete the game; and if they can be replaced by a set of cards with a comparable system of distinctive features. In other words, solitaire is a *code* in which the various cards are differentiable *paradigmatically* from each other by suit and number and placeable or organizable *syntagmatically* into columns in specific ways, in which they can be replaced by other kinds of cards with comparable features.

A code can be thought of as being like a formatted computer disk. The format of a *phonological code*, for instance, provides the differential phonic features (sounds) along with a finite set of combinatory syllable patterns for making words. Often, a *code* is made up of many constituent structural systems or codes (also called *subsystems* or *subcodes)*. For instance, the *language code* consists of *phonological, morphological, syntactic,* and *semantic* subcodes, each with its own type of paradigmatic, syntagmatic, and analogical formats.

Knowledge of a code allows an individual to construct appropriate messages with the resources of the code. A face-to-face conversation, for instance, involves not only the simultaneous deployment of the subsystems of language (phonological, morphological, etc.), but also those that compose gestural, facial, and various other nonverbal codes. The verbal message is thus "woven together" with the resources of different codes. This "weaving together" is called a *text.* A *text* is a collation of signs taken from one or more codes in order to construct and communicate a message. When someone says something to someone else, writes a letter, or wears a certain kind of dress for an occasion, s/he is engaged in text-making. Routine conversations, musical compositions, stage plays, poems, dance styles, ceremonies are but a few examples of the many kinds of texts that people make on a regular basis, as individuals or as groups. These can only be understood fully if the codes used to make them are known. The term *message* refers to *what* one wishes to communicate with a text; the term *text* refers more specifically to *how* the message is constructed.

Texts bear meaning in specific *contexts*. The term *context* refers to the real-world conditions—physical, psychological, social, etc.—that influence, shape, and even determine how a text is made or what a text means. Consider a discarded and damaged beer can. If someone were to come across this item on a sidewalk on a city street, s/he would no doubt view it as a piece of garbage or rubbish. But if the person saw the very same object on a pedestal, displayed in an art gallery, "signed" by some artist, and given a title such as "Waste," then s/he would be inclined to interpret its meaning in a vastly different way. S/he would, in fact, interpret it most likely as an artistic text, decrying a throw-away or materialistic society. Clearly, the can's physical context of occurrence and social frame of reference—its location on a sidewalk vs. its display in an art gallery—will determine what it means.

It is now possible to define the signifying order more formally. The *signifying order* is the overall system, or *macrocode,* that supplies the signs, the specific codes in which they are organized structurally, and the texts they make possible to the members of a culture. This interrelationship can be illustrated graphically as follows:

The Signifying Order

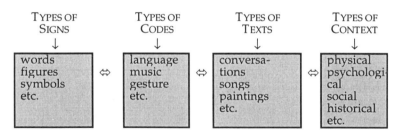

3.9 THE DIMENSIONALITY PRINCIPLE

Research in semiotics has shown that *representation* unfolds in terms of three *dimensions* which, as we discussed above (§3.3), Peirce called *firstness, secondness,* and *thirdness.* We will refer to this as the *dimensionality principle* throughout this book.

Consider, for instance, the *temporal* aspect of representation. In this case, a sign's meaning in a specific instance is inferable relative to three temporal dimensions, which can be represented graphically as axes in three-dimensional space: (1) a synchronic (firstness) axis that provides its attendant meaning; (2) a diachronic (secondness) axis that provides its latent historical meanings; and (3) a dynamic (thirdness) axis that entails the potential for new meaning pursuant to its use in the specific instance:

Temporal Dimensionality

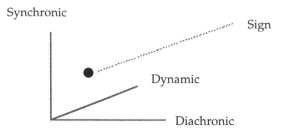

Consider, as a second example, the type of dimensionality that can be called *notational*. This constitutes a representation space in which the various meanings of a sign are inferable relative to three notational axes: (1) a denotative (firstness) axis that provides its intended meaning; (2) a connotative (secondness) axis that allows for the sign's extended uses according to context; and (3) an annotative (thirdness) axis that entails the individual's own understanding of the sign's meanings. The sign's position relative to the axes determines its specific meaning: if it is closer to the firstness axis it is primarily denotative (intended meaning); if it is closer to the secondness axis it is primarily connotative (extended meaning); and if it is closer to the thirdness axis it is primarily annotative (personal meaning).

Notational Dimensionality

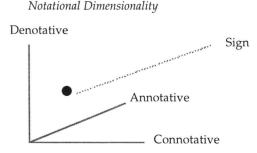

Consider, finally, a third type of dimensionality that can be called *structural*. This constitutes a representation space in which the various meanings of a sign are inferable relative to three structural axes: (1) a paradigmatic (firstness) axis that entails a selection operation; (2) a syntagmatic (secondness) axis that entails a combination operation; and (3) an analogical (thirdness) axis that entails a replacement operation:

Structural Dimensionality

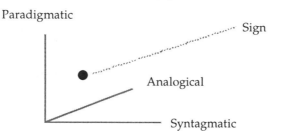

These dimensionalities can be summarized as follows:

DIMENSIONALITY	FIRSTNESS AXIS	SECONDNESS AXIS	THIRDNESS AXIS
TEMPORAL	synchronic	diachronic	dynamic
NOTATIONAL	denotative	connotative	annotative
OPERATIONAL	paradigmatic	syntagmatic	analogical

The dimensionality principle makes it explicit that there is an inter-connectedness among the multifarious dimensions of representation and signification. It also allows us to establish a commonality among different representational systems. Because all such systems are composed of the same kinds of dimensionalities, the principle provides a basis for showing an interrelation among all areas of knowledge-making, from language to science and the arts. A digit in numerical representation, for instance, has the exact same structural features in dimensional terms that, say, a noun in language has—i.e. both are signs that exist in temporal, notational, and operational three-dimensional spaces, deriving their forms, functions, and meanings in terms of these dimensionalities. The difference between a digit and a noun is thus not to be located in structural patterns, but in the different cognitive functions of the representational systems to which they pertain. This is why, despite their different functions, both are understandable in exactly the same way. In essence, the dimensionality principle makes it obvious why such seemingly diverse forms of representation as poetry and mathematics are not mutually exclusive—with adequate exposure to both, people will be able to extract meaning from either one of them in remarkably similar ways.

3.10 STRUCTURAL EFFECTS

The signifying order is both restrictive and liberating in human terms. It is restrictive in that it imposes upon individuals born into a specific culture an already-fixed system of signification. This system will largely determine how people come to understand the world around them—i.e. in terms of the language, music, myths, rituals, technological systems, and other codes that they learn in social context. But the signifying order is also liberating because paradoxically it provides the means by which individuals can seek new meanings on their own. The artistic, religious, scientific, and philosophical texts to which individuals are exposed in social contexts, moreover, open up the mind, stimulate creativity, and engender freedom of thought. As a result, human beings tend to become restless for new meanings, new messages. For this reason, codes are constantly being modified by new generations of artists, scientists, philosophers, and others to meet new demands, new ideas, new challenges.

Leaving aside this knack for creativity for the moment, the fact remains that culture *structures* beliefs, attitudes, worldview, and even sensory perception to varying degrees. As a concrete example, the reader should look at the following classic visual illusion. As s/he can probably confirm for h/erself, most people living in Western societies will see line **AB** as longer than line **CD**:

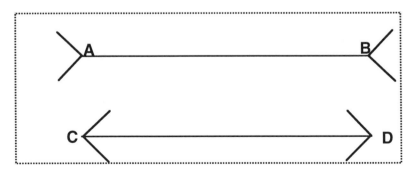

In actual fact the lines **AB** and **CD** are equal in length, but the orientation of the arrowheads fools the Western eye into seeing **AB** as longer than **CD**. In rural Uganda, on the other hand, psychologists have found that people see the lines as equal in length (Simon 1976: 19-20). The factor behind this illusion is that Western individuals are accustomed to seeing drawings in *perspective*. In painting *perspective* is the technique of creating an illusion of depth or length in two-dimensional surface drawings. As a historical footnote, it should be noted that the craft of perspective drawing dates back to the Renaissance, after the Italian artist Filippo Brunelleschi (1377–1446) discovered and then entrenched this technique in Western painting.

Visual illusions provide strong evidence in favor of the notion of *structural effect*, i.e. of the notion that signifying orders *structure* perception, beliefs, worldview. Consider, as another example, color perception. The light spectrum consists of a continuous gradation of hue from one end to the other. According to some physicists, there are potentially 8 million gradations that the human eye is capable of distinguishing. If one were to put a finger at any point on the spectrum, there would be only a negligible difference in gradation in the colors immediately adjacent to the finger at either side. Yet a speaker of English describing the spectrum will list the gradations as *purple, blue, green, yellow, orange,* and *red*. This is because the speaker has been conditioned by the English language to classify the content of the spectrum in specific ways. There is nothing inherently "natural" about the speaker's organizational scheme; it is a reflex of English vocabulary, not of Nature.

By contrast, speakers of other languages are predisposed to see other color categories on the very same spectrum. Speakers of Shona, an indigenous African language, for instance, divide it up into *cipswuka, citema, cicena,* and *cipswuka* (again), and speakers of Bassa, a language of Liberia, segment it into just two categories, *hui* and *ziza*. The relative proportional widths of the gradations that these color categories represent vis-à-vis the English categories can be shown graphically as follows:

English	purple	blue	green	yellow	orange	red
Shona	cipswuka	citema		cicena	cipswuka	
Bassa	hui				ziza	
Potential Number of Categories	8 million gradations					

So, when an English speaker refers to, say, a ball as *blue*, a Shona speaker might refer to it as either *cipswuka* or *citema*, and a Bassa speaker as *hui*. But this does not stop an English speaker from relating h/er categories to those of the other two languages. The specific color categories one has acquired in a cultural context in no way preclude the ability to perceive the color categories of other cultures. This is, indeed, what a learner of another language ends up doing when s/he studies the new color system: i.e. s/he learns how to reclassify the content of the spectrum in terms of the new categories. Moreover, in all languages there exist signifying resources for referring to more specific gradations on the spectrum if the situation should require it. In English the words *crimson, scarlet, vermilion,* for instance, make it possible to refer to gradations of *red.* But these are still felt by speakers to be *subcategories* of red, not distinct color categories on their own. They are related *hyponymically* to each other (above, §3.4).

In 1969, the psycholinguists Berlin and Kay argued, moreover, that differences in color terms are only superficial matters that conceal general underlying principles of color perception. Using the judgments of the native speakers of twenty widely divergent languages, Berlin and Kay came to the conclusion that there were "focal points" in basic (single-term) color systems which clustered in certain predictable ways. They identified eleven universal colors, or focal points, which corresponded to the English words *red, pink, orange, yellow, brown, green, blue, purple, black, white,* and *gray.* Not all the languages they investigated had separate words for each of these colors, but there emerged a pattern that suggested to them the existence of a fixed way of perceiving color across cultures. If a language had two colors, then the focal points were equivalents of English *black* and *white.* If it had three color terms, then the third one corresponded to *red.* A four-term system had either *yellow* or *green,* while a five-term system had both of these. A six-term system included *blue;* a seven-term system had *brown.* Finally, *purple, pink, orange,* and *gray* were found to occur in any combination in languages which had the previous focal points. Berlin and Kay found that languages with, say, a four-term system consisting of *black, white, red,* and *brown* did not exist. Berlin and Kay's *universal color system* can be represented as follows:

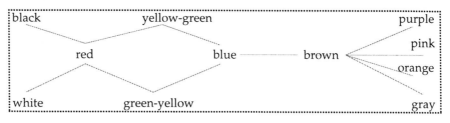

The intriguing implications of this research were pursued vigorously in the 1970s by many psychologists. Eleanor Rosch (1975), for instance, demonstrated that the Dani people of West Irian, who have a two-color system similar to the Bassa system described above, were able to easily discriminate eight focal points. Using a recognition-memory experiment, Rosch found that the Dani recognized focal colors better than non-focal ones. She also found that they learned new colors more easily when the color names were paired with focal colors. Such findings suggested to Rosch that languages provided a guide to the interpretation of color, but they did not affect its perception in any way.

But many problems remain to this day with the conclusions reached by color researchers. For one thing, the fact that the eleven focal points posited by Berlin and Kay corresponded to the color terms of their own language (English) is suspicious. Could the researchers have been predisposed by their own language to gloss all other terms according to the English categories? Many of the terms Berlin and Kay listed, some critics have pointed out, turn out to be borrowings (color terms taken and/or adapted from other languages), which would greatly undermine their theory.

Semiotically speaking, color terms are verbal signifiers, and the categories they encode are their referents. This means that people are predisposed to attend primarily to the gradations (referents) they have learned to discriminate through the color signifiers they know. This is a practical strategy; otherwise, millions of signifiers would need to be invented to classify the spectrum in terms of all the possible discriminations that can be made. But this simple semiotic explanation also makes it clear that to learn new ways of classifying the spectrum, all one has to do is learn new signifiers or invent new ones.

The underlying purpose of the foregoing discussion has been to show that the *meanings* captured by one signifying order in no way tell the complete story about the world. The signifying order always leaves gaps, offering up only a portion of what is potentially knowable in the world. Indeed, a little reflection will reveal that an infinite number of *signifiers* could be created without any *signifieds*. This is exactly what young children do when they make up "nonsense words," creating them seemingly only for the pleasure of making imitative, pleasant, or humorous sound effects. The great British writer of children's books Lewis Carroll (1832–1898) invented his own nonsense language, in his poem *Jabberwocky*, to show that the English language as constituted does not tell all there is to tell about reality. Using signifiers such as *brillig, slithy, tove, wabe* and others (from *Through the Looking Glass*, 1871: 126-129), Carroll showed that it is an easy thing to make up legitimate words that seem to beg for legitimate meanings.

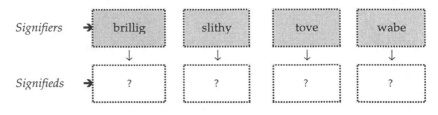

In effect, Carroll had coined signifiers without signifieds; i.e. words that suggested ideas by virtue of the fact that they sounded like English words. Actually, Carroll provided his own *signifieds* for these words as follows to make his point even stronger:

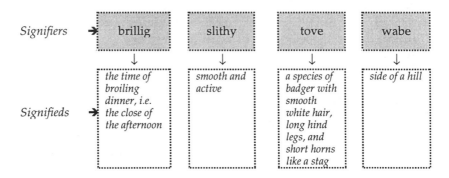

Analogously, there are infinitely many *signifieds* that are not captured by a language. Indeed, there are still no words in English for "side of a hill," "smooth and active," and other *Jabberwocky* concepts. Here are a few other examples of potential signifieds not captured by existing English words:

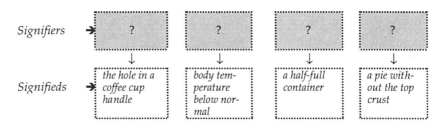

However, even though gaps exist in a signifying order, humans have the ability to fill them any time they wish. They do this typically by inventing new signs, altering already-existing ones to meet new demands, borrowing signs from other signifying orders. One can always find ways to refer, for instance, to the above signifieds by paraphrase or some other verbal strategy—e.g. *a pie without the top crust = a*

top-crustless pie. But the lack of signifiers to *enshrine* these concepts implies that they will not be anticipated by speakers of English within the scheme of things.

The notion of *structural effects* is not a theory of mind; it simply acknowledges what effects signs have on human thinking. In actual fact, there are creative forces constantly at work in individual human beings. The philosopher Giambattista Vico (chapter 2, §2.1) termed these the *fantasia* and the *ingegno*. The former is the capacity that allows human beings to imagine literally anything they desire freely and independently of biological or cultural processes; it is the creative force behind new thoughts, new ideas, art, science, and so on. The latter is the capacity that allows human being to convert their new thoughts and ideas into expressive representational structures—metaphors, stories, works of art, scientific theories, etc. So, although human beings are indeed shaped in large part by their particular biology and by the social system in which they are reared, they are also endowed with creative faculties that seem, in our opinion, to be well beyond the capacities of the current sciences of biology and psychology to explain. The human being is, indeed, a true enigma among living species.

Part II

The Semiotic Study of Culture

We think only in signs. These mental signs are of mixed nature; the symbol-parts of them are called concepts... A symbol, once in being, spreads among peoples. In use and in experience, its meaning grows.

Charles Peirce (1839–1914)

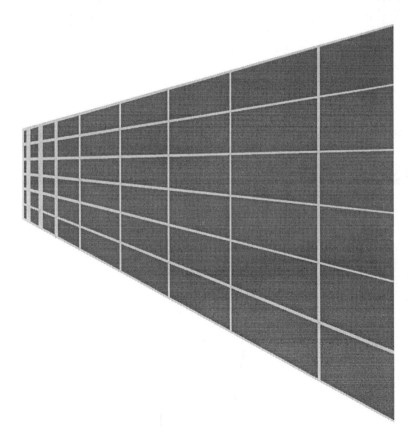

4

THE BODY

*Cultural life is then viewed as a series
of texts intersecting with other texts,
producing more texts.*

Harvey (1990: 49)

4.0 PRELIMINARY REMARKS

Humans convey over two-thirds of their ideas and feelings through the body, producing up to 700,000 physical signs, of which 1000 are different bodily postures, 5000 are hand gestures, and 250,000 are facial expressions (Morris et al. 1979). Logically, the first area to come into the purview of semiotics encompasses the many codes fashioned from the properties of the body. Technically speaking, the study of these codes falls under the rubric of *nonverbal semiotics.*

The social function of bodily codes is to regulate Self-Other relations; i.e. to ensure that the ways in which people interact in their cultural spheres, and in society generally, are regular and fluid. These codes have evolved in the human species as structural systems designed to maintain cooperation and harmony. Consider the following typical, but hardly trivial, vignette that illustrates how Self-Other relations are regulated in a routine situation by a context-appropriate bodily code.

> • An individual in the United States is about to step into an elevator of a skyscraper on the ground floor. Inside, s/he sees three people, all obvious strangers to each other.
>
> • How does s/he know this? S/he knows this because the individuals in the elevator are near or leaning against the walls of the elevator, facing the door or looking down at the ground, and silent.
>
> • Once inside, the individual knows that s/he is expected to assume a similar posture; i.e. to face the door or look down at the floor to avoid eye contact with the others and, of course, to maintain silence.

In short, if s/he is an active participant in American culture, s/he knows the code that is appropriate to this situation. If the individual decides to act in some other way—e.g. to face the others, to look right at them—the others would become uneasy or angry, because they would see h/er behavior as either conflictual or disturbed. To cope with the transgressor's breach of conduct, they would more than likely ignore h/er actions completely, as if they hadn't occurred.

Across cultures, bodily codes are the result of a perception of the body as something more than physical substance. Winks, hand gestures, facial expressions, postures, and other bodily actions all communicate something culturally relevant in particular social situations. The body is, in fact, a major source of signification and communication and thus a major target of semiotic inquiry. There are five major types of bodily codes, each of which will be looked at in this chapter: *kinesic, facial, proxemic, tactile,* and *gestural. Kinesic codes* are fashioned from bodily movements, postures, etc. believed to bear meaning during social interaction; *facial codes* are based on the expressive qualities of the face and on eye contact; *proxemic codes* are fashioned from the distances people feel they should maintain between each other and the orientation that their bodies should assume during interaction; *tactile codes* are based on the meanings that certain touch patterns are felt to have in social situations; and *gestural codes* are made from the properties of the hand.

As in all areas of semiotic investigation, the analyst is guided by three basic questions in h/er search to understand nonverbal representational behavior (Chapter 2, §2.1): (1) *What* does a certain nonverbal sign, code, or text mean? (2) *How* does it mean what it means? (3) *Why* does it mean what it means? The semiotician seeks answers to these questions essentially by observing people being themselves in their social ambiances. The observational activities of the semiotician-as-people-watcher, however, are not random. They are guided by five specific goals:

1. identifying the basic signifying properties structuring the observed behaviors (iconicity, indexicality, etc.);

2. relating these to the signifying order;

3. documenting and explaining the structural effects that bodily codes have on individuals;

4. investigating how these codes are interconnected throughout the signifying order;

5. utilizing the findings or techniques of any cognate discipline (anthropology, psychology, etc.) that are applicable to the situation at hand.

In pausing to look over the important terrain of bodily-based meaning-making, this chapter constitutes the first stop on our journey through the landscape of culture. In other treatments of nonverbal behavior, the reader will likely see a different organization of the topics; but the goal of most is very much the same as ours—to highlight the role of the body in social interaction.

4.1 NONVERBAL SEMIOSIS AND COMMUNICATION

Before dealing with bodily codes, it is necessary to look at nonverbal semiosis and communication generally, an area of investigation which has itself become a major subfield of theoretical semiotics. The work of Thomas A. Sebeok (1920–), one of this century's leading semioticians and linguists, has been highly instrumental in expanding the perimeter of this subfield to include the study of semiosis and communication across species. In what is known as the *biosemiotic* movement, Sebeok has shown that in studying cross-species semiosis, we end up getting a clearer look at what makes human semiosis unique.

Research by animal ethologists has shown how remarkably rich and varied animal communication systems are. They have identified, for instance, birdcalls for courting, mating, hunger, food bearing, territoriality, warning, and distress, and elaborate vocal signals that whales and dolphins deploy to communicate over long distances underwater. Biosemiotics aims to investigate all such patterns, seeking to understand how animals are endowed by their nature with the capacity to use specific types of signals for survival (*zoosemiosis*), and thus how human semiosis (*anthroposemiosis*) is both similar to and different from animal semiosis. The objective of this new branch of semiotics is, thus, to distill common elements of semiosis from its manifestations across species, integrating them into a taxonomy of notions, principles, and procedures for understanding this phenomenon in its globality.

The study of animal semiosis and communication actually traces its roots to Darwinian evolutionary biology (Darwin 1859), and especially to Darwin's 1872 contention that animal behavior constituted a viable analogue for human mental functioning. By the end of the nineteenth century, psychology took a decidedly Darwinian turn. The early experiments in this field led to the classical theory of conditioning in humans. The Russian psychologist Ivan Pavlov (1902), for instance, rang a bell while he presented meat to a dog. Initially, only the meat stimulus, not the ringing of the bell, evoked an instinctive salivation response in the dog. However, after repeated bell ringings, Pavlov found that the bell alone would evoke salivation. The dog had obviously "learned" to associate the sound of the bell with the presence of meat. The dog's learning event was called, appropriately, a *conditioned response*. It was then claimed that humans too learned in a similar way. Intrigued by such findings, work on animal intelligence was pursued with great fervor during the first quarter of the twentieth century. Robert Yerkes (1916), for instance, succeeded in showing that monkeys and apes had the capacity to transfer their conditioned responses to novel learning tasks. And in 1925 Wolfgang Köhler showed that apes could even devise spontaneous solutions to problems without previous conditioning.

The goal of these early comparative psychologists was to generalize the findings from the animal experiments to human learning. The assumption was that the same laws of conditioning applied across all species and, therefore, that universal principles of learning and problem-solving could be inferred from observing animal behavior. Some psychologists continue to work under this very assumption. However, by the middle of the twentieth century, the use of animals as convenient substitutes for people in the laboratory came under attack and a new movement emerged, known as *ethology*, stressing that animals and people lived in separate worlds, and that animals should be studied within their natural habitats.

Soon after, some researchers became intrigued by the possibility of teaching human systems of communication to animals. This led to the widely known "ape language experiments" that started in the 1950s. Although there have been reports of some symbolic activity, of some comprehension of humor, and of some control of sentence structure, these experiments have not yet established the capacity for human language or for human symbolicity in primates.

These experiments were ingenious above all else in the ways in which they got around the incapability of gorillas and chimpanzees to speak because of the fact that they lack the requisite vocal organs. The first experimenters, for instance, chose American Sign Language (ASL) as the code for teaching apes human language. One of the first subjects was a female chimpanzee named Washoe whose training by the Gardner husband and wife team (B. T. Gardner and R. A. Gardner 1969, R. A. Gardner and B. T. Gardner 1975) began in 1966 when she was almost one year of age. Remarkably, Washoe learned to use 132 ASL signs in just over four years. What appeared to be even more remarkable was that Washoe began to put signs together to express a small set of ideas. Inspired by the results obtained by the Gardners, others embarked on an intensive research program, aiming to expand upon their teaching procedures, that is still ongoing today. The Premacks (e.g. Premack and Premack 1983), for example, whose work actually began as far back as 1954 with a five-year-old chimpanzee named Sarah, taught their subject a form of written language. They instructed Sarah to arrange and respond to vertical sequences of plastic tokens on a magnetic board which represented individual words: e.g. a small pink square = "banana," a small blue triangle = "apple," etc. Sarah eventually developed the ability to respond to combinations of such symbols, which included references to abstract notions.

Although there was an initial wave of enthusiasm over such results, with the media reporting on them on a regular basis, there really has emerged no solid evidence to suggest that chimpanzees and gorillas are capable of verbal behavior and symbolicity in the same way that humans are, or of passing on to their offspring what they have learned from their human mentors. These experimenters appear to refuse to accept the inevitable fact that most of human representational activity is species-specific.

Nevertheless, the study of primate communication in itself remains a fascinating area of scientific investigation that falls well within the purview of biosemiotics. The objective in biosemiotics, however, is not to determine whether primates can speak like humans, but rather to learn what semiosic capacities they share with humans. It is likely that certain properties or features of semiosis cut across species, while others are specific to one or several species. Determining the universality or specificity of particular semiosic properties is a much more realizable goal than determining if animals are able to speak. Sebeok, for instance, has documented the manifestations of iconicity in vastly different species—suggesting that it is a cross-species property. As a case-in-point, he has singled out termite mound constructions. These mounds have extremely hard walls, constructed from bits of soil cemented with saliva and baked by the sun. Inside the walls are numerous chambers and galleries, interconnected by a complex network of passageways. The ventilation, drainage, and heat required for hatching the eggs are obtained from the fermentation of organic matter, which is stored in the chambers serving as nurseries. Of more than 55 species common in the US, the majority build their nests underground. The subterranean termites are extremely destructive, because they tunnel their way to wooden structures, into which they burrow to obtain food. Upon closer scrutiny, termite mound constructions reveal that they are hardly without semiosic properties. These mounds, in fact, mirror the constituents of the termite's social evolution, even after the colony itself has become extinct. In semiotic terms, it can be said that these mounds are iconic "expressions" of the genetically imprinted social system of these insect architects. This is an example of *unwitting iconicity* manifesting itself in Nature as a concomitant of a specific life scheme.

Biosemiotics takes its impetus from the work of the biologist Jakob von Uexküll (1909), who provided empirical evidence to show that an organism does not perceive an object in itself, but according to its own particular kind of mental *modeling system* (chapter 3, §3.2). This allows the organism to interpret objects and events in a biologically unique way and, subsequently, to respond to them in semiosically specific ways. For von Uexküll, the modeling system of a species routinely converts its external world experiences, which can be called *cognizing states,* into internal states of knowing and remembering in terms of the particular features of that system, which can be called *recognizing states.* This in no way implies that animals do not have consciousness, emotions, or intelligence, nor that they are incapable of communicating their feelings, drives, and urges effectively. Rather, it means that their cognizing and recognizing states are vastly different from human ones. Moreover, while semiosis is a feature of all life forms, representation is not. There is no evidence to even hint that an animal can (or desires to) understand the meanings that we humans extract from a painting, feel the moods evoked by a Beethoven piano sonata, comprehend the intent of a narrative, and so on.

The goal for biosemiotics is thus not to determine whether or not it is possible to teach animals human representational systems, but to learn whether interspecies communication, without human intervention, is part of Nature's overall plan. While we may not be able to communicate with other species in the same ways that we do with each other, there is a level at which we do indeed "make contact" with some species. There is no doubt, for instance, that a house cat and a human enter into a rudimentary form of communication on a daily basis. Sharing the same living space, and relying on each other for affection, they do indeed communicate their feeling-states to each other in a patterned fashion. They do this by sending out signals and by utilizing bodily based modes of communication. Tones of voice, postures, movements are the signifiers that are forged from their mutually-developed "interspecies communication code." This code reflects the deployment of basic semiosic strategies that appear to cut across human and feline communication systems, emerging adaptively from the shared experiences of the two species.

Hockett's Typology

Among the first to emphasize the differences between human and animal systems was the American linguist Charles Hockett (1960). He did this by elaborating a set of 13 design features of verbal communication against which it was possible to compare systems across species:

Design Feature	Properties and Manifestations
1. Auditory-vocal	This feature refers to the fact that language involves mainly auditory and vocal processes, as opposed to visual, tactile, or other modes of communication.
2. Broadcast transmission and directional reception	This feature refers to the fact that a verbal signal can be heard by any auditory system within ear range, and to the fact that the source can be located with the ears' direction-finding capacity.
3. Rapid fading	This feature refers to the fact that auditory signals are transitory and do not await the hearer's convenience.
4. Interchange-ability	This feature refers to the fact that speakers of a language can reproduce any linguistic message they can understand.
5. Total feedback	This feature refers to the fact that speakers of a language hear and can reflect upon everything that they say (unlike the visual displays often used in animal courtship signaling).
6. Specialization	This feature refers to the fact that the sound waves of speech have no function other than to signal meaning.
7. Semanticity	This feature refers to the fact that the elements of the linguistic signal convey meaning through their stable reference to real-world situations.
8. Arbitrariness	This feature refers to the fact that there is no necessary dependence of the verbal signal on the nature of the referent.
9. Discreteness	This feature refers to the fact that speech uses a small set of sound elements (phonemes) that form meaningful oppositions with each other.
10. Displacement	This feature refers to the fact that language has the capacity to refer to situations remote in space and time from their occurrence.
11. Productivity	This feature refers to the fact that messages in language are constructed by using old elements to produce new ones.
12. Traditional transmission	This feature refers to the fact that language is transmitted from one generation to the next primarily through a process of teaching and learning (not by genetic inheritance).
13. Duality of patterning	This feature refers to the fact that verbal sounds have no intrinsic meaning in themselves but combine in different ways to form elements (e.g. words) that do convey meanings.

Hockett's typology has made possible a concrete comparison of animal and human communication systems on the basis of specific features. As mentioned above, the bodily-based mode of communication is the one that perhaps most cuts across communication systems. However, even with the deployment of this versatile communicative mode, there is no way for a human to communicate a broader range of feeling-states to an animal—states that are implied, for instance, by words such as *embrace, guide, hold, kiss, spank, tickle,* etc. Interspecies communication is realizable, but only in a very restricted sense. It can occur in some modes, partially or totally, to various degrees according to species. If the design features of the communicative modes of the two species are vastly different, however, then virtually no message transmission is possible.

In addition to design features, communication systems can be compared in terms of the *media* with which, or through which, messages are transmitted. Again, human transmission differs from animal transmission in that it includes artifactual and mechanical media in addition to the natural media:

> • *natural media* are biologically-based media: e.g. the voice (speech), the face (expressions), and the body (gesture, posture, etc.);
>
> • *artifactual media* are human-made media: e.g. books, paintings, sculptures, letters, etc.;
>
> • *mechanical media* are also human-made media: e.g. telephones, radios, television sets, computers, videos, etc.

A verbal message, for instance, can be delivered through *natural* transmission, if it is articulated with the vocal organs; or else it can be transmitted by means of markings on a piece of paper through the *artifactual* medium of writing; and it can also be converted into radio or television signals for *mechanical* (electromagnetic) transmission. There is no evidence of any use of artifactual or mechanical media in animal species.

Sebeok's Typology

Another perceptive method of comparing human and animal communication systems has been fashioned by the semiotician Thomas A. Sebeok. His insightful typology includes the following six crucial features:

1. *Innate Modeling Capacities:* This refers to the fact that all organisms possess species-specific inner modeling capacities that allow them to respond in kind to their outer experiences.

2. *Vocality:* This refers to the fact that signals and messages can be transmitted vocally or nonvocally. Bird communication, for instance, is vocal; bee-dancing is nonvocal.

3. *Verbality:* This refers to the fact that verbal communication is unique to the human species. All other communication systems in Nature are nonverbal. Language is verbal, but not necessarily vocal (e.g. it can be communicated also by means of alphabet characters, gestures, etc.); *speech*, on the other hand, is both vocal and verbal.

4. *Wittingness:* This refers to the fact that certain messages are unwitting (e.g. the signals sent out by pupil responses); others are witting, showing purposeful and intentional behavior.

5. *Hemisphericity:* This refers to the fact that human communication involves bilaterality, i.e. the cooperation of the functions associated with the left and right hemispheres.

6. *Formation:* This refers to the fact that communication systems are *formed* in the organism by exposure to appropriate input in social context and are subject to change or even *dissolution* over time. In all species other than the human, systems are formed primarily through the biological channel; only human beings acquire their ability to communicate both from biology and from culture.

The value of this typology lies in providing the specific biological and psychological categories for separating human from animal communication capacities. Communication in animal species serves a survival function. The exchange of signals helps animals find food, migrate, or reproduce. But humans have developed complex forms of communication that are used not only to ensure survival, but also to express ideas and emotions, to tell stories and remember the past, and to negotiate with one another. There is no evidence to suggest that an animal understands the meanings that we humans communicate on a daily basis.

4.2 KINESIC CODES

Kinesic codes regulate how people behave physically in certain social situations. They are a product of cultural history and convention. Recall the elevator vignette described above (§4.0). This time, imagine that the stomach of one of the passengers sends out one of those uncontrollable growls that result from hunger, digestion, or some other bodily process. Undoubtedly, s/he will feel embarrassed or uneasy, even though s/he knows that s/he has no control over a sound emitted naturally by the body. This is because the *kinesic code* that applies to the "elevator situation" does not permit any sound to break the measured silence in the cubicle. So, as a socially redeeming strategy the individual might excuse h/erself, make an ironic or facetious remark about the sound, attempt to hide it by making some more kinesically acceptable noise (like clearing h/er throat), or ignore it completely as if it hadn't occurred.

The sounds made by the body—sneezing, coughing, burping, etc.—and the fluids that issue forth from it are interpreted in terms of the kinesic codes that regulate a specific situation. These codes also prescribe what body image is socially acceptable. In contemporary Western society, for instance, the "slim, lean look" is a condition for attractiveness for both males and females. The margin of flexibility from any idealized thinness model is larger for males than it is for females, but males must additionally strive to develop a muscular look.

Kinesic codes are derived from the particular type of anatomy that characterizes the human body. The details of skeletal structure distinguishing *Homo sapiens* from its nearest primate relatives—the gorilla, chimpanzee, and orangutan—stem largely from a very early adaptation to a completely erect posture and bipedal striding walk. The uniquely S-shaped spinal column places the center of gravity of the human body directly over the area of support provided by the feet, thus giving stability and balance in the upright position (chapter 1, §1.3). So, many bodily movements and postures are inherited through our bipedal evolutionary legacy. But the break with this legacy can be seen in the cross-cultural tendency to walk and assume postures in ways designed to generate social meaning. In social contexts, bodily posture and body image are perceived to be part of Self-presentation, not Self-preservation.

Consider posing. In courtship displays, for instance, the posing actions that males and females execute are hardly spontaneous. They are in fact regulated by culture-specific kinesic codes. The minimal units that make up such codes are called *kinesthemes* (or *kinemes*), in analogy with *phonemes* (the minimal units of sound in a language). Courtship kinesthemes can be discerned, for example, in flirting situations in which strangers attracted to each other sexually commonly participate. In North American culture, the male in such a situation attempts typically to look "virile" by assuming a form of posing involving the cocking of the head, an exaggerated tone of voice, and a pseudo-nonchalant attitude towards the female suitor as he casts glances towards her. The female, on the other hand, will typically tilt

her head down and to the side as she looks away. This is meant to attract the attention of the male. By cocking the head and looking up
shyly at a potential suitor, the female establishes a closer affective linkage with the male. Raising the shoulder, arching the back, tossing the
head in one sweeping motion, and playing with the hair are all female
courtship kinesthemes in such situations. A female might also tuck her
hair behind her ear (if she wears longer hair) to expose her neck, an
alluring erogenous zone for males. Taking notice of a specific female, a
particular male will react by engaging in exaggerated movements—linking his hands behind his head with his chest out, laughing
loudly, swaying markedly, etc. Similar codes exist across cultures. The
meanings of the kinesthemes are highly variable and annotative (chapter 3, §3.5), but they nonetheless cohere into a coded system of signification that tends to regulate interaction in courtship situations.

Courtship displays in all species may look comical or absurd to
outsiders, but to the members of the species concerned they constitute a
crucial kinesic mode of communication at a key stage in the enactment
of reproductive urges. In humans, these displays make sense only if the
appropriate physical and social contexts are present during courtship
or flirtation. So, while human kinesic codes may be residues of some
ancient animal signaling mechanism, as some sociobiologists suggest,
the great diversity that is evident in human courtship displays across
cultures suggests that they are not mere contemporary versions of in-
stinctual mating behaviors. Rather, they are shaped in large part by
human notions of gender and romance and are, therefore, constantly
subject to change. In the human species, courtship is not only a reflex of
biology, but also a product of history and tradition. Like any code of
the signifying order, it is the outcome of Nature and Culture cooperat-
ing in a type of partnership that is found nowhere else in the animal
realm.

Kinesic codes also mediate people's perception of which bodily
parts or zones are erogenous. More technically, some bodily parts are
perceived across cultures as kinesic signifiers that connote specific
erotic signifieds. In her fascinating book *The Gift of Touch* (1983), Helen
Colton has documented how such codes influence people's view of
which female bodily parts are erotic. She did this by asking females
living in diverse societies the following question: If a stranger were to
come upon you taking a bath, then what bodily part or area would you
cover? As Colton found out, the answer depended on the culture in
which the woman was reared:

> - An Islamic woman would cover her face.
> - A Laotian woman would cover her breasts.

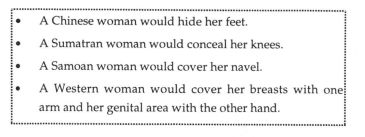

- A Chinese woman would hide her feet.
- A Sumatran woman would conceal her knees.
- A Samoan woman would cover her navel.
- A Western woman would cover her breasts with one arm and her genital area with the other hand.

With regard to this topic, the semiotician Michel Foucault (1926–1984) argued persuasively that the "sins of the flesh" are hardly universal. They too must be defined culturally. The Puritans of England, for instance, saw any form of sexual contact or gazing in a marriage situation as a kind of "necessary sin." "Sexual temptation" is still felt by some people to be "sinful." This is why many current-day conservative politicians are wont to condemn "obscene materials," young people's "lack of morals," and the "scourge of sexual sins," even when they seem to be actively engaged in sexual activities hypocritically behind the scenes. On the other hand, the many "hedonistic" rites and practices of our own and other cultures exalt and glorify the eroticism of the human body. Obviously, what is "obscene" behavior to some is "natural" or "desirable" behavior to others. While sexual urges are based in biology, perceptions of what is or is not erotic, sinful, or obscene are ensconced in cultural traditions and habits.

Humans, like other animals, sense and respond instinctively to the maleness or femaleness of another human. Across the animal realm, such responses are elicited by sexual signals during estrus (going into heat). From an evolutionary perspective, however, the human species has developed a sexuality independent of estrus. Other animals experience chemical and physical changes in the body during estrus which stimulate desire. People are the reverse. They normally experience desire through mental stimulation first and then experience estrus-type changes in the body. Thus, what is *sexual* is literally in the mind of the beholder.

But the human story of sex does not end there. Throughout the world, certain behaviors are perceived as constituting male and female sexuality. These result in the *gender* codes that define "masculinity" and "femininity" within a tribe or society. This is why gender behaviors vary considerably: e.g. in Western society, men are often expected to be the "sex-seekers," to initiate courtship, and to show an aggressive interest in sex; but among the Zuñi peoples of New Mexico, these very same actions and passions are expected of the women.

In terms of the *dimensionality principle* (chapter 3, §3.9) a representamen that stands for something sexual, erotic, etc. constitutes a sign that will be interpreted in terms of (1) its physical sex designations (firstness), (2) its sexuality annotations (secondness), and (3) its gender implications (thirdness):

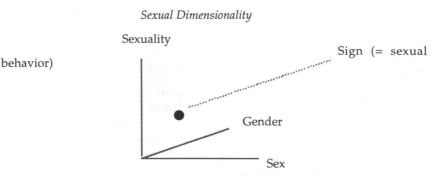

Sex is a firstness process that implies an either/or relation (male vs. female); *sexuality* is a secondness psychological reaction, developed in terms of individual and culturally based patterns of behavior; *gender* is a thirdness conventional code influencing what the sign (behavior) entails in social terms. Note that if a person alters h/er biological *sex*, by surgery and hormone treatment, then that person's *sexuality* patterns will change accordingly. Culturally, too, the person's *gender* will be redefined as a "new sexual persona," and s/he will start behaving in gender-coded ways.

4.3 FACIAL CODES

In 1963 the psychologist Paul Ekman established the Human Interaction Laboratory in the Department of Psychiatry at the University of California at San Francisco for the empirical study of facial expression. He was joined by Wallace V. Friesen in 1965 and Maureen O'Sullivan in 1974. Over the years, Ekman and his team have been able to link specific facial actions to different aspects of emotion. A facial action is called a *viseme* (or *videme*). Ekman has shown that a specific viseme can be broken down into components—eyebrow position, eye shape, mouth shape, nostril size, etc.—which in various combinations determine its meaning (which is generally connotative in social situations). Ekman found that very little visemic variation exists in the facial *codes* of different cultures. Indeed, he has shown that it is possible to write a "grammar" of the face that shows less cross-cultural variation than do language grammars.

Psychologists have also found that specific individuals are responsive sexually to certain particular kinds of faces and not to others from puberty onwards. One explanation as to why such preferences surface at puberty is the formation of what the psychologist Money (1986) calls "lovemaps" in the mind. These are mental images that determine the kind of face that will evoke sexual arousal and love moods (such as infatuation) in an individual. Lovemaps are developed during childhood in response to various experiences and influences. At adolescence, they unconsciously generate an image of what the ideal sweetheart should be like, becoming quite specific as to details of the physiognomy and facial appearance of the ideal lover.

All this suggests that the face is perceived as a signifier standing for the Self. This would explain why people prepare the face for presentation to social audiences, decorating it according to situation. Facial decorations and alterations constitute *representational* activities regulated by facial grooming and appearance codes. From the beginning of time, human beings have "made up" their faces to convey sexual persona. As the anthropologist Helen Fisher (1992: 272-273) has aptly remarked, in fact, the archeological evidence reveals that the cosmetic making up of the face is a characteristic representational activity that goes right back to our Cro-Magnon ancestors, who would apparently decorate their faces, plait their hair, and don garlands of flowers to show off sexually for one another around the fire's glow.

Facial decoration is also characteristic of fertility and passage rites. For example, the pubescent males of the Secoya people who live along the Río Santa Naría in Peru wear a sprig of grass through their nasal septum (the partition that divides the two nasal cavities) for the traditional circumcision rite of passage. In some tribal Gê societies of Brazil, when a young man becomes a father for the first time a saucer-like plate, which may reach a diameter of four inches, is inserted through the flesh of his lower lip to symbolize his passing from boyhood to manhood. Although Westerners might consider such forms of facial alteration disfiguring or mutilating, one must not forget Western practices like ear-piercing, nose-piercing, and even straightening, capping, or bleaching the teeth—all of which might appear just as mutilating to other peoples.

It is interesting to note that the perception of the face as a purveyor of persona permeates the signifying orders of cultures throughout the world—a pattern that reflects what we will call the *interconnectedness principle* in the remainder of this book. This principle posits that a specific meaning (or signified) considered vital by members of a culture will be encoded in various verbal and nonverbal ways throughout the culture's signifying order—in language, in bodily codes, in artistic practices, etc. The interconnectedness of the "face-as-persona" concept shows up not only in facial codes and representational activities but also, for example, in language, as can be seen in expressions such as the following:

> 1.   We argued *face* to *face*.
> 2.   Don't show your *face* on my property again.
> 3.   He criticized the supervisor to her *face*.
> 4.   Put on a happy *face*.
> 5.   You wear your feelings on your *face*.
> 6.   You can see his hypocrisy on his *face*.
> 7.   He's just another pretty *face*.

This same concept shows up as well in portraiture practices. These inhere in the visual representation of a subject whose facial appearance, as depicted by the artist, is typically interpreted by viewers as a visemic clue provided by the artist for understanding the subject's character, social position, profession, etc. The *interconnectedness principle,* as we shall see in the final chapter (§12.2), provides a basic framework for studying the ways in which the codes of a signifying order are linked holistically together by basic concepts such as this one.

Eye Contact

Of particular importance to social interaction is eye contact. Across cultures, the length of time involved in making eye contact conveys what kind of relationship people have with each other. Staring is often interpreted as a challenge or flirtation. Making eye contact early or late during a verbal exchange will indicate the kind of relationship one wishes to have with the interlocutor. Narrow eyelids communicate pensiveness, whereas the eyebrows made to come nearer together communicate thoughtfulness, and when made to rise, surprise.

Clearly, eye contact and eye configuration patterns may in part be anchored in evolution and anatomy, but there are many aspects that are culture-specific—southern Europeans will tend to look more into each other's eyes during conversation than do North Americans; in some cultures males do not look into female eyes unless they are spouses or members of the same family; and so on. The minimal units of gazing and looking that are meaningful in a culture can be called *ocularemes* (again in analogy with *phonemes*). In North American culture, for instance, where the male is expected to be the sex seeker, ocularemic patterns such as *gazing, staring, gaping, glaring, peering,* and *ogling* are expected more often than not of the male. *Gazing* refers to prolonged looking that is often indicative of sexual wonder, fascination, awe, or admiration. *Staring* is an audacious or insolent form of gazing. *Gaping* refers to a prolonged open-mouthed look reflecting sexual amazement or awe. *Glaring* is a harder, more piercing form of staring. *Peering* is looking narrowly, searchingly, and seemingly with difficulty. *Ogling* is staring in an amorous, usually impertinent manner. In effect, Western cultural history dictates that men should be the gazers and women the ones looked at. Although this has been changing since the late 1960s, the remnants of this cultural trend are still found throughout the signifying order—in language, courtship behaviors, artistic representations, etc.

4.4 PROXEMIC CODES

Proxemic codes regulate the distances people maintain between each other and the ways they orient their bodies when interacting in social situations. For example, when strangers of the opposite sex in our society are introduced to each other, each one knows not only to extend the right hand to initiate a handshake, but also how far to stand from the other. They would also not touch any other part of the body—arms, face, etc.

Such codes are the product of the interaction between biological mechanisms and cultural tradition. This is why they vary widely across the world. At sporting events or theaters, for instance, North Americans usually slide into a crowded aisle while facing forwards with their back to the people already seated, avoiding eye contact; Russians, on the other hand, face the people already seated. People in other cultures stand closer to each than we do during social contact. The semiotic gist of the story is that interpersonal space is imbued with meaning and that the social behaviors that are considered to be the norm within specific kinds of spaces are regulated by proxemic codes that must be learned in cultural context.

The term *proxemics* was coined by the anthropologist Edward T. Hall (1966) as the study of the cultural, behavioral, and sociological aspects of spatial distances between individuals. At a firstness level, proxemic structures are reflective of the biological mechanism known as *territoriality*, one of several mechanisms by which animals control access to critical resources, such as food or nesting sites. All animal species compete for territories, either fighting actual battles or performing ritual combats as tests of strength. Each species has the biological means of seeking out appropriate territories for its survival, of marking them, and of defending them. Intrusion into the territory is perceived instinctively as a signal of aggression. Cats, for example, mark the boundaries of their proclaimed territory by urination, and are prepared to challenge any intrusions into the territory aggressively. We do an analogous thing, by the way, by marking off our own appropriated territory (home) by various props (doors, fences, landmarks, etc.). And like other animals, we are willing to protect the territories we occupy with aggression.

The territoriality mechanism became the target of behavioral psychologists in the middle of the twentieth century, when their experiments received much media attention because of the implications they seemed to have at the time for life in modern crowded urban centers. The gist of these experiments can be outlined as follows. When two laboratory rats were enclosed in the same cage, the researchers found that they would instinctively seize areas of approximately equal dimensions. When a third rat was introduced into the same cage, then a tripartite arrangement of subdivided areas would seem to be negotiated among the three rats. However, there always seemed to be some initial reluctance to do so, as signaled by minor altercations among the three rats at the beginning of the negotiations. As each extra rat was introduced progressively into the same environment, more reluctance and aggression would ensue until a "critical mass" would apparently be reached at which the rats in the cage would either fight aggressively and relentlessly or demonstrate some form of aberrant behavior. The implications for urban overcrowding that those experiments apparently had were not missed by journalists and reporters. They also seemed to provide an explanation as to why some people "snap," as the expression goes, when this critical mass is surpassed; and why others seek rational solutions such as escaping into the suburbs, moving into the country, etc.

Another implication that was derived from the above experiments was the fact that we all need to maintain a boundary around ourselves for our protection and sanity. Hall (1966) was among the first to see the relevant implications and, thus, to investigate the patterns and dimensions of the zones people establish and maintain between each other when interacting. He noted that these could be measured very accurately, allowing for predictable statistical variation, and that the boundary dimensions varied from culture to culture. Each meaningful interpersonal zone can be called a *proxeme* (in analogy with *phoneme*, *kinestheme*, etc.). In North American culture, Hall found that a distance of under six inches between two people was perceived as an "intimate" distance, while a distance from 1.5 to 4 feet was the minimum perceived as safe. Intruding upon the limits set by this boundary causes considerable discomfort. For example, if a stranger were to talk at a distance of only several inches away from someone, s/he would be considered rude or even aggressive. If the "safe" distance were breached by some acquaintance, on the other hand, the breach would be interpreted as a sexual advance.

More specifically, Hall identified four types of culturally elaborated proxemes: *intimate, personal, social,* and *public.* He further subdivided these into "far" and "close" phases:

Intimate Proxeme (0 in. – 18 in.)

- At intimate distance, all the senses are activated and the presence of the other person or persons is unmistakable. The close phase (0 in. – 6 in.) is an emotionally-charged zone reserved for love-making, comforting, and protecting; the far phase (6 in. – 18 in.) is the distance at which family members and close friends interact. Touch is frequent at both phases of intimate distance.

Personal Proxeme (1.5 ft. – 4 ft.)

- This is the minimum comfortable distance between non-touching individuals. In the close phase (1.5 ft. – 2.5 ft.), one can grasp the other by extending the arms. The far phase (2.5 ft. – 4 ft.) is defined as anywhere from one arm's length to the distance required for both individuals to touch hands. Beyond this distance the two must move to make contact (e.g. to shake hands). In essence, this zone is reserved for informal contact between friends. It constitutes a small protective space that separates the Self from the Other.

Social Proxeme (4 ft. – 12 ft.)

- This distance is considered non-involving and non-threatening by most individuals. The close phase (4 ft. – 7 ft.) is typical of impersonal transactions and casual social gatherings. Formal social discourse and transactions are characteristic of the far phase (7 ft. – 12 ft.). This is the minimum distance at which one could go about one's business without seeming rude to others.

Public Proxeme (12 ft. and beyond)

- At this distance, one can take either evasive or defensive action if physically threatened. Hall notes that people tend to keep at this distance from important public figures or from anyone participating at a public function. Discourse at this distance will be highly structured and formalized (lectures, speeches, etc.).

Proxemic codes are interconnected with the other codes of the signifying order (the *interconnectedness principle*). Utterances such as "Keep your distance," "They're very close," "We've drifted far apart," "You're trespassing into my personal space," "I can't quite get to him," "Please keep in touch," etc. are all verbal reflexes of proxemic signifieds. Incidentally, research has demonstrated consistently that the relative ages, genders, levels of familiarity, and social roles of the individuals involved in an interpersonal encounter, as well as the perceived attractiveness of an interlocutor, are factors that influence proxemic zones in interactive settings.

Bodily orientation is also regulated by a proxemic code. If someone is standing up at the front of an audience, s/he is perceived as more important than those sitting down. Speeches, lectures, classes, musical performances, etc. are oriented in this way. Officials, managers, directors, etc. sit behind a desk to convey importance and superiority. Only their superiors can walk behind the desks to talk to them. To show friendliness, the person behind the desk will have to come out and sit with h/er interlocutor in a different part of the room.

4.5 TACTILE CODES

In most cultures, one of the constituents of greeting involves a form of handshaking. This is an example of a social behavior regulated by a *tactile code*, i.e. a code that regulates the patterns of touch in interpersonal situations. In modern urban centers, and in Western culture generally, people rarely touch each other. Some clinical psychologists have even attributed most of our anxieties and emotional syndromes to this apparent cultural fear and abhorrence of touch. The modern fields of *dance* and *touch therapy* have been developed, in fact, as a means to help people express themselves and relate to others through movement and touch.

The minimal units of touch (where to touch, duration of the touch, etc.) can be called *tactemes* (in analogy with *phonemes, kinesthemes,* etc.), and the type of communication that is based on touch is known more technically as *haptic*. The most common form of haptic communication is handshaking. The zoologist Desmond Morris (1969) claims that the Western form may have started as a way to show that neither person was holding a weapon. It thus became a "tie sign," because of the bond it was designed to create. Throughout the centuries, this sign became a symbol of equality among individuals, being used to seal agreements of all kinds. Indeed, refusing to shake someone's outstretched hand continues, to this day, to be interpreted as a sign of aggressiveness or as a challenge. Predictably, this form of haptic greeting reveals a high degree of cross-cultural variation. People can squeeze the hand (as Europeans and North Americans do), shake the other's hand with both hands, shake the hand and then pat the other's back or hug h/er, lean forward or stand straight while shaking, and so on. But haptic communication is not limited to handshake greetings. Other manifestations of haptic behavior include patting someone on the arm, shoulder, or back to indicate agreement or to compliment; linking arms to indicate companionship; putting one's arm around the shoulder to indicate friendship or intimacy; holding hands with family members or a lover to express intimacy; hugging to convey happiness at seeing a friend or a family member; and so on.

Anthropologists are unclear as to why tactile and haptic codes vary so much across cultures. In our opinion, it is due to differing perceptions of the Self. People in some cultures seem to think of themselves as literally "contained" in their skin. The zones of privacy that define "Self-space" in these cultures, therefore, include the clothes that cover the skin. On the other hand, in other cultures the Self is felt to be located down within the body shell, resulting in a totally different perception and coding of proxemic, tactile, and haptic behaviors. As a consequence, people in these cultures are in general more tolerant of crowds, of noise levels, of the touching of hands, of eye contact, and of body odors than most North Americans are (Hall 1966).

One aspect of tactile behavior that is shrouded in evolutionary mystery is "lip touching" in the human species, known, of course, more commonly as *kissing*. When the lips of both people touch, kissing is perceived normally as erotic. But not all kissing is, of course, erotic. It can be a way of showing affection to children, friends, pets, etc. But erotic kissing is particularly interesting as an evolutionary and cultural phenomenon. It seems to be a kind of mock-suckling or mock-feeding of the sexual partner, implying vulnerability, closeness, and sensuality. This is perhaps why prostitutes may be willing to perform a variety of sexual acts for hire, but generally draw the line at kissing. However, erotic kissing is not universal. It is not common in China or Japan, for instance; it is completely unknown in some African tribal societies. Traditional Inuit and Laplander societies are more inclined to rub noses than to kiss.

4.6 GESTURAL CODES

Gesture is representation and communication involving the hands, the arms, and to a lesser extent, the head. Gesture is found in humans and primates. For example, chimpanzees raise their arms in the air as a signal that they want to be groomed; they stretch out their arms to beg or invite; and they have the ability to point to things (Beaken 1996: 51). These gestures are, evidently, purposeful and regulatory of the actions of other chimps. But the number of gestural signifiers of which chimpanzees are capable is limited. Human gesturing, on the other hand, is productive and varied. It encompasses, for instance, the many sign languages used in communities of the hearing-impaired, the alternative sign languages used by religious groups during periods of imposed silence, the hand signals used by traffic personnel, and the hand and arm movements used to conduct an orchestra. Some gestures can have quite specific meanings, such as those for saying good-bye or for asking someone to approach. Other gestures more generally accompany speech, such as those used to emphasize a particular point. Although there are cross-cultural similarities in gesture, substantial differences also exist both in the extent to which gesture is used and in the interpretations given to its particular uses. In 1979, Desmond Morris, together with several of his associates at Oxford University, examined 20 gestures in 40 different areas of Europe. The research team found some rather fascinating things. For instance, they discovered that many of the gestures had several meanings, depending on culture: e.g. a tap on the side of the head can indicate completely opposite things—"stupidity" or "intelligence"—according to cultural context; the head gestures for "yes" and "no" used in the Balkans seem inverted to other Europeans; and so on.

Gestures can be witting and unwitting. The former are the manual signals that people produce spontaneously across cultures to indicate affective states and intentions—e.g. clenching the hand to convey anger; lifting the arm to cover the face for protection; and so on. Witting gestures span the entire range of semiosic properties: e.g. referring to a round object by moving the hands in opposite directions—one clockwise and the other counter-clockwise—is an example of iconic gesturing; pointing to something with the index finger or with a tilt of the head is, of course, an example of indexical gesturing; and the conventionalized hand movements people use in greeting, agreeing, negating, halting, insulting, etc. are instances of symbolic gesturing. Many semioticians and linguists consider gesture to be a more fundamental form of communication than vocal language. This would explain why gesture is the default mode of communication when one doesn't speak the language of the people of a country one is visiting. For example, if the visitor needed to describe an automobile in that situation, s/he would typically use the hands to portray a steering wheel and the motion used to steer a car, accompanying this, perhaps, with a vocal sound imitative of a motor. This anecdotal scenario not only suggests that gesture is a more fundamental mode of communication, but also that its essentially iconic modality makes it a much more universal, and less culture-dependent, system of message-making.

Many linguists claim that gesture and speech are linked in human evolution. The use of the hands—the dominant limbs in the human species, given their physiological structure for grasping and pointing—was made possible when the human species evolved into one that walks upright. The liberation of the hands from the requirements of locomotion allowed early humans not only to make tools and to use fire deliberately, but also to use their hands for gesturing. The capacity to point out beings, objects, and events in the immediate environment, so as to convey their existence and location to others, conferred upon our early bipedal ancestors a new and powerful psychological control over their environment and over their own lives.

The transition from manual to vocal language is explained, typically, by theorists in terms of an imitation and substitution process by which gestural signs were transferred osmotically to the vocal apparatus. The version of gesture theory that has become a point of departure for all subsequent ones was actually formulated by the philosopher Jean Jacques Rousseau (1712–1778) in the middle part of the eighteenth century. Rousseau became intrigued by the question of the origins of language while seeking to understand what he called the "noble savage." Rousseau proposed that the cries of nature that early humans must have shared with the animals, and the gestures that they must have used simultaneously, led to the invention of vocal language. He explained the evolutionary transition in this way—when the accompanying gestures proved to be too cumbersome, their corresponding cries were used to replace them completely. However, Rousseau did not provide any scientific evidence to support his theory. In the early twentieth century, Richard Paget (1930) accepted Rousseau's idea, refining it as follows. Gestural signs became vocal ones, Paget claimed, through vocal simulation: i.e. manual gestures were purportedly copied unconsciously by positions and movements of the lips and tongue, and the continual apposition of gestures and vocal movements led eventually to the replacement of the former by the latter. But again, Paget provided no evidence to support his explanation.

Such theories raise two rudimentary questions that they seem incapable of answering: (1) What made the transition from gestural to vocal signs attainable or even desirable? (2) Why has gesture survived as a communicative system? Actually, the most suggestive indirect evidence that gesture may in fact have been the evolutionary antecedent of vocal language is the very fact that it has survived and can satisfy all basic communicative needs. The psychological literature has documented, moreover, that children invariably pass through an initial stage of pointing and iconic gesturing before they develop language (Lieberman 1984). Incidentally, some fascinating experiments have shown that speakers who are requested not to use vocal speech to communicate with each other can easily create a gesture language within a very short period of time (Singleton, Morford, and Goldin-Meadow 1993, Morford, Singleton, and Goldin-Meadow 1995). This suggests rather strongly that gesture contains all the structural features that are needed to make verbal messages.

Gesticulants

The findings of the linguist David McNeill (1992) show, much more precisely, how gesture is intrinsically interconnected with vocal language. After videotaping a large sample of people as they spoke, McNeill came to the inescapable conclusion that the gestures that accompany speech, which he called *gesticulants*, are hardly inconsequential to the act of communication. Gesticulants exhibit images that cannot be shown overtly in speech, as well as images of what the speaker is thinking about. This suggested to him that speech and gesture constitute a single integrated referential/communication system that allows a person to get the message across effectively.

McNeill proceeded to classify gesticulants into five main categories. First, there are *iconic* gesticulants, which, as their name suggests, bear a close resemblance to the referent or referential domain of an utterance: e.g. when describing a scene from a story in which a character bends a tree back to the ground, a speaker observed by McNeill appeared to grip something and pull it back. His gesture was, in effect, a visual icon of the action talked about, revealing both his memory image and his point of view (he could have taken the part of the tree instead).

Second, there are *metaphoric* gesticulants. These are also pictorial, but their content is abstract, rather than iconic. For example, McNeill observed a male speaker announcing that what he had just seen was a cartoon, simultaneously raising up his hands as if offering his listener a kind of object. He was obviously not referring to the cartoon itself, but to the genre of the cartoon. His gesture represented this genre as if it were an object, placing it into an act of offering to the listener. This type of gesticulant typically accompanies utterances that contain expressions such as *presenting an idea, putting forth an idea, offering advice*, and so on.

Third, there are *beat* gesticulants. These resemble the beating of musical tempo. The speaker's hand moves along with the rhythmic pulsation of speech, in the form of a simple flick of the hand or fingers up and down, or back and forth. Beats are indexes, marking the introduction of new characters, summarizing the action, introducing new themes, etc. during the utterance.

Fourth, there are *cohesive* gesticulants. These serve to show how separate parts of an utterance are supposed to hold together. Beats emphasize sequentiality, cohesives globality. Cohesives can take iconic, metaphoric, or beat form. They unfold through a repetition of the same gesticulant form, movement, or location in the gesture space. It is the repetition itself that is meant to convey cohesiveness.

Fifth, there are *deictic* gesticulants. As mentioned in the previous chapter (§3.6), deixis is the term used by semioticians to designate all kinds of pointing or indicating signs. Deictic gesticulants are aimed not at an existing physical place, but at an abstract concept that had occurred earlier in the conversation. These reveal that we perceive concepts as having a physical location in space.

McNeill's work gives us a good idea of how the gestural mode of representation intersects with the vocal one in normal discourse. As Frutiger (1989: 112) has also observed, accompanying gestures reveal an inner need to support what one is saying orally: "If on a beach, for example, we can hardly resist drawing with the finger on the smooth surface of the sand as a means of clarifying what we are talking about."

McNeill's gesticulant categories are actually subtypes of the more generic category of gesticulant known as an *illustrator*. Other categories are *emblems*, *affect displays*, *regulators*, and *adaptors*:

- *Illustrators:* As just discussed, these accompany and literally illustrate vocal utterances. Examples: circular hand movements when talking of a circle; moving hands far apart when talking of something large; moving both the head and hands in an upward direction when saying *Let's go up.*

- *Emblems:* These directly translate words or phrases. Examples: the *Okay* sign, the *Come here* sign; the hitchhiking sign; waving; and many obscene gestures.

- *Affect Displays:* These communicate emotional meaning. Examples: the typical hand movements and facial expressions that accompany happiness, surprise, fear, anger, sadness, contempt, disgust, etc.

- *Regulators:* These monitor, maintain, or control the speech of someone else. Examples: hand movements indicating *Keep going, Slow down, What else happened?*

- *Adaptors:* These are gesticulants that satisfy some need. Examples: scratching one's head when puzzled; rubbing one's forehead when worried; and so on.

Sign Languages

Many societies have developed or adopted gesture codes for the use of hearing- or speech-impaired individuals. These are known generally as *sign languages*—the term *sign* being used as a synonym for *gesture*. These are languages in the real sense of the word, since they share many structural and communicative features with vocal languages. The spatial and orientational use of hand movements, as well as facial expressions and body movement, make up the grammar and lexicon of sign languages. In American Sign Language (ASL), for instance, the sign for "catch" involves one hand (in the role of agent) moving across the body (an action) to grasp the forefinger of the other hand (the patient). ASL signifiers are made by one or both hands, which assume distinctive shapes and movements. A number of manual communication systems use the sign vocabulary of ASL in combination with other hand movements to approximate the syntax of Standard English.

Sign languages are also used by hearing peoples for various purposes. One of the best-known examples is the sign language developed by the Plains peoples of North America as a means of communication between tribes with different vocal languages. The manual signs represent things in nature, ideas, emotions, and sensations. For example, the sign for a white person is made by drawing the fingers across the forehead, indicating a hat. Special signs exist also for each tribe and for particular rivers, mountains, and other natural features. The sensation of cold is indicated by a shivering motion of the hands in front of the body; and the same sign is used for winter and for year, because the Plains peoples count years in terms of winters. Slowly turning the hand, relaxed at the wrist, means vacillation, doubt, or possibility; a modification of this sign, with quicker movement, is the question sign. This sign language is so elaborate that a detailed conversation is possible using the gestures alone (Mallery 1972).

4.7 CLOTHING AS EXTENSION OF THE BODY

Throughout cultures, one comes across representations of the body—in painting, in narratives, etc.—which reveal that it is perceived typically as being imbued with moral, social, and aesthetic significance. In ancient Greece the body was glorified as a source of pleasure; in ancient Rome it was perceived as a source of moral corruption. As a consequence, the two cultures represented the body in different ways. The Christian Church has always played on the duality of the body as a temple and as an enemy of the spirit. The perception of the body as something morally significant is typical of tribal cultures too. As the anthropologist Helen Fisher (1992: 253-254) observes, even in the jungle of Amazonia Yanomamo men and women wear clothes for sexual modesty. A Yanomamo woman would feel as much discomfort and agony at removing her vaginal string belt as would a North American woman if one were to ask her to remove her underwear. Similarly, a Yanomamo man would feel just as much embarrassment at his penis accidentally falling out of its encasement as would a North American male caught literally "with his pants down."

Clothing and decorating the body for social presentation are forms of representation. For example, the wearing of jewelry is typically representative of sexual or romantic meanings. When a young Zulu woman falls in love, she is expected to make a beaded necklace resembling a close-fitting collar with a flat panel attached, which she then gives to her boyfriend. Depending on the combination of colors and bead pattern, the necklace is a courtship text designed to convey a specific type of romantic message: e.g. a combination of pink and white beads in a certain pattern would convey the message *You are poor, but I love you just the same* (Dubin 1987: 134).

The wearing of *clothes* constitutes a fundamental means of extending the meanings of the body. Like any human object or artifact, clothes are interpreted as signs: i.e. as signifiers standing for something else (personality, social status, etc.). At a biological level, clothes have a very important function indeed—they enhance our survivability considerably. They are, at this denotative level, human-made extensions of the body's protective resources; i.e. they are additions to our protective bodily hair and skin thickness. As Werner Enninger (1992: 215) aptly points out, this is why clothing systems vary according to geography and topography: "The distribution of types of clothing in relation to different climatic zones and the variation in clothes worn with changes in weather conditions show their practical, protective function." But as is the case in all human systems, clothes invariably take on a whole range of connotations in social settings. These are established on the basis of the various *dress codes* (from Old French *dresser* "to arrange, set up") that inform people how to clothe themselves in social situations. In terms of the *dimensionality principle*, therefore, clothes denote bodily protection (i.e. they extend bodily protective functions), taking on specific connotative meanings in social settings in terms of a culture's various dress codes:

Clothing Dimensionality

Extend bodily protection

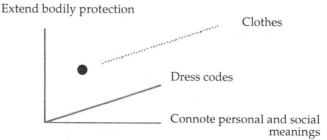

Clothes

Dress codes

Connote personal and social meanings

Predictably, dress codes vary across cultures. To someone who knows nothing about Amish culture, the blue or charcoal *Mutze* of the Amish male is just a jacket. But to the Amish the blue *Mutze* signals that the wearer is between 16 and 35 years of age, the charcoal one that he is over 35. Similarly, to an outsider the Russian *kalbak* appears to be a brimless red hat. To a rural Russian, however, it means that the wearer is a medical doctor. It is interesting to note, too, that clothing texts, like other representational activities, can be used to lie about oneself: e.g. con artists and criminals can dress in three-piece suits to look trustworthy; a crook can dress like a police officer to gain a victim's confidence, and so on. To discourage people from deceiving others through clothing, some societies have even enacted laws that prohibit misleading dressing and that define who can dress in certain ways. In ancient Rome, for instance, only aristocrats were allowed to wear purple-colored clothes; and in many religiously oriented cultures differentiated dress codes for males and females are regularly enforced.

For some semioticians and cultural historians, the history of clothing fashions is the history of a culture. Let us take, therefore, a rapid and highly selective trip through the maze of Western fashion history as a case-in-point. After the fall of the Western Roman Empire in 476 AD, invaders from the north introduced fitted tunics and hoods into Western clothing styles. Shortly thereafter, the élite of the Byzantine Empire adopted Oriental traditions of dress, with no apparent concession to sexual attraction or to utility. After Charlemagne (742?–814 AD) became Holy Roman Emperor in 800, a relatively uniform style of dress appeared in Europe. Charlemagne's own everyday attire consisted of an undertunic and an overtunic, with breeches cross-gartered to the knee. This introduced the "tunic style" to other European monarchs. Court ladies also started wearing long tunics, under supertunics hitched up to show the tunics beneath. A cloth veil concealed the hair. These garments made up the basic wardrobe of the European aristocracy throughout the Middle Ages.

In the 1100s the Crusades had a startling effect on fashion, as crusaders brought back luxurious Oriental fabrics and new styles. The Oriental long, trailing tunic became the main form of aristocratic dress in the 1300s and evolved into the doublet, which survived into the 1600s as the basic male outer garment. Its modern version is the waistcoat or vest. The period also produced an early form of the corset for women. Throughout the Middle Ages, long skirts reached to the floor to hide women's ankles.

In the Renaissance, the development of new fabrics and materials brought about a desire for elaborate clothing styles. By the early 1600s, fashion had literally become the craze with lace edges, frills at the neck and sleeves, collars that eventually became the cravat and the necktie, and breeches for men. This period also saw the introduction of the wig for men. Light colors and fabrics characterized the 1700s, typified by the loose gown. Soft lace replaced the starched, formal ruffs of the previous century. With the French Revolution (1789–1799) came radical changes, as men began wearing trousers for the first time in six hundred years. No basic change in men's clothing has taken place since. Women's fashion reverted to what was deemed the "classical style," a look featuring thin fabrics and bare arms—emphasizing a new sexual freedom for females.

Up until the nineteenth century fashion was, clearly, the privilege of the aristocracy. The Industrial Revolution, however, projected fashion for the masses into the realm of economic possibility. Since then fashion crazes for everyone have become an intrinsic feature of the social landscape. Outside the Western world, however, clothing styles continue to be anchored in religious and/or tribal traditions. Where non-Western cultures have come into conflict with Western ideas, traditional garments have often been displaced. Nevertheless, in Africa, the Middle East, and the Far East many aspects of traditional dress have survived.

The broad range of connotations associated with dress codes are inextricably interconnected with other codes of the signifying order. Until the early 1950s, females in Western culture rarely wore pants. The expression "the one who wears the pants in the family" meant, denotatively and connotatively, the male. With the change in social role structures during the decades of the 1950s and 1960s, women too began to wear pants regularly, sending out the new social messages that this entailed. The reverse shift in styles has never occurred. Except in special ritualistic circumstances—e.g. the wearing of a Scottish kilt—men have not worn skirts in modern-day Western cultures since the French Revolution. If they do, then we label the act "transvestitism," with the particular kinds of negative connotations that this evokes.

During the 1950s, a new dress code based on age cropped up in Western society that mirrored an emerging social trend—the advent of an adolescent subculture. That was, in fact, the period when the clothes worn by the first rock'n roll musicians and adolescent media personages became the dress models for teenagers to emulate. With the entrenchment of teenage lifestyles from the mid-1960s onwards, a corresponding diversification of clothing styles ensued. For example, in the mid-1970s teens wishing to be members of so-called "punk groups" would have had to dye their hair with bizarre colors and cut it in unconventional ways; they would have had to wear unusual clothes and various kinds of props (e.g. safety pins stuck through their nostrils) to send out counter-culture messages. Although punk fashion started as a

political statement by working class youths in England, by the time its
symbolism was marketed to a larger segment of the teen subculture, it
ended up being all things to all classes: e.g. the fascist insignia used by
English punks lost its ideological overtones, becoming a "put-on"
aimed at provoking adults of a middle-class, bourgeois mentality.

Clearly, like any code, fashion is interconnected with the other
components of the signifying order. Discourse also frequently reflects
its meanings. Here are some examples that are self-explanatory:

1. I *dressed down* for such a casual occasion.
2. They *dressed up* and went to the prom.
3. The plane doesn't land for another hour, so keep your *shirt* on.
4. The only thing those swindlers didn't take was the *shirt* off my back.
5. You would understand my decision if you put yourself in my *shoes*.
6. The *shoe* is on the other foot.
7. Wait for the other *shoe* to drop.

4.8 NUDITY

The human being is the only animal that does not "go nude," so to
speak, without triggering off some form of social repercussion (unless,
of course, the social ambiance is that of a nudist camp). Indeed, nudity
can only be interpreted culturally. We are all born "nude," but we soon
learn that nudity has negative connotations. Moreover, what is considered "exposable" of the body will vary significantly from culture to
culture, even though the covering of genitalia seems, for the most part,
to cross cultural boundaries.

To see how powerful the meanings of nudity are, consider the "art"
of strip-teasing (male and female). A semiotician would ask: *What* does
it represent? *Why* do we attend (or desire to attend) performances
whose sole purpose is the removal of clothing to reveal the genitals
and, in the case of female strip-teasing, also the breasts? The semiotician would, of course, seek answers to these questions in the domain of
the signifying order. To start with, in order to understand nudity, one
must consider it in comparison with its paradigmatic counterpart,
clothing.

Strip-teasing is an act of alluring "clothing-removal." In an audience setting it has, first and foremost, something of a pagan ritualistic

quality to it. The dark atmosphere, the routines leading up to the act, and the predictability of the performance itself, with its bodily gyrations and mimetic emphases on sexual activities, are suggestive of sexual theater—i.e. of a hedonistic performance worshipping carnality and sexuality. There is no motive for being at such performances, really, other than to indulge our fascination with the sexuality that the clothing conceals. As the psychoanalyst Sigmund Freud (1856–1939) suggested, by masquerading the sexual body society has guaranteed, paradoxically, that people will desire to look at it through representations and performances that range from nude drawings to strip-teasing. Covering the body is an act of modesty. But clothing has in effect imbued it with a kind of secret desirability below the covered surface. So, at a strip-tease performance, the shedding of clothes does several symbolic things at once: it removes our imposed moral restrictions on sexuality; it reveals those covered bodily parts that have become so desirable; it engages us in carnal ritualizing.

Visual artists have also always had a fascination with the nude figure. The ancient Greek and Roman nude statues of male warriors, Michelangelo's (1475–1564) powerful *David* sculpture, and Rodin's (1840–1917) nude sculpture *The Thinker* are all suggestive of the potency of the male body. It is this suggestiveness that enhances male sexuality, not the size of the penis (as is popularly believed). On a "weakling" body, male genitals are hardly ever perceived as sexual, no matter what size they are. On the other side of this semiotic paradigm, the female nude has typically been portrayed as soft, sumptuous, and submissive —something to be gazed at. It is, in fact, this system of depiction that feminist social critics reacted to in the 1980s and 1990s. All of this makes it rather evident that nudity is much more than bare flesh, semiotically speaking.

The modern-day fascination with erotic materials, magazines, and videos is a contemporary testament to our age-old fascination with nudity as a signifying phenomenon. Those who see danger in such materials, and seem to be prepared to become everyone else's "moral guardians" by censoring them, are probably more overwhelmed by the connotative power of nudity than most others. Censorship is more dangerous than sexual depictions. Censorship-minded people attempt to control the form and contents of representational activities, by claiming to have the best interests of society at heart. In actual fact, they are simply rationalizing their fear of sexuality. Gazing at the human body depicted in sexual poses or activities reveals, in our opinion, the signifying value that nudity and sexuality have in our culture, no more and no less. Only when such depictions are restrained does a perilous fascination with gazing surface. In the world of representational behavior, nudity is indeed a very powerful signifying phenomenon.

Aware of this, some have even gone so far as to advocate the practice of not wearing clothes. The proponents of nudism maintain that clothing should be abandoned when not absolutely necessitated by the rigors of the weather, as clothing serves to focus erotic attention on the body, thereby exciting an unhealthy interest in sex. The shame customarily associated with nakedness in much of modern society results, according to nudists, from centuries of cultural conditioning against complete exposure of the body in public. Nudism, by correcting in its practitioners this false sense of shame, aims to enhance their self-assurance and furnish them with a new appreciation of the essential beauty and dignity of the human body. Whatever the case, the interplay between clothing and nudity as signifying systems cannot be ignored. They are intertwined and interconnected with the entire signifying order of a culture.

4.9 BODILY ART: DANCING

Dancing is common to all peoples and cultures. It is an art form based on bodily kinesthemes and gestures connected to each other textually through pattern and rhythm, and usually performed to music. Dance serves three main functions in human life:

1. It can be a form of aesthetic communication, expressing emotions, moods, or ideas, or telling a story. Classical Western ballet is an example of aesthetic dancing.

2. It can be a part of ritual, serving religious communal functions. In Java, for example, spirit-possession dances remain a part of village life. Sub-Saharan African societies engage in masked dances to exorcise spirits.

3. It can be a form of recreation, serving various psychological and social needs, or simply as an experience that is pleasurable in itself.

Evolutionary psychologists see dancing as a residue of movement for survival. (It is harder to attack moving prey.) This animal mechanism purportedly explains why it is virtually impossible to remain motionless for any protracted period of time. When we are forced to do so by the situation, our body reacts against it. There is, of course, some truth to this theory. During the public performance of a lengthy slow movement of a classical piano sonata, for example, it is almost impossible for audience members to keep perfectly still or not to cough or make some other kind of vocal sound. These involuntary reactions result in all likelihood from a latent need for movement. But why this need was converted in early cultural contexts into dancing defies explanation in biological terms. The reason behind the origin of dance as *art* remains a mystery. Throughout the world dance, like all art, serves a spiritual need—the need to seek meaning in life. Art somehow provides assurance beyond rational comprehension that there is a design and purpose to life beyond physical survival.

The best known form of aesthetic dancing is *ballet*, which originated in the courts of Italy and France during the Renaissance, becoming primarily a professional discipline shortly thereafter. The basis of ballet is a turned-out position of the legs and feet with corresponding arm positions. Certain relationships of the arms, legs, head, and torso produce an aesthetic, harmonious effect. A ballet may be choreographed either to music especially composed for it or to music already existing. The plot of a ballet is called its *libretto* or *scenario*. Ballet choreographers may use narratives from literature, drama, and films. Plotless ballets, on the other hand, are intended to create a mood, interpret a musical composition, or celebrate dancing for its own sake.

Early precursors to ballets were the lavish court dances of Renaissance Italy. Professional ballet dancers first appeared in the mid-1600s, with the art form being developed extensively during the reign of Louis XIV of France (1643–1715). Louis established the Académie Royale de Danse, a professional organization for dancing masters. At first dancers were men; professional female dancers appeared in 1681. During the second half of the eighteenth century the Paris Opéra was still dominated by male dancers. By the end of the century, and by the time of the romantic nineteenth century, ballet became dominated by women.

In the 1920s and 1930s popular dance forms, such as jazz and modern dance, enriched ballet's form and stylistic range. Two great American ballet companies were founded in New York City in the 1940s: the American Ballet Theater and the New York City Ballet. Since the mid-twentieth century, ballet companies have been founded in many cities throughout the United States and Canada. Beginning in 1956, Russian ballet companies such as the Bolshoi Ballet and the Saint Petersburg Ballet began performing in the West.

The universality of dance is evidence of its importance to human life. People frequent discos, take dance lessons, and enroll their children in ballet school because they feel that dancing satisfies some basic need of human life. As the American philosopher Susanne K. Langer (1895–1985) suggested, beautiful movements in dance have no specific purpose other than to engender in people the sense of beauty and of the sublime—both of which seem to be needed by human beings to satisfy an intrinsic need. As the saying goes, art is "food for the soul."

5

LANGUAGE

*A human language is a system of re-
markable complexity. To come to
know a human language would be an
extraordinary intellectual achievement for a creature not specifically
designed to accomplish this task.*

Chomsky (1975: 4)

5.0 PRELIMINARY REMARKS

Language (from Latin *lingua* "tongue") is truly a wondrous endowment. Without its development in the human species, culture as we know it would have been inconceivable. The knowledge preserved in books, and to which anyone can have access if one
knows the appropriate verbal codes, constitutes the intellectual scaffold
sustaining social and technological growth. It is no exaggeration to say
that if somehow all the books in the world were to be destroyed over-
night, human beings would have to start all over re-coding knowledge
linguistically. Writers, scientists, educators, law-makers, etc. would
have to come together to literally "rewrite" knowledge. In oral cultures,
too, language is the primary means through which traditions, skills,
and knowledge are codified and passed on to subsequent generations.
People the world over are told in words how and what things are.

Language has always been felt to constitute the capacity that, more
than any other, sets humankind apart from all other species. There is a
deeply felt conviction within us that if we were ever able to solve the
enigma of how language originated in our species, then we would possess a vital clue to the mystery of life itself. The Bible starts off, as a
matter of fact, with "In the beginning was the Word," in acknowledg-
ment of this deeply-entrenched belief. Throughout the centuries, the
debate has revolved around whether the Word was a gift from a divine
source or a unique accomplishment of the human mind. In ancient
Greece, actually, language and mind were considered indistinguishable. Indeed, the Greek term for "speech"—*logos*—designated not only
articulate discourse but also the rational faculty of mind. For the

Greeks, it was *logos* that transformed the brute human animal into a reflective thinker.

Language is essentially a representational system made up of words (or, more accurately, *morphemes*). But what is a *word*? Take, for instance, *green*. First, a word must be a legitimate verbal signifier structurally. And, indeed, *green* qualifies as a signifier because it is made up of legitimate English *phonemes*, joined in an appropriate fashion (i.e. according to English syllable structure). The signifier *deñ*, on the other hand, would not be an acceptable signifier because it contains a phoneme, represented by the alphabet character *ñ*, that does not exist in English. Hence, it would violate paradigmatic structure. Nor would *gpeen* be a permissible signifier, even though each of its sounds is an acceptable phoneme, because it would violate syntagmatic syllable structure (the sequence *gp* does not occur in English to start a syllable). Now, *green*, being a legitimate signifier and having been assigned a particular function in the signifying order, will entail a meaning range that involves denotative, connotative, and annotative dimensions. As a *qualisign* (chapter 3, §3.3) it denotes, of course, a specific gradation on the light spectrum; its extensional connotations encompass concepts such as *envy* ("She's *green* with envy"), *hope* ("The grass is always *greener* on the other side"), *youthfulness* ("He's at the *green* age of eighteen"), etc. Annotatively, *green* elicits various reactions in its users, within a specific range of meanings: e.g. some people love the color, others find it bland. But language is not just a collection of words with their meanings. It also entails knowing how to join words into *sentences* and *discourses*.

Our trip through the cultural landscape has reached a very important site with this chapter—the one inhabited by *Homo loquens*, the speaking animal and the closest ancestor of *Homo culturalis*. Studying the properties of language formally is the task of the science of linguistics (chapter 2, §2.5). The focus of the cultural semiotician, on the other hand, is on the relation of the verbal code to the signifying order. As was the case in the study of bodily semiosis (chapter 4), the focus of semiotic research is on the main signifying properties of language and on how language mediates and regulates thought and social interaction.

5.1 THE ORIGINS OF LANGUAGE

There is no more effective code for representing the world in its intricate detail and for making and communicating sophisticated messages than the verbal one. Language makes it possible to summon up past events, to refer to incidents that have not as yet occurred, to formulate questions about existence, to answer them, to conjure up fictional worlds, to give thoughts and actions a preservable form. What is this extraordinary code? Is it a species-specific genetic endowment, developed over many years of adaptive trial and error? Or is it something that the human species invented in an attempt to fulfill some basic need?

The answer, in our view, is affirmative to both of these questions. Language is surely the result of some innate faculty; but it is also something that humanity could have easily done without in order to survive as a species. Moreover, there seems to be no biological reason for its utilization by humans to formulate questions about existence and about themselves. Language is not an innate mental organ, as some linguists claim. Indeed, if we were somehow to shut off subsequent generations from language, there is virtually no doubt that the human species would have to start all over reinventing it. Organs, on the other hand, cannot be reinvented in our progeny. What we inherit from our biological heritage is not a language organ, but the capacity for verbal semiosis—a capacity tied to our *secondary modeling system* (chapter 3, §3.2).

The lengths to which some have gone to throw light on the enigma of language origins are quite extraordinary. It is reported by the Greek historian Herodotus that in the seventh century BC the Egyptian king Psamtik (663–610 BC) devised an experiment to determine the original language of humanity. He gave two new-born babies of ordinary people to a shepherd to nurture among his flocks. The shepherd was commanded not to utter any speech before them. The children were to live by themselves in a solitary habitation. At appropriate hours the shepherd was instructed to bring goats to them, give them their fill of milk, and carry out the necessary tasks to ensure their survival. After two years the shepherd brought the babies, raised in the prescribed manner, before Psamtik. The first word uttered by the two sounded like *becos*—the ancient Phrygian word for bread. The over-anxious Psamtik immediately declared Phrygian to be the mother tongue of humanity. Whether or not Psamtik's experiment ever took place at all is an open historical question. But even if it had, it certainly would not have proved anything. The babbling sounds made by the children–in probable imitation of each other–were interpreted, or more accurately misinterpreted, as constituting the word *becos* by Psamtik.

The enigma of language origins has spawned countless speculations throughout the millennia. This is why the Linguistic Society of Paris imposed its notorious ban in 1866 on all discussions related to this question, as did the Philological Society of London a half century later in 1911. In the early 1970s, however, interest in this conundrum was rekindled, as a result of the intriguing and suggestive findings that were being accumulated in such interrelated fields of inquiry as archeology, paleography, animal ethology, sociobiology, psychology, neurology, anthropology, semiotics, and linguistics. Language scientists came to see these as tantalizing bits and pieces for solving the puzzle of language origins.

One possibility is that language developed from *echoism*, i.e. from attempts of early humans to imitate natural sounds and react vocally to emotions. Indirect evidence for echoism as an originating force can be discerned in the onomatopoeic words and interjections that make up the core vocabularies of all languages. But echoism on its own fails to explain the evolutionary transition from onomatopoeic words to the development of syntax and discourse. Nevertheless, echoism cannot be dismissed entirely as a factor in language origins. After all, there really is no way to determine whether or not sound imitation played a much more pivotal creative role in prehistoric times than it does today. Moreover, as we saw in the previous chapter (§4.6), the probable apposition of manual signs with osmotic vocal imitations of their referents may have been the factor that led over time to the replacement of the former by the latter.

Another possibility is that speech grew out of the chants that the members of the first hominid groups vocalized to maintain harmony as they worked together. As social needs increased, so did the means for communicating them. But, then, what mental feature could have sparked the process by which chanting became full language? Moreover, as Sebeok (1986) suggests, communication is not a necessary function of language, since humans have many nonverbal means of communicating available to them. And as Chomsky (1975: 57) has aptly remarked, "there seems no reason to single out communication among the many uses to which language is put."

One of the first to investigate the question of language origins rigorously was the linguist Morris Swadesh (1971), who started by dividing the evolution of language into four primary periods that corresponded to the Eolithic (the dawn stone age), Paleolithic (the old stone age), Neolithic (the new stone age), and Historical (the last 10,000 years) periods. He then suggested that all languages in the world today sprang from one source during the Paleolithic period when Neanderthals still survived. This scenario was challenged on several counts. But Swadesh's method showed, once and for all, that a scientific approach to the age-old puzzle of language origins was conceivable. Using data from archeology and anthropology, together with a detailed knowledge of previous work on language change and reconstruction, Swadesh demonstrated how a credible primal scene could be drafted, and how the transition to contemporary language behavior could be explained plausibly.

Swadesh's work was also instrumental in rekindling the nine-teenth-century interest in language comparison—the meticulous com-parison of the structures and systems of related languages in order to make hypotheses about their common ancestor or *proto-language*. By the end of the nineteenth century language scientists had amassed suffi-cient evidence to suggest that most of the modern Eurasian languages had evolved from a single language. They called this language Proto-Indo-European (PIE), hypothesizing that it was spoken long before the first civilizations of 5000 years ago, and that it had split up into differ-ent languages in the subsequent millennium. The formation of lan-guages from one source came to be known as *diversification*. Shortly thereafter, linguists started to apply the same comparison techniques to other language families. The motivating idea behind such efforts was that it would be possible eventually to piece together the mother tongue of humanity through the reconstruction of various proto-languages.

The work on PIE has made it the most useful proto-language for modern theories of language origins, for the simple reason that knowl-edge about it is detailed and extensive. Already in the nineteenth cen-tury, linguists had a pretty good idea both of what PIE sounded like and of what kind of vocabulary it had. PIE had words for animals, plants, parts of the body, tools, weapons, and various abstract notions. It is this stock of reconstructed lexical items that has helped contempo-rary linguists paint a fairly good picture of the semantic range of one of the first vocabularies utilized by human beings.

By going further and further down the branches toward the "trunk" or "roots" of the proto-linguistic tree, modern-day reconstruc-tionists have been better and better able to formulate viable hypotheses about what one of the first proto-languages spoken by humans—which they have designated "Nostratic" (from Latin *noster* "ours")—might have been like. Actually, the idea of a common linguistic ancestor was bandied about within traditional reconstructionist circles. Pedersen (1931: 338), for instance, suggested the term *Nostratian* as "a compre-hensive designation for the families of languages which are related to Indo-European." The value of the current work on Nostratic lies in the fact that it has put in front of contemporary linguists a kind of proto-lexicon of human language that can be assessed to generate hypotheses about how language originated.

Language vs. Speech

Although in colloquial parlance we rarely distinguish between *language* and *speech*, in actual fact the two are different. *Speech* is a physiological phenomenon. It involves the use of the organs of the vocal apparatus

—the tongue, the teeth, the epiglottis, etc.—to deliver *language*, which is a mental code. Language is commonly delivered as speech; but it can also be expressed through other media, such as the alphabetic and the gestural ones. One can have language without speech, as do individuals with impaired vocal organs, because it exists as a mental code. But one cannot, clearly, have speech without language.

There is a strong possibility that language developed before speech in the human species. The evidence, however, is indirect. At birth, the larynx in human infants is high in the neck, as it is in other primates. Infants breathe, swallow, and vocalize in ways that are physiologically similar to gorillas and chimps. But, some time around the first three to six months of life, the infant's larynx starts to descend gradually into the neck, dramatically altering the ways in which the child will carry out laryngeal physiological functions from then on. Nobody knows why this descent occurs. It is an anatomical phenomenon that is unique to humans. This new low position means that the respiratory and digestive tracts now cross above the larynx. This entails a few risks: food can easily lodge in the entrance of the larynx, and humans cannot drink and breathe simultaneously without choking. But in compensation, it produces a pharyngeal chamber above the vocal folds that can modify sound.

The lowered larynx makes it possible for human beings to articulate sounds with the vocal apparatus. The specific sounds that are used in a language to make up vocal signifiers are called *phonemes*. The *phoneme* is a minimal unit of sound that allows people who speak a language to differentiate its words. For example, what keeps words such as *sip* and *zip* distinct is the first sound. The *phonemic* difference between *s* and *z* can be discerned in the vibration of the vocal cords in the larynx. Putting an index and middle finger over the larynx and articulating these two sounds will immediately make the difference between *s* and *z* quite evident—the cords vibrate during the pronunciation of *z*, but not of *s*. The two sounds are otherwise articulated in the same way.

Phonemic distinctions are perceived by the hearing center of the brain and produced through its motor pathways via a complex system of coordination between brain and vocal organs. There are twelve cranial nerves. Seven of these link the brain with the vocal organs. Some perform a motor function, controlling the movement of muscles, while others perform a sensory function, sending signals to the brain. The larynx controls the flow of air to and from the lungs, so as to prevent food, foreign objects, or other substances from entering the trachea on their way to the stomach. The ability to control the vocal folds makes it possible to build up pressure within the lungs and to emit air not only for expiration purposes, but also for the production of sound.

These physiological conditions were prerequisites for the development of vocal speech in the species too. Interestingly, research on the
casts of human skulls has established that the lowering of the larynx
did not take place earlier than 100,000 years ago. This is fairly persuasive evidence that there may have been language without speech in
pre-*Homo Sapiens* species. The most probable mode of delivery of language was gesture. When speech became physiologically possible, it is
likely that it was used in tandem with the previous gestural signs, not
replacing them completely. This is the most likely reason why we still
use gesture as a default mode of communication (when vocal speech is
impossible), and why we gesticulate when we speak.

5.2 PROPERTIES OF LANGUAGE

Language comes naturally to us. We acquire it without effort or training during our infancy. Indeed, the only requirement for learning any
language is adequate exposure to samples of it from birth to about two.
So natural is speech to us, in fact, that we hardly ever consider what it
is that we are doing when we speak. This is perhaps why the linguist
Noam Chomsky (1986) goes so far as to claim that language is a physical organ, as congenital to the human being as, say, flight is to a bird.
Language is to thinking as our eyes and our noses are to seeing and
smelling. Is Chomsky right?

For Chomsky, all languages are designed according to a universal
grammar (UG) present in the brain at birth. Exposure to specific samples of speech in infancy allows the child to determine the particular
principles of the UG that are relevant to the language being acquired.
This implies that all natural languages are built on the same basic neural plan and that differences among languages are explainable as
choices of rule types from a fairly small inventory of possibilities
—choices impelled by cultural processes. This would explain rather
neatly the universality and rapidity of language acquisition—when the
child learns one fact about a language, the child can easily infer other
facts about the language without having to learn them one by one.

As persuasive as UG theory is, in our view, it is significantly
flawed because it has been restricted to accounting for the development
of *grammar* in the child. As such, it ignores a much more fundamental
creative force in early infancy—iconicity—which involves a process of
creative imitation. Moreover, it is legitimate to ask if there is a UG only
for verbal language, as Chomsky insists. A semiotician would instantly
ask, however: What about the acquisition of nonverbal representational
capacities? Since nonverbal codes are found throughout the world and
developed during infancy without any training, does the brain there-

fore also possess universal nonverbal grammars? If the role of culture is simply to set the parameters that determine the specific verbal grammar that develops in the child, could it not also set, say, the specific melodic and harmonic parameters that determine the specific forms of musical knowledge that develops in the child?

Vocal Iconicity

As mentioned, perhaps the greatest weakness in the UG approach to explaining language development is its dismissal of the role that imitation and iconicity play in childhood verbal development. Imitation is observable already at the age of six months when children start to emit monosyllabic utterances (*mu, ma, da, di,* etc.). These are imitations of what children have heard in social context. They are called *holophrastic* (one-word) utterances in the relevant literature, and have been shown to serve three basic functions: (1) naming an object or event; (2) expressing an action or a desire for some action; (3) conveying emotional states. Holophrases are typically monosyllabic reductions of adult words—*da* for *dog, ca* for *cat,* etc. Over 60% will develop into nouns, and 20% will become verbs, and during the second year many of them will be doubled—*wowo* "water," *bubu* "bottle", *mama* "mother." These early efforts are, clearly, the result of an innate imitative modeling propensity. The developmental evidence thus suggests that iconicity is a primary semiosic force that guides the early development of language.

Iconicity, however, does not disappear from language after childhood. It can be seen in the tendency of adults to deploy it unwittingly in everyday speech acts. Vocal iconicity, for example, manifests itself typically:

- in the use of *alliteration* (the repetition of sounds) for various effects: *sing-song; no-no,* etc.;

- in the *lengthening* of sounds for emphasis: "Yesssss!" "Noooooo!" etc.;

- in the use of *intonation* to express emotional states, to emphasize, to shock, etc.: "Are you absolutely sure?" "Noooooo way!";

- in *sound-modeling,* as in the language of cartoons and comic books: "Zap!" "Boom!" "Pow!" etc.;

- in *onomatopoeic* descriptions of people and things: e.g. a snake or person with snake-like characteristics is described as *slithery, slippery, sneaky,* etc.;

- in the *raising* of the voice to convey a state of anger; in an increased *rate of speech* to convey urgency; in *whispering* to imply conspiracy; etc.;

- in the use of *alliterative idioms* for effect: e.g. "gaggle of geese," "huff and puff," "sterner stuff," "cute kid," etc.

Morris Swadesh (above, §5.1) was a pioneer in the study of such sound modeling phenomena, which he included under the general rubric of *sound symbolism*. He drew attention, for example, to such *sound symbolic* features as the presence in many of the world's languages of [i]-type vowels to express "nearness," in contrast to [a]- [o]- and [u]-type vowels to express the opposite notion of "distance." Such coincidences suggested to him that the notion of nearness tends to be represented unconsciously by the relative nearness of the lips in the articulation of [i] and other front vowels, while the complementary notion of distance tends instead to be represented by the relative openness of the lips in the pronunciation of the [a], [æ], [u] and other mid and back vowels. Examples of this paradigmatic differentiation abound in many languages. Here are some from English:

NEARNESS CONCEPTS	DISTANCE CONCEPTS
here = [hiːr]	there = [ðæːr]
near = [niːr]	far = [faːr]
this = [ðis]	that = [ðæt]

The psychologist Roger Brown (1970: 258-273) also studied the influence of sound symbolism in word-formation and word-perception in the 1960s and 1970s. In one of his classic studies, he asked native speakers of English to listen to pairs of antonyms from a language unrelated to English and then to try guessing, given the English equivalents, which foreign word translated which English word. The subjects were asked to guess the meaning of the foreign words by attending to their sounds. When he asked them, for example, to match the words *ch'ing* and *chung* to the English equivalents *light* and *heavy*, not necessarily in that order, Brown found that about 90% of English speakers correctly matched *ch'ing* to *light* and *chung* to *heavy*. He concluded that the degree of translation accuracy could only be explained "as indicative of a primitive phonetic symbolism deriving from the origin of speech in some kind of imitative or physiognomic linkage of sounds and meanings" (Brown 1970: 272).

Grammatical Iconicity

Iconicity is not just a factor in word-formation; it manifests its influence at all levels of language. The linguist Ronald Langacker (e.g. 1987, 1990), for instance, suggests that certain aspects of sentence structure are, in effect, generated by what can be called an *iconic reflex system*. Nouns, for instance, trace a "region" in mind-space. This is why a count noun is imagined as referring to something that encircles a bounded region, whereas a mass noun is visualized as referring to something that occurs in a non-bounded region. Thus, for example, a noun like *leaf* evokes a mental picture of a bounded referent, whereas the noun *water* elicits an image of a non-bounded referent. So, *leaves* can be counted, *water* cannot. This entails an *iconic reflex systematization* in the forms and functions of these signs. This is why *leaf* has a plural form (*leaves*), and *water* does not (unless the referential domain is metaphorical); this is also why *leaf* can be preceded by an indefinite article (*a leaf*), *water* cannot; and so on. Similar reflex patterns can be found in other representational systems—in painting, for instance, water is represented either with no boundaries or else as bounded by other figures (land masses, the horizon, etc.); leaves, on the other hand, can be depicted as separate figures with circumscribable boundaries.

As this line of research shows, grammar is really an iconic code, "summarizing," so to speak, our direct perception of things in the world. Consider further the relation between an active and passive sentences such as "Alexander ate the apple" and "The apple was eaten by Alexander." In the active sentence, the subject (*Alexander*) is in the foreground of the mind's eye, while the object (*apple*) is in the background. The action implied by the verb (*eating*) is spotlighted as an activity of the subject. The overall mental view that active sentences convey is, therefore, one of the subject as a "perpetrator" or "executor" of the action. A change from active to passive, however, changes the position of the foreground and the background in the mind's eye. The passive sentence brings the apple to the foreground, relegating the eater, Alexander, to the background. The action of eating is now spotlighted on the object, the "receiver" of the action. As this simple example shows, passive sentences are hardly just stylistic variants of active ones. They give us, in effect, a different mental angle from which to see the same action in mind-space.

This account of grammar is highly compatible with what is now known about the fixed chronological stages that the child passes through on h/er way to speaking in sentences, and it gives us a good account of how sentence composition reflects the child's experience of the world. It is beyond the scope of the present discussion to engage in a critical discussion of the relevant research. Suffice it to say here that from a semiotic perspective it suggests that sentence-forming structures such as conjunctions and prepositions are acquired with facility, not because they are built into the brain's UG as general principles, but because the child learns early on that they are perspectival tools. This is probably why sentence grammar and the ability to draw and to enjoy music emerge in tandem in the child. The child learns early on that language allows h/er to respond to the world in the same way that a drawing or a melody does. Incidentally, this is perhaps why we can understand stories in virtually the same ways that we understand music or paintings. A painting is much more than an assemblage of lines, shapes, and colors, and melodies are more than combinations of notes and harmonies. Similarly, a sentence in language is much more than an assemblage of words and phrases built from some rule system in the brain. We use the grammatical elements at our disposal to model the world in ways that parallel how musicians use melodic elements and painters visual elements to model it.

Verbal Indexicality

As we saw in chapter 3 (§3.6), along with iconicity, indexicality is a major property in semiosis and representation. Across the world's languages, one commonly finds (1) words like *this, that, here, there, up, down* that allow people to refer to the relative location of things; (2) words like *before, after, now, then, yesterday, tomorrow* that allow people to refer to events that are in temporal relation to each other; and (3) pronouns like *I, you, he, she, the one, the other* that allow people to refer to the participants in a situation. In the literature about child language, verbal indexical signs appear later than iconic ones, as might be expected, since they are secondness signifying structures. Indeed, the dimensionality principle can be used to explain rather nicely the sequence of events in child language development, with iconicity (a firstness form of semiosis and representation) emerging first, indexicality (a secondness form) next, and finally full symbolicity (a thirdness form).

The manifestations of verbal indexicality are not limited to the three referential domains described above. They can be seen as well in how people sometimes refer to abstract concepts. We suggested above the term *iconic reflex system* to refer to the presence of iconically motivated forms in grammar. So too it can be suggested that the forms, or *reflexes*, indexicality leaves in grammar can be characterized in terms of an *indexical reflex system*. Verbal constructions such as *think up, think over*, and *think out* are products of this system:

1. When did you *think up* that preposterous idea?
2. You should *think over* carefully what you have just said.
3. *Think out* the entire problem before coming to a solution.
4. I cannot *think straight* today.
5. Go ahead and *think* that problem *through*.

Even though these verbal constructions have abstract referents, they nonetheless evoke images of location and movement. The construction *think up* elicits a mental image of upward movement, thus portraying the abstract referent as an object being extracted physically from a kind of mental terrain; *think over* evokes the image of scanning with the mind's eye; *think out* elicits an image of extracting something so that it can be held up to the scrutiny of the mind's eye; *think straight* elicits an image of direct, and thus logical, movement (from one point to another via a straight linear path); and *think through* evokes an image of continuous, unbroken movement through space. These constructions allow users to locate and identify abstract ideas in relation to spatio-temporal contexts, although such contexts are purely imaginary. It's as if these imaginary indexical referents allow us to locate thoughts in the mind, with the mind having the physical features of a territory and thoughts having those of physical objects within it.

5.3 LANGUAGE AND THOUGHT

The notions of *iconic* and *indexical reflex systems* raise the question of the relation of language to thought. Do the grammars of specific languages influence or determine how children come to view the world? Do expressions like *think up* and *think over*, for example, condition users of English to think in certain ways? The idea that language and thought are interlinked generally falls under the rubric of the *Whorfian hypothesis* (WH), after the American anthropological linguist Benjamin Lee Whorf (1897–1941), even though versions of this notion can be found before Whorf (chapter 2, §2.5). The WH posits that language structures predispose native speakers to attend to certain concepts as being necessary. But, as Whorf emphasized, this does not mean that innovation in language is impossible. On the contrary, we can use language to invent new categories of reference any time we want. For example, if for some reason we wish, or need, to refer to "adolescent boys between the ages of 13 and 16 who smoke," then by coining an appropriate word, such as *groon*, we would in effect etch this concept into our worldview, because the presence of the word *groon* in memory, as Whorf argued, would predispose us to see its meaning as somehow necessary. When a boy with the stated characteristics came into view, therefore, we would immediately recognize him as a *groon*.

To see how language and thought are intertwined, it is instructive to compare two languages in a specific way to determine how they encode a particular concept, say, "device for keeping track of time." In Italian, for instance, the word *orologio* is used to encode it. In English, on the other hand, two words exist, *watch* and *clock*, which are distinguished in terms of the collocation of the referent: *watch* refers to a device that is carried, worn, or put on bodies (on wrists, around the neck, in pockets, etc.), while *clock*, on the other hand, refers to an object that is placed in specific locations—on a table, on a wall, etc.—and not carried around. This does not mean that collocation distinctions do not exist in Italian. In this specific case they are conveyed by another language structure: *da + place*, with *da* meaning approximately "for": *orologio da polso* = wristwatch ("watch for wrist"), *orologio da tavolo* = table clock ("clock for table"), and so on. Historically speaking, the emergence of different categories of language to refer to time suggests different perceptions of time. The word *watch* originated in the 1850s when people started strapping clocks around their wrists. Since then people in the West seem to have, in a sense, become fixated on "watching" time pass. As the psychologist Robert Levine (1997) discovered, this fixation is typical of cultures that distinguish between clocks and watches, less so of others. Burmese monks, for instance, hardly need *watches* to inform them when it is time to get up. They get up when there is enough light to see the veins in their hands. In Mexican society, showing up "on time" is often cause for ridicule, rendering watches virtually useless. Language reflects such cultural perceptions at the same time that it projects them into discourse and, thus, reinforces them. So, the gist of the semiotic story of "device for keeping track of time" is that keeping accurate time, at least in the past, has been more of a preoccupation in English-speaking cultures than it has been in Italian and other cultures, and that this has been encoded in their respective language systems.

Whorf suggested that the function of language was to allow people to classify experience and that it thus was an organizing grid through which humans came to perceive and understand the world around them. When we name something, we are classifying. What we are naming belongs to no class until we put it in one. For this reason, the WH raises some interesting questions about social inequalities and the structure of the language that encodes them. In English, sexist terms like *chairman*, *spokesman*, etc. were often cited in the past as examples of how language predisposed its users to view certain social roles in gender terms. Feminist critics have maintained that English grammar was originally organized from the perspective of those at the center of the society—the men. This is why we still tend to say that a woman marries into a man's family, and why at wedding ceremonies expressions such as "I pronounce you man and wife," are still used by some. In the not-too-distant past, and perhaps still today in many areas of Western society, women were defined in relation to men. Similarly damaging language is the kind that excludes women, such as "lady atheist" or "lesbian doctor," implying that atheists and doctors are not typically female or lesbian.

By the way, in some other societies the reverse is true. Investigating grammatical gender in the Iroquois language, Alpher (1987) found that in this language the feminine gender is the default one, whereas masculine items are marked by a special subject prefix. This is the converse of gender categories in most languages with a gender system. Alpher relates this to the fact that the Iroquois society is matrilineal —traditionally women hold the land, pass it on to their heirs in the female line, are responsible for agricultural production, control the wealth, arrange marriages, and so on. Iroquois grammar too is organized from the viewpoint of those at the center of the society—in this case the women.

One of the more interesting implications of the WH is the view that language models the world in the same way that visual art does. To a semiotician this is a particularly interesting implication because it would not only confirm the notion of an interconnectedness among the various codes of the signifying order, but also assign a much more prominent role to the brain's primary modeling system in language (chapter 3, §3.2). The philosopher Ludwig Wittgenstein (1889–1951), too, saw sentences as representing features of the world in the same way that pictures did. The lines and shapes of drawings show how things are related to each other; so too, he claimed, do the ways in which words are put together in sentences. It is relevant to note, however, that Wittgenstein had serious misgivings about his so-called "picture theory" of language. Before his death he became perplexed by the fact that language could do much more than just construct propositions about the world. So, he introduced the idea of *language games*, by which he claimed that there existed a variety of linguistic games (describing, reporting, guessing riddles, making jokes, etc.) that went beyond simple pictorial representation.

5.4 NAMES

Like the body (chapter 4), language is felt across cultures to be an extension of persona. This would explain why language is used universally to identify people. Throughout the world people are given *names*, i.e. words that stand for them as individuals. A *name* has both indexical and symbolic properties because, like a pronoun, it identifies the person and, usually, h/er ethnic origin; it is symbolic because, like any word, it is a product of historical forces and thus tied to conventional systems of signification. Less often, names are coined iconically. Trivial but instructive examples of this can be seen in the names we tend to give household animals—*Ruff, Purry*, etc.

The study of names falls more properly under a branch of both semiotics and linguistics called *onomastics* (from Greek *onoma* "name"). The phenomenon of name-giving in the human species is indeed a fascinating one on many counts. Across cultures, a neonate is not considered a full-fledged member of the culture until s/he is given a name. The naming of a newborn infant is h/er first rite of passage in society, by which s/he is identified as a separate individual with a unique personality. If a person is not given a name by h/er family, then society will step in to do so. A person taken into a family, by marriage, adoption, or some other means, is also typically assigned the *family name*. From childhood on, the individual's sense of Self is felt somehow to be embedded in h/er name. In traditional Inuit tribes, for instance, an individual is perceived to have a body, a soul, and a name; a person is not seen as complete without all three. A few years ago, a British television program, *The Prisoner*, played on this very same perception. It portrayed a totalitarian world in which people were assigned numbers instead of traditional names—*Number 1, Number 2*, etc. The idea was, obviously, that a person could be made to conform to the will of the state and to become more controllable by state officials if s/he did not have a name. The whole series was, in a sense, a portrayal of the struggle that humans feel to discover the meaning of Self. The use of numerical identification of prisoners and slaves is, in effect, a negation of their Selfhood and, ultimately, of their worth.

In Western society, the Judeo-Christian influence on first names has been especially strong. In some countries, like Brazil, a child must be given an appropriate Christian name before s/he can be issued a birth certificate. Although this might seem like an extreme measure, in all cultures name-giving is constrained by traditions and conventions. In some parts of Western society, name-giving is a much more open and unregulated process. But even in the West, it is shaped by several customs and trends—e.g. children are often named after the months (*May*), precious stones (*Ruby*), after popular contemporary personalities (*Elvis, Marilyn*), after flowers (*Blossom*), after places (*Georgia*), or after personages in the classical myths (*Diana, Jason*). New names are frequently coined from variant spellings (*JoEtta, Beverleigh*), or even completely invented. The late rock musician and composer Frank Zappa

(1940–1993), for instance, named his daughter *Moon Unit* and his son *Dweezil*.

Until the late Middle Ages, one personal name was generally sufficient as an identifier. Duplications, however, began to occur so often that additional names became a necessity. Hence, *surnames* were given to individuals (literally "names on top of a name") to keep their identities distinct. These were either indexical, in that they identified the individual in terms of h/er place of origin or parentage, or descriptive (qualisigns), in that they referred to some personal or social feature (e.g. occupation) of the individual (or of h/er family). In England, for example, a person living near or at a place where apple trees grew might be called "John where-the-apples-grow," hence, *John Appleby*. Such topographic surnames abound in English-speaking cultures—e.g. *Wood, Woods, Moore, Church, Hill, Rivers*, etc. Descendant surnames, or names indicating parentage, were often formed by prefixes such as *Mac-, Mc-* in Scottish or Irish names or *Ap-* in Welsh names, or by suffixes such as *-son* in English names, *-sen* or *-dottir* in Scandinavian names—e.g. *Johnson* or *Jensen*, "son of John," *Maryson*, "son of Mary," *Jakobsdottir*, "daughter of Jacob." Surnames reflecting medieval life and occupations also formed a productive source of individualization, *Smith* being the foremost with equivalents in Spanish (*Ferrer*), German (*Schmidt*), and Hungarian (*Kovacs*). Other surnames derived in a similar fashion are *Farmer, Carpenter, Tailor, Weaver,* etc.

Name-giving is extended across cultures to encompass inanimate referents. When this is done, the objects somehow take on, as if by magic, an animate quality of their own. Throughout the world, naming objects and artifacts is felt to bestow upon them a mysterious life force. So fundamental is our association between name-giving and life that this should come as no surprise. So, when brand products or tropical storms, for instance, are given names they seem to take on a human personality that is meant to appeal to specific consumers. The names given to cosmetics and beauty products frequently evoke connotations of beauty, cleanliness, sophistication, and naturalness: *Moondrops, Natural Wonder, Rainflower, Sunsilk, Skin Dew*. Sometimes they convey scientific authority: *Eterna 27, Clinique, Endocil, Equalia*. Men's toiletries are often descriptive: *Brut, Cossak, Denim, Aramis, Devin*. Cars are also given descriptive names: *Jaguar, Mustang, Triumph, Princess*.

5.5 WRITING

Language manifests itself as speech, i.e. as articulated sounds (see above, §5.1). But speech can also be represented visually in the graphic medium. The use of visual signs to represent speech is known as *writ-*

ing. In evolutionary terms writing did not develop as a simple substitute for speech. The earliest graphic signs so far discovered were unearthed in western Asia from the Neolithic era. They are elemental shapes on clay tokens that were probably used as image-making forms or casts (Schmandt-Besserat 1978, 1992).

The earliest writing systems were all independent of speech and not alphabetic or syllabic in nature. They were pictorial. In the ancient civilization of Sumer around 3500 BC, for instance, pictorial writing was used to record agricultural transactions and astronomical observations. Most of the Sumerian *pictographs* represented nouns such as stars and animals, with a few for such qualisigns as "small," "big," and "bright." A few centuries later, this pictographic system was expanded to include verbs: *to sleep*, for example, was represented by a person in a supine position. To facilitate the speed of writing, the Sumerians eventually streamlined their pictographs and transformed them into symbols for the actual sounds of speech. These were written down on clay tablets with a stylus in a form of writing known as *cuneiform*.

Pictographs are images of objects, people, or events—for example, a drawing of the sun stands for the spoken word *sun*. Pictographic forms of writing are still in existence today even in alphabet-using cultures: e.g. the images of males and females painted on bathroom doors are examples of pictographs. More abstract forms of pictographic signs are called *ideographs* (or *ideograms*). These may bear some resemblance to their referents, but assume much more of a conventional knowledge of the relation between signifier and signified on the part of the user. International symbols for such things as public telephones, washrooms, etc. are all ideographic. More abstract ideographs are known as *logographs* (or *logograms*). These show a highly-evolved form of symbolicity which, nevertheless, has a basis in iconicity. A logographic system combines various pictographs for the purpose of indicating non-picturable ideas. Thus, the Chinese pictographs for *sun* and *tree* are combined to represent the Chinese spoken word for *east*.

By about 3000 BC the ancient Egyptians also used a pictographic script—known as *hieroglyphic*. But in their case, the pictographs were becoming more alphabetic, standing for parts of words. Hieroglyphic writing was used to record hymns and prayers, to register the names and titles of individuals and deities, and to record various community activities—*hieroglyphic* derives from Greek *hieros* "holy" and *glyphein* "to carve."

From such pictographic-ideographic systems emerged the first *syllabaries*. These were systems of signs for representing syllables. They were developed by the Semitic peoples of Palestine and Syria from the ideographs of the Egyptian system during the last half of the second millennium BC. Syllabaries are still used in some cultures. Japanese, for example, is still written with two complete syllabaries—the *hiragana* and the *katakana*—devised to supplement the characters originally taken over from Chinese.

The emergence of syllabaries on the scene bears witness to the fact that, once writing became a flourishing enterprise in the ancient civilizations, it was convenient for it to be produced without pictures. The transition from pictorial to sound representation—the *alphabet principle*—came about to make writing rapid and efficient in its use of space. So, for example, instead of drawing the full head of an ox (1) only its bare outline was drawn; which (2) stood for the ox; which (3) eventually came to stand for the word for ox (*aleph* in Hebrew); and which (4) finally stood just for the first sound in the word (*a* for *aleph*). Stage (4) occurred around 1000 BC when the ancient Phoenicians systematically created the first true alphabetic system for recording sounds. The Greeks adopted the Phoenician alphabet and started the practice of naming each symbol by such words as *alpha, beta, gamma*, etc., which were imitations of Phoenician words: *aleph* "ox," *beth* "house," *gimel* "camel," etc. Alphabetic writing has become the norm in Western cultures. But in every alphabetic symbol that we now use to record our thoughts abstractly, there is an iconic history and prehistory that has become dim or virtually unseeable because our eyes are no longer trained to extract pictorial meaning from it.

Alphabetic writing is a truly remarkable achievement. It has made possible the recording and transmission of knowledge. Indeed, in Western culture to be an alphabet-user is to be literate and thus educated. So close is the link between the two that we can scarcely think of knowledge unless it is recorded in some alphabetic form and preserved in some book form for posterity; nor can we think of a person as educated unless we know that s/he can read and write verbal texts competently. In order to read and write, one must follow a sequence of characters arranged in a particular spatial order. For example, English writing flows from left to right, Hebrew from right to left, and Chinese from top to bottom. In all alphabet-using cultures, the ability to read and write does not emerge spontaneously. The child must be trained to recognize the alphabetic system and use it systematically to encode and decode written texts.

Besides its intrinsic value, the ability to read has economic consequences in modern societies. Adults who are better-than-average readers are more likely to have high-paying jobs. The growing technologization of society has brought along with it increasing demands for literacy, which the schools are hard pressed to meet. The reading ability needed to comprehend materials important to daily living, such as income tax forms and newspapers, has been estimated to be as high as the twelfth-grade level in North America. Some efforts have been made to simplify forms and manuals, but the lack of sufficient reading ability definitely impairs a person's capacity to function in modern society.

5.6 DISCOURSE

The semiotician seeks information on a culture's verbal code in itself as a system of representation, and also on how it is used for communication. The study of "language in action," so to speak, is called *discourse analysis*. Discourse is coded behavior. Like kinesic codes (chapter 4), it is designed to regulate Self-Other relations in social situations, and to allow individuals to present the Self strategically to Others (Di Pietro 1987). Needless to say, collecting data on discourse must be guided by some theoretical framework. Here, we will describe one framework that is particularly useful for compiling such data, namely the one devised by the Moscow-born linguist and semiotician Roman Jakobson (1896–1982), who carried out most of his work in the United States. Jakobson identified six "constituents" that characterize all speech acts (Jakobson 1960):

1. an *addresser* who initiates the communication of a message;

2. a *message* that s/he recognizes must refer to something other than itself;

3. an *addressee* who is the intended receiver of the message;

4. a *context* that permits the addressee to recognize that the message is referring to something other than itself: e.g. if someone were crying out "Help," lying motionless on the ground, then one would easily understand that the message is referring to a concrete situation;

5. a mode of *contact* by which physical, social, and psychological connections are established between the addresser and addressee;

6. a *code* providing the signs and structural information for constructing and deciphering messages.

Jakobson then pointed out that each of these constituents correlates with a different communicative function:

1. *emotive*: implies the presence of the addresser's emotions, attitudes, social status, etc. in the message;

2. *conative*: implies the intended effect—physical, psychological, social, etc.—that the message is expected to have on the addressee;

3. *referential*: implies a message constructed to convey information ("Main Street is two blocks north of here");

4. *poetic*: implies a message constructed in some aesthetic fashion ("Roses are red, violets are blue, and how's it going with you?");

5. *phatic*: implies a message designed to establish social contact ("Hi, how's it going?");

6. *metalingual*: implies a message designed to refer to the code used ("The word noun is a *noun*").

Jakobson's analysis of discourse goes well beyond the positing of a situation of simple information transfer, as the bull's-eye model of communication discussed in chapter 2 implies (§2.3). It involves determining *who* says *what* to *whom; where* and *when* it is said; and *how* and *why* it is said. This implies that discourse is motivated and shaped by the setting, the message contents, the participants, and the goals of each interlocutor. Discourse thus makes an emotional claim on everyone in the social situation. It can thus be characterized as a form of acting, of presenting persona through language.

An interesting area of discourse that can be used to illustrate how to apply the Jakobsonian model to the study of verbal communication is adolescent speech. Jakobson's emotive and conative functions are particularly dominant in shaping teenage talk (Danesi 1994). The emotive function shows up, for example, in increased rates of speech delivery, in overwrought intonation patterns, in emphatic voice modulations, etc.—e.g. "He's sooooo cute!" "She's faaaaar out!" "That's amaaaazing!" etc. Utterances such as "We called her up (?) (intonation like a question)...but she wasn't there (?) (same intonation)...so we hung up (?) (same intonation)" show a pattern of a rising emotive tone of voice, as if each sentence were interrogative. Called colloquially by the media "uptalk," this feature is, in effect, an implicit tag questioning strategy. A *tag* is a word, phrase, or clause added to a sentence to emphasize a point, to seek approval, to ascertain some reaction, etc.—e.g. "She's coming tomorrow, *isn't she?*" "That was a good course, *right?*" etc. The "uptalk" pattern demonstrated by adolescents is, in effect, a tag question without the tag. This emotive trait probably indicates the need of teenagers to ensure the full conative participation of their interlocutors. There is nothing particularly surprising about this feature of adolescent discourse. Adult speech can also be highly emotive. Adults commonly lengthen sounds for emphasis and regularly use intonation patterns to express emotional states, to emphasize something, to shock someone, etc. The difference between adult and adolescent speech lies in the degree and extent to which emotivity characterizes the discourse.

The poetic function can also be discerned frequently as a feature of adolescent discourse. In the mid-1980s words such as *loser, gross-out, air-head, slime-bucket,* and others were in widespread use in North American teen language. Words like *vomatose, thicko, burger-brain, knob* gained currency in the 1990s. But no matter from what generation of teens the words come, the poetic function reflects a need to describe others and meaningful social situations in highly connotative ways. Adolescents are keenly sensitive to bodily appearance and image, as well as to the perceived sociability of peers. At puberty changes in physical appearance are perceived as traumatic. Consequently, teenagers are concerned that everyone is constantly observing them. To offset this preoccupation with Self-image, they talk defensively about how others act, behave, and appear. Language is thus used as an evaluative grid for assessing peer appearance and sociability, as a strategy for deflecting attention away from the Self.

As the brief foregoing discussion shows, Jakobson's model provides a useful grid not only for classifying and interpreting actual discourse tokens as they occur in real-life situations, but also for understanding the fact that discourse is frequently a highly emotive form of behavior whose primary purpose appears to be the regulation of Self-Other relations in social interaction.

The Interconnectedness of Discourse

Discourse is interconnected with all the other codes and representational practices of the signifying order (*interconnectedness principle*). For example, it is discernible in ritualistic situations—the Catholic Mass is spoken; sermons, prep rallies, and other ceremonial gatherings are anchored in speeches, either traditionally worded or specifically composed for the occasion; and so on. The use of language in ritual is not to create new meanings, but to assert communal sense-making, to ensure cultural cohesion. Societies are held together as a result of such verbal rituals. People typically love to hear the same speeches, songs, stories at specific times during the year (at Christmas, at Passover, etc.) in order to feel united with the other members of the culture. These are the formulaic texts that the language code allows its users to construct for the occasion. They are passed on from generation to generation with little or no modification.

From the beginning of time, language has been thought to have special powers. The name of God has been a closely guarded secret in many cultures, if indeed it was known or allowed to be uttered at all. Cultural shamans were thought to possess magical word knowledge that could control objects, people, spirits, and natural events. The magical force of language is still woven into the formulas, incantations, and litanies of names of all religions. At a Roman Catholic Mass, for example, the speaking of the words "This is my body" is thought to identify the moment when the communion bread is changed into the body of Christ. Prayer and invocations of various types are thought to be able to cure disease, ward off evil, bring good to oneself and harm to an enemy. And when we give a name to someone in a religious ceremony, the infant is believed to be the recipient of spiritual life. This is why Ernst Cassirer (1946: 34-36) saw language, myth, and ritual as having a common origin:

> The word, like a god or a daemon, confronts man not as a creation of his own, but as something existent and significant in its own right, as an objective reality. As soon as the spark has jumped across, as soon as the tension and emotion of the moment has found its discharge in the word or the mythical image, a sort of turning point has occurred in human mentality; the inner excitement which was a mere subjective state has vanished, and has been resolved into the objective form of myth or of speech.

As Cassirer (1946: 38) goes on to explain, the power of language lies in its ability to fix something in the mind, so that it does not "fade away again when the spoken word has set its seal upon it and given it definite form." This impulse to name is at the root of religious experience; and indeed a large number of creation myths feature the *Word* as the force behind creation.

Words in their origin were probably perceived as sacred acts. Those who possessed knowledge of words also possessed supernatural or magical powers. In many early cultures, even knowing the name of a deity was purported to give the knower great power—e.g. in Egyptian mythology, the sorceress Isis tricked the sun god, Ra, into revealing his name and, thus, gained power over him and all other gods. In some cultures, the name given to the individual has a life and a historical reality independent of the individual, bringing with it all the qualities of the previous individuals who shared that name. The ancestors bearing that name are perceived to weave a sort of magical protective aura on the individual named after them. The Inuit, for instance, believe that a newborn baby cries because it wants its name, and will not be complete until it gets it. In some traditional Inuit tribes, an individual will not pronounce h/er name, fearing that this senseless act could break the magical spell of protection that it brings with it. As Espes Brown (1992: 13) puts it: "the fact that when we create words we use our breath, and for these people and these traditions breath is associated with the principle of life; breath is life itself. And so if a word is born from this sacred principle of breath, this lends an added sacred dimension to the spoken word."

Belief in the magical powers of language is not limited to oral tribal cultures. It abounds even in modern technological cultures. "Speak of the devil," we say in common parlance, and "he will appear." When someone sneezes, uttering "Bless you" is meant to ward off sickness. Verbal contact—"Hi, how's it going?"—which Malinowski (1922) called *phatic communion*, is so common that we have forgotten that it has a basis in ritual. As Ann Gill (1994: 106) puts it, language and magic are intrinsically intertwined:

> By portraying experience in a particular way, words work their unconscious magic on humans, making them see, for example, products as necessary for success or creating distinctions between better or worse—be it body shape, hair style, or brand of blue jeans. Words create belief in religions, governments, and art forms; they create allegiances to football teams, politicians, movie stars, and certain brands of beer. Words are the windows of our own souls and to the world beyond our fingertips. Their essential persuasive efficacy works its magic on every person in every society.

The other side of sacredness is *taboo*. This word comes from the tribal language Tongan where it means "holy, untouchable." Taboos exist in all cultures, because there are certain forms of language that a society prefers to avoid. These are generally related to sexuality, the supernatural, excretion, death, and various aspects of social life. For example, among the Zuñi of New Mexico, the word *takka* "frogs" is prohibited during ceremonies. In our own culture, so-called four-letter words are generally considered obscene, but they can be perceived as taboo if uttered in sacred places like churches, sanctuaries, etc.

5.7 VERBAL ART: POETRY

The poems, stories, and plays that individuals throughout the world have created, and continue to create, are testaments to the need for verbal art in human life. Of all the verbal art forms, poetry is the most fundamental. *Poetry* can be defined as verbal art based on the acoustic, rhythmic, and imagistic properties of words so as to provide insight into the intrinsic nature of things. The philosopher Vico (chapter 2, §2.1) saw poetry as the primordial form of language. Vico called the first speakers "poets," which etymologically means "makers," because he claimed that they formed their first concepts poetically—e.g. as images of a god or a hero. The ancient Greeks, for instance, formed the concept of "valor" poetically through the character of the hero Achilles in the *Iliad*. This same pattern of knowing is noticeable in children, who invariably acquire their first concepts through poetic story figures

—through god-like and heroic characters who embody them. But these embodiments are not merely fanciful nor principally subjective.

Poetry is essentially "vocal music," since it is marked by rhythm and tone. Although poetry eventually gained an independent existence in our culture, in many others poetry and music are still conceived of as identical. Some of the earliest written examples of poetic texts found by archeologists in ancient Sumer, Babylon, and other areas of the Middle East appear to confirm that poetry originated alongside music and drama as a communal expression to seek favor from, or give praise to, the gods. The musical aspect of poetry is still visible in many cultures. For example, in the Navajo culture, poetic forms are still used as incantations for rain. But even in our modern technological culture, ritualistic uses of poetry abound—e.g. we use poetic language on greeting cards, on special kinds of invitations, to impart knowledge to children, in advertising jingles, and so on.

The poet's words reverberate in our minds. Sound is what shapes the sense in poetry. Poetry is thus evidence that the senses work intermodally in the production of fundamental meanings. The term that is used to refer to intermodality is *synesthesia*—the process by which several sensations are evoked in tandem. Synesthetic effects can be discerned in expressions such as "loud red," "bright tone," etc. The term *aesthesia*, on the other hand, is commonly used to refer to the activation of all the sensory modalities in a holistic way. When we call the appreciation of art an "aesthetic experience," we literally mean that we sense and feel the meaning of a work of art as a whole.

Interest in the nature and function of poetry goes back to ancient times. In the *Republic*, Plato asserted that poets were divinely inspired, but he regarded poetry as a pallid imitation of the actual world. Aristotle, on the other hand, in the *Poetics*, argued that poetry was the greatest of all the creative arts, representing what is universal in human experience. The Roman poet Horace (65–8 BC), in his critical work *Ars Poetica*, maintained that the function of poetry was to please and instruct. In his essay *On the Sublime*, the rhetorician Longinus (213–273 AD) stressed that poetry was a means through which spiritual, moral, or intellectual knowledge could be achieved. In the Middle Ages, the great Italian poet Dante (1265–1321) showed the world how poetry was intertwined with the human spirit and the flux of history. In his masterpiece, the *Divine Comedy*, which he began around 1307 and completed shortly before his death, Dante took his readers on an imaginary journey through hell, purgatory, and heaven. In each of these three realms Dante meets with mythological, historical, and contemporary personages. Each character is symbolic of a particular fault or virtue, either religious or political; and the punishment or rewards meted out to the characters reflect, annotatively, Dante's portrayal of human actions as meaningful in the universal scheme of things. Dante is guided through hell and purgatory by Virgil, who is, to Dante, the symbol of reason, and through paradise by Beatrice, the woman Dante loved. The work of modern poets throughout the world has been inspired by Dante's masterpiece.

6

METAPHOR

*Midway between the unintelligible
and the commonplace, it is metaphor
which most produces knowledge.*

Aristotle (1952a: III, 1410b)

6.0 PRELIMINARY REMARKS

Metaphorical expressions are so common and widespread that
people hardly ever notice the omnipresence in discourse of
metaphor and its indispensableness when explaining some
abstract concept, especially to children. The examples and stories we
tell children, in fact, are essentially *metaphorical* narratives. These allow
us to make abstractions communicable to children in concrete ways. No
wonder, then, that interest in metaphor has become so widespread in
those disciplines studying the human mind.

Although interest in figurative language is ancient, the experimental study of its relation to cognition and communication is a relatively
recent phenomenon. And it has soared. Indeed, since about the mid-
1950s the amount of linguistic and psychological research on metaphor
has been mind-boggling. A while back, the literary scholar Booth (1979:
23) remarked that if one were to count the number of bibliographical
entries on metaphor published in the year 1977 alone, one would be
forced to surmise that by the year 2039 there would be "more students
of metaphor on Earth than people." The first effort to provide a bibliographical basis to the burgeoning scientific study of metaphor was
Warren Shibbles' mammoth 1971 volume *Metaphor: An Annotated Bibliography and History*, which contained some 4,000 entries. In 1985 Noppen compiled an exhaustive bibliography of post-1970 publications,
which he updated in 1990 with Hols (Noppen 1985, Noppen and Hols
1990). But despite the enormous amount of interest in metaphor among
scholars, by and large people still think of metaphor as a stylistic device
of poets and writers for decorating messages or making them more effective. Nothing could be farther from the truth. If the recent scientific
work on metaphor is even partially correct, then metaphor can no
longer be viewed as verbal ornamentation. On the contrary, it is the

sum and substance of abstract thinking. George Lakoff and Mark John-son (1980: 3) put it as follows:

> Metaphor is for most people a device of the poetic imagina-tion and the rhetorical flourish—a matter of extraordinary rather than ordinary language. Moreover, metaphor is typi-cally viewed as characteristic of language alone, a matter of words rather than thought and action... We have found, on the contrary, that metaphor is pervasive in everyday life, not just in language but in thought and action.

In this chapter, our trip through the cultural landscape brings us to the site where *Homo metaphoricus* resides. Semioticians have always known about the unique signifying power of this ancestor of *Homo cul-turalis*. But, as mentioned, it is only in the last few decades that the same view of metaphor has been spreading to other scholarly domains. The study of metaphor, sometimes called *metaphorology*, has always been a major branch of semiotics.

6.1 WHAT IS METAPHOR?

From ancient times to today, the use of figures of speech, or *tropes*, has been seen primarily as a stylistic strategy employed by orators and writers to strengthen and embellish their orations and compositions. In addition to metaphor—which is defined traditionally as the use of a word or phrase denoting one kind of idea or object in place of another word or phrase for the purpose of suggesting a likeness between the two (e.g. "Love is a rose")—rhetoricians have identified the following primary tropes:

- *Climax* is an arrangement of words, clauses, or sentences in the order of their importance, the least forcible com-ing first and the others rising in potency until the last: "It is an outrage to scoff at her; it is a crime to ridicule her; but to deny her freedom of speech, what shall I say of this?"

- *Anticlimax* is the opposite trope, namely the sequencing of ideas that abruptly diminish in importance at the end of a sentence or passage, generally for satirical effect: "I will shoot him down first, and then I will talk to him."

- *Antithesis* refers to the juxtaposition of two words, phrases, clauses, or sentences contrasted or opposed in meaning in such a way as to give emphasis to contrast-ing ideas: "To err is human, to forgive divine."

- *Apostrophe* is the technique by which an actor turns from the audience, or a writer from h/er readers, to address a person who usually is either absent or deceased, or to address an inanimate object or an abstract idea: "Hail, Freedom, whose visage is never far from sight."

- *Euphemism* is the substitution of a delicate or inoffensive term or phrase for one that has coarse, sordid, or other unpleasant associations, as in the use of *lavatory* or *rest room* for *toilet*.

- *Exclamation* is a sudden outcry expressing strong emotion, such as fright, grief, or hatred: "Oh vile, vile, person!"

- *Hyperbole* is the use of exaggeration for effect: "My friend drinks oceans of water."

- *Litotes*, on the other hand, is the technique of understatement so as to enhance the effect of the ideas expressed: "Franz Boas showed no inconsiderable analytical powers as an anthropologist."

- *Simile* is the technique of specific comparison by means of the words *like* or *as* between two kinds of ideas or objects: "You're as light as a feather."

- *Metonymy* is the use of a word or phrase for another to which it bears an important relation, as the effect for the cause, the abstract for the concrete, etc.: "She's the head of our family."

- *Conceit* is an elaborate, often extravagant metaphor or simile for making an analogy between totally dissimilar things: "Love is a worm."

- *Irony* refers to a dryly humorous or lightly sarcastic mode of speech, in which words are used to convey a meaning contrary to their literal sense: "I really love the pain you give me."

- *Onomatopoeia* is the imitation of natural sounds by words: *the humming bee, the cackling hen*, etc.

- *Oxymoron* is the combination of two seemingly contradictory or incongruous words: "My life is a living death."

- *Paradox* is a statement that appears contradictory or inconsistent: "She's a well-known secret agent."

- *Personification* is the representation of inanimate objects or abstract ideas as living beings: "Necessity is the mother of invention."

- *Rhetorical Question* is a questioning strategy that is intended not to gain information but to assert more emphatically the obvious answer to what is asked: "You do understand what I mean, don't you?"

- *Synecdoche* is the technique whereby the part is made to stand for the whole, the whole for a part, the species for the genus, etc.: "The President's administration contained the best brains in the country."

Since the 1970s, the trend in linguistics and psychology has been to consider metaphor, metonymy, synecdoche, and irony as manifestations of separate cognitive processes, rather than as types of tropes. As will become evident in this chapter, the reason for this is that they are manifestations of how the mind probably produces abstract concepts.

Aristotle was the one who coined the term *metaphor*—itself a metaphor (*meta* "beyond" + *pherein* "to carry"). The great Greek philosopher saw the power of metaphorical reasoning in how it allowed people to produce knowledge. However, he affirmed that, as knowledge-productive as it was, its primary function was stylistic, a trope used by orators and writers to spruce up their more prosaic and literal ways of communicating. Remarkably, this latter position became the rule by which metaphor came to be judged in Western society. But as a seminal 1977 study by Pollio, Barlow, Fine, and Pollio showed clearly, Aristotle's former view was in effect the correct one. Those researchers documented the fact that speakers of English uttered, on average, 3,000 novel verbal metaphors and 7,000 idioms per week. Shortly thereafter, it became clear to scientists that metaphor was hardly an optional flourish on literal language. On the contrary, they started to discover that it actually mirrored the cognitive processes that underlie abstract concepts.

Defining metaphor semiotically poses an interesting dilemma. In the metaphor "The professor is a snake," there are two referents, not one, which are related to each other:

- There is the primary referent, *professor*, which is known as the *topic* (or *tenor*) of the metaphor.

- Then there is a second referent, *snake*, which is known as the *vehicle* of the metaphor.

- Their coupling creates a new meaning, called the *ground*, which is not the simple sum of their two meanings.

Thus, since each referent is itself a sign (*professor* = [A_1 ≡ B_1], *snake* = [A_2 ≡ B_2]), *metaphor* can be defined as a complex sign manifesting the following representational structure:

$$\{[A_1 \equiv B_1] \equiv [A_2 \equiv B_2]\}$$

However, it is not the denotative meaning of the vehicle that is transferred to the topic, but rather its connotations and annotations. So, the [A_2 ≡ B_2] in the above formula does not stand denotatively for *snake*, but rather for the culture-based characteristics perceived in snakes, namely [B_2 = "slyness," "danger," "slipperiness," ...]. It is this complex system of historically-inherited connotations that are mapped onto the topic. So, in effect, in metaphor the connotations of [B_2] replace the denotative meaning of the topic. Metaphor can now be defined formally as the relation:

[A_1 ≡ B_2], where B_2 = connotative meanings associated with A_2

Metaphor reveals a basic tendency of the human mind to think of certain referents in terms of others. The question now becomes: Is there any psychological motivation for this? In the case of "The professor is a snake," the probable reason for correlating two apparently unrelated referents seems to be the *de facto* perception that humans and animals are interconnected in the natural scheme of things. Indeed, as we shall see in this chapter, metaphor is the strongest evidence that exists in support of what we have called the *interconnectedness principle* in this book. It reveals a knack in humans for establishing similarities among dissimilar things, interconnecting them within mind-space. Among the first to point this out was Vico (chapter 2, §2.1). Before Vico, metaphor was viewed as a manifestation of *analogy* (chapter 3, §3.7). Analogy is an inductive form of reasoning that asserts that if two or more entities are similar in one or more respects, then a probability exists that they will be similar in other respects. For Vico, on the other hand, metaphor was hardly a manifestation of analogical reasoning; it revealed how humans go about creating analogies.

6.2 CONCEPTUAL METAPHOR

The first modern-day researchers to argue on a scientific basis that metaphors are the data that reveal how abstract thinking occurs were the linguist George Lakoff and the philosopher Mark Johnson in their groundbreaking 1980 book, *Metaphors We Live By*. Lakoff and Johnson documented meticulously the presence of metaphor in everyday thought and discourse, thus disavowing the mainstream view within linguistics that metaphorical utterances were simple figurative alternatives to literal ways of speaking. According to the traditional account of discourse in linguistics, an individual would purportedly try out a literal interpretation first when s/he hears a sentence, choosing a metaphorical one only when a literal interpretation is not possible from the context (Grice 1975). But as it turns out, this is not the case.

First, Lakoff and Johnson assert what Aristotle claimed two millennia before, namely that there are two types of concepts—*concrete* and *abstract* (chapter 3, §3.4). But the two scholars add a remarkable twist to the Aristotelian notion—namely that abstract concepts are built up systematically from concrete ones through metaphorical reasoning. They then proceed to rename abstract concepts *conceptual metaphors*, defining them as generalized metaphorical formulas that characterize specific abstractions. For example, the expression "The professor is a snake" is really a token of something more general, namely, *people are animals*. This is why we can also say that *John* or *Mary* or whoever we want is a *snake, gorilla, pig, puppy*, and so on. Each specific metaphor ("John is a gorilla," "Mary is a snake," etc.) is not an isolated example of poetic fancy. It is really a manifestation of a more general metaphorical idea—*people are animals*. Such formulas are what Lakoff and Johnson call *conceptual metaphors*:

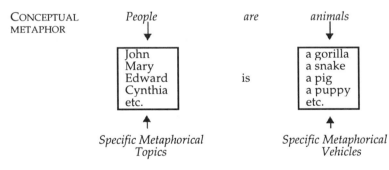

Each of the two parts of the *conceptual metaphor* is called a *domain*: *people* is the *target domain* because it is the abstract topic itself (the "target" of the conceptual metaphor); and *animals* is the *source domain* because it represents the class of vehicles, called the *lexical field*, that delivers the metaphor (the "source" of the metaphorical concept). An *abstract concept* can now be defined simply as a mapping of one domain onto the other. This model of concept-formation suggests that abstract concepts are formed systematically through such mappings and that specific metaphors are pointers to the source domains. So, when we hear people talking, for instance, of *ideas* in terms of *circles, points,* etc., we can easily identify the source domain they are deploying as *geometrical figures/relations:*

1. Those ideas are *circular.*
2. I don't see the *point* of your idea.
3. Her ideas are *central* to the discussion.
4. Their ideas are *diametrically opposite.*

The conceptual metaphor in this case is *ideas are geometrical figures/relations.* Conceptual metaphors are, as Lakoff and Johnson so aptly call them, "metaphors we live by." To get a firmer sense of what these are all about, consider the topic of *argument.* The most commonly used vehicles for conceptualizing arguments in our culture are the connotations associated with *war,* hence the conceptual metaphor *argument is war.* This shows up in such common utterances as the following:

5. Your claims are *indefensible.*
6. You *attacked* all my *weak points.*
7. Your criticisms were right *on target.*
8. I *demolished* his argument.
9. I've never *won* an argument.
10. She *shot down* all my points.
11. If you use that *strategy,* I'll *wipe you out.*

What does talking about argument in this way imply? It means, as Lakoff and Johnson suggest, that we actually "win" or "lose" arguments, and that our reactions towards the argument situation unfold as if we were involved in an actual physical battle: we attack a position, lose ground, plan strategy, defend or abandon a line of attack, etc. In a phrase, the *argument is war* conceptual metaphor structures the actions we perform when we argue and influences the feelings we experience during an argument.

Image Schema Theory

Lakoff and Johnson trace the psychological source of conceptual metaphorizing to *image schemas.* These are mental snapshots of our sensory experiences of locations, movements, shapes, etc. They are the mental links between sensory experiences and mental concepts. Image schemas are, in effect, "figured-out experiences" that permit us not only to recognize patterns inherent in certain sensations, but also to anticipate certain consequences and to make inferences and deductions from them. Schemas are *mental maps* that can reduce a large quantity of sensory information into general patterns. Image schema theory suggests, therefore, that the source domains enlisted in delivering an abstract topic were not chosen originally in an arbitrary fashion, but derived, rather, from the experience of events. The formation of a conceptual metaphor, consequently, is the result of an experiential induction. This is why metaphors often produce aesthetic or synesthetic effects, and this would explain why metaphorical utterances are more memorable than others.

The image schema is not a "replica." It is a *Gestalt structure* (Johnson 1987), a kind of "mental icon" of an experience. Schemas can be associative, fictitious, or narrative—e.g. the concept of *love*, for instance, implies an associative image schema (a face, a vignette, etc.); a *winged table* implies a fictitious schema that is nevertheless easy to imagine; an encounter that occurred in the recent past with someone implies a narrative image schema, i.e. a schematization of the episodes of the encounter in temporal sequence.

Image schemas, moreover, are not only picturable mental icons of experiences. They can be iconic of any sensory modality. Think, for example, of the following:

12. the sound of thunder

13. the feel of wet grass

14. the smell of fish

15. the taste of toothpaste

16. the sensation of being uncomfortably cold

17. the sensation of extreme happiness

The image schema associated with (12) has an auditory quality to it, rather than a picturable *Gestalt*. Similarly, the schema associated with (13) has a tactile quality, the one with (14) an olfactory quality, the one with (15) a gustatory quality, the one with (16) a kinesic quality, and the one with (17) an emotional quality.

Image schemas are so automatic that we are hardly ever aware of their control over conceptualization. But they can always be elicited easily. If someone were to be asked to explain the expression "I'm feeling *up* today," s/he would likely not have a conscious image schema involving an upward orientation, which can be abbreviated to [verticality]. However, if that same person were asked the following questions —"How far up do you feel?" "What do you mean by up?" etc.—then s/he would no doubt start to visualize the [verticality] schema. In effect, image schemas are evidence of "abstractive seeing," as the philosopher Susanne Langer (1948) so aptly put it. As an example, consider the following image schema of an *obstacle* or *impediment:*

IMPEDIMENT IMAGE SCHEMA

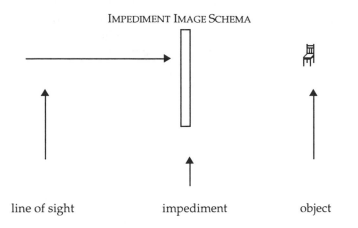

line of sight   impediment   object

Several abstract scenarios are now visualizable in terms of this [impediment] schema: one can *go around* the [impediment], *over* it, *under* it, or *through* it, or one can *remove* it and continue on towards the object. On the other hand, the [impediment] could successfully impede someone, so that s/he would have to *stop* at the [impediment] and *turn back*. All of these actions can be easily seen within mind-space. Now, it is easy to see why this schema has become the source of a host of abstract ideas in our culture:

18. We *got through* that difficult time.
19. Jim felt better after he *got over* his cold.
20. You want to *steer clear of* financial debt.
21. With the bulk of the work *out of the way*, he was able to call it a day.
22. The rain *stopped* us from enjoying our picnic.
23. You cannot *go any further* with that idea; you'll just have to *turn back*.

Lakoff and Johnson identify several basic types of image schemas. The first one involves mental *orientation*. This type of schema underlies concepts that are derived from our physical experiences of orientation —*up vs. down, back vs. front, near vs. far*, etc. The [verticality] and [impediment] schemas discussed above are two examples of orientational schemas. The second type involves *ontological* thinking. This produces conceptual metaphors in which activities, emotions, ideas, etc. are associated with entities and substances: e.g. *the mind is a container* as in "I'm *full* of memories." The third type of schema is an elaboration of the other two. This produces *structural metaphors* that extend orientational and ontological concepts: e.g. *time is a resource* is built from *time is a resource* and *time is a quantity*, as in "My time is *money*." Here is just a sampling of how image schemas underlie various concepts:

happiness is up/sadness is down

> 24. I'm feeling *up* today.
> 25. She's feeling *down*.
> 26. That *boosted* my spirits.
> 27. My mood *sank*.
> 28. That gave me a *lift*.

health and life are up/sickness and death are down

> 29. I'm at the *peak* of my health.
> 30. She *fell* ill.
> 31. Life is an *uphill* struggle.
> 32. Lazarus *rose* from the dead.
> 33. Her health is *sinking* fast.

knowledge is light/ignorance is darkness

> 34. I was *illuminated* by that professor.
> 35. I was left in the *dark* about what happened.
> 36. That idea is very *clear*.
> 37. That theory is *obscure*.
> 38. His example *shed light* on several matters.

ideas are buildings

> 39. That is a *well-constructed* theory.
> 40. His views are on *solid ground*.
> 41. That theory needs *support*.
> 42. Their viewpoint *collapsed* under criticism.
> 43. She put together the *framework* of a theory.

ideas are plants

44. Her ideas have come to *fruition*.
45. That's a *budding* theory.
46. His views have contemporary *offshoots*.
47. That is a *branch* of mathematics.

ideas are commodities

48. He certainly knows how to *package* his ideas.
49. That idea just won't *sell*.
50. There's no *market* for that idea.
51. That's a *worthless* idea.

As Lakoff and Johnson emphasize, we do not detect the presence of image schemas in such common expressions because of repeated usage. For example, we no longer interpret the word *see* in sentences such as "I don't *see* what you mean," "Do you *see* what I'm saying?" in image schematic terms, because they have become so familiar to us. But the association between the biological act of seeing outside the body and the imaginary act of seeing within mind-space was the original source of the conceptual metaphor *seeing is understanding/believing/thinking*, which now permeates common discourse:

52. There is more to this than *meets the eye*.
53. I have a different *point of view*.
54. It all depends on how you *look* at it.
55. I take a *dim view* of the whole matter.
56. I never *see eye to eye* on things with you.
57. You have a different *worldview* than I do.
58. Your ideas have given me great *insight* into life.

Cultural Models

For the present purposes, the last relevant point made by Lakoff and Johnson in their truly fascinating book is that cultural groupthink is built on conceptual metaphors, since these coalesce into a system of abstract thinking that holds together the entire network of associated meanings in the culture. This is accomplished by a kind of "higher-order" metaphorizing—that is, as target domains are associated with many kinds of source domains (orientational, ontological, structural), the concepts they underlie become increasingly more complex, leading to what Lakoff and Johnson call *cultural* or *cognitive models*. To see what this means, consider the target domain of *ideas* again. The following three conceptual metaphors, among many others (as we have seen), deliver the meaning of this concept in three separate ways:

ideas are food

59. Those ideas left a *sour taste* in my mouth.
60. It's hard to *digest* all those ideas at once.
61. Even though he is a *voracious* reader, he can't *chew* all those ideas
62. That teacher is always *spoonfeeding* her students.
63. That idea has *deep roots*.

ideas are persons

64. Darwin is the *father* of modern biology.
65. Those medieval ideas continue to *live on* even today.
66. Cognitive linguistics is still in its *infancy*.
67. Maybe we should *resurrect* that ancient idea.
68. She *breathed* new life into that idea.

ideas are fashions

69. That idea went out of *style* several years ago.
70. Those scientists are the *avant-garde* of their field.
71. Those revolutionary ideas are no longer in *vogue*.
72. Semiotics has become truly *chic*.
73. That idea is old *hat*.

Recall from examples cited above that there are other ways of conceptualizing *ideas*—e.g. in terms of *buildings, plants, commodities, geometry,* and *seeing*. The constant juxtaposition of such conceptual metaphors in common discourse produces, cumulatively, a *cultural model* of *ideas* that has a specific *Gestalt* structure. This can be shown graphically as in Figure 6.1.

Several of the source domains for this model—e.g. *food, people,* and *fashion*—are relatively understandable across cultures: i.e. people from non-English-speaking cultures could easily figure out what statements based on these domains mean if they were translated or relayed to them. However, there are some source domains that are more likely to be culture-specific, such as, for instance, the *geometrical figures* domain, and thus beyond easy comprehension. This suggests that there are different degrees or "orders" of concepts. The *ideas are food* concept, for example, is a lower-order concept because it connects a universal physical process—*eating*—to an abstraction—*thinking*—directly. But the *ideas are geometrical figures* concept reveals a higher-order form of conceptualization, since geometrical figures and notions are themselves concepts that are learned in a cultural context.

Figure 6.1

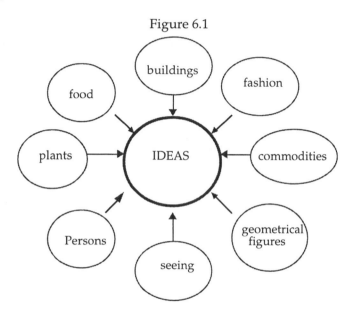

The Background to Conceptual Metaphor Theory

Lakoff and Johnson did not devise *conceptual metaphor theory*, as it is now called, in a vacuum. They developed it from the work conducted in several disciplines and from the deliberations of several key scholars in the twentieth century. The experimental investigation of metaphor was initiated by the linguist Karl Bühler (e.g. 1951 [1908]) and his associates (e.g. Staehlin 1914) at the turn of the century, who collected intriguing data on how subjects paraphrased proverbs. In the 1950s and 1960s an increasing number of psychologists started to look at such issues as the effects of metaphor on concept-formation (e.g. Asch 1950, Osgood and Suci 1957, Brown, Leiter, and Hildum 1957), the neurological processes involved in metaphor processing (e.g. Weinstein 1964), the effects of context on the choice of literal or metaphorical expressions (Koen 1965), and the role of imagery in metaphor (e.g. Asch 1958, Werner and Kaplan 1963). Even the behaviorist psychologist B. F. Skinner, in his highly controversial treatment of language development

Verbal Behavior (1957), had the insight to include verbal metaphors in his overall theory of verbal behavior.

But it is the work of the literary critic I. A. Richards (1893–1979) in which *conceptual metaphor theory* finds its philosophical source. In his widely-read and influential 1936 book, *The Philosophy of Rhetoric*, Richards argued convincingly that the meaning created by a metaphor was an open-ended one, not simply a sum of the parts. Metaphor produced a unique kind of semantic "interaction" between two domains. Like two chemicals mixed together in a test tube, the result of mixing two domains [A₁] and [B₂] (above, §6.1) creates a dynamic semantic interaction that retains properties of both domains but also has unique ones of its own. Max Black (1962) added, later, that the two domains were to be regarded as "systems" rather than as discrete units.

Richards' crucial work opened the way for the serious investigation of metaphor within the social sciences. The 1955 study by the Gestalt psychologist Solomon Asch, for instance, showed that metaphors derived from the vocabularies of sensation of several phylogenetically-unrelated languages (*warm, cold, heavy*, etc.) used the same sensory modality for different referential domains. For example, he found that *hot* stood for *rage* in Hebrew, *enthusiasm* in Chinese, *sexual arousal* in Thai, and *energy* in Hausa. As Brown (1958: 146) aptly commented shortly after the publication of Asch's study, "there is an undoubted kinship of meanings" in different languages that "seem to involve activity and emotional arousal." Empirical work on metaphor proliferated in the 1970s and 1980s. As Winner (1982: 253) has stated, if nothing else, the research literature has established that if "people were limited to strictly literal language, communication would be severely curtailed, if not terminated." By the early 1990s there was little doubt in the minds of many linguists and psychologists that metaphor was a guide to the workings of human abstract thinking.

6.3 OTHER TROPES

Since the early 1970s, the practice in cognitive linguistics (chapter 2, §2.5) has been to use the term *metaphor* to encompass various kinds of tropes. Within this new analytical framework, *personification* ("My cat speaks English"), for instance, would be seen as a particular kind of *metaphor*, namely one in which the target domain [A₁] refers to an animal or inanimate object and the source domain [B₂] refers to traits that are associated with human beings. In a nutshell, any cognitive process that involves a *mapping* from a source to a target domain is now classified under the category of *metaphor*; any that does not is viewed separately:

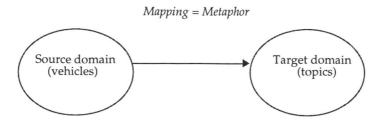

Mapping = Metaphor

Metaphor can now be defined as the ability of the human brain to convert experience into abstraction via the *mapping* of some source domain onto a target domain to produce an abstract concept. There are two tropes that are regularly considered separately from metaphor in concept-formation—*metonymy* and *irony*—because they do not entail such a mapping process. *Metonymy* is a cognitive process by which the name of one thing is used in place of that of another associated with or suggested by it (e.g. *the White House* for *the President*). In concept-formation terms, it can be defined as the process of using a part of a domain to represent the whole domain:

Metonymic Concept-Formation

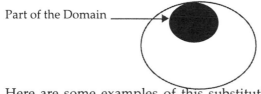

Here are some examples of this substitutive process (Lakoff and Johnson 1980: 35-40):

> 74. She likes to read *Dostoyevski* (= the writings of Dostoyevski).
> 75. He's in *dance* (= the dancing profession).
> 76. My mom frowns on *blue jeans* (= the wearing of blue jeans).
> 77. New *windshield wipers* will satisfy him (= the state of having new wipers).

There is a special subtype of metonymy, known as *synecdoche*, that is particularly productive in concept-formation. This is defined as the process by which the part is used to represent the whole, and vice versa:

> 78. The *automobile* is destroying our health (= the collection of automobiles).
> 79. We need a couple of *strong bodies* for our teams (= strong people).
> 80. I've got a new *set of wheels* (= car).
> 81. We need *new blood* in this organization (= new people).

In parallelism with the notion of *conceptual metaphor*, we suggest the term *conceptual metonym* to refer to generalized metonymical formulas such as *the face is the person* that inform both common discourse and the entire meaning system inherent in the signifying order of a culture:

> 82. He's just another pretty *face*.
> 83. There are an awful lot of *faces* in the audience.
> 84. We need some new *faces* around here.

Conceptual metonyms are abstractions, and like conceptual metaphors they are interconnected to other domains of meaning-making in a culture. The distribution of the concept *the face is the person* throughout the meaning pathways of the signifying order is the reason why portraits, in painting and photography, focus on the face. The face is, in effect, a metonym for personality. Here are some other examples of conceptual metonyms:

the part for the whole

> 85. Get your *butt* over here!
> 86. The Blue Jays need a *stronger arm* in right field.
> 87. We don't hire *crew cuts*.

the producer (brand) for the product

> 88. I'll have a *Heineken*.
> 89. We bought a *Ford*.
> 90. He's got a *Rembrandt* in his office.

the object used for the user

> 91. My *piano* is sick today.
> 92. The *meat and potatoes* is a lousy tipper.
> 93. The *buses* are on strike.

the controller for the controlled

> 94. *Napoleon* lost at Waterloo.
> 95. *Montreal* won a lot of Stanley Cups.
> 96. A Mercedes rear-ended *me*.

the institution for the people responsible

> 97. *Shell* has raised its prices again.
> 98. The *Church* thinks that promiscuity is immoral.
> 99. I don't approve of *Washington's* actions.

the place for the institution

> 100. The *White House* isn't saying anything.
> 101. *Milan* is introducing new jackets this year.
> 102. *Wall Street* is in a panic.

Irony also does not entail a mapping process. Rather, it constitutes a highlighting strategy based on the use of words to convey a meaning contrary to their literal sense ("I love being tortured"). It is, more formally, a cognitive strategy by which a concept [**A**] is highlighted through its opposite [-**A**]: [**A** ≡ -**A**]. This process creates a discrepancy between appearance and reality, thus creating a kind of "meaning tension by contrast."

There is a second type of irony, which can be defined simply as the use of words or statements to criticize someone in a biting, mocking way. This type constitutes a powerful discourse technique that allows someone to make a powerful comment on a situation. For instance, adolescents in Western culture use it typically as a verbal tactic for critiquing others (Danesi 1994)—hence the coining of words such as *mega-bitch, geekdom, party animal, dude, dog* "unattractive person," *wimp dog* "male with little personality." Another function of irony in adolescence is humor—hence expressions like *M.L.A.* = *massive lip action* "passionate kissing", *barf* " vomit," *blimp boat* "obese person."

6.4 METAPHOR AND GRAMMAR

Is there any connection between conceptual metaphors/metonyms and grammar? The traditional view is that grammatical rules are arbitrary and that meaning is objectively determinable in the syntactic structure

of language. The work on metaphor summarized above, however, provides reasons why this view is no longer tenable. And, indeed, some
cognitive linguists have started to provide a truly fascinating theoretical framework for relating grammatical categories to concept-formation
processes (e.g. Langacker 1990, Taylor 1995).

As a concrete example of how grammar and metaphor might be
interrelated, consider the use of the prepositions *since* and *for* in sentences such as the following in English:

> 103. I have been living here *since* 1990.
>
> 104. I have known Lucy *since* September.
>
> 105. I have not been able to sleep *since* Monday.
>
> 106. I have been living here *for* fifteen years.
>
> 107. I have known Lucy *for* nine months.
>
> 108. I have not been able to sleep *for* five days.

An analysis of the expressions that follow *since* reveals that they
belong to a source domain based on an image schema of *time* as a
[point on a line]. The specific *points* in sentences (103)-(105) are "1990,"
"September," "Monday." The schema can be shown graphically as follows:

Time = [point on a line]

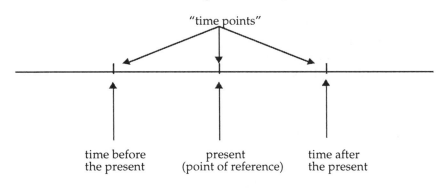

"time points"

| time before
the present | present
(point of reference) | time after
the present |

The expressions that follow *for*, on the other hand, belong to a
source domain based on an image schema of *time* as a [quantity]. The
specific *quantities* in sentences (106)-(108) are: "fifteen years," "nine
months," "five days." This can be shown graphically as differences in
the capacity of *containers*:

Time = [quantity]

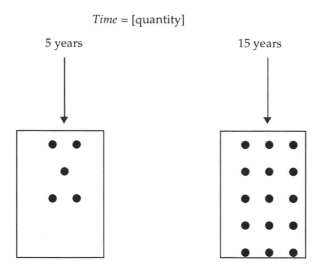

5 years   15 years

These image schemas are the sources for the two conceptual metaphors *time is a point* and *time is a quantity*. These can now be seen to have a specific effect at the level of grammar—expressions introduced by *since* are reflexes of the conceptual metaphor *time is a point*; those introduced by *for* are reflexes of the conceptual metaphor *time is a quantity*. This is, in fact, the kind of *rule of grammar* that interconnects conceptual metaphors/metonyms and parts of speech.

Take, as one other example, the selection of certain verbs in particular types of sentences in Italian. The verb *fare* "to make" is used in reference to a weather situation—*fa caldo* "it makes hot," *fa freddo* "it makes cold." The physical state of "being hot" or "being cold" is conveyed instead with the verb *essere* "to be" when referring to objects—*è caldo* "it is hot," *è freddo* "it is cold"—and with *avere* "to have" when referring to people—*ha caldo* "s/he is hot," *ha freddo* "s/he is cold." The use of one verb or the other—*fare, essere,* or *avere*—is motivated by an underlying image schematic conceptualization of bodies and the environment as containers. So, the [containment] context in which the *heat* or *cold* is located determines the verbal category to be employed. If it is in the environment, it is "made" by Nature *(fa freddo)*; if it is in a human being, then the body "has" it *(ha freddo)*; and if it is in an object, then the object "is" its container *(è freddo):*

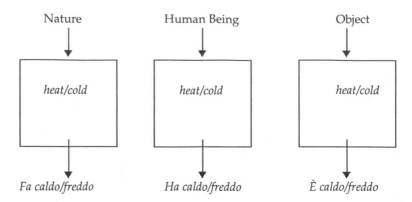

It is interesting to note that in Italian "being right," "being sleepy," etc. are also conceptualized as "contained" substances. This is why to say "I am right," "I am sleepy," etc. in Italian one must say *ho ragione* ("I have reason"), *ho sonno* ("I have sleepiness"), etc.

A metaphorical theory of grammar can now be envisaged. This would posit that the "history of derivation" of a specific language category in the organization of some (perhaps most) sentences (1) starts out as an *experiential* form, that is (2) converted into an image schema (e.g. [verticality], [containment], [impediment], etc.) that is then (3) converted into an appropriate *conceptual metaphor/metonym* (e.g. *happiness is up, the body is a container*, etc.) that, (4) finally, is *grammaticalized* (reflected grammatically) and/or *lexicalized* (reflected lexically):

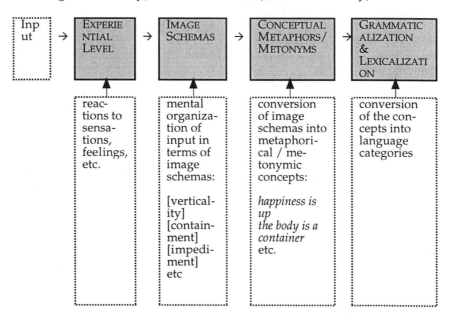

As a practical example, take the schema [verticality]. Humans the world over experience the sensation of [verticality] as an *up* and *down* view of things. This experience is a consequence of the fact that we stand, climb, look up, look down, and so on. The [verticality] schema is a mental shorthand of the experience, becoming the source of the conceptual metaphor *happiness is up*. This is then grammaticalized and lexicalized according to the type of sentence organization required —e.g. "I'm feeling up today" (lexicalization), "Great!" (intonation up).

6.5 METAPHOR AND THE SIGNIFYING ORDER

Conceptual metaphors and metonyms are not only the most likely sources of grammaticalization and lexicalization processes in a language, but they are also interconnected with the other codes of the signifying order, providing the "conceptual glue" that keeps the whole system of culture together (chapter 12, §12.2). Paradoxically, while metaphor holds existing cultural systems together, it is also the source of innovation in such systems. This is because, as Vico argued convincingly, the metaphorical capacity is tied to *fantasia*, the imaginative and creative faculty of mind that predisposes human beings to search out and forge new meanings constantly. Indeed, novel metaphors are being created all the time. If someone were to say "Those ideas are a cup of coffee," it is unlikely that the reader would have heard this expression before. But its novelty forces us to reflect upon its meaning. The vehicle used, a *cup of coffee*, is a common object of everyday life and therefore easily perceivable as a source for thinking about *ideas*. The metaphor now compels us to start thinking of *ideas* in terms of the kinds of physical, gustatory, social, and other attributes that are associated with a *cup of coffee*. For this metaphor to gain currency, however, it must capture the fancy of many other people for a period of time. Then and only then will its novelty have become worn out and will it become the basis for a new conceptual metaphor: *ideas are drinking substances*. After that, expressions such as "Your idea is a cup of tea," "That theory is a bottle of fine wine," and the like will become similarly understandable as offering different perspectives on *ideas*.

In terms of the signifying order, the work of Lakoff and Johnson suggests that the system of conceptual metaphors that is found in a culture constitutes, in effect, a *metaphorical code*. The study of metaphorical codes across cultures is beginning to show that they possess many features in common, especially with respect to the formation of what we have called "lower-order" concepts (above, §6.2). Indeed, the universal features of such codes invite the question of the relation of metaphor to the emergence of conceptual thinking in the human species. Recall the *seeing is believing* conceptual metaphor ("I have a different *point of view*," "I never *see eye to eye* with him," etc.). This has been documented across societies as a fundamental source of cultural models of *belief* (e.g. Viberg 1983, Danesi 1990). In evolutionary terms, the crystallization of such models in human thought suggests that vision was originally at the root of many of our abstract notions. Indirect evidence for this hypothesis can be discerned in the presence of conceptual formulas such as *thoughts are movable objects* and *thinking is visual scanning* in languages across the world (Danesi and Santeramo 1995):

thoughts are movable objects

> 109. *Work* that idea *over* in your mind.
> 110. *Turn* that thought *over* in your mind.
> 111. You should *rearrange* your thoughts carefully.
> 112. *Put* your thoughts *in order* before going forward with your plans.

thinking is visual scanning

> 113. You must *look over* what you've written.
> 114. I must *look into* what you've told me a bit further.
> 115. She *saw right through* what you told her.
> 116. I'm going to *see* this thing completely *out*.
> 117. You should *look into* that philosophy further.

These suggest that thoughts, like objects, can be moved, arranged, located, etc., or else seen, looked into, scanned, etc. As Walter Ong (1977: 134) has also pointed out, the presence of such formulas in human thought suggests that "we would be incapacitated for dealing with knowledge and intellection without massive visualist conceptualization, that is, without conceiving of intelligence through models applying initially to vision."

Metaphorical codes are overarching systems of meaning that constitute "conceptual organizing grids" for the entire signifying order of a culture. Our own courtship rituals, for example, reflect the *love is a sweetness* metaphor ("She's my sweetheart," "I love my honey," etc.) in nonverbal ways: e.g. sweets are given to a loved one on St. Valentine's Day; matrimonial love is symbolized at a wedding ceremony by the eating of a cake; we sweeten our breath with candy before kissing our loved ones; etc. The *justice is blind* metaphorical concept can be discerned in the fact that outside or inside courtrooms statutes of "Justice" have blindfolds. The metaphorical concept *the scales of justice*, too, is commonly symbolized by corresponding sculptures of scales near or inside justice buildings.

Incidentally, Emantian (1995) has documented cross-cultural similarities in the ways in which sexual desire is metaphorized. In Chagga, a Bantu language of Tanzania, the same *love* concept found in our culture—*love is a sweetness*—manifests itself constantly in discourse about sex and romance. In Chagga the man is perceived to be the eater and the woman his *sweet food,* as can be detected in expressions that mean, in translated form, "Does she taste sweet?" "She tastes sweet as sugar honey" (Emantian 1995: 168).

Metaphorical codes are powerful shapers of worldview because they are so understandable. They make thinking easy. They are automatic, effortless, and established by community consensus. More often than not, they are guides to a culture's past. A common expression like "He has fallen from grace" would have been recognized instantly in a previous era as referring to the Adam and Eve story in the Bible. Today we continue to use it with only a dim awareness (if any) of its Biblical origins. Expressions that portray life as a journey—"I'm still a long way from my goal," "There is no end in sight," etc.—are similarly rooted in Biblical narrative. As the literary critic Northrop Frye (1981) aptly pointed out, one cannot penetrate such expressions, or indeed most of Western literature or art, without having been exposed, directly or indirectly, to the original Biblical stories. These are the source domains for many of the conceptual metaphors we use today for judging human actions and offering advice, bestowing upon everyday life a kind of implicit metaphysical meaning and value.

Proverbs too are extended metaphors that people employ to provide sound practical advice when it is required in certain situations:

118. You've got too many fires burning (= advice to not do so many things at once).
119. Rome wasn't built in a day (= advice to have patience).
120. Don't count your chickens before they're hatched (= advice to be cautious).
121. An eye for an eye and a tooth for a tooth (= equal treatment is required in love and war).

Every culture has similar proverbs, aphorisms, and sayings. They constitute a remarkable code of ethics and of practical knowledge that anthropologists call "folk wisdom." Indeed, the very concept of *wisdom* implies the ability to apply proverbial language insightfully to a situation. Preaching, too, would hardly be persuasive if it were not embedded in the metaphorical code of a culture. An effective preacher is one who knows how to structure h/er oration around a few highly understandable conceptual metaphors: e.g. *sex is dirty, sex is punishable by fire,* etc. These guide the preacher's selection of words, illustrations, turns of phrase, practical examples, etc.—"You must cleanse your soul of the filth of sex"; "You will burn in Hell, if you do not clean up your act"; etc.

Scientific reasoning too is intertwined with the metaphorical code. Science often involves things that cannot be seen—atoms, waves, gravitational forces, magnetic fields, etc. So, scientists use their metaphorical know-how to get a look, so to speak, at this hidden matter. That is why waves are said to *undulate* through empty space, atoms to *leap* from one quantum state to another, electrons to *travel in circles* around an atomic nucleus, and so on. Metaphors are evidence of the human ability to see the universe as a coherent structure. As physicist Robert Jones (1982: 4) aptly puts it, for the scientist metaphor serves as "an evocation of the inner connection among things." When a metaphor is accepted as fact, it enters human life, taking on an independent conceptual existence in the real world, suggesting ways to bring about changes in and to the world. Even the nature of experimentation can be seen in this light. Experimentation is a search for connections, linkages, associations of some sort or other. As Rom Harré (1981: 23) has pointed out, most experiments involve "the attempt to relate the structure of things, discovered in an exploratory study, to the organization this imposes on the processes going on in that structure."

All this really could not be otherwise. Whereas individual signs entail referential domains for humans to reflect upon, utilize, and store as knowledge, metaphor is the form of thought humans use to interconnect such domains into increasingly layered orders of meaning —layers upon layers of metaphors. One metaphor suggests another, which suggests another, and so on. The central feature of human thinking is the fluid application of existing metaphorical concepts to new situations.

7

SPACE

Buildings speak the language of the commercial sign system of the surrounding city.

Jameson (1991: 39)

7.0 PRELIMINARY REMARKS

The fact that all social groups build and design the abodes and public edifices of their villages, towns, and cities in characteristic ways is a clear indication that places, buildings, and spaces are felt throughout the world to have culture-specific meanings and functions. Indeed, a building is hardly ever perceived by the members of a society as simply a pile of bricks, wood, straw, etc. put together to provide shelter. Rather, its shape, size, features, and location are perceived to be signifiers that refer to a range of meanings that are as interconnected to the signifying order of a culture as are those associated with, say, facial expressions, cosmetics, and words for abstract ideas.

In this chapter, our trip through the landscape of culture takes us through the domain of the *built and inhabited social environment*. This is the home of *Homo faber*, the maker. On this leg of our journey, we will stop to look at several fascinating semiotic aspects of places, spaces, and buildings. We will discuss, among other things, the function of *maps* as special kinds of *signs* and the nature and role of *spatial* and *architectural codes* in communal life. In this area of cultural analysis, too, we remind the reader that the semiotician's research efforts are guided by five primary goals:

1. identifying the basic signifying properties connected with spatial and architectural codes (iconicity, indexicality, etc.);

2. relating these to the signifying order and to processes of representation (e.g. *dimensionality*);

3. documenting and explaining the structural effects that spatial and architectural codes have on individuals;

4. investigating how these codes are interconnected
    throughout the signifying order (the *interconnectedness
    principle*);

5. utilizing the findings or techniques of any cognate disci-
    pline that are applicable to the situation at hand.

7.1 SHELTERS

Animals reside in territories that they have appropriated as their own,
or in some negotiated arrangement with other animals, so that they can
procure their shelter, alimentation, and habitation needs. But, unlike
other species, humans also manifest a unique compulsion to *represent* in
meaningful ways the territories in which they are located as social
groups, i.e. they demonstrate the tendency to imbue their territories
with meanings extracted from the resources of their signifying orders.

As we saw previously (chapter 4, §4.4), biologists define *territoriality* as an innate survival mechanism that allows an animal to gain access to, and defend control of, critical resources such as food and nesting sites that are found in certain habitats. The Austrian zoologist
Konrad Lorenz (1903–1989) was among the first scientists to identify
and document the patterns animals display in marking the boundaries
of their territories. Such patterns, he proposed, were an important part
of an animal's repertory of survival strategies, as critical, in evolutionary terms, as its physiological characteristics. Lorenz (1952) also suggested that human aggression and warfare were explainable as residual
territoriality impulses. Lorenz's controversial theory gained widespread popularity through a best-selling book written in 1966 by
Ardrey, *The Territorial Imperative*—a book that subsequently generated
a heated debate in academia and society at large on the nature and origin of human aggression. The notion of territoriality in human life continues to receive much support because of its intuitive appeal
—intrusions into appropriated territories (e.g. into one's home, car,
etc.) are indeed perceived typically by human beings as signals of aggression, in the same way that a cat, for example, would likely react to
another cat intruding upon the boundaries it has proclaimed by urination.

The territoriality mechanism endows an animal species with the
ability to secure a survival space within the habitat to which it has become adapted. But in the human species the story does not stop there.
Consider, for instance, the procuring of a *shelter* within a habitat. Many
animals have the ability to construct appropriate shelters within their
habitats to protect themselves from the elements and to procure a safeguard against intruding enemies: e.g. beavers build dams of stick, mud,

brushwood, and/or stone to widen the area and increase the depth of water around their habitats; marmots (groundhogs) make burrows in the ground where they can hibernate safely during the winter; and the list could go on and on. Human shelter-making, however, presupposes more than survival. As implied by the *dimensionality principle* (chapter 3, §3.9), a shelter is perceived to have a meaning not only along a biological (*firstness*) axis as an abode for enhancing survival, or as a means of supplementing the body's protective biological resources, but also as an extension of Self (*secondness*) and as a *sign* with meanings derived from the various *architectural codes* that are present in a culture (*thirdness*):

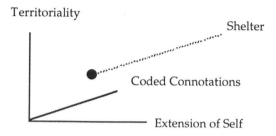

7.2 MAPS

Since ancient times, human societies have invariably represented the territories in which they are located with visual signs, known as *maps*, made with indexical (indicating where places are), iconic (representing places in topographical relation to each other), and symbolic (notational system) signifiers.

Making a map is such a straightforward task that virtually anyone who has been exposed to the concept of the map can make one on the spot. Here's a simple illustration. Let's say a stranger wants to get to a certain destination. The stranger is at location **A**, which is at the intersection of two streets, one running north and south, the other east and west. H/er goal is to go to a location **B**, which we know is west two blocks and north three blocks of location **A**. An easy way to show h/er how to get to **B** is to draw h/er a map. On the map, the location **A** is the point of intersection of two lines at right angles—the intersecting streets. Compass directions can also be added to the map to reinforce its orientation indexicality. Finally, two equally-calibrated units added to the east-west line can be used to represent two blocks west (to the left) of **A**; and three equally-calibrated units added to the north-south line starting from that point can be used to represent three blocks north. This will show the stranger how to reach the desired location, **B**:

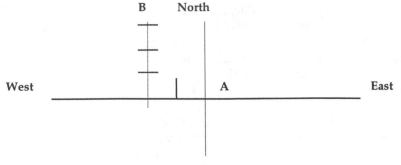

A *map* can be defined, semiotically, as a complex sign made with three kinds of signifiers:

- A map is, overall, an *indexical* sign, since it indicates where the territory is located on the *terra firma*.

- Its layout is *iconic*, because it shows the features in a territory in topographical relation to each other.

- It involves *symbolicity* because it is interpretable on the basis of a conventional notational system (e.g. *key, scale,* etc.).

Some semioticians prefer to define a map as a *text*. Actually, a map can function both as a *sign* standing for a specific territory and a *text* conveying a message or point of view about that same territory. Maps thus have *structural effects* on how social groups perceive and interpret represented territories (chapter 3, §3.10). To illustrate how a map can produce such effects, we direct the reader's attention to the technique of cylindrical projection in Western map-making—a method for making two-dimensional maps by projecting the globe onto a flat surface. Developed by the Flemish geographer Gerardus Mercator (1512–1594), this technique consists in wrapping a cylinder around the globe, making it touch the equator, and then projecting (1) the lines of latitude outward from the globe onto the cylinder as lines parallel to the equator, and (2) the lines of longitude outward onto the cylinder as lines parallel to the prime meridian (the line that is designated 0° longitude, passing through the original site of the Royal Greenwich Observatory in England). The resulting two-dimensional map represents the world's surface as a rectangle with parallel lines of latitude and parallel lines of longitude (which are perpendicular to those of latitude).

Because of the curvature of the globe, the latitude lines on the map nearest the poles appear closer together. This distortion makes certain land masses appear smaller than they are. This, in turn, tends to produce a structural effect on perception, by which *larger land mass = better, more powerful, more important, etc. land mass*, and thus tends to condition how people come to see the relative value of the territories represented by this kind of map. Indeed, the very concept of *worldview* derives from the fact that the ways in which we come to *view* the *world* are, in part, a consequence of how that *world* is represented *for viewing* by the maps we make of it.

Although modern technology now makes it easy to construct three-dimensional maps, traditionally the term *map* has always designated a two-dimensional representation of an area; three-dimensional maps are more accurately known as *models*. All civilizations have developed map-making techniques to meet a host of social purposes. In Western culture, these were elaborated and refined in tandem with and in relation to the rise and growth of the physical and mathematical sciences. The basic type of Western map shows the natural features of the area covered as well as cultural features—e.g. political boundaries, such as the limits of towns, countries, and states. Developed in parallel with this basic type are the many special-purpose maps that have been devised with specialized functions in mind: e.g. maps for the special needs of navigation and exploration, to show political divisions, to show the physical structure of an area, to indicate crop distribution and/or density patterns, to show population levels, etc. Cartographers have invented a great variety of signifiers to suit various representational needs. These are generally summarized and defined in the map's key or legend, which is, more accurately, a *code* in the semiotic sense of the word.

Since Mercator invented the cylindrical projection method, most Western map-making techniques have been devised in accordance with the principles of Cartesian coordinate geometry. These allow the cartographer to represent the earth as a two-dimensional plane covered with lines of longitude and latitude. By convention, longitude is marked 180° east and 180° west from 0° at Greenwich, England. Latitude is marked 90° north and 90° south from the 0° parallel of the equator. Points on a map can be accurately defined by giving degrees, minutes, and seconds for both latitude and longitude; these correspond to real points on the earth. Indeed, the whole concept of map-making involves the representation of "real spaces" (the signified domain) in terms of "map spaces" (the signifier domain) with higher or lesser degrees of fidelity.

Distances are represented with the technique of *scaling*, which allows for the portrayal of the distance between two points on the earth as the distance between the two corresponding points on the map: e.g. a scale of 1:100,000 means that one unit measured on the map (say 1 cm.)

represents 100,000 of the same units on the earth's surface. A high degree of accuracy can be achieved in scaling through the use of aerial and satellite photography. The varying heights of hills and mountains, and the depths of valleys, are portrayed instead with the technique known as *relief*. In earlier maps, this consisted in making small drawings of mountains and valleys on the maps. But this method was extremely imprecise and thus came eventually to be supplanted by the use of contour lines. The shapes of these lines provide accurate (iconic) representations of the shapes of hills and depressions, and the lines themselves show actual elevations, so that closely spaced contour lines indicate steep slopes. Other methods of indicating elevation include the use of colors, tints, hachures (short parallel lines), or shadings. When colors are used for this purpose, a graded series of tones is selected for coloring areas of similar elevations. Shadings or hachures, neither of which show actual elevations, are more easily interpreted than contour lines and are sometimes used in conjunction with them for achieving greater fidelity in representation.

How do we decode a map? To say "I am here, but I want to get to there" on a map involves understanding (1) that *here* and *there* are indexes in map space standing for points in real space: [*a point on a map* _ *a physical location in a real territory*], and (2) that the movement from *here* to *there* on a map stands for the corresponding movement between two points in real space. In this way, maps make it possible to plan a journey through real space with amazing accuracy, since the journey has in effect already been envisaged intellectually in terms of the map space. This is why maps have greatly enhanced humankind's ability to know the world, having allowed people to literally "envision" real-world places in their minds.

The History of Cartography

The first known maps were made by the Babylonians around 2300 BC. Carved on clay tablets, they consisted largely of land surveys made for the purposes of taxation. More extensive regional maps, drawn on silk and dating from the second century BC, have been found in China. The precursor of the modern map, however, is believed to have been devised by the Greek philosopher Anaximander (c. 611–c. 547 BC). It was circular and showed the known lands of the world grouped around the Aegean Sea at the center and surrounded by the ocean. Anaximander's map constituted one of the first attempts to think beyond the immediate territorial boundaries of a particular society—Greece—even though Anaximander located the center of the universe in the Aegean Sea. Then, around 200 BC, the Greek geometer and geographer Eratosthenes (chapter 3, §3.6) introduced the technique of parallel lines to indicate latitude and longitude, although they were not evenly and accurately spaced. Eratosthenes' map represented the known world from present-day England in the northwest to the mouth of the Ganges River in the east and to Libya in the south. About 150 AD, the Egyptian scholar Ptolemy (c. 100–c. 170 AD) published the first textbook in cartographic methodology, entitled simply *Geographia*. Even though they contained a number of errors, his were among the first maps of the world to be made with the mathematical technique of projection. At about the same time in China, map-makers were also beginning to use mathematically accurate grids for making maps.

The next step forward in cartographic methodology came in the medieval era when Arab seamen showed the world how to make highly accurate navigational charts, with lines indicating the bearings between ports. Then, in the fifteenth century, influenced by the publication of Ptolemy's maps, European map-makers laid the foundations for the modern science of cartography. In 1507, for instance, the German cartographer Martin Waldseemüller (c. 1470–c. 1522) became the first to apply the name *America* to the newly identified trans-Atlantic lands, separating America into North and South—a cartographic tradition that continues to this day—and differentiating the Americas from Asia. In 1570 the first modern *atlas*—a collection of maps of the world—was put together by the Flemish cartographer Abraham Ortelius (1527–1598). The atlas, titled *Orbis Terrarum*, contained 70 maps.

Undoubtedly, the most important development in the sixteenth century came when the Flemish Gerardus Mercator (1512–1594) developed the technique of cylindrical projection in 1569. As mentioned above, this allowed cartographers of the era to portray compass directions as straight lines, at the expense, however, of the accurate representation of relative size. This technique led, in the first half of the seventeenth century, to the development of more precise methods of determining latitude and longitude. By the eighteenth century, the modern-day scientific principles of map-making were well established. With the rise of nationalism in the nineteenth century, a number of European countries conducted topographic surveys to determine political boundaries. In 1891, the International Geographical Congress proposed the political mapping of the entire world on a scale of 1:1,000,000, a task that has occupied cartographers up to the present day. Throughout the twentieth century, advances in aerial and satellite photography, and in computer modeling of topographic surfaces, have greatly enhanced the accuracy and fidelity of map-making.

But to the semiotician, no matter how great the representational fidelity of scientifically produced maps, they are still signs that reflect cultural worldview. Maps of American aboriginal cultures, for instance, differ from Western maps, not in objectivity, but in how they portray spaces and territories culturally. Whereas Western map-making is based on the principles of Cartesian geometry, which segments the map space into determinable points and calculable distances, aboriginal map-making is based instead on portraying the interconnectedness among the parts within the map space through a distortion of distance, angulation, and shape. The end result is that Western maps represent the world as an agglomeration of points, lines, and parts, related to each other in terms of the mathematics of the Cartesian plane; aboriginal maps represent the world instead as a holistic unsegmentable entity. Both types of map produce structural effects—Western maps provide a "discrete point" Cartesian view of the world, aboriginal ones a more holistic sacred view.

The Western map space has, indeed, even produced structural effects on how planners have designed modern cities. Not only does the layout of the city of New York, for instance, mirror the Cartesian map space, but the city also names its streets largely in terms of the grid system: e.g. *52nd and 4th* refers to the intersection point of two perpendicular lines in the city grid. The same effects manifest themselves also in how architects and planners draw such things as blueprints, floor plans, city sewer systems, suburban subdivisions, etc. In a fundamental semiotic sense, modern cities and buildings are the "structural byproducts" of the worldview that has been produced by the widespread use of the techniques that have shaped Western map-making since the early sixteenth century.

Exploration

Although they were devised originally as socially meaningful representations of specific territories, maps have also served another deep-seated need of the sapient animal—exploration, i.e. the need to know what lies beyond one's immediate world. Across the ages, explorers went on their quests to find new territories with maps in hand. Indeed, the practice of exploration requires not only thorough knowledge of ships or other crafts, but also considerable experience with reading and making maps.

The reason why maps have allowed human beings to travel and seek out unknown territories is that they are made in part with the same *symbolic* properties that geometry, algebra, and other symbol-using representational systems possess (chapter 3, §3.6). In the same way that the sciences of geometry and trigonometry have allowed human beings to solve engineering problems since ancient times, the science of cartography has allowed explorers to solve travel problems with amazing accuracy. As representations of real spaces, maps allow humans to take intellectual journeys whose imagined trajectories on the map space can then be reenacted in the world of real space to see where they lead. Maps have, in effect, allowed humans to model the physical world in ways that have suggested to them beforehand how to travel within that world.

Exploration involves the determination of position and direction. Position is a point on the earth's surface that can be identified (i.e. fixed) in terms of the grid or coordinate system of Cartesian geometry, i.e. with lines of latitude and longitude. Direction is the position of one point relative to another. In the Cartesian plane, the shortest distance between two points is a straight line, and since any line in the plane is a hypotenuse, then its length can be determined easily. In this way, Cartesian-designed maps allow explorers to fix points and determine distances to regions of the plane (the earth's surface) that are as yet unknown. Suppose, for instance, that the known world is located in the upper left quadrant of the Cartesian plane. Points shown in that map space—p_1, p_2, p_3, ...—can be located accurately in real space with the technique of scaling. Now, assume that the unknown world is in the lower right quadrant. With this map, an explorer can literally chart h/er trip to that world because s/he can calculate the distance needed to reach some imaginary point in the map space of that world, say p_2, by simply determining the length of the line in the map space from h/er starting point, say p_1 to p_2 and then converting that measurement to real-world units, using the scale established for the upper quadrant:

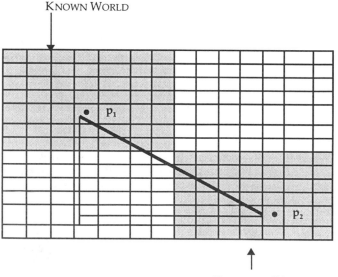

KNOWN WORLD

p_1

p_2

UNKNOWN WORLD

Clearly, the explorer setting out on a journey to p_2 will not know what s/he will encounter along the way, nor will she know in advance if p_2 is a land mass or a body of water. But s/he can still take that journey with a high degree of assurance that s/he will be able to find h/er intended destination, no matter what it is.

In sum, the science of cartography has allowed *Homo culturalis* to explore the terrestrial world with amazing ease. What is even more remarkable is that the same science has permitted *Homo culturalis* to describe the positions of heavenly bodies and to calculate their distances from Earth with accuracy. Suffice it to say here that mapping outer space involves the use of techniques that correspond to terrestrial point-fixing in terms of latitude and longitude lines. Simply put, the positions of stars relative to one another are regarded as points on a celestial map; the motion of the sun, the moon, and the planets is then indicated as a mean rate of progression across the celestial space. It is truly mind-boggling to think that with the aid of a simple representational device (the map), *Homo culturalis* has already been able to set foot on the moon and will no doubt be able to visit other places in the skies in the not-too-distant future.

7.3 SPATIAL CODES

At a denotative level, buildings and places are perceived to be reflexes of shelter and territoriality. But in the larger social context, they are invariably imbued with connotations that emanate from the *spatial codes* of a culture's signifying order. There are three types of spatial codes—*public*, *private*, and *sacred*. *Public* spatial codes are those that relate to sites where communal or social interactions of various kinds take place; *private* spatial codes are those that relate to places that individuals have appropriated or designated as their own; and *sacred* spatial codes relate to those locales that are purported to have metaphysical, mythical, or spiritual qualities. Like all codes, these too regulate behavior in social situations: e.g. one must knock on the door of a friend's house to announce one's presence, but one does not knock on the door of a retail store; one may sit and wait for someone in a foyer, atrium, or lobby, but one does not normally wait for someone in a public washroom; one can walk on a public sidewalk, but one cannot walk on someone's porch without permission; when one enters a sacred place like a church or chapel, one feels and behaves differently than when one enters a bank or a stadium; and so on.

Although people experience physical space in similar ways throughout the world, the meanings assigned to spaces in social territories will vary. An outsider would have to learn how to interpret, respond to, and behave appropriately in the public, private, and sacred places of a culture before becoming a functional member of that culture (Gallagher 1993).

7.4 PUBLIC SPATIAL CODES

In the wilderness, places are perceived by all species as survival spaces; i.e. as spaces in which sustenance and shelter can be procured. But in cultural contexts, the space appropriated by a tribe or society is felt additionally by its members to be a communal body. This is why societies are often described by people as being healthy, sick, vibrant, beautiful, ugly, etc. And, indeed, outsiders habitually judge a society at first sight on how the public places appear to the eye—as neat, dirty, organized, disorganized, etc. And this is why when someone defaces public places, s/he is felt to have violated the entire community. Conflicts between tribes or nations are, in actual fact, often triggered by such acts against the communal body.

Within the communal body, public places are set aside so that members of a society can gather as groups for reasons of entertainment, recreation, celebration, etc. They provide appropriate locales where ritualistic behaviors can unfold. The spatial codes that relate to such places are coordinated with the kinesic and proxemic codes described in chapter 4 (§4.2, §4.4). This is why the way one dresses for church is typically different from the way one dresses for work, the way one behaves in a restaurant is different from the way one behaves at home, and so on. This interconnectedness among the various codes of the signifying order is what gives coherence and overall purpose to social activities and routines, producing recognizable structural effects on how people experience places—e.g. the space in one's home feels more personal than the space in a bank. At a party, a feast, a ceremony people assume the social personae that they are either assigned or expected to play, i.e. they know what clothes to wear, what behaviors are appropriate, etc. The end result is that the public event is felt as a collective bodily experience. Participation at such gatherings is necessary for the maintenance of social solidarity and traditions.

Public places set aside for the display and exchange of goods are characteristic of all cultures. In many large contemporary urban societies, this function is served by shopping malls. But the mall has become much more than just a locus for the acquisition of market goods. The modern mall satisfies several psychic and social needs at once. It is perceived as a safe and purified space for human socialization and is thus felt to be a haven for combating loneliness and boredom; it provides a theatrical atmosphere proclaiming the virtues of a consumerist utopia;

it imparts a feeling of security and protection against the world of cars, mechanical noises, and air pollution outside; it shields against rain, snow, heat, cold; it conveys a feeling of control and organization. In a phrase, the mall is placeless and timeless—there is no appearance of aging or experience of time passing in its ambiance.

Malls are self-contained consumerist fantasylands, where one can leave the problems and hassles of daily life literally "outside." In the controlled "inside" environment of the mall everything is clean, shiny, cheery, and ever so optimistic. The mall is commonly experienced as a nirvana of endless shopping, cosmeticized and simplified to keep grisly reality out of sight and out of mind. And as one can with a remote-controlled television set, one can "switch" from scene to scene—from clothing store to coffee stand, to pinball parlor, to lottery outlet—with great ease.

The mall subtext is essentially *shopping = paradise on earth*. But this is ultimately an empty, vacuous message. Very few people will claim that their experiences at shopping malls are memorable, rewarding, or meaningful. Indeed, they do not remember them for very long once they have left.

7.5 PRIVATE SPATIAL CODES

In the same way that public spaces are perceived to be the parts of a communal body, so too private spaces are felt typically to be extensions of Self-space. A home, whether a crude hut or an elaborate mansion, is a shelter providing protection from weather and intruders. It is felt to be an extension of the body's protective armor. Indeed, when one steps inside, one feels as if one has entered into one's own body. When people build and decorate their homes, they are primarily engaged in making images of themselves to suit their own eyes. The identification of Self with the home is characteristic of all cultures.

In tribal societies the house tends to be a single volume, a room for all activities, reflecting an uncomplicated experience of Self. It is usually built directly against neighboring structures and often close to the tribal meeting-house or religious site as well. In China, on the other hand, the walled-in form of the courtyard house, which has persisted for centuries, reflects the need for privacy that is inherent in Chinese social traditions and perceptions of Self. But rows of single-volume dwellings, each with a small court or garden, are also found in China, reflecting a different type of Self-perception. At the other end of the scale are the imperial palace compounds, of which the Forbidden City in Beijing is the outstanding example. The various buildings of these compounds, laid out to form a vast, symmetrical complex, constitute a symbolic text supporting the divine claims of the emperors and the society they governed.

Within the home, the rooms are themselves meaningful spaces eliciting a specific constellation of emotive connotations. Concealing bedrooms seems to have a biological basis. Humans are extremely vulnerable when sleeping, and so it is certainly judicious, if not essential, to keep sleeping areas hidden from view. This is perhaps why people are especially protective of their bedrooms, which are felt to be the most vulnerable and secretive part of Self-space. In this private space, an individual unwinds, relaxes, and expresses h/er inner Self through decoration and personal objects. The bedroom is a refuge and asylum from the outside world. Only intimates are allowed to share that space symbolically. This is why when someone steals something from a bedroom, or defiles it in some way, it is felt to be a personal violation. When people cannot procure a personalized space, as in public housing projects, prisons, etc., it should come as no surprise to find that they tend to lose respect for their place and even for themselves, thus engaging in defacement and vandalism.

It is instructive to note that the Industrial Revolution was a turning point in Western society, in the meanings assigned to the private home. The city poor lived in reasonable, well-built rows of small houses. But it was the emerging middle class that attained the economic ability to buy land and to build fairly comfortable large houses. In the twentieth century, new transportation systems, and the desire of the middle class to own a plot of land, produced suburbs, where the majority of independently situated family houses are found today. As population increased, technology responded. By the late nineteenth century the construction of houses had become a major architectural subject, studied by ranking architects. Small one-story dwellings, each on its own tract of land, proliferated especially in America. Large ornate houses became fairly common, closely adjacent to neighbors in the older cities, standing alone in the newer towns and the suburbs. Distinctive styles of domestic architecture rose in popularity and waned shortly thereafter.

Houses that broke with historical architectural styles were slow to be accepted. As early as 1889 the American architect Frank Lloyd Wright (1869–1959) built a house embodying new concepts of spatial flow from one room to another. He and others, both in Europe and in the United States, soon moved towards a domestic architectural style of metric forms and simplified surfaces largely free of decoration. Contemporary changes in painting and sculpture were allied to this movement, and by the 1920s *modernist* architecture, though by no means universally accepted, had arrived. By the 1950s the *modernist* house—a more or less standard, one-floor, two- or three-bedroom house—was commonplace in North America.

7.6 SACRED SPATIAL CODES

Sacred places are sites where humans believe they can secure some form of contact with or proximity to the divinities. The codes that relate to these places are also interconnected with the kinesic and proxemic codes of the signifying order. In a Catholic church, for example, a confessional is felt to be a very intimate enclosure. Therefore, it cannot be lit or be made amenable to social interaction. It signifies a space in which one is expected to look into the dark depths of the soul. The altar area is perceived as more sacred and therefore less traversable than the area containing the pews. As a table for eating spiritually along with Christ, it was once put against the wall of the church with the priest facing it and with his back to the people. This removed the priest and the whole Mass from the people, making it more detached and ethereal. The language spoken was Latin, which further imbued the whole ceremony with a far-removed and, yet, seemingly spiritual quality. Nowadays the altar and the priest face the faithful. Interaction is encouraged by this new configuration. There is a greater feeling of "communion" among the people, not just of "communion with God." The change in the orientation of the altar reflected, clearly, a change in emphasis on the part of the Church and its faithful.

Every culture has its designated sacred spaces, usually with some building on them. The place and building are designed for worship of the deities. In tribal societies, one building was enough to host the congregation; but in large urban societies, many such buildings are needed. These all have the same goal of making the individuals of a culture feel that they have entered a special place. Indeed, the word *church* originates from New Testament Greek *ekklesia*, meaning "those called out," i.e. those called by God away from their daily life to form a new and spiritually deeper relation with the divine.

The salient characteristic of all sacred spaces is that they are designed to impart a feeling that they do not belong to the real world, that they are places where the divinities can be reached, and where miracles and supernatural events are occasionally expected to take place. The Madonna appeared to St. Bernadette at Lourdes in 1858, and the grotto where she carried out Her dialogue with the peasant girl has ever since been considered sacred and thought to be able to cure disease and bring spiritual healing. Similar places exist throughout the world.

7.7 ARCHITECTURAL CODES

Building styles and practices are inevitably influenced by the available technologies in a culture, but the primary functions of buildings remain the same the world over—to protect against intrusions, to circumvent gravity, and to avoid discomforts caused by an excess of heat, cold, rain, or wind. The codes that relate to buildings and their designs are called *architectural*. Architecture is to building as literature is to writing practices. Buildings are, indeed, like works of art, testifying to the nature of the society that produced them.

Beyond shelter, buildings are constructed with certain broad social purposes in mind—as signs of identity, status, power, sacredness, etc. Temples, churches, mosques, for instance, are designed to allow people to celebrate the mysteries of religion and to provide assembly places where gods can be propitiated and where people can be instructed in matters of belief and ritual. Fortresses and castles are designed with defense in mind. Palaces, villas, and skyscrapers are created to display power and wealth.

Architectural practices mirror social organization and lifestyle. A proliferation of building types, for instance, reflects the complexity of modern life. In large urban centers, more people live in mass housing and go to work in large office buildings; they spend their incomes in large shopping centers, send their children to different kinds of schools, go to specialized hospitals and clinics when sick, linger in airports on the way to distant hotels and resorts, etc.

The aesthetic response to buildings and architectural space is complex. It differs from that of sculpture or painting because the observer can be inside the art text (the building) or stand outside it. It is affected by the emotional responses the observer may have to the materials used, by the way they have been assembled, and by the lighting conditions. Features such as windows, doors, floor design, and ceiling height, too, affect the observer aesthetically. Movement through the spaces within a building also has narrative force, since the parts of a building are interpreted as being as structured as the parts of a sentence or a novel. Buildings are thus "read" as texts with annotative meanings.

Consider how the height of a building can convey a specific kind of meaning. This minimal unit of meaning of an architectural code can be called an *architecteme* (in analogy with *phoneme*, *kinestheme*, etc.). The cities built during the medieval period had one outstanding architectemic feature—the tallest building noticeable along their skyline was the church. The spires on medieval churches rose majestically upwards to the sky. This design feature reflected the fact that there is something overpowering about looking up at tall buildings, making one feel small and insignificant by comparison. The height of churches thus came to symbolize the power and wealth of the clergy. But, as the clergy began losing social clout after the Renaissance, cities were gradually redes- igned architecturally to reflect the new cultural order. Today, the tallest buildings in sprawling urban centers are certainly not churches. The tallest structures in cities like Dallas, Toronto, Montreal, New York, Chicago, Los Angeles are owned by large corporations and banks. Wealth and power now reside literally and symbolically in these insti- tutions. Inside these mammoth structures the social dynamics mirror an *up-down* conceptual system: the jobs and positions with the lowest value are at the bottom of the building; the more important ones are at the top. The company's executives reside, like the gods on Mount Olympus, on the top floor. The atmosphere on this level is perceived to be rarefied and other-worldly. This architectural symbolism is the rea- son why we use such expressions as *to work one's way up, to make it to the top, to climb the ladder of success, to set one's goals high,* etc.

Historical Sketch of Western Architecture

The Assyrian city of Khorsabad, built during the reign of Sargon II (722–705 BC) and excavated in 1842, is one of the oldest city sites to have been found, and has become the basis for studying the architec- ture and social order of the Mesopotamian world. Many of the architec- tural trends in the West trace their origins to the building styles and practices of ancient Greece and Rome. Both were noteworthy for gran- diose urban design, as exemplified by the Parthenon (448–432 BC) which crowns the Athenian Acropolis and Hadrian's Villa (125–132) near Tivoli.

From the fourth century until the early Renaissance, Christianity dominated social systems, including architectural trends, prompting the building of many new churches. Byzantine churches, domed and decorated with mosaics, proliferated throughout the Byzantine Empire. The secularizing trends of the Renaissance brought about a revival of the principles and styles of ancient Greek and Roman architecture. The Italian architect Filippo Brunelleschi (1377–1446) was the first to revive the classical forms, championing a new architecture based on mathe- matics, proportion, and perspective. In 1418 he was commissioned to build the dome of the unfinished Florence Cathedral. His design for the dome was a great innovation, both artistically and technically (Figure 7.1).

Brunelleschi also developed the technique of *perspective* in Western art and architecture (chapter 3, §3.10). In the sixteenth century, Rome became the leading center for architectural innovation. Saint Peter's Basilica in the Vatican was the most important of many sixteenth-century architectural projects. Toward the middle part of the century such leading Italian architects as Michelangelo, Baldassare Peruzzi, Giulio Romano, and Giacomo da Vignola started the trend of using the classical Roman elements in ways that became known as the *mannerist* style, characterized by arches, columns, and entablatures that enshrined the techniques of perspective and depth in Western architecture. The best known architect of the period was the sculptor Gianlorenzo Bernini (1598–1680), designer of the great oval piazza in front of St. Peter's Basilica.

Figure 7.1

Duomo, Florence
Italian Cultural Institute

In the eighteenth century a new style arose, called *rococo*, reflecting a new affluence and elegance in society at large. But little less than a century later, with the advent of the Industrial Revolution, a new world order came into existence, accompanied by architectural trends that set the stage for the growth of industrialized building trends and the widespread use of cast iron and steel. At the beginning of the twentieth century, the American architect Louis Sullivan (1856–1924) and his apprentice Frank Lloyd Wright (1869–1959) designed the first true skyscrapers. The "art of the modern skyscraper" was an invention of the so-called *Bauhaus school* (based in Weimar, Germany, around 1919–1925), which brought together architects, painters, and designers from several countries to formulate the goals of the visual arts in the modern age, under its first director Walter Gropius (1883–1969). The Bauhaus style prevailed throughout the 1940s, 1950s, and most of the 1960s. Often referred to with the term *modernism*, its approach can be seen in the chaste elegance and subtle proportions of the Seagram Building (1958) in New York. Gropius wanted to rebuild the landscape by stripping it of its past symbolism, substituting a geometrically pure style that intentionally excluded references to the past. The Bauhaus School envisioned a working-class architectural landscape. Buildings were to be fashioned as box-like forms so as to eliminate all the symbols of traditional power. Out of this movement, modern office towers, housing projects, hotels, and other public buildings were built with the same basic cubic blueprint.

Between about 1965 and 1980, architects started to reject modernism, which they found to be too monolithic and formulaic, promoting a new style that came to be known as *postmodern*. The postmodern architects wanted to inject individuality, intimacy, complexity, humor, and irony into building design. The American architect Robert Venturi (1925–), for instance, defended the new vernacular architecture—gas stations, fast-food restaurants, etc.—and attacked the modernist establishment with incisive criticism. By the early 1980s, postmodernism had become the dominant trend in American architecture and an important phenomenon in Europe as well. Its success in the US owed much to the influence of Philip C. Johnson (1906–). His AT&T Building (1984) in New York City instantly became a paragon of postmodern design (Figure 7.2).

The postmodern office towers built during the 1980s aspired to a similar high stylistic profile, striving for an individualistic flamboyance. Vivid color and other decorative elements were effectively used to build everything from office towers to private houses. Today's new office buildings emphasize high-tech and glamorous professions. Once again the city landscape, and thus the mindscape that it mirrors, are changing.

City Design

The origin of cities is to be found in super-tribal settlements that came onto the scene around 5,000–6,000 years ago (chapter 1, §1.5). To protect themselves and their food supplies against predatory nomads, animals, and changes in climate, the people in these settlements built their dwellings within a walled area or a naturally fortified place, such as the acropolis of ancient Greek cities. Because the availability of water was also a key consideration, these early settlements were usually located around, near, or along a river. Gradually, the expanding configuration of buildings and spaces of the settlement created the need for a specialization of labor. Markets developed in which artisans could exchange their specialties for other kinds of goods. And the powerful religious sphere contributed crucially to the intellectual and educational life of the early cities, making them centers of commerce, learning, and technology.

Figure 7.2

The spread of the city in Europe was a result of the breakup of feudalism. At the beginning of the sixteenth century Europe had six or seven cities of 100,000 or more inhabitants; at the end of the century it had twice as many. During the seventeenth century, although the population of Europe remained stationary, that of the cities increased. But it was not until the late nineteenth century that the process of urbanization, i.e. of more and more people moving into cities at the expense of rural districts, became a general trend. Its principal causes were the development of the factory system, improvements in transportation, and the mechanization of agriculture, which reduced the need for farm labor. Many modern cities have, in fact, been planned as industrial centers near sources of raw materials. In 1890, barely 16 percent of the population of the United States lived in cities of 100,000 or more. In 1990 just over one-fourth of the population did so, and three-fourths of the total population lived in cities and towns of 2500 or more.

City design reflects cultural values, beliefs, and emphases. In ancient Greece, religious and civic citadels were oriented in such a way as to give a sense of aesthetic balance to the inhabitants—streets were arranged in a grid pattern and housing was integrated with commercial and defense structures. In the Renaissance, the design of cities around piazzas was in sharp contrast to the narrow, irregular streets of medieval cities. Renaissance city planners stressed wide, regular radial streets forming concentric circles around a central point, with other streets radiating out from that point like spokes of a wheel. To this day, the downtown core is known as *centro* in Italy, reflecting this Renaissance view of cities as circles.

After the Industrial Revolution the concept of the grid started to gain a foothold on city designs. The grid system of design conveys rationalization, efficiency of movement, and facility of localization. But since the middle part of the twentieth century, many new city designs have emerged. Hotels and other recreational buildings (e.g. casinos) are taking on some of the symbols of power that were once associated exclusively with the banks and the corporations The city of Las Vegas is a classic example of a city designed to cater to the craving for recreation and consumption. The tall hotel towers that mark its landscape are symbols of a world of fast money, quick recreational fixes, and consumerist delights.

8

ART

Art is indistinguishable from life.

Hassan (1987: 39)

8.0 PRELIMINARY REMARKS

The capacity to draw and extract meaning from pictures, to make and enjoy music, to dance, to put on stage performances, to write poetry, is a truly extraordinary and enigmatic endowment of the species. The "art instinct" allows everyone, regardless of age, to indulge in the entire range of feelings and spiritual emotions that truly differentiate humans from other life forms. It is indisputable evidence of the workings of what Vico called *fantasia* (chapter 2, §2.1) Artistic expressions are passed on from generation to generation throughout the world as precious tokens of culture because they are perceived universally as transcending time, as saying something true and profound about the human condition.

Defining *art* is as impossible as defining *culture*. Indeed the two are often used as synonyms, or more accurately, as hyponyms, whereby one subsumes the other (chapter 3, §3.4). Art is something that everyone recognizes, but that no one can quite define. It involves a disciplined, skilled form of representation that entails a distinctive way of looking at the world. The word *art*, in fact, derives from the Latin *ars*, meaning "skill." This is why this word is used frequently as a synonym for *skill*—e.g. the "art of gardening," the "art of chess." In its broader meaning, however, it involves not only specialized skill, but also a creative imagination and a point of view about the world that is etched into the artistic text.

In classical and medieval times, poets were praised and recognized for their artistic endeavors, whereas musicians, painters, sculptors, and other artists who used physical skills were considered less important and, therefore, remained anonymous. However, from the Renaissance on, as all human activities came to be valued, those skilled in the visual and performing arts gradually gained greater recognition and social prestige, and thus the right to authorship. By the eighteenth century, a more sophisticated public felt the need to distinguish between art that was purely aesthetic and art that was practical or ornamental. Thus, a distinction was made between the fine arts—including literature, music, dance, painting, sculpture, and architecture—and the decorative or applied arts—such as pottery, metalwork, furniture and carpet making, etc.—which for a time were demoted to the rank of crafts. Because the prestigious École des Beaux-Arts in Paris taught only the major visual arts, the term *art* has sometimes been narrowed in the West to mean only drawing, painting, architecture, and sculpture. However, since the mid-twentieth century, greater appreciation of all types of art, of non-Western art, and of folk artistic traditions has expanded the view of what constitutes art considerably.

Many scholars believe that art originally had a ritualistic and mythological function. The notion of artists as individualists and eccentric creators is a relatively modern one. In ancient cultures, art was created to be used as part of ceremonies meant to please the gods. It was made by all members of the community, rather than by professionals alone. In traditional aboriginal cultures of North America art continues, in fact, to be perceived as one aspect of community rituals that are designed to ensure a good harvest or to celebrate a significant life event such as a birth or a marriage. But even in modern Western cultures, art continues to reverberate with ritualistic overtones. At a performance of a classical piece of music in a concert hall, for instance, there is ristualistic silence. At a rock concert, on the other hand, there is communal shouting and physical involvement. Hanging a painting in an art gallery invites an individualistic appreciation; but drawing something on a city wall invites social participation (graffiti, commentary, modifications, etc.).

The subfield of semiotics that deals with art is called *aesthetics*; the related subfield of art interpretation is called *hermeneutics*. The two are concerned with such phenomena as human responses to sounds, forms, and words and with the ways in which the emotions condition such responses. In this chapter, therefore, our trip through culture reaches the site inhabited by *Homo aestheticus*. Actually, we have already met this species of *Homo* on previous stops—in our discussions of dancing (chapter 4, §4.9), poetry (chapter 5, §5.7), and architecture (chapter 7, §7.7). Here, we will limit the discussion to some of h/er other artistic skills.

8.1 THEORIES OF ART

The first aesthetic theory of any scope was that of Plato, who believed that art was an imitation of ideal forms. However, he also felt that art encouraged immorality, and that certain musical compositions caused laziness and immoderacy. He thus suggested banishing some types of artists from society. Aristotle also saw art as imitation, but not in the Platonic sense. The role of art, thought Aristotle, was to complete what Nature did not finish, separating the form from its content, such as the human bodily form from its manifestation in people, and then transferring that form onto some physical medium, such as canvas or marble. Thus, art was not pure imitation, but rather a particular representation of an aspect of things that had the capacity to profoundly affect the human observer and thus eventually transform the social order. In his *Poetics*, Aristotle argued that tragedy, for instance, so stimulates the emotions of pity and fear that by the end of the play the spectator is purged of them. This *catharsis*, as he called it, makes the audience psychologically healthier and thus more capable of happiness.

The third-century philosopher Plotinus (205–270 AD), born in Egypt and trained in philosophy at Alexandria, also gave far more importance to art than did Plato. In his view, art reveals the true nature of an object more accurately than ordinary experience does, thus raising the human spirit from the experience of the mundane to a contemplation of universal truths. According to Plotinus, the most precious moments of life are those mystical instants when the soul is united, through art, with the divine. Aesthetic experience is thus intertwined with mystical experience.

Art in the Middle Ages was considered to be primarily a servant of religious sentiments. It was during the Renaissance that art reacquired its more secular functions. The Renaissance saw little difference between the artist and the scientist. Indeed, many were both—Leonardo da Vinci was a painter, writer, and scientist, Michelangelo a visual artist and writer, to mention but two. It was only after the Enlightenment and the Romantic movement that an unfortunate, artificial split came about, pitting artists against scientists. The view of the artist as a unique kind of genius impelled by h/er own creative energies to free h/erself from the shackles of culture is also very much a product of Romanticism. In ancient times artists were merely laborers, paid by rulers for their services. Ancient Egyptian architects, for instance, were hired to build structures designed to glorify the pharaoh and life after death. In pious medieval Europe, visual artists and playwrights were hired by the Church to create art texts designed to extol Christian themes. The choice to be an artist was a matter of social custom, not of some esoteric inclination at birth. Artists, like other people, customarily followed their fathers' profession. It was only after the eighteenth century that the choice to become an artist became an individual one.

So, why is art so effective emotionally, no matter who produces it or at which period of time it is produced? Perhaps the best-known, and most widely-accepted, contemporary theory for explaining the potency of art is the one put forward by the American philosopher Susanne Langer (1895–1985) during the middle part of the twentieth century. We do not experience art, she emphasized (Langer 1957), as individual bits and pieces (notes, shapes, words, etc.), but as a totality. It is only when an individual tries to understand rationally what the art work means that the holistic experience is transformed by reasoning and language into one in which its parts can be taken apart, discussed, critiqued, etc. like the individual words in a sentence. But, no matter how many times people try to understand the aesthetic experience discursively, it somehow remains larger than the sum of its parts. One can analyze the opening movement of Beethoven's *Moonlight Sonata* as a series of harmonic progressions and melodic figures based on the key of C# minor. But the elements of melody and harmony come into sharp focus as components of the work only upon a close discursive analysis of the sonata's structure. When one hears it played as an artistic performance, one hardly focuses on these bits and pieces. One cannot help but experience the music holistically. And this is what makes it emotionally "moving," as the expression goes. This can be compared to the pleasant sensation that comes from looking at an equilateral triangle. Our gratifying response to that figure derives not from the fact that it is made up of three equal lines, but from the way these lines are arranged to define the figure itself. The three lines considered separately or in some other arrangement (e.g. placed over each other) would not evoke any particular emotional or aesthetic response in the observer.

Langer remarked, further, that because of its profound emotional qualities, great art transforms human beings and cultures permanently. It is truly a "mirror of the soul," as the saying goes. Humanity has never been the same since, for example, Michelangelo sculpted his *David*, since Shakespeare wrote his *King Lear*, since Beethoven composed his Ninth Symphony. Indeed, the spiritual meanings in great art works can be discovered and rediscovered across time, across cultures. Art texts become a permanent part of the evolution of the human species, permanently etched in the spiritual blueprint of humankind.

8.2 THEATER

The word *performance* is used to refer to the physical means employed for enacting an art text for an audience. Performances are generally given spatial prominence through a raised stage, and they generally involve using props and paraphernalia such as costumes, masks, musical instruments, and artifacts of various kinds. They are put on according to a socially defined tradition, i.e. they are scheduled, set up, and prepared in advance; they have a beginning and an end; they unfold in terms of a structured sequence of parts (e.g. acts in a play); and they are coordinated for public participation. Performances are both reflective and constitutive of cultural meanings: they both shed light upon the values of the culture and critique them. They are also intrinsically interconnected with the signifying order. This is why citations from Shakespeare or Molière, allusions to actions in famous plays, references to dramatic characters for explaining certain aspects of human nature (Oedipus, Antigone, Hamlet, Ophelia, Lear) are commonplace in ordinary discourse.

The performing arts include theater, dancing, singing, playing instrumental music (or combinations of these, as in musicals and opera), mime, vaudeville, circus acts, pageantry, and puppetry. In this section we will focus on the *theater*. This can be defined as an enactment of some event in Nature, in life, or in society, put on by actors on a stage, around which an audience can view and/or hear the performance. In general, theater puts on display actions and events that we somehow consider vital to our existence.

The term *theater* is used to describe both the performance itself and the location where it takes place. Stages and auditoriums have had distinctive forms in every era. New theaters today tend to be flexible and eclectic in design, incorporating elements of several styles. A theatrical performance, however, need not occur in an architectural structure designed as a theater, or even in a building. Many earlier forms of theater were performed in the streets, in open spaces, in market squares, in churches, or in rooms and buildings not intended for use as theaters. Much of contemporary experimental theater, too, rejects the formal constraints of traditional stage theaters, attempting to create the sense of auditorium through the actions of the performers and the natural features of the acting space.

The dramatic text in theater is usually verbal, but it can also be based purely on bodily movement. The latter genre is referred to more precisely as *pantomime,* or the art of theater based on facial expressions and bodily movements rather than on a verbal text. In the great open-air theaters of ancient Greece and Rome, where the audience could see more easily than it could hear, pantomime became an important element of verbal theater as well, leading to the use of stylized pantomimic gestures to portray character in Western theatrical art.

Most scholars trace the origin of *drama* to ancient ceremonial practices. The dramatic nature of religious traditions can still be discerned, for example, in the Catholic Mass and the Easter reenactment of the *Via Crucis.* The early tribal performances were intended probably as fertility or harvest rites, i.e. as performances intended to appease the gods. Even in ancient Greece the first dramas revolved around tales of the gods. The plays of Aeschylus (c. 525–456 BC), Sophocles (c. 497–405 BC), and Euripides (c. 485–406 BC) were drawn from myth and legend, though their focus was not a simple performance of the mythic story line, but rather a consideration of the tragedy of human actions. The actors of those dramas wore masks, a practice which also had a ritualistic source. Masks are expressive devices, shifting the focus from the actor to the character, thus clarifying aspects of theme and plot as well as imparting a sense of greater universality to the character. In modern theater, make-up has taken over the functions of masks.

Comedy was developed in ancient Greece alongside drama for criticizing and satirizing both individuals and society in general. The first great comedic playwright was, no doubt, Aristophanes (c. 445–385 BC), who became famous for satirizing both public figures and the gods, to the delight of large audiences. The comedic approach became even more popular in the Roman plays of Plautus (c. 250–184 BC) and Terence (c. 185–159 BC). But, with the fall of the Roman Empire in 476 AD, the emerging Christian church saw the theater as too bawdy and scatological and discouraged it for more than five hundred years, promoting instead a liturgical form of theater based on Bible stories. By the fifteenth century, this form of drama had evolved into the *morality play*, which was a self-contained drama performed by professional actors, and which dealt, typically, with the theme of the individual's journey through life. Theater had become over the centuries less and less participatory and more and more reflective as an art form

Comedic theater was revived by the movement known as the *commedia dell'arte*, an improvised comedy that arose in sixteenth-century Italy and spread throughout Europe in the next two hundred years. The six to twelve players in the *commedia* wore half-masks to portray the exaggerated features of a character. They did not use a script; rather, they improvised comedies both on outdoor, impromptu stages and in conventional staging areas. Each actor played the role of a stereotypical character as, for instance, Harlequin, the clownish valet; the Doctor, who used meaningless Latin phrases and often suggested dangerous remedies for other characters' imagined illnesses; and Pulcinella, who concocted outrageous schemes to satisfy his animal-like cruelty and lust. Unlike traditional theater, *commedia* troupes featured skilled actresses rather than males playing the female characters. From this collection of stock characters, each troupe was able to put on hundreds of plots. *Commedia* actors also developed individual comic routines, called *lazzi*, which they could execute on demand, especially when it was felt that a sudden laugh was needed. For instance, a *commedia* performer might pretend to trip and tumble into a pail of bath water during the exit sequence.

Along with the *commedia*, modern theater generally started in the Renaissance when satirical plays such as *The Mandrake*, by Niccolò Machiavelli (1459–1527), revived the ancient world's penchant for farce, bawdiness, and satire. By the mid-sixteenth century a new, dynamic secular theatrical practice had developed, leading to the plays of Shakespeare and Molière. The most important concept in Renaissance art was *verisimilitude*—the appearance of truth. Characters were depicted as ideal types, rather than as idiosyncratic individuals, and the sense of time, place, and action in the play was imbued with realism. Many of the plays had a single plot, which took place within a 24-hour period, and occurred only in one locale. The rationale was that a theater audience, knowing it had been sitting in one place for a limited time, would not believe a play that spanned several days or locations.

By the eighteenth century, Western theater was becoming even more realistic with the emergence of the Romantic movement in the arts. In its purest form, this movement concentrated on a search for the spiritual nature of humankind through art, the only form of human knowing that would allow humankind to transcend the limitations of the physical world and find truth. One of the best examples of romantic drama is *Faust* (Part I, 1808; Part II, 1832), by the German playwright Johann Wolfgang von Goethe (1749–1832). Based on the classic legend of a man who sells his soul to the devil, this play depicts humankind's attempt to master all knowledge and power in its constant struggle with the universe.

As plays attracted larger and larger audiences, playwrights became more and more involved in writing about bourgeois life, focusing on the psychological realism of the characters and showing concern for social problems. They sought to present a slice of life on the stage. This new realistic trend in theater led to the notion of the *director* as the person who interprets the text, determines acting style, suggests scenery and costumes, and gives the production a cohesive style. Through much of the history of drama the director was the playwright. During the late Romantic period, however, the director was instead often the leading actor of the company—the actor-manager. Duke George II of Saxe-Meiningen, who presided over the players in his ducal theater in Meiningen, Germany, in the 1880s, is generally regarded as the first modern director.

From the time of the Renaissance to the late nineteenth century, theater had been striving for total realism, or at least for the illusion of reality. As it reached that goal at the threshold of the twentieth century, a multifaceted, antirealistic reaction erupted. Paralleling modern visual art and musical movements, playwrights at the turn of the century started turning out symbolist, abstract, and ritualistic dramatic texts in an attempt to revitalize the theater. Throughout the first half of the century, movements such as futurism, Dadaism, and surrealism sought to bring new artistic and scientific ideas into theater. But the most popular and influential nonrealistic genre of the first part of the twentieth century was absurdism. The subtext in all absurdist drama was that of humanity as lost in an unknown and unknowable world, where all human actions become senseless and absurd. Absurdism was at its peak in the 1950s, but continued to influence drama through the 1970s.

Waiting for Godot

Absurdist drama is psychologically powerful. Take, as a case-in-point, the play *Waiting for Godot*, published in 1952 by the Irish-born playwright and novelist, Samuel Beckett (1906–1989. It is a powerful indictment of the wretchedness of the human condition. *Waiting for Godot* caught the modern imagination because, like the two tramps in the play, people in the twentieth century seemed to have literally "lost faith," having become cynical about the meaning of human existence. Even today, the play challenges our ingrained belief that there is a meaning to life, insinuating that all our meaning-generating systems (language, religious concepts, etc.) are no more than illusory screens we have set up to avoid the truth—that life is an absurd moment of consciousness on its way to extinction.

The play shows two tramps stranded in an empty landscape attempting to pass the time in a series of banal activities reminiscent of slapstick comedians or circus clowns. The two tramps, Vladimir and Estragon, seem doomed forever to repeating their senseless actions and words. They call each other names; they ponder whether or not to commit suicide; they reminisce about the senseless past; they threaten to leave each other but cannot; they perform silly exercises; and they are constantly waiting for a mysterious character named Godot who never comes. A strange pair, named Lucky and Pozzo, appear, disappear, reappear, and finally vanish in the second act, which is virtually a duplicate of the first. Pozzo whips Lucky, as if he were a cart horse. Lucky kicks Estragon. The two tramps tackle Lucky to the ground to stop him from shrieking out a deranged parody of a philosophical lecture. Vladimir and Estragon go back to talking about nothing in particular, and wait with no purpose whatsoever for Godot. Their dialogue is meaningless, a chain of silly clichés. Allusions to the Bible narrative and scenery are sardonic and absurd—there is a bare tree on stage in a parody of the Biblical tree of life, the tramps constantly engage in meaningless theological discourse satirizing the questions raised by the Bible, etc. The play ends with the two tramps still waiting. "In the beginning was the Word," announces Genesis; "the Word is hollow," Beckett's play retorts. There is no meaning to life, nor will there ever be. Life is meaningless, a veritable circus farce!

But despite the play's nihilism, people seem paradoxically to discover meaning in it. The tramps are perpetually waiting for Godot—a name coined as an obvious sarcastic allusion to God. Godot never comes, in the play. But deep inside us, as audience members, we yearningly hope that Beckett is wrong, and that on some other stage, in some other play, the design of things will become known to us—that God will indeed come.

Waiting for Godot is a parody of the medieval Christian worldview shaped by the Judeo-Christian Bible, a play that questions traditional assumptions about certainty, identity, and truth. The play satirizes the fact that words can refer only to other words, and that statements about anything subvert their own meanings. It thus assails the traditional assumption we make that language can express ideas without changing them. This is why some critics view *Waiting for Godot* as a critique of classic theater, which drew its stories and characters from myth or ancient history. The clear objective of the ancient dramas was to consider humanity's place in the world and the consequences of individual actions. The classical actors—all men—wore costumes of everyday dress and large masks. Movement and gesture were stately and formal. The plays emphasized supernatural elements, bloody violence, and obsessive passions. *Waiting for Godot* is a cynical reenactment of this kind of theater. Its story and characters—all men—are there to consider humanity's place in the world. But the play finds very little to consider and sees very little in the idea that individual actions have consequences. The play has no plot, no passion; the actions portrayed are inane; and the language used is incongruous.

Absurdist drama wanted to eliminate much of the cause-and-effect relationship among events, reduce language to a game and thus minimize its communicative power, reduce characters to archetypes, make places nonspecific, and portray the world as alienating and incomprehensible. *Waiting for Godot* is perhaps the best known absurdist play of the century. It is a disturbing parody of theater and the Christian worldview at once. There is only a void out there, no afterlife, no heaven or hell, blurts out the play. Human history has no beginning or end. Human beings fulfill no particular purpose in being alive. Life is a meaningless collage of actions on a relentless course leading to death and to the return to nothingness.

But Beckett's bleak portrait somehow forces us to think about the very questions it appears to discard. Like the six characters in Luigi Pirandello's 1921 play *Six Characters in Search of an Author*, we nonetheless desire to continue our search for an author to write us into existence. Paradoxically, Beckett's play stimulates in us a profound re-evaluation of the meaning of consciousness and particularly of human spirituality. We may be condemned to waiting for Godot, and the rational part of our mind might tell us that existence is absurd, but at a more profound level we sense that there is a spiritual reality that can only be felt, not understood.

Post-Absurdist Trends

Whatever the trend in theatrical style, drama constitutes an intrinsic component of all cultures and is highly interconnected with a culture's signifying order. The ancient tragedies showed how humans and the gods struggled, interacted, and ultimately derived meaning from each other. Medieval morality plays put on display principles of human conduct that informed the populace about what was meaningful to them. Shakespeare's great tragedies brought the struggle of Prometheus in Aeschylus' drama down to more earthly dimensions in the figures of a Hamlet, a King Lear, a Macbeth. The theatrical code in a culture is, as mentioned, highly interconnected with the other codes. This is why we commonly say that people "act out" their feelings, that they "play roles," that they "walk in and out of a situation" (like a dramatic scene), that they "wear masks" to hide their true selves, and so on. As Shakespeare himself aptly put it, "All the world's a stage."

Today, the functions of the theater have been largely replaced by *cinema* (below, §8.5), although so-called "experimental" theater attracts a fairly large following. Many experimental playwrights of the 1960s and 1970s wrote plays using language as a game, as sound, as a barrier, as a reflection of society. In a play such as *American Buffalo* (1976) by David Mamet (1947–), for instance, little action occurs and the focus is on mundane characters and events. The language is fragmentary, as it is in everyday conversation. And the settings are indistinguishable from reality. The intense focus on seemingly meaningless fragments of reality creates a nightmarish effect for the audience. But by the 1990s, theater in much of the Western world seems to have entered into a period of stasis, rather than experimentation, giving way to cinema as the primary form of theatrical-narrative art in the culture. Musical theater has also emerged as a popular entertainment art form. Already in the 1920s musicals were transformed from a loosely connected series of songs, dances, and comic sketches to a story, sometimes serious, told through dialogue, song, and dance. The form was extended in the 1940s by the team of Richard Rodgers (1902–1979) and Oscar Hammerstein II (1895–1960) and in the 1980s by Andrew Lloyd Webber (1948–) with such extravagantly popular works as *Cats* (1982) and *Phantom of the Opera* (1988).

It should be mentioned, as a final word, that theatrical practices in Asia—in India, China, Japan, and Southeast Asia—have been significantly different from post-Renaissance Western practices. The central idea in Asian performance art is a blend of literature, dance, music, and spectacle. The theater is participatory—the audience does not actually take part in the performance, but participation unfolds like a shared experience. The performances are often long, and the spectators come and go, eating, talking, and watching only their favorite moments. Asian theater was discovered by the West in the late nineteenth century, influencing acting, writing, and staging among the absurdists and many others.

8.3 MUSIC

Music is an art form involving the organized movement of sounds through a continuum of time. Music plays a role in all societies, and it exists in a large number of styles, each characteristic of a geographical region or a historical era. Indefinite border areas exist, however, between music and other sound phenomena such as poetry (chapter 5, §5.7). For this reason, societies differ in their opinion of the musicality of various sounds. Thus, chanting, half-spoken styles of singing, or sound texts created by a computer program may or may not be accepted as music by members of a given society or group. Muslims, for example, do not consider the chanting of the Koran to be music, although to Western ears the structure of the chant is similar to that of secular singing. Often, it is the social context in which the sounds occur that determines whether or not they are to be regarded as music. Industrial noises, for instance, are not perceived as musical unless they are presented as part of a concert of experimental music in an auditorium, with a composer.

Various strata of musical art may exist, according to culture: (1) classical music, composed and performed by trained professionals originally under the patronage of courts and religious establishments in the West; (2) folk music, shared by the population at large; and (3) popular music, performed by professionals, disseminated through electronic media (radio, television, records, film) and consumed by a mass public. But the boundaries among these strata are not clear—e.g. melodies from the realm of classical music are sometimes adopted by the folk community, and vice versa.

Although an isolated cuneiform example of Hurrian (Hittite) music of 2000 BC has been tentatively deciphered, the earliest Western music known is that of the ancient Greeks and Romans, dating from about 500 BC to 300 AD. Fewer than a dozen examples of Greek music survive, written in a notation that has still not been deciphered with certainty. Greek and Roman theories of the nature and function of music, however, are discussed at length in the writings of such philosophers as Pythagoras, Aristotle, Plato, and Boethius. These philosophers believed that music originated with the god Apollo, the musician Orpheus, and other mythological figures, and that it reflected in microcosm the laws of harmony that rule the universe. They also believed that music influences human thoughts and actions. The rhythm of Greek music was closely associated with language. In a song, the music was composed to duplicate the rhythms of the text. In an instrumental piece it was made to follow the rhythmic patterns of the various poetic meters. The internal structure of Greek music was based on a system of sound modes that combined a scale with special melodic contours and rhythmic patterns. A similar organization exists today in Arabic and Indian music. Because each Greek mode incorporated rhythmic and melodic characteristics, listeners could distinguish between them. Greek philosophers wrote that each mode possessed an emotional quality and that listeners would experience this quality on hearing a composition in that mode.

Opinions differ as to the original motivation for, and the spiritual value of, music. In some African societies music is seen as the faculty that sets humans apart from other species; among some Native Americans it is thought to have originated as a way for spirits to communicate with human beings. In Western society music is regarded generally as an art form. But in some others it is considered to be of low value, associated with sin and evil, and thus something to be restricted or even prohibited. This view is not unknown to America, where attempts in the 1950s to ban rock'n' roll were based on the argument that it was an obscene and sinful form of musicality.

The minimal unit, or signifier, of musical organization is the *tone*—a sound with specific pitch and duration. Musical texts are put together by combining individual tones to make melodies and harmonies, on the structural plan of regularly recurring beats. The makers of musical texts are known, appropriately enough, as composers, since the principal creative act in music is based on arranging sounds into meaningful texts known as compositions. Innovation is an important criterion of good composing in Western society, but is less so in other societies. Creative acts in music also include improvisation, or the creation of new music in the course of performance. Improvisation usually takes place on the basis of some previously determined structure, such as a tone or a group of chords; or it occurs within a set of traditional rules, as in the *ragas* of India or the *maqams* of the Middle East. Performance, which involves a musician's personal interpretation of a previously composed piece, has smaller scope for innovation.

Music everywhere is used frequently to accompany other activities. It is, for example, universally associated with dance. It is a major component in many types of religious services, secular rituals, and theater. In some societies it is also an activity carried on for its own sake. In Western society, for example, music is often listened to at concerts, on the radio, etc. In a fundamental sense music is an "international language," since its grammar is not based on word meanings and combinations, but on melody, rhythm, and harmony. Like gesture codes, these seem to be more understandable across cultures than verbal languages are, and fit much more easily into frames of meaning that transcend specific cultures.

8.4 VISUAL ART

The paintings of animals found on cave walls and roofs, and the artifacts that exploded onto the scene in Europe over 30,000 years ago, bear witness to the productivity of visual representation. These are the "fossil records," so to speak, of humanity's first attempts at visual knowing. The capacity for visual art is etched into the human blueprint. The research on childhood development shows that at about the same time that children utter their first words they also start scribbling and doodling. Although children, with parental prompting, may learn to label the rough figures they make as, say, "suns" or "faces," they do not set out to draw anything in particular, but instead seem spontaneously to produce forms that become refined through practice into precise, repeatable shapes. The act of drawing in childhood appears to be pleasurable in itself; usually identification is provided, if at all, only after the child finishes drawing. Of course, shapes eventually suggest "things" (signifieds) to the child as h/er ability to use symbols develops, but in the beginning, pleasure and satisfaction occur without larger or more explicit associations of meaning. This form of representational activity in childhood is truly an example of "art for art's sake."

Drawing involves transferring perceived forms onto some surface, representing them with lines and shapes. These are the minimal elements of visual representation which can be called *pictoremes*, in analogy with *phoneme*, *kinestheme*, etc. Linear pictoremes can be straight, round, curved, etc. and used in various combinations to make up all kinds of visual signifiers. Three straight lines, for instance, can be joined up in specific ways to represent a triangle, the letter "H," or a picnic table iconically:

triangle   the letter "H"   picnic table

Virtually everything we see can be represented by a combination of lines and shapes: e.g. a cloud is a shape, a horizon is a line. Other visual signifiers include *value, color,* and *texture. Value* refers to the darkness or lightness of a line or shape. It plays an important role in portraying dark and light contrasts. *Color* conveys mood, feelings, atmosphere. This is why we speak of "warm," "soft," "cold," "harsh" colors. *Texture* refers to the sensation of touch evoked imagistically when we look at some surface.

Lines and shapes can also be combined to create an illusion of depth. In the following plane figure there are 12 lines. The way they are put together, however, makes us believe that they represent a three-dimensional box:

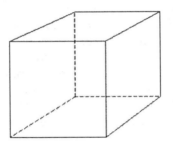

The figure has been drawn with straight lines drawn on a two-dimensional surface (the page). Yet we interpret it as a three-dimensional box. This is both because of the use of *perspective* representation and of dotted lines. Such techniques allow us to portray three-dimensional spaces convincingly on two-dimensional surfaces. In perspective representation, the flat surface of the painted picture is known as the *picture plane*; the horizon line is the horizontal *eye-level line* that divides the scene in the distance; and the *vanishing point* is located on the horizon line where parallel lines in the scene appear to converge. The person who developed the technique of *perspective* was, as mentioned previously, the Italian architect Filippo Brunelleschi (chapter 3, §3.10).

What Is Art?

The question of the function of visual art has become part of a general social debate as contemporary Western art galleries routinely put controversial "abstract" paintings and sculptures on display. One of the most famous versions of this debate was initiated by Andy Warhol (1928–1987), the American pop artist who produced paintings and silk-screen prints of commonplace images, such as soup cans and photographs of celebrities. Take, for example, his painting of a Campbell's soup can (1964).

When asked *what* it means, people will either (1) say that it means nothing, or (2) give responses such as "It is a symbol of our consumer society," "It represents the banality and triviality of contemporary life," etc. The latter pattern of responses suggests that we tend to interpret human-made artifacts as "works of art" because meanings and values are attributed to them by those who make them, by the society in which they live, and by those who look at them in later years. But, in our view, "art" that does not evoke the sense of consciousness associated with reflective human emotion is bound to have little lasting value. True art transcends the social, the present, and the purely conventional. It is an expression of a search for meaning in life that makes consciousness both agonizing and ecstatic at once.

The modern idea of visual art as something to be appreciated individualistically by viewing it in a gallery or museum belies the fact that art in its origins had a public function. Art was meant to decorate the public square or to commemorate some meaningful event. The idea of "private" and "authored" art is a modern idea that took shape in the late Renaissance. And only after the Romantic nineteenth century did the idea of the "art gallery" as the appropriate locus for appreciating art emerge as an *idée fixe*. Created for display in a public space, art was originally always open to contributions from the denizens of the area, making the interpretation of a work an open-ended one. Only in a gallery setting is interpretation controlled by the original maker of the art. Any contributions to the art text would be considered defacement.

Photography

One of the more interesting visual art forms of the contemporary world is photography. The earliest photographs on record were made by the French physicist Nicéphore Niepce (1765–1833). Then in 1831 the French painter Louis Daguerre (1789–1851) succeeded in developing a positive photographic image. From then on, the technology needed to develop modern photography was developed with great rapidity. The first camera for public use was produced by the American George

Eastman (1854–1932) in 1889. During the 1950s, new manufacturing processes greatly increased the speed, or light sensitivity, of both black-and-white and color film. The decade was also marked by the introduction of electronic devices called light amplifiers, which intensify dim illumination, making possible the recording on photographic film of even the faint light of very distant stars. Such advances in mechanical devices systematically raised the technical level of both amateur and professional photography.

Photography became an art form almost from the instant it was invented. Indeed, from the 1860s through the 1890s it was conceived of as an alternative to drawing and painting, allowing for greater fidelity. In other words, photography was viewed as a shortcut to traditional visual art. The Swedish photographer Oscar Gustave Rejlander (1813–1875) and the English photographer Henry Peach Robinson (1834–1901), for instance, emulated painting forms with their cameras. Like the painter, they claimed, the photographer inevitably makes a selection of what is to be recorded. This selection may be planned ahead of time or calculated on the spot. Lighting, focus, and camera angle may be manipulated to alter the appearance of the image; the developing and printing processes may be modified to produce desired results; or the photograph may be combined with other media to produce a composite art form.

Photography has become much more than an ersatz form of painting in modern technological cultures. In our society today it mediates how we remember people, events, and things. The photographs that adorn our tables and walls are, in effect, visual mementos and testimonials of who we are. Photographs capture a fleeting and irretrievable moment in time, extracting it from the flux of change that characterizes human life. Such captured moments have strong appeal because they provide eyewitness evidence, so to speak, that we do indeed exist in some enduring form, at least in the photographic space—this is why, in Michelangelo Antonioni's 1966 movie masterpiece, *Blow-Up*, the search for clues to a crime in a blow-up of a photograph is interpretable as a metaphor for the search for clues to our own existence in our photographic images.

8.5 CINEMA

The example of *Blow-Up* leads to the topic of *cinema*, which has become the art form to which most people today respond most strongly and to which they look for recreation, inspiration, and insight. Movies are aesthetically powerful because they juxtapose dialogue, music, scenery, and action in a visual-narrative way.

Most cinema historians trace the origin of cinema to the year 1896, when the French magician Georges Méliès made a series of films that explored the narrative potential of the new medium. In 1899, in a studio on the outskirts of Paris, Méliès reconstructed a ten-part version of the trial of French army officer Alfred Dreyfus and filmed *Cinderella* (1900) in 20 scenes. He is chiefly remembered, however, for his clever fantasies, such as *A Trip to the Moon* (1902), in which he exploited the new possibilities for offering perspective that the movie camera afforded. His short films were an instant hit with the public and were shown internationally. Although considered little more than curiosities today, they are significant precursors of an art form that was in its infancy at the time.

The theatrical fantasies of Méliès influenced the American inventor Edwin S. Porter, often called the father of the silent film, when he produced the first major American silent film, *The Great Train Robbery*, in 1903. Only eight minutes long, it greatly influenced the development of motion pictures because of its intercutting of scenes shot at different times and in different places to form a unified narrative, culminating in a suspenseful chase. With the production of D. W. Griffith's *The Birth of a Nation* (1915), small theaters sprang up throughout the United States, and cinema emerged as a *de facto* art form. Most films of the time were short comedies, adventure stories, or filmed records of performances by leading actors of the day.

Between 1915 and 1920, grandiose movie palaces proliferated throughout the United States. The film industry moved gradually to Hollywood. Hundreds of films a year poured from the Hollywood studios to satisfy the ever-increasing craving of a fanatic movie-going public. The vast majority of them were Westerns, slapstick comedies, and elegant romantic melodramas such as Cecil B. DeMille's *Male and Female* (1919). In the 1920s movies starring the comedian Charlie Chaplin ushered in the golden age of silent film.

After World War I, motion-picture production became a major American industry, generating millions of dollars for successful studios. American films became international in character and dominated the world market. Artists responsible for the most successful European films were imported by American studios, and their techniques were adapted and assimilated by Hollywood.

The transition from silent to sound films was so rapid that many films released in 1928 and 1929 had begun production as silent films but were hastily turned into sound films, or "talkies" as they were called, to meet the growing demand. Gangster films and musicals dominated the new "talking screen" of the early 1930s. The vogue of filming popular novels reached a peak in the late 1930s with expensively mounted productions of classic novels, including one of the most popular films in motion-picture history, *Gone with the Wind* (1939).

The trend toward escapism and fantasy in motion pictures was strong throughout the 1930s. A cycle of classic horror films, including *Dracula* (1931), *Frankenstein* (1931), and *The Mummy* (1932), spawned a series of sequels and spin-offs that lasted throughout the decade. One of the most enduring films of the era was the musical fantasy *The Wizard of Oz* (1939), based on a book by L. Frank Baum—a children's movie with a frightful theme that reflected the emerging cynicism of society at large, namely, that all human aspirations are ultimately make-believe, that the Wizard at the end of the road of life is really a fraud, a charlatan. The fun of living is getting to Oz, not finding out the truth about Oz.

One American filmmaker who came to Hollywood from radio in 1940 was the writer-director-actor Orson Welles, who experimented with new camera angles and sound effects that greatly extended the representational power of film. His *Citizen Kane* (1941) and *The Magnificent Ambersons* (1942) influenced the subsequent work of virtually every major filmmaker in the world. From the late 1940s to the mid-1970s, Italian cinema achieved an intimacy and depth of emotion that radically transformed cinematic art, with Roberto Rossellini's *Open City* (1945); Vittorio De Sica's *The Bicycle Thief* (1949); Pier Paolo Pasolini's *The Gospel According to Saint Matthew* (1966); Federico Fellini's *La Strada* (1954), *La Dolce Vita* (1960), *8 1/2* (1963), and *Juliet of the Spirits* (1965); Michelangelo Antonioni's *L'Avventura* (1959) and *Red Desert* (1964); Bernardo Bertolucci's *The Conformist* (1970) and *1900* (1977); and Lina Wertmuller's *Swept Away* (1975) and *Seven Beauties* (1976).

One of the most distinctive and original directors to emerge in post-World War II international cinema was Sweden's Ingmar Bergman (1918-), who brought an intense philosophical and intellectual depth to his films, treating the themes of personal isolation, sexual conflict, and religious obsession. In his film *The Seventh Seal* (1956) he probed the mystery of life and spirituality through the trials of a medieval knight playing a game of chess with Death. In *Wild Strawberries* (1957) he created a series of poetic flashbacks reviewing the life of an elderly professor. He dissected the human condition starkly in a series of films—*Persona* (1966), *Cries and Whispers* (1972), *Scenes from a Marriage* (1973), and *Autumn Sonata* (1978)—which excoriated the futile penchant in the human species to search for meaning in existence.

In the 1950s and 1960s the use of color virtually eclipsed the black-and-white film. But some filmmakers still preferred black and white, striving for "naked" realism. Such black and white films as *Psycho* (1960) by Alfred Hitchcock, *The Last Picture Show* (1971) by Peter Bogdanovich, *Raging Bull* (1980) by Martin Scorsese, *Zelig* (1983) and *Shad-*

ows and Fog (1992) by Woody Allen, and *Schindler's List* (1994) by Steven Spielberg have become classics.

Of the many directors of the last part of the twentieth century, perhaps no one has been as successful at exploiting the film medium as a versatile art form as has Steven Spielberg (1947–). His *Jaws* (1975), about a killer shark that terrorizes a small beach community, became the model for a number of films in which fear-inspiring creatures threatened helpless victims. His *Close Encounters of the Third Kind* (1977) and *E.T.* (1982) capitalized on a widespread fascination with the possibility of extraterrestrial life. His other multimillion-dollar blockbusters include *Raiders of the Lost Ark* (1981), *Indiana Jones and the Temple of Doom* (1984), and *Indiana Jones and the Last Crusade* (1989), all imitative of the serial cliffhangers of the 1930s. Most of Spielberg's films rely heavily on high-tech special effects, especially his *Jurassic Park* (1993), which features frighteningly realistic computer-generated dinosaurs. Within the first four weeks of its release, *Jurassic Park* became one of the highest-grossing films up to that time, only to be surpassed by James Cameron's *Titanic* (1998) a few years later.

The 1980s and 1990s saw a revolution in the home-video market, with major releases being made available for home viewing almost immediately after they left the movie theater. This development, combined with the advent of cable television, which features relatively current films on special channels, seemed to threaten the long-term survival of movie theaters and created a climate similar to that of the early 1950s, when television began to challenge the popularity of motion pictures. As a result, film companies increasingly favored large spectacles with fantastic special effects in order to lure the public away from home videos and back to the big screen. But despite the challenge from video, the traditional movie theater has remained as popular as ever—a testament to the power of cinema as an art form for the modern imagination.

Blade Runner

Cinema talks to the modern psyche in ways that perhaps theater cannot. As an example, consider Ridley Scott's 1982 classic movie *Blade Runner*, based on a science fiction story titled *Do Androids Dream of Electric Sheep?* by Philip K. Dick (1928–1982). This movie still attracts considerable interest from moviegoers of all kinds.

Before discussing this movie, it is necessary to deal first with the science fiction genre itself. Unlike traditional forms of fiction, this genre looks at the effects of science or future events on human beings. Although this has ancient roots—e.g. in his *True History* (160 AD) Lucian of Samosata dealt with a trip to the moon; the seventeenth cen-

tury British prelate and historian Francis Godwin also wrote of travel
to the moon; the English statesman Sir Thomas More wrote about an
idealized world in *Utopia* (1516)—science fiction as we now know it
traces its origins to the Industrial Revolution period when, in her
novel *Frankenstein* (1818), the British novelist Mary Shelley
(1797–1851) explored the potential of science for good or evil. After
the publication of this novel, the science fiction genre emerged as a
new form of popular fiction. The first writer to specialize in this new
genre was the French author Jules Verne (1828–1905). His highly
popular novels include *Journey to the Center of the Earth* (1864) and
Around the World in Eighty Days (1873). The first major English writer
of science fiction was H. G. Wells (1866–1946), whose *Time Machine*
(1895), *The Island of Dr. Moreau* (1896), and *The War of the Worlds* (1898)
became instant classics.

   In the twentieth century the popularity of science fiction grew with
the publication of *Brave New World* (1932) by Aldous Huxley
(1894–1963) and *Nineteen Eighty-four* (1949) by George Orwell
(1903–1950). These two novels set the stage for *Blade Runner*, which was
scripted in the 1980s style of science fiction writing, called cyberpunk.
The targets of cyberpunk writers were dehumanized societies dominated by technology and science, and the fallibility of scientists.

   Blade Runner deals, actually, with an ancient theme: What if we
could bring machines to life? What would they be like? Against the de-
pressing backdrop of a futuristic choking urban landscape, Rick Deckard is one of a select few law-enforcement officers, nicknamed "blade
runners," who have been trained to detect and track down "replicants,"
powerful humanoid robots who had been engineered to do the work of
humans in space. But some of the replicants have gone amok. They
have somehow developed the mental characteristics of humans and
have started to ask fundamental philosophical questions about their
own existence made urgent by the limited lifespan programmed into
them. A desperate band of these killer replicants has made its way back
to Earth, seeking to have their programmed deaths reversed. They are
looking for the sinister corporate tycoon responsible for their creation,
so that he can give them new life. Deckard's assignment is to track
down these runaway replicants and terminate them.

   The movie is about neither genetic engineering nor the dream of
bringing machines to life. It is about the nature of humanity. The movie
asks if "humanity" is itself a concept, the concoction of some invisible
tycoon. It is relevant to note that the method used by Deckard to detect
whether a suspect is human or replicant is reminiscent of the classic
Turing test proposed by artificial intelligence theorists (chapter 2, §2.4).
Interestingly, we are never sure if Deckard is himself a human or a replicant. This ambiguity is an intrinsic part of the movie's narrative.

Deckard's search unfolds in an urban wasteland where punk mutants control the streets while the pathetic inhabitants of endless blocks of gloomy high-rises remain glued to their TV sets. Deckard relies on a VCR, complete with stop action and precision image-enhancers, to track the replicants through dark alleys abandoned to the forces of anarchy.

In this scenario the replicants, paradoxically, are more "human" than the human characters. Deckard even falls in love with one of them, Rachel, whose name alludes obviously to the Biblical Rachel. She helps him track down his prey, falling in love with him. Deckard is saved at the end by a replicant who shows him mercy, one of the quintessential human qualities. Not only the replicants, but the mannequins in the movie as well, are all icons of the human form. Indeed, one of the replicants is killed sardonically by a mannequin. Human-like toys are also seen from time to time. But there is one feature that differentiates human anatomy from artificially-made anatomies—the eye. Deckard's version of the Turing test involves identifying the particular kinds of responses that only the human eye is capable of. Replicants use their eyes exclusively to see; humans use them as well to show feeling and spirituality. Aware of the mysterious power of the human eye, the replicants kill their maker by poking out his eyes.

The film asks basic questions about the nature of the emotions and human memory. Awareness of Self is largely autobiographical. This is why false memories were implanted in Rachel, leading her to believe that she was truly "human."

The film makes many ironic references to the Biblical narrative of Western society. Near the end, a replicant wearing only a white cloth around his waist, in obvious parody of the Crucifixion scene, saves Deckard's life at the cost of his own. The white dove that appears when the replicant dies is laden with religious symbolism. Finally, when Deckard and Rachel escape the gruesome city scene to the countryside, the dark, gloomy atmosphere suddenly clears up, the sun comes out, and a "new Biblical dawn" arises.

Blade Runner asks the fundamental questions of philosophy in a new way: What is a human being? What is real? Is there any meaning to existence? It does so by making the replicants mirror images of human beings, transforming their struggle to know who they are into a reflection of our own struggle. It is interesting to note that as we embark upon the twenty-first century, the themes that *Blade Runner* explored have become popular ones in society at large. Many of the same themes are examined by TV science fiction programs with large followings.

8.6 POSTMODERN ART

In closing this chapter, a few comments are in order with respect to a movement in the art world known as *postmodernism*, especially since it became for a while in the 1980s and 1990s a topic of substantial interest to cultural semioticians. Recall that the term *postmodernism* was coined by architects to designate a response against the earlier modernist style (of skyscrapers, tall apartment buildings, etc.) that had degenerated into sterile and monotonous formulas (chapter 7, §7.7). Postmodern architects called for greater individuality, complexity, and eccentricity in design, along with allusions to historical symbols and patterns. Shortly after its adoption in architecture, the notion of postmodernism started to catch on more broadly, becoming a more general movement in philosophy and the arts.

To understand the philosophical roots of this movement it is instructive to step back in time to the Christian medieval era. The worldview of most people of that era was focused on a firm belief in an afterlife with God. The typical medieval individual probably saw h/erself as being put on earth by God to prove h/erself worthy of reunification with God in Heaven. This state of affairs was necessitated when humanity's first parents, Adam and Eve, were ejected from the Garden of Eden because of their sin. Humanity then had to regain favor with God. To show sin-prone humanity how to atone for its sins, God sent His Son, Jesus Christ, the Savior of humanity, who will come a second time to restore the original state of innocence at the end of the world. This Biblical worldview found its greatest artistic expression in the *Divine Comedy*, written by Dante Alighieri (chapter 5, §5.7).

The religious narrative imparted a form of reassurance to most people alive in the medieval era. After the Renaissance and certainly after the Enlightenment, however, a more secular worldview took hold of people living in Western culture. This did not, however, eliminate the religious narrative from the signifying order completely. Statistics show that even today the majority of people living in the West are convinced that the world has a design and a purpose that is beyond science to know, and that there probably is a Being at the "center" of the design, who is the "author" of the human story.

In the nineteenth century, the dizzying growth of technology and the constantly increasing certainty that science could eventually solve all human problems on its own terms brought about a radically different philosophical outlook in Western culture. At mid-century, Darwin introduced the controversial notion of natural selection, which posed a serious challenge to the traditional Christian worldview (chapter 1, §1.1). By the end of the century, the now famous assertion that "God is dead," by the German philosopher Friedrich Nietzsche (1844–1900), acknowledged the radical change in worldview that science and especially Darwinian evolutionary theory had brought about. Nietzsche meant, of course, that the grip which the medieval Christian narrative had had on Western society had finally been loosened. By the middle part of the twentieth century, the critique of all aspects of that narrative had begun in full earnest. *Postmodernism* was just around the corner.

Among the cultural symptoms of the new worldview in the domain of art were the absurdist movement discussed above (§8.2) and the postmodernist art movement which, like its counterpart in architectural design, called for greater individuality, complexity, and eccentricity. But the essence of postmodern technique in all the arts was irony and parody, and the belief that there was nothing beneath the parodies. As the sociologist Zygmunt Bauman (1992: vii-viii) has perceptively remarked, postmodernism constitutes "a state of mind marked above all by its all-deriding, all-eroding, all-dissolving *destructiveness.*"

Koyaanisqatsi

A well-known example of postmodern art technique in the area of cinema is Godfrey Reggio's brilliant 1983 film *Koyaanisqatsi*—a film without words that unfolds through a series of discontinuous, narrativeless images. On the one hand, the movie shows us how narrativeless, disjunctive, and distracted the twentieth-century world has become; on the other hand, it is an example of what postmodern art is like, a parody of documentary-style films and TV programs. The film has no characters, plot, dialogue, commentary: in a word, nothing recognizable as a narrative. The camera juxtaposes contrasting images of cars on freeways, atomic blasts, litter on urban streets, people shopping in malls, housing complexes, buildings being demolished, etc. We see the world as the TV camera sees it. It is a turgid, gloomy world with no purpose or meaning whatsoever. People run around like mindless robots. To emphasize the insanity of a world characterized by countless cars, decaying buildings, and crowds bustling aimlessly about, Reggio incorporates the mesmerizing music of Philip Glass (1937–) into his technique. The music acts as a guide to understanding the images, interpreting them tonally. We can feel the senselessness of human actions in such a world in the contrasting melodies and rhythms of Glass' music. His slow rhythms tire us with their heaviness, and his fast tempi—which accompany a demented chorus of singers chanting in the background—assault our senses. When this musical-imagistic frenzy finally ends, we feel an enormous sense of relief.

In a certain sense, the whole film can be conceived of as a musical sonata with an opening part or exposition, a middle developmental section, and a final recapitulation with coda. The film starts off with a glimpse into a vastly different world—the world of the Hopi peoples of Arizona. This is a world firmly embedded in a holistic view of existence, a view that does not separate social life from Nature. Glass' choral music in this exposition is spiritual, sacred, profound. It inspires reverence for the human and the natural as one inseparable reality. This stands in dark contrast to the development of the filmic sonata—a cornucopia of dissonant images of a decaying, senseless, industrialized world. Then we are taken back, at the end, to the Hopi world. As in any recapitulation, the opening profound strains of the choir come back, hauntingly, awesomely, and with a warning this time (the coda) which is projected onto the screen:

koyaanisqatsi (from the Hopi language)

1. crazy life
2. life in turmoil
3. life out of balance
4. life disintegrating
5. a state of life that calls for another way of living

As this movie clearly shows, the postmodern movement in art offered a break from traditional narrative art. As Jean-François Lyotard (1984: xxiv) states, in postmodern art "narrative function is losing its functors, its great heroes, its great dangers, its great voyages, its great goal." However, in making Western culture more aware of its narrative presuppositions and its preoccupation with words, postmodernism engenders a reconsideration of Western belief systems. As mentioned at the start of this chapter, *art* and *culture* are inextricably intertwined. They are two sides of the same coin. Both have evolved to satisfy the need for meaning in the human species. It should come as little surprise, therefore, that as postmodern art lost its grip on the artistic imagination by century's end, so too did cultural trends start to become much less deconstructive of or ironic about the past. At the threshold of the twenty-first century, the Western signifying order, like all other signifying orders, has proven to be a highly dynamic and adaptive tool, serving basic human needs that are not significantly different than were those felt by the members of the first tribal societies.

9

OBJECTS

*Are we machines of the kind that re-
searchers are building as "thinking
machines"? In asking this kind of
question, we engage in a kind of projection—understanding humanity by
projecting an image of ourselves onto
the machine and the image of the machine back onto ourselves. In the tradition of artificial intelligence, we
project an image of our language activity onto the symbolic manipulations of the machine, then project that
back onto the full human mind.*

Winograd (1991: 220)

9.0 PRELIMINARY REMARKS

In human life, there is virtually no *object* or *artifact* that is not imbued
with meaning. Indeed, objects constitute particular kinds of signifiers with a broad range of connotative and annotative signifieds
across the world's cultures. In this chapter, our trek through the landscape of culture takes us through the domain of objects, yet another site
inhabited by *Homo faber* (chapter 7), the ingenious maker of things.
Moreover, we will visit the neighboring abode of a recent descendant
of *Homo culturalis*—*Homo technologicus*, the maker of machines.

Like all the other dimensions and components of culture, the meanings of objects and machines are coded in terms of the signifying order
and, therefore, reveal the same kinds of signifying properties that characterize, say, clothing, bodily presentation, language, buildings, etc.
Studying why people make things, how they design their objects, what
role these play in the evolution of a culture, is another important part
of cultural semiotics. Although the terms *object* and *artifact* are often
used interchangeably, they are distinguished in both semiotics and archeology as follows: *objects* are things found in the environment, *artifacts* are things made by humans. This distinction, however, is not necessary here, since our purpose is to focus on the meanings that things
in general embody.

9.1 OBJECTIFICATION

The objects that are made and used in a culture are hardly randomly produced "things." They cohere into a system of signification that mirrors, in microcosm, the meaning dimensionalities of the entire signifying order. This is why archeologists reconstruct ancient societies on the basis of the artifacts they discover at a site. The jewelry, clothes, furniture, ornaments, tools, toys, etc. that they find there are the bits and pieces that allow them to reconstruct the ancient society's *system of objects* that, in turn, allows them to reconstruct the society's signifying order to various degrees of completeness. Artifacts provide truly valuable clues as to what the signifying order of an extinct culture was probably like. Especially significant in the study of ancient signifying orders is the analysis of objects that were thought to possess mysterious powers. Although all objects are thought to have intrinsic value across the world's cultures, there are some that are thought to possess magical qualities.

Fetishism

An extreme manifestation of this belief is referred to as *fetishism*—the conviction that some inanimate objects, known as *fetishes* (from Portuguese *feitiço* "artificial, charm," from Latin *facticius* "artificial"), are imbued with supernatural attributes. The fetish is typically a figure modeled or carved from clay, stone, wood, or some other material, resembling a deified animal or some sacred thing. Sometimes it is the animal itself, or a tree, river, rock, or place associated with it. In some societies belief in the powers of the fetish is so strong that fetishism develops into idolatry. In such cases, the fetishistic belief is actually an extreme form of *animism*—the view that spirits either inhabit or communicate with humans through material objects.

    Animism is not limited to tribal or pre-modern cultures. On the contrary, it is alive and well even in modern Western cultures, whether or not people realize it. In addition to the fetishes that incite sexual urges or fantasies in some people—feet, shoes, intimate female apparel—there are many behaviors in our culture that can only be explained as the manifest effects of a latent form of animism. In the 1970s, for example, American society went mad for "pet rocks." Many considered this fad simply a quick way to make money, foisted upon a gullible public spoiled by consumerism. But to some semioticians, that craze was, in effect, clear evidence of a latent form of animism. The same animistic tendencies can be seen in the common view held by even modern-day people that some objects are unexplainably magical. This is why, if they are lost, then impending danger is feared. If, however, they are found serendipitously—as for instance when one finds a "lucky penny"—then it is believed that the gods or Fortune will look auspiciously upon the finder.

Objectification

Animism is, actually, a manifestation of an unconscious psycho-semiosic process that can be called *objectification*. This refers to the fact that people perceive objects as having a necessary logic and *raison d'être* all their own, of which their makers may not be aware: i.e. their existence is believed to be already implicit in the formless matter of the universe, assuming actual material shape through human agents. This ingrained belief system would explain why objects are perceived to be related "genealogically" to each other—the making of one leading to the making of another and then to the making of yet another, and so on. Like works of art, objects are felt to be *reifications* (reflections) of innate forms of thought that seek expression in real-world physical forms. In *dimensionality* terms, objectification can thus be explained as the perception of an object as (1) something material, (2) whose particular (paradigmatically differentiable) shape is but one manifestation of the forms inherent in the human mind, that (3) generates a meaning in relation to the other objects and codes in a culture:

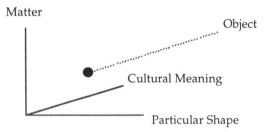

Objectification manifests itself in many behaviors and beliefs. One such belief is the perception that some objects are extensions of the physical Self. The jewelry people wear, the personal objects that individuals possess to adorn their abodes, and the like are all signifiers of physical persona. In Western culture this applies as well to the automobile, which is experienced by many as an extension of the body and thus as a protective shell of the Self (Richards 1994). In the public world of traffic, it creates a space around the physical body which is as inviolable as the body itself. Interestingly, but not unexpectedly, this manifestation of objectification is not confined to Western culture. The anthropologist Basso (1990: 15-24) found that the Western Apache of east-central Arizona, for instance, also perceive the car as a body. The

Apache even use the names of body parts to refer to analogous automobile parts: e.g. the hood is called a "nose," the headlights "eyes," the
windshield "forehead," the area from the top of the windshield to the
front bumper "face," the front wheels "hands and arms," the rear
wheels "feet," the items under the hood "innards," the battery "liver,"
the electrical wiring "veins," the gas tank "stomach," the distributor
"heart," the radiator "lung," and the radiator hoses "intestines."

9.2 DOLLS: A CASE-IN-POINT

A truly interesting manifestation of objectification that merits separate
treatment here, because of the interest it has generated among cultural
semioticians, is discernible in the kinds of meanings that toys have.
This form of objectification is at times as extreme as any form of religious fetishism. Consider, for instance, what happened during the 1983
Christmas shopping season in the United States and Canada. That period is now often described by cultural historians as the Christmas of
the "Cabbage Patch" doll craze. Hordes of parents were prepared to
pay almost anything to get one of those dolls for their daughters.
Scalpers offered the suddenly and unexplainably out-of-stock dolls for
hundreds of dollars through classified ads. Adults fought each other in
lines to get one of the few remaining dolls left in stock at some toy
stores.

How could a simple doll have caused such mass hysteria? In our
view, only an extreme form of objectification, bordering on fetishism,
could have possibly triggered it. To see why this is so, consider more
closely what toys mean. Children have always played with objects. In
the child's mind broom handles can be imagined to be swords, rocks
balls, and so on. A toy, on the other hand, is an adult-made object imbued with the connotations that childhood has in a culture. Toys, as the
logo for a major toy chain states, are indeed us *(Toys "R" Us)*. Dolls are
particularly meaningful because they are icons of the human figure to
higher or lesser degrees of fidelity. As early as 600 BC dolls were made
with movable limbs and removable garments, so as to reinforce their
representation of human anatomy. When parents buy or make a doll,
they are, in effect, giving their child an ersatz sibling or playmate. Dolls
have been found in the tombs of ancient Egyptian, Greek, and Roman
children. Evidently the objective was to provide the children with a
lifelike human form, so that they could, in effect, play with someone
else in the afterlife.

Interestingly, in many societies dolls also have religious and ritualistic functions. In the Hopi culture, for instance, *kachina* dolls are given
as sacred objects to children as part of fertility rites. Even in Christian

practices, dolls have been used since the Middle Ages to represent the Holy Family in the Nativity scene, as part of Christmas observations. In Mexico, dolls representing Our Lady of Guadeloupe are ceremonially paraded every year. And in some cultures of the Caribbean, it is believed that one can cause physical or psychological damage to another person by doing something injurious to a doll constructed to resemble that person.

The commercialization of dolls as both fashion icons and play-things for children can be traced to Germany in the early fifteenth century. The fashion dolls were made to depict the clothing of German women. Shortly thereafter, manufacturers in England, France, Holland, and Italy also began to produce dolls dressed in fashions typical of their respective locales. The more ornate ones were often used by rulers and courtiers as gifts. By the seventeenth century, however, simpler dolls, made of cloth or leather, were being used primarily as playthings by children.

During the eighteenth century, the human iconicity of dolls was improved considerably as manufacturing systems became more tech-nologized. The fashion dolls looked so lifelike that they were often used to illustrate clothing style trends and were sent from one country to another to display the latest fashions in miniature form. After the Industrial Revolution, dolls became commonplace toys. Before then, most people lived in agricultural communities or settings. Children barely out of infancy were expected to share the workload associated with tending to the farm. There was, consequently, little distinction between childhood and adult roles—children were considered to be adults with smaller and weaker bodies. During the Industrial Revolu-tion the center of economic activity shifted from the farm to the city. This led to the emergence of a new social order with different role cate-gories and assignments. The result was that children were left with few of their previous responsibilities, and a new view of them surfaced. Children were proclaimed to be vastly different from adults, needing time to learn at school and to play. Child labor laws were passed and public education became compulsory. Protected from the harsh reality of industrial work, children came to assume a new identity in society at large as innocent, faultless, impressionable, malleable beings. The toys that were manufactured for the use of children soon became part of this new *mythology* (cultural perception) of childhood (chapter 10, §10.3).

Dolls came to be viewed as the playmates of little girls. By the early part of the twentieth century, it was assumed that all female children would want to play with dolls, and toys came to connote *gender identity* (chapter 4, §4.2). Noteworthy design innovations in dolls manufactured between 1925 and World War II included sleeping eyes with lashes, dimples, open mouths with tiny teeth, fingers with nails, and latex-rubber dolls that could drink water and wet themselves. Since the 1950s, the association of lifelike dolls with female gender identity has been entrenched further by both the quantity of doll types being produced and their promotion by media advertising techniques (chapter 11, §11.4). Since their launch in 1959, the "Barbie" dolls, for instance, have become a part of the system of objects that are associated with little girls growing up in North America. Incidentally, the Barbie dolls also started the trend of buying clothing and accessories for dolls, thus enhancing their human iconicity even more.

The Cabbage Patch dolls were, in fact, intended to be virtually indistinguishable from the real thing. They even came with "adoption papers," and each doll was given a name, taken at random from 1938 Georgia birth records. Like any act of naming, this conferred upon each doll a human personality. And, thanks to computerized factories, no two dolls were manufactured alike. No wonder, then, that the Cabbage Patch doll shortage created such frenzy—a pattern that has been repeated regularly, to varying degrees, at Christmas time ever since. Having toys is perceived as an intrinsic feature of the social and emotional life of children. So, in the same way that a parent would panic if the child's physical life were threatened because of the lack of, say, food, the "Cabbage Patch parent" found h/erself panicking over the possibility of h/er child's social and emotional life being threatened because of the lack of what was, at a denotative level, just a toy.

9.3 FOOD

Some semioticians distinguish between an object proper, or inanimate material, and material of plant or animal origin, such as food. Although the topic of food is often given a separate treatment in semiotic manuals, we will deal with it under the rubric of objectification because our interest here is in the meanings associated with all types of things, including food.

At a biological level, survival without food is impossible. So, at a denotative level food is perceived to be a survival substance. But, once again, given the semiosic and representational nature of the human species, food and eating invariably take on a whole range of connotations and annotations in social settings. The term that is often used to designate the meanings that food entails is *cuisine*. This refers to what we eat, how we make it, and what it tells us about the makers and eaters. At the level of culture, cuisine is perhaps more precisely definable as the system of *food codes* that are found alongside, and interconnected with, the other codes in the signifying order. In terms of the *dimensionality principle*, food denotes a survival substance at a *firstness* level; it takes on specific annotative meanings for the individual at a *secondness* level; and it is imbued with social meanings derived from a culture's food codes at a *thirdness* level:

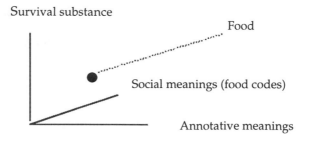

Survival substance

Food

Social meanings (food codes)

Annotative meanings

The "Raw" vs. the "Cooked"

The anthropologist Claude Lévi-Strauss (1964) made an important distinction between raw and cooked food in the evolution of *Homo culturalis*. He saw the advent of cooking as the event that transformed human group life into cultural life. All animals eat food in its raw form, including the human animal; but only *Homo culturalis* cooks h/er food. According to Lévi-Strauss this transformation was accomplished by two processes—roasting and boiling—both of which were among the first significant technological accomplishments of early human cultures. Roasting is more primitive than boiling because it implies direct contact between the food and a fire. So, it is slightly above "the raw" in evolutionary terms. But boiling reveals an advanced form of technological thinking, since the cooking process in this case is mediated by a pot and a cooking liquid. Boiling was the event that led to the "cooked" form of eating. Interestingly, in some parts of the world the distinction between "the raw" and "the cooked" has been enshrined into the signifying order to connote social relations. In Hindu society, for instance, the higher castes may receive only raw food from the lower castes, whereas the lower castes are allowed to accept any kind of cooked food from any caste.

To get a sense of the intrinsic relation between cooking and culture, it might be instructive to imagine a "Robinson Crusoe" situation, i.e. an imaginary scenario drafted in imitation of Daniel Defoe's (1660?–1731) famous novel, *The Life and Adventures of Robinson Crusoe*, which appeared in 1719. This is a fictional tale of a shipwrecked sailor, based on the adventures of a seaman, Alexander Selkirk, who had been marooned on an island off the coast of Chile. The novel chronicles Crusoe's ingenious attempts to overcome the island's hardships. It has become one of the classics of children's literature.

We can suppose that, like Robinson Crusoe, a person has somehow been abandoned alone on an isolated island in the middle of nowhere to fend for h/erself. Without the support and security of a social ambiance, h/er first instincts will, of course, lead h/er to survive in any way that s/he can. In this situation, h/er need for food and water takes precedence over all else. When h/er need becomes desperate, s/he will hardly be fussy about how the "raw food" she finds on the island will taste. In effect, s/he will eat anything that will not kill h/er. The eating of raw food in such a drastic situation has only one function—to secure survival.

Now, suppose that after living alone on the island for a few days the person discovers other similarly-abandoned individuals, each one on some remote part of the island, all of whom speak the same language as s/he does. Since there is strength in numbers, the decision is made to live as a group. To reduce the risk of not finding enough food for everyone to eat, the group decides that it is wise to assign responsibility for the hunting and gathering of food to specific persons. Others are then assigned the task of developing the basic technology for cooking the food. Others still are given the task of actually cooking the food. These role assignments are determined by mutual consent, say, according to the demonstrated abilities of each individual when s/he was living alone. After a period of time, what will emerge from these role agreements is a proto-culture, based on a division of labor. As time passes, other social agreements and arrangements are established. At that point, it is quite likely that the cooking of food will become more and more routinized and even adapted to meet changing taste preferences among the individuals.

The purpose of this vignette has been to exemplify how raw food is tied to survival and cooked food to culture. Indeed, it might even be claimed, as it is by some anthropologists, that the cooking of food was the event that led to the invention of culture. When especially favorable food sources became available, early humans settled in permanent, year-round communities, learning to domesticate plants and animals for food, transportation, clothing, and other uses. With greater population concentrations and permanent living sites, cultural institutions developed, united by religious ceremonies and food exchanges. These early cultures soon developed complex belief systems with regard to the supernatural world, i.e. with regard to the forces of Nature and of the gods. Food thus became a part of ritual and a staple of symbolic life.

Food Symbolism

The above evolutionary scenario would explain why food reverberates with symbolism and why the world's religious ceremonies revolve around it. The *raison d'être* of the Catholic Mass, for instance, is to partake of bread that has become the consecrated body of Christ. But even in the secular domain, we schedule breakfast, lunch, and dinner events ritualistically on a daily basis. In a phrase, the symbolic meanings of food are interconnected with the other meaning pathways charted by the signifying order of a culture. This is why we talk of the *bread of life*, of *earning your bread*, and so on. In many European languages words for *bread* are often synonymous with life. The word *companion*, incidentally, comes from Latin and means literally the person "with whom we share bread." Bread is, evidently, as much symbol as it is food.

Many of the symbolic meanings derive from mythic and religious accounts of human origins. The Christian story of Adam and Eve, for instance, revolves around the eating of an apple. In actual fact, the Hebrew account of the Genesis story tells of a forbidden fruit of knowledge, not an apple. The representation of this fruit as an apple can be traced to medieval Christian visual depictions of the Eden scene, when painters and sculptors became interested in the Genesis story. In the Koran, on the other hand, the forbidden fruit is a banana. Now, the Biblical symbolism of the apple as forbidden knowledge, continues to resonate in our culture. This is why the apple tree symbolizes the tree of knowledge; why Apple Computer has chosen this fruit to symbolize its quest for knowledge; why we have expressions such as *the apple of one's eye*.

Ramses II of Egypt cultivated apples in orchards along the Nile in the thirteenth century BC. The ancient Greeks also cultivated apple trees from the seventh century BC onwards, designating the apple "the golden fruit," since Greek mythology, like Christian, assigned it a primordial significance. The apple was given to Hera from the Garden of the Hesperides as a wedding present when she married Zeus.

Edibility

Predictably, the meanings that foods entail produce *structural effects* (chapter 3, §3.10). The fact that in our culture rabbits, cats, and dogs, for instance, are felt to be household pets, forces us to perceive cooked rabbit, cat, and dog meat as inedible. On the other hand, we eat bovine (beef steaks, hamburgers, etc.), lamb, and poultry meat routinely, with no discomfort. Predictably, such cultural perceptions are not universal. In India, a cow is classified as sacred and, therefore, as inedible. Incidentally, this is the basis of our expression *sacred cow* to refer to some-

thing unassailable and revered. Anglo-American culture does not classify foxes or dogs as edible food items, but the former is reckoned a
delicacy in Russia, and the latter in China. Need it be mentioned that
some people even eat human meat (a practice known more precisely as
anthropophagitism or cannibalism)?

Edibility is more a product of culture than it is of Nature. Outside
of those which have a demonstrably harmful effect on the human organism, the types of flora and fauna that are considered to be edible or
inedible vary greatly among different cultures. Perceptions of edibility
have a basis in history, not digestive processes. We cannot get nourishment from eating tree bark, grass, or straw. But we certainly could
get it from eating frogs, ants, earthworms, silkworms, lizards, and
snails. Most people in our society would, however, respond with disgust and revulsion at the thought of eating such potential food items.
This notwithstanding, there are societies where they are not only eaten
for nourishment, but also considered to be delicacies. Our expression *to
develop a taste for* some food reveals how closely tied edibility is to cultural perception. If we were left alone on that hypothetical Robinson
Crusoe island described above (§9.1), the question would certainly be
one of not of taste, but of survival at any taste.

The specific kinds of tastes that one finds meaningful in social settings can be called *gustemes* (in analogy with *phoneme, narreme*, etc.). We
perceive gustemic differences in cuisine as fundamental differences in
worldview and lifestyle—as differences between "us" and "them." In
our society we eat fish with great enjoyment, but we do not eat the eyes
of fish, which we find distasteful, by and large. But those living in
many other societies do. To see others eat the eyes tends to cause discomfort or queasiness within many of us. It is a small step from this
unpleasant sensation to a perception of the eaters as barbaric. It is interesting to note that when we do come to accept the gustemes of others, we then reclassify their cuisine as an exotic delicacy.

Eating Events

Food codes are interconnected with the other codes of the signifying
order. The complex rules of how to prepare food and when to eat it, the
meanings that specific dishes have vis-à-vis social class, the subtle distinctions that are constantly made in the ways food items are cooked,
etc. are all coded in terms of the signifying order. For this reason, food
codes also regulate how eating events are expected to unfold: e.g. they
regulate the order in which dishes are presented, what combinations
can be served in tandem, how the foods are to be placed on the table,
who has preference in being served, who must show deference, who
does the speaking and who the listening, who sits where, what topics

of conversation are appropriate, etc. In effect, as Visser (1991: 107) remarks, "dinner invitations can be fraught with hope and danger, and dinner parties are dramatic events at which decisions can be made and important relationships initiated, tested, or broken."

Eating events are crucial to the establishment and maintenance of social relations and harmony. There exists virtually no society that does not assign an area of the domestic abode to their occurrence. All societies, moreover, impose a discrete set of table manners that relate to differing types of eating events. For example, if someone has never eaten spaghetti before, then s/he will have to learn how. Incidentally, in nineteenth-century Naples, from where the modern-day version of this dish comes (Visser 1991: 17-18), people ate spaghetti by raising each strand of pasta in their fingers, throwing back their heads, and lowering the strands into their mouths without slurping. Today, the correct manner of eating spaghetti is to twirl it around the fork, in small amounts, and then to insert the fork into the mouth as one does with any other food eaten with a fork.

Codes of table manners generally also involve the correct deployment of flatware. Specialized knives, spoons, forks, and other implements for eating and serving food have until recent times been the privilege of the aristocracy. In ancient Egypt, Greece, and Rome knives and spoons were made of precious materials and often decorated. The Romans also possessed skewers that were forerunners of the fork. From the Middle Ages until the Renaissance, the knife remained the principal table utensil. Forks came into common table use in Italy in the 1500s. At the same time spoons made the transition from kitchen utensils to table items, and flatware came to be used by all peoples of all classes. During the nineteenth century numerous other items of flatware were created, along with variations on the three basic implements, such as teaspoons, butter knives, and salad forks.

Cultures vary widely in the degree of sociability they associate with the eating event. At one end of the sociability continuum some cultures see eating as a private act; at the other end, other cultures see it as necessarily a social event, never, outside of special circumstances, to be performed in private. Many cultures, as well, have a kind of "pecking order" designed to indicate the social class or position of the eaters. In our culture, eating in a high-class restaurant entails the activation and deployment of a whole set of complementary codes, from dress to language, that are meant to create a whole range of subtle and not-so-subtle messages about oneself.

9.4 OBJECTIFIED CONSCIOUSNESS

Technology is the general term used for describing the systematic processes by which human beings fashion objects and machines to increase
their understanding of, and control over, the material environment.
The term is derived from the Greek words *tekhne,* which refers to an
"art" or "craft," and *logia,* meaning an "area of study," hence the meaning of *technology* as the "craft of object-making." Many historians of culture argue that technology has not only become an essential condition
of advanced civilizations, but also refashioned the signifying orders of
such civilizations into a global culture, which has now developed its
own dynamism and does not respect geographical limits or social systems. Technology, in a phrase, has transformed cultural systems permanently, frequently with unexpected social consequences.

Gutenberg's Galaxy

The growth of technology since the Renaissance has indeed had profound consequences on the evolution of the signifying orders of humankind, creating the conditions for their coalescence into a worldwide
signifying order or *metaculture,* whose defining characteristic is the in-
ternationalizing of codes—a leveling process that has led since the
middle part of the twentieth century to a widening adoption among the
peoples of the earth of standard languages, symbol systems, ways of
doing things, etc. The term *modern culture* is in fact indistinguishable
from both *technological culture* and *global culture.* From a semiotic standpoint, the salient feature of today's global culture is the high degree of
objectification that it engenders in people and thus the perception that
knowledge is *objectifiable.*
   The event that started the globalization of culture was, no doubt,
the invention of print in the fifteenth century and the subsequent widespread use of the book to codify knowledge. The forerunners of books
were the clay tablets, impressed with a stylus, used by the Sumerians,
Babylonians, and other peoples of ancient Mesopotamia. These were
followed by the scrolls of the ancient Egyptians, Greeks, and Romans,
which consisted of sheets of papyrus, a paper-like material made from
a pith of reeds, formed into a continuous strip and rolled around a
stick. The strip, with the text written with a reed pen in narrow, closely
spaced columns on one side, was unrolled as it was read. Later, during
the fourth to first centuries BC, a long roll was subdivided into a number of shorter rolls, stored together in one container. In the first century
AD, this was replaced by the rectangular *codex,* the direct ancestor of
the modern book. The codex, used at first by the Greeks and Romans
for business accounts and schooling, was a small, ringed notebook con-

sisting of two or more wooden tablets covered with wax, which could be marked with a stylus, smoothed over, and reused many times. It was easier for readers to find their place in a codex, or to refer ahead or back. In the Middle Ages, codices were used primarily in the observance of the Christian liturgy. Indeed, the word *codex* is part of the title of many ancient handwritten books on topics related to the Bible.

Literacy introduces a level of abstraction in human interaction that forces people to separate the maker of knowledge from the knowledge made. And this in turn leads to the perception that knowledge can exist on its own, spanning time and distance. This is precisely what is meant by the term *objectivity:* knowledge unconnected to a knower. Before literacy became widespread, humans lived primarily in oral-auditory cultures, based on the spoken word. The human voice cannot help but convey emotion, overtly or implicitly. So, the kind of consciousness that develops in people living in oral cultures is shaped by the emotionality of the voice. In such cultures, the knower and the thing known are seen typically as inseparable. On the other hand, in literate cultures, the kind of consciousness that develops is shaped by the structural effects produced by the writing medium. The written page, with its edges, margins, and sharply defined characters organized in neatly-layered rows or columns, induces a linear-rational way of thinking in people. In such cultures, the knowledge contained in writing is perceived as separable from the maker of that knowledge primarily because the maker of the written text is not present during the reading and understanding of h/er text, as s/he is in oral communicative situations. The spread of literacy through the technology of print since the Renaissance has been the determining factor in the objectification of knowledge in the modern world and thus the main factor in the process of globalization.

Because of this, the great communications theorist Marshall McLuhan (1911–1980) characterized the modern world as the "Gutenberg Galaxy," after the German printer Johannes Gutenberg (1400?–1468?), who is considered the inventor of movable type. Through books, newspapers, pamphlets, and posters, McLuhan argued, the printed word became, after the fifteenth century, the primary means for the propagation of knowledge and ideas. More importantly, given the fact that the book could cross political boundaries, the Gutenberg press set in motion the globalization of culture. Paradoxically, however, as McLuhan (1962) observed, this process did not simultaneously lead to the elimination of tribalism in the human species—one of the evolutionary milestones that led to the invention of culture (chapter 1, §1.3). On the contrary, he claimed that it was impossible to "take the tribe out of the human being", so to speak, no matter how advantageous a technologized global culture would seem to be. McLuhan insisted that tribal tendencies resonate continually within the psyche of modern-day people, constituting the root cause of the sense of alienation that many modern individuals tend to feel living in large impersonal social settings.

Babbage's Galaxy

By the start of the twentieth century, the great advances made in technology had objectified human consciousness and cultural signifying orders to a high degree throughout a large part of the world. A second technologically-engendered cultural revolution occurred at mid-century that, by century's end, had objectified consciousness even further—namely, the revolution set in motion by the astounding technological accomplishments in electronics and, especially, in computer science. Since the 1980s, the computer has become so interconnected with the signifying orders of modern cultures that it is accurate to say that we live no longer in "Gutenberg's Galaxy" but in "Babbage's Galaxy," to coin an analogous term after the person who invented the first true computer—Charles Babbage (1792–1871). Today's personal computers can store the equivalent of thousands of books. Within seconds, anyone with a modem can access an enormous store of human information. Almost every text we consider meaningful or practical has been transferred to computer memory systems. Print technology opened up the possibility of founding a "world civilization"; computer technology has brought that possibility closer and closer to realization.

The first general-purpose all-electronic computer was built in 1946 at the University of Pennsylvania by the American engineer John Presper Eckert, Jr., and the American physicist John William Mauchly. Called ENIAC, for *Electronic Numerical Integrator And Computer*, the device contained 18,000 vacuum tubes and could perform several hundred multiplications per minute. ENIAC's program was wired into its processor, so that reprogramming required manual rewiring. The development of transistor technology and its use in computers in the late 1950s allowed the advent of smaller, faster, and more versatile machines than could be built with vacuum tubes. Because transistors use much less power and have a much longer life, this development alone was responsible for the improved machines called "second-generation computers." Late in the 1960s the integrated circuit was introduced, making it possible for many transistors to be fabricated on one silicon board, with interconnecting wires plated in place. In the mid-1970s, with the introduction of large-scale integrated circuits with many thousands of interconnected transistors etched into a single silicon board, the modern-day personal computer was just around the corner.

Modern computers are all conceptually similar, regardless of size. The features of their design and operation have become modern-day analogues of human mental design and operation, as we discussed in the second chapter (§2.4). So, it is worthwhile here to cast a schematic glance at these features. The physical and operational system of the computer is known as its hardware. This is composed of five distinct components:

- a *central processing unit* made up of a series of chips that perform calculations and that time and control the operations of the other elements of the system;

- *input devices*, such as a keyboard, that enable a computer user to enter data, commands, and programs into the central processing unit;

- *memory storage devices* that can store data internally (RAM) and externally (tapes, disks, etc.);

- *output devices*, such as the video display screen, that enable the user to see the results of the computer's calculations or data manipulations;

- a *communications network*, called a "bus," that links all the elements of the system and connects the system to the external world.

The computer's hardware system is directed by a *program*. This is a sequence of instructions that tells the hardware what operations to perform on data. Programs can be built into the hardware itself, or they may exist independently in a form known as software. A general-purpose computer contains some built-in programs or instructions, but it depends on external programs to perform useful tasks. Once a computer has been programmed, it can do only as much or as little as the software controlling it at any given moment enables it to do. A wide range of applications programs are in use, written in special *machine, computer*, or *programming* languages.

As discussed in chapter 2 (§2.4), the design features of the computer lend themselves as convincing analogues for the structure and functioning of the human mind. This is why in cognitive science and artificial intelligence circles parallel-processing computers have been constructed with the specific purpose of duplicating the complex functions of human thought. But it is wrong, in our view, to assume a similarity between human and machine hardware systems. The former grow out of lived experience and historical forces; the latter have been invented by humans themselves. The idea that computers can think like humans is really no more than a modern-day version of animism that can be called *machinism* or *computerism*—namely, the view that our machines are us (humanoids) and that we are machines (protoplasmic replicators).

This new manifestation of objectification has become an all-pervasive one. In part, it has been energized by the remarkable advances in the technology of computer hardware, software, and networks. In Babbage's Galaxy, such networks reinforce the illusion that knowledge and information exist independently of their makers, even more so than did the book in Gutenberg's Galaxy. But human signs are not like computational data that can be neatly dismissed as true or false. Rather, they provide perspective, emotivity, and other impenetrable aspects of human knowing. Essentially, the human mind cannot study or reproduce itself.

The science of artificial intelligence is providing a highly technical theoretical apparatus for modeling certain aspects of human cognition in computer software. But it will never be able to answer the question of what the mind is. As the philosopher Vico (in Bergin and Fish 1984: 123) aptly put it, human beings can never really understand what they themselves have not made. Since human beings have not made the mind, there is no way that they will ever really understand it. Many theories have been devised to explain it. But it is difficult to separate theory-making from the activity of thinking itself. The result is always unsatisfactory. In our view, the science of semiotics provides a much more practicable agenda for studying the mysteries of the mind, for the simple reason that the mind reveals itself in the forms and contents of signs, codes, myths, stories, works of art, and other expressive phenomena, including computer languages.

In his book *Mental Models* (1983), the psychologist P. N. Johnson-Laird provided a useful framework for talking about the mind. According to Johnson-Laird, there are three basic types of machine consciousness:

1. "Cartesian machines" that do not use symbols and lack awareness of themselves;

2. "Craikian machines" (after Craik 1943) that construct models of reality, but lack self-awareness;

3. self-reflective machines that construct models of reality and are aware of their ability to construct such models.

The computer software designed to simulate human mentality produces types (1) and (2) forms of consciousness. But only human beings are capable of the type (3) form. Unlike a Cartesian or a Craikian machine, a human being is not only capable of constructing models of h/er mind, but is aware of doing so. Indeed, we become conscious when we engage in mentally simulating our thoughts and experiences.

The computer is one of *Homo culturalis's* greatest intellectual achievements. It is an extension of h/er rational intellect. As a maker of objects and artifacts, s/he has finally come up with a machine that will eventually take over most of the arduous work of ratiocination. This could then leave h/er imagination much more time to search out new associations in poetry, art, and music of which only human creatures with a human body, a human mind, and reared in a human culture are capable. The caveat issued by the art historian Arnheim (1969: 73) is still valid today: "There is no need to stress the immense practical usefulness of computers. But to credit the machine with intelligence is to defeat it in a competition it need not pretend to enter."

In Sumerian and Babylonian myths there were accounts of the creation of life through the animation of clay (Watson 1990: 221). The idea of bringing inanimate matter to life has, in fact, captivated the human imagination since at least the beginnings of recorded history. Since the publication of Mary Shelley's grotesque and macabre novel *Frankenstein* in 1818, the idea that robots could be brought to intelligent life has been pursued relentlessly. *Homo technologicus*, the ingenious and resourceful descendant of *Homo culturalis*, now finds h/erself at the center of everything. But as William Barrett (1986: 160) aptly notes, despite h/er great intellectual resources, s/he is essentially an unsatisfied and unsatisfiable descendant. The reason for this is simply that objectified consciousness is a disembodied consciousness, at odds with the human being's true sensorial, emotional, and imaginative nature.

9.5 OBJECTIFIED ART

There is one other manifestation of objectification that merits some discussion here by way of conclusion. In a society where objects of all kinds are being produced for mass consumption, there arises an incessant craving for new objects. The semiotician Roland Barthes (1915–1980) referred to this excessive form of objectification as "neomania" (Barthes 1957). To encourage the acquisition of objects, obsolescence is, in fact, regularly built into the marketing strategies of a product, so that the same product can be sold again and again under new guises. This is why advertisers rely on a handful of Epicurean themes—happiness, youthfulness, success, status, luxury, fashion, beauty—to peddle their products. The implicit message in all advertising is that solutions to human problems can be found in buying and consuming.

The emphasis on consumerism has even spawned its own art forms. Shortly after World War II, a new artistic movement, called *pop art* (short for *populist art*), for instance, was in fact inspired by the mass production and consumption of objects. For pop artists, the factory, supermarket, and garbage can became their art school. But despite its apparent absurdity, many people loved pop art, no matter how controversial or crass it appeared to be. In a certain sense, the pop art movement bestowed on people the assurance that art was for mass consumption, not just for an élite class of *cognoscenti*. Some artists duplicated beer bottles, soup cans, comic strips, road signs, and similar objects in paintings, collages, and sculptures; others simply incorporated the objects themselves into their works. In a phrase, pop art is the product of the imagination of *Homo technologicus*. But ultimately, it is a transitory art. Along with pop music, blockbuster movies, bestseller novels, television programs, fashion shows, and most commercial products, it is destined to become quickly obsolete.

The pop art movement emerged in the 1940s and 1950s, when painters like Robert Rauschenberg (1925–) and Jasper Johns (1930–) wanted to close the gap between traditional art and the mass-culture aesthetics of consumerist life. Rauschenberg constructed collages from household objects such as quilts and pillows, Johns from American flags and bull's-eye targets. The first full-fledged pop art work was *Just What Is It That Makes Today's Home So Different, So Appealing?* (1956, private collection) by the British artist Richard Hamilton. In this satiric collage of two ludicrous figures in a living room, the pop art hallmarks of crudeness and irony are emphasized.

Pop art developed rapidly during the 1960s, as painters started to portray brand-name commercial products, with garish sculptures of hamburgers and other fast-food items, blown-up frames of comic strips, or theatrical events staged as art objects. Pop artists also appropriated the techniques of mass production. Rauschenberg and Johns had already abandoned individual, titled paintings in favor of large series of works, all depicting the same objects. In the early 1960s the American Andy Warhol (1928–1987) carried the idea a step further by adopting the mass-production technique of silk-screening, turning out hundreds of identical prints of Coca-Cola bottles, Campbell's soup cans, and other familiar subjects, including identical three-dimensional Brillo boxes (chapter 8, §8.4).

Using images and sounds that reflect the materialism and vulgarity of modern consumerist culture, pop artists seek to provide a view of reality that is more immediate and relevant than that of past art. They want the observer to respond directly to the object, rather than to the skill and personality of the artist. Ultimately, however, the pop art movement may be no more than one of the symptoms of life in Babbage's Galaxy, which psychologists call *alienation*—a sense of rootlessness, stemming from excessive forms of materialism.

10

NARRATIVE

> *Myths have a quasi-objective collective existence, unfold on their own "concrete logic" with supreme disregard for the vagaries of individual thought, and reduce any particular consciousness to a mere function of themselves.*
>
> Eagleton (1983: 104)

10.0 PRELIMINARY REMARKS

The human penchant for life-stories is an integral part of human consciousness. People all over the world cannot help but think of their lives as stories and proceed to tell them as such. Autobiographical stories have an inherent logic all their own that imparts sense and purpose to the teller's life, not simply mirroring what happened to the teller during h/er lifetime, but exploring and interpreting it for h/er. Such storytelling is as fundamental to human psychic life as breathing is to physical life. Indeed, the "narrative instinct" is as much a part of the constitution of *Homo culturalis* as are any of h/er physical instincts.

The workings of the narrative instinct are also manifested in the founding stories, known more specifically as *myths*, that form the basis of all cultural life. These are to cultural character what life-stories are to personal character. Only after a culture has grown to maturity is there any question as to the "truth" embodied in its myths. For example, it was only after the ancient culture of Greece had matured that there emerged a debate over the truthfulness of its founding myths. Plato, for example, criticized these trenchantly, exalting reason instead as the only trustworthy means for probing reality. But neither the ancient debate nor the entrenchment of the rational scientific method after the Renaissance succeeded in eliminating the need for myth in Western civilization. On the contrary, even today there is an urgent penchant in all human beings to make use of and produce narrative accounts —factual and fictional—to explain who we are and why we are here. The details of the stories change from culture to culture, but they all reflect the same *narrative structure*: i.e. the same kinds of thematic units, plot lines, character types, etc. The study of this structure in ancient myths comes under the semiotic rubric of *mythology*, and the general study of storytelling under that of *narratology*.

In this chapter, our journey through the realm of culture takes us to the region inhabited by *Homo mythologicus*, the storyteller. We will stop in various areas of this region to look at the many fruits that the narrative instinct has yielded and continues to allow human beings to harvest. Studying the ways in which narratives give sense and purpose to human existence is, needless to say, a fundamental focus of any semiotic approach to the study of culture.

10.1 NARRATIVE REPRESENTATION

A *narrative* is a *text* that is constructed to describe a sequence of events or actions that are felt to be logically connected to each other or causally intertwined in some way. The narrative sequence may be purely fact-based, as in a newspaper report, a psychoanalytic session, etc., or fictional, as in a novel, a fairy-tale, etc. Needless to say, it is often difficult, if not impossible, to determine the boundary line between fact and fiction. Indeed, even in the recounting of life-stories, fiction is often intermingled with fact in order to give the stories more coherence and thus credibility. Incidentally, this is called the "Othello effect" by psychologists, who characterize it as a kind of lying in order to emphasize the truth.

The narrative text typically shows a three-layer structure; i.e. its meaning is anchored in (1) the main *text*, (2) a *subtextual* layer, and (3) an *intertextual* layer. The term *subtext* designates any implicit narrative within the text that is not immediately accessible to interpretation. A subtext is, in other words, a text within the main text, which is subject to the interpretation of the listener/reader. An *intertext* is a narrative to which a text alludes by implication. It is a text from outside the main text. Access to that intertext requires knowledge of the signifying order. Subtextuality and intertextuality reveal that the narratives of the signifying order are interconnected with each other (the *interconnectedness principle*). For example, the main text of the movie *Blade Runner* (chapter 8, §8.5) unfolds as a science fiction detective story, but its subtext is, arguably, a religious text—the search for a Creator. This interpretation is bolstered by the many intertextual allusions to Biblical themes and symbols in the movie. Many narratives are constructed in this way. Understanding the narrative, therefore, is dependent upon the listener's/reader's knowledge of the culture's intertextuality, i.e. of the culture's network of existing texts to which the maker of a text alludes.

In dimensionality terms, the narrative is perceived as a text at a firstness level, i.e. as something constructed to convey meaning. At a secondness level, the meanings the maker of the narrative is presumed to want are perceived as implicit within the text. This is the subtextual dimension, which is in large part subject to secondness (individual) interpretations of the text. At a thirdness level, the narrative reveals what textual resources already existing in the signifying order the narrative-maker has drawn upon, linking h/er narrative to the culture's meaning pathways (intertextuality):

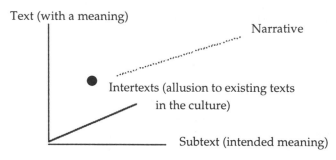

Narrative texts can be verbal, nonverbal, or a combination of both. An example of a verbal narrative is a short story; an example of a non-verbal narrative is a silent movie that tells the story through image sequences; and an example of combined verbal-nonverbal narrative is a comic book. The three structural features of all narratives are *plot*, *character*, and *setting*. The *plot* is basically what the narrative is all about; it is a kind of macro-referent, to which the narrative draws attention. *Character* refers to the embodiment of human personality features in the people who are the perpetrators and/or participants in the plot. The *setting* is the location where, and the time when, the plot takes place. The teller of the story is called the *narrator*. The narrator can be a character of the narrative, the author of the narrative, or some other person. Each type of narrator provides a different perspective on the story for the reader. The reader can thus feel a part of the narrative, looking at the action as if s/he were in it (*looking from within*); or aloof from it, looking at the action as if from the outside (*looking from without*).

The novel *Flatland: A Romance of Many Dimensions*, written by the literary critic Edwin A. Abbott (1838–1926), is an exceptional case-in-point of a narrative that provides the reader literally with both perspectives. The characters of the novel are personified geometrical figures, known as Flatlanders, living in a two-dimensional universe called Flatland. Flatlanders can only see each other as dots or lines, even if they are, from our vantage point as readers, circles, squares, triangles, etc. The novel provides us with this perspective by projecting us into the mind of a Flatlander. To grasp what kind of perspectival view this entails, one should imagine Flatland as the flat surface of a table. A Flatlander can see figures in only one dimension: i.e. as dots or lines depending on their orientation (*looking from within*). For example, if one looks at a paper circle lying on the table, with the eyes level with the table's surface, s/he will see the edge of the circle as a line. The same applies to any other shape. The only way, then, to distinguish a circle from a straight line, an ellipse, or any other figure is to view Flatland from a vantage point above it, i.e. to look down at the shapes from above the table. This three-dimensional viewing of the figures constitutes a *looking from without* perspective. It literally provides the reader with a different view of Flatland and its inhabitants. Similarly, although the perspective in most novels is not "virtual" as it is in *Flatland*, the reader's understanding of any narrative is invariably conditioned by one of these two mental vantage points—*looking from within* and *looking from without*.

Fiction

By and large, people think of narrative as *fiction* (from Latin *fingere* "to form, make, put together"). But fictional narration did not become prevalent until the Middle Ages. That was the era when people started inventing romances, novellas, and, a little later, novels. Before the Middle Ages, people may have indeed created fictional stories, such as fables, tales, and legends, but these did not serve the same function that fiction has fulfilled since the medieval era—the telling of stories for the sake of the telling. The ancient dramas, fables, tales, etc. were not fictional in the post-medieval sense. They were imaginative portrayals of mythic themes.

But there is some evidence that fictional narrativity has ancient roots nonetheless. Papyri from the fourth Egyptian Dynasty report on how King Cheops (2590–2567 BC) delighted in hearing the fictional stories that his sons told him. The Greek statesman and general Aristides (530?–468? BC), moreover, wrote a collection of what we would now call short stories about his hometown, Miletus, to celebrate the Greek victory over the Persians at Salamis. The Latin *Golden Ass* of Apuleius (125?–200? AD) was also a fictional narration aimed at providing social and moral commentary. But by and large the ancient world told tales of the gods or of human foibles. These were hardly perceived as fictional. Fiction became a standard narrative craft only after the Middle Ages, especially after the Italian Giovanni Boccaccio (1313–1375) wrote the *Decameron* (1351–1353), a collection of 100 fictional tales set against the gloomy background of the Black Death, as the bubonic plague that swept through Europe in the fourteenth century was called. The *Decameron* is the first real example of fiction in the modern sense. To escape an outbreak of the plague, ten friends decide to take refuge in a country villa outside Florence. There they entertain one another over a period of ten days with a series of stories told by each member of the party in turn. Each day's storytelling ends with a *canzone*, a short lyric poem. The *Decameron* is thus crafted from fictional stories, unfolding as a penetrating analysis of human character.

Ever since, fictional narration has been a yardstick for probing human actions and human character. This is probably because its structure (*plot-character-setting*) is felt to reflect the structure of real-life events, of which the narrator may not even be consciously aware: i.e. the narration is felt to be already implicit in the form of the actions and events that are manifest in actual human lives. In a sense, narrative creates reality as a sequence of purposeful actions connected by its very structure to each other.

The reality-inducing effect of narrative structure was evident a few decades ago in a popular program on American television called *Wild Kingdom*. The show purported to explain animal behavior in scientific terms. Each week, a film would be made of animals eating, hunting, mating, etc. Unedited, the actions of the animals caught on film would hardly make up a meaningful story line. But with the help of film editors and scriptwriters the program produced an intriguing narrative account of the actions dispersed randomly on the unedited film. Although the program's creators may have extracted their ideas from scientific sources, the particular ways in which they explained the animals' actions constituted a human plot. The result was a weekly dose of human narrative about animals put together by the program's film editors, directors, and scriptwriters.

Vladimir Propp

The serious study of narrative structure in semiotics can be traced to the work of Vladimir Propp (1928), who argued persuasively that ordinary discourse was built upon this very structure. According to Propp, there exist a relatively small number of "narrative units," or plot themes, which go into the make-up of a "plot grammar." The term sometimes used to refer to these units is *narrames*. Propp then went on to suggest that plot grammar was as intrinsic to human cognitive processes as was linguistic grammar.

Propp's theory would, in effect, explain why narrative is the medium through which children learn about the world. Stories of imaginary beings and events allow children to make sense of the real world, providing the intelligible formats that mobilize the child's natural ability to learn from context. The psychologist Jerome Bruner (1986) has argued, similarly, that narrative thinking underlies how we come to understand ourselves and the social world in which we live. Narratives give pattern and continuity to the child's raw perception and experience. They impart the sense that there is a *plot* to life, that the *characters* in it serve some meaningful purpose, and that the *setting* of life is part of the human condition. Children respond to plot, character, and setting without training. They instinctively understand any discourse that links events in a narrative way. By age four or five, children are able to manage and negotiate narratives by themselves, especially during play, when they create imaginary narratives designed to allow others watching them a framework for interpreting their actions.

A. J. Greimas

After Propp, the semiotician who most influenced the study of narrative was Algirdas Julien Greimas (1917–1992). Greimas' main contribution to the theory of narrative was his discovery that the stories of different cultures were devised with virtually the same stock of actions, characters, motifs, themes, and settings. These make up what he called a "narrative grammar." This grammar, Greimas remarked, seems invariably to involve:

- a *subject* (the hero of the plot)

- who desires an *object* (a person, a magic sword, etc.)

- and who encounters an *opponent* (a villain, a false hero, a trial situation, etc.)

- and then finds a *helper* (a donor)

- who then gets an *object* from a *sender* (a dispatcher)

- and gives it to a *receiver*;

- etc.

In order to explain the passage from these categories, which Greimas called *actants*, to actual narrative discourse, he posited the presence of a "generative trajectory" in the human mind that maps the actants onto other constituents of a social interaction to produce the discourses that make up a large portion of human communication. An actant can be converted into various story roles at a certain number of specified positions on its narrative trajectory. At the actual level of telling, one actant can be represented by several actors, and several actants by one and the same actor. In a mystery novel, for instance, the subject, or hero, may have several enemies, all of whom function actantially as an opponent. In a love story, a male lover may function as both object and sender. A simple application of actantial theory to a novel such as *Madame Bovary* (1857) by Gustave Flaubert (1821–1880) would go somewhat like this:

> • *subject*   = Emma
>
> • *object*   = happiness
>
> • *sender*   = romantic literature
>
> • *receiver*   = Emma
>
> • *helper*   = Léon, Rodolphe
>
> • *opponent*   = Charles, Yonville, Rodolphe, Homais, L'heureux.

10.2 MYTH

The word *myth* derives from the Greek *mythos* "word," "speech," "tale of the gods." A myth is a narrative in which the characters are gods, heroes, and mystical beings, the plot revolves around the origin of things or around dramatic human events, and the setting is a metaphysical world juxtaposed against the real world. In the beginning stages of human cultures, myths functioned as genuine narrative theories of the world. This is why all cultures have created them to explain their origins: the Zuñi people, for instance, claim to have emerged from a mystical hole in the earth, thus establishing their kinship with the land; Rome was said to have been founded by Romulus, who as an infant had to be suckled by a wolf, thus alluding to a certain fierceness; and the list could go on and on. Myths create a metaphysical knowledge system for explaining human origins and actions. And this system is the one to which we instinctively resort even today for imparting knowledge of values and morals initially to children. It also manifests itself latently in other ways. Climatologists, for example, refer to the warming of the ocean surface off the western coast of South America that occurs every 4 to 12 years as a person, *El Niño* ("the little one" in Spanish). Although modern people do not believe *El Niño* to be a person, they nonetheless find it somehow more appropriate to blame an imaginary being for certain weather repercussions. The difference between a current-day imaginary being like *El Niño* and an early cultural one is that the latter was believed to be a real being (a god, a hero, etc.).

Types of Myth

The most important myth in a culture, known as the *cosmogonic* myth, explains how the world came into being. In some cosmogonic accounts, the world is created from nothing; in others it emerges from the lower worlds. *Eschatological* myths, on the other hand, describe the end of the world. These usually predict the destruction of the world by a divine being who will send human beings either to a paradisiacal existence or to one of eternal torment, depending on the ways in which people have lived their lives. An apocalypse, i.e. a universal fire and a final battle of the gods, is a central theme of eschatological mythology. To counteract the apocalypse, many cultures tell myths of birth and rebirth which inform people how life can be renewed or which tell them about the coming of an ideal society or of a savior. Myths of the *culture hero* are also common. These describe beings who discover a cultural artifact or technological process that radically changes the course of history.

Rarely do we realize how much of the representational fabric of modern cultures is cut from myth. From the Germanic and Roman myths we have inherited, for instance, the names of most of the days of the week and months of the year: e.g. Tuesday is the day dedicated to the Germanic war god Tiu; Wednesday to the chief god Wotan, Thursday to Thor, Friday to the goddess of beauty Frigga; and Saturday is dedicated to the Roman god Saturn, *January* to Janus, and so on. Our planets bear a similar pattern of nomenclature: Mars is named after the Roman god of war, Venus after the Roman god of love, etc. The residues of mythic thinking can also be seen in the fact that we continue to read horoscopes, implore the gods to help us, cry out against Fortune, and so on.

The narrative structure of myths imparts coherence and plausibility to forms of cultural representation. The characters in myths are the beings that early peoples imagined to be the perpetrators of, or masterminds behind, the events that occur in Nature and in human life. Notions of destiny, fate, fortune, etc. are all derivatives of this form of thinking. The mythic plots revolved around the actions of these characters. For example, to explain climatological events, the ancient Romans invented Neptune, the god of the sea and brother of Jupiter, the supreme god of the skies. Originally a god of springs and streams, Neptune became identified with the Greek god of the sea, Poseidon. The myth of Neptune is a story created to explain the interconnectedness of natural phenomena, thus giving a metaphysical coherence to the world. The French anthropologist Claude Lévi-Strauss (1908–) even saw myth as the original source for the parts of speech in language. Lévi-Strauss (1978) pointed out that certain clusters of relationships in myth, as expressed in the narrative text, conform to the systematic order of the language's structure.

Views of Myth

The Italian philosopher Giambattista Vico (chapter 2, §2.1) claimed that the original mythic stories led to the foundation of the first cultural spheres and institutions (chapter 1, §1.6). The gradual increase of control humans had over their environment and the increasing complexity of human institutions were then reflected in the functions that new gods assumed. For Vico, myth was constructed on the basis not of a rational logic but of what he called a poetic logic, a form of thinking based upon, and guided by, conscious bodily experiences that were transformed into generalized ideas. The course that humanity runs, according to Vico, goes from an early mythical age, through a heroic one, to a rational one. Each age has its own kind of culture, art, language, social institutions, and narratives—the poetic mentality, for instance, generated myths; the heroic one, legends; and the rational one, narrative history.

In myth, psychoanalysts find traces to the psychic motivations and complexes of individuals. Sigmund Freud (1913), for instance, saw the conflicts recounted in myths as attempts to come to grips with unconscious psychic life. In the myth of Oedipus—the king who was abandoned at birth and unwittingly killed his father and then married his mother—he found a narrative paradigm for explaining a subconscious sexual desire in a child for the parent of the opposite sex, usually accompanied by hostility to the parent of the same sex. Carl Jung (1965) saw in such stories evidence for a collective unconscious in the human species which seeks expression through narrative. The American mythologist Joseph Campbell (1904–1987) added that the mythic characters were essentially the first archetypes (chapter 1, §1.2)—literally, original models of abstract concepts.

Two interesting views of myth were set forth by the Romanian-born historian of religion Mircea Eliade (1907–1986) and the French sociologist Émile Durkheim (1858–1917). In Eliade's interpretation, myth reveals an explanation of the nature of being. This is why modern peoples use mythic stories to rediscover and reexperience their own nature. Durkheim rejected the notion that myth arises in response to extraordinary manifestations of Nature. To Durkheim, Nature was a model of regularity and thus predictable and ordinary. He concluded that myths arose as emotional responses to social existence, thus constituting a narrative moral code and a system of historical reasoning. Myths and the rituals stemming from them sustain and renew moral systems, keeping them from being forgotten, and they bind people socially. Durkheim thus argued for a psychic continuity between myth and religious experiences. He explained the remarkable similarity among the world's myths with a pre-Jungian theory of "collective conscious," by which the basic ingredients of myth—the plots, characters, actions, themes, etc.—were actually part of the human brain and thus common to every human being. These mythic patterns were molds, or templates, from which the different myths were made:

> The collective conscious is the highest form of the psychic life, since it is the consciousness of the consciousness. Being placed outside and above all individual and local contingencies, it sees things in this permanent and essential aspect, which it crystallizes into communicable ideas...it alone can furnish the mind with the molds which are applicable to the totality of things and which make it possible to think of them (Durkheim 1912: 12).

Most semioticians would agree with Durkheim. The work in narratology has revealed, above all else, that the narrative structure of myths provides the categories of the plot grammars that underlie all the stories we tell, from the ancient tragedies to the detective stories of today. In this explanatory framework, stories are said to have a denotative surface structure and an unconscious mythical one. The surface level narrates the story as a series of connected real-time events or images. But the events themselves, and the nature of their connectivity, are reflexes of the mythic categories hidden below; i.e. the surface elements cohere into a *signifier* that has an underlying mythic *signified* that works at a subtextual level. As Key (1989: 149) has aptly put it: "Humans label consciously, but symbolic significance remains at an unconscious level."

The anthropologist Bronislaw Malinowski (chapter 1, §1.1) further refined this sociological and evolutionary conception of myth. For Malinowski, myth fulfilled an indispensable function—it expressed, enhanced, and codified belief, safeguarding morality by providing practical rules for the guidance of individuals. So, Malinowski suggested, the mythical perception of plants, for instance, was the practical and cultural basis for the domestication of plant life, and agriculture itself became part of a perception both of cosmic order and of the structure of society. Certain other myths and rites had as their function the replenishment of life. Such myths and rites were so generalized in their relation to the signifying order that religious and mythical meaning was given to the entire culture. For example, in Indo-European cultures myth reflects a tripartite structure that is extended to the social structure, with a priest or ruler at the top of a hierarchy, warriors in the middle, and farmers, herdsmen, and craftsmen at the base. These classes are correlated with cosmic deities; and in the narrative plots of the myths the interrelationships, antagonisms, and conflicts among these three classes are dramatized. This structure operates as an archetypal language for the statement of ideal meanings within Indo-European cultures. In effect, Malinowski argued that, in its primitive form, myth was not merely a story, but a lived reality. It was not fictional, and like any sacred story it lives on in our rituals, governing our modes of perception and controlling our conduct.

The German philosopher Ernst Cassirer (1946) allied himself, instead, with those who saw myth as arising from an emotional response to Nature—awe of thunder, fear of lightning, etc. He stressed, however, that myth was not identical with the emotion from which it arose, but that it was the expression—the objectification—of the emotion. In this expression or objectification, the identity and basic values of the group were given an absolute meaning.

The most popularized studies of myths in the twentieth century were those of the American scholar Joseph Campbell (e.g. 1949, 1969). In his bestselling books, Campbell combined insights from Jungian psychoanalysis, theories of history, and linguistic analysis to formulate a general theory of the origin, development, and unity of all human cultures. If there is thunder in the sky, and one lacks the notion of "thunder," then it can be explained as the angry voice of a god; if there is rain, then it can be explained as the weeping of the gods; and so on. A myth is a telling of events that holds past, present, and future together for a specific culture. For this reason, Campbell claimed, the earliest myths constituted the foundational fabric of culture.

10.3 MYTHOLOGIES

The gist of the work in semiotic mythology suggests that the original mythic themes and symbols continue to reverberate in the signifying orders of modern-day societies. To distinguish between the original myths and their modern-day versions, the semiotician Roland Barthes (1915–1980) designated the latter *mythologies* (1957). Mythologies are modern-day reflexes of mythic themes, plots, and characters. In early Hollywood westerns, for instance, the mythic theme of good vs. evil manifested itself in various symbolic and expressive ways: e.g. cowboy heroes wore white hats and villains black ones.

A mythology often manifests itself as ritualistic behavior. Sports events, for example, are mythological dramas pitting the good (the home team) against the bad (the visiting team). The whole fanfare associated with preparing for a "big event," like the Super Bowl of American football, has a ritualistic quality similar to the pomp and circumstance that the mythic armies engaged in before going out to battle and war. Indeed, the whole event is perceived to be a mythic battle. The symbolism of the home team's (army's) uniform, the valor and strength of the players (the heroic warriors), and the skill and tactics of the coach (the army general) have a powerful effect on the home fans (one of the two warring nations). The game (the battle) is somehow felt to unfold in metaphysical terms, i.e. as a struggle of Herculean proportions between the forces of good and evil in the universe. Sports figures are exalted as heroes or condemned as villains.

A mythology can also take the form of a concept or social trend. Childhood, for instance, emerged as a mythology during the Industrial Revolution, when for the first time in Western social history children were considered to be at a stage of life as yet uncorrupted and untainted by civilization (chapter 9, §9.2). This concept did not exist in previous eras, nor is it a universal one today in other cultures. Children are different from adults, not any better or worse. They may lack adult social, cognitive, and linguistic skills, but their behavior ranges considerably. The image of children as pure and innocent is part of a *mythology*, not a psychology or sociology, of childhood. A child has no awareness whatsoever of being pure or innocent—adults do. In medieval and Renaissance paintings there are no children as such, at least not in the mythological way we think of them today. The new social order brought about by the Industrial Revolution, and the idealized notions of childhood expressed by the Romantic artists of the nineteenth century, generated the mythology, proclaiming children vastly different from adults, giving them a new pristine identity as innocent, faultless, impressionable, malleable creatures.

Barthes emphasized that most of our rituals and social concepts are mythological. Whether or not people are conscious of this, Barthes' theory would explain rather well why it is that so many of us become involved emotionally in such spectacles as sports events and such notions as childhood. As Barthes claimed, mythologies tap psychically into ancient themes that continue to inform our daily life schemes. If Barthes is right, then mythological thinking, which originally served a mystical and cosmological function—explaining what the universe is all about and how we fit into the scheme of things—has gradually taken on sociological and pedagogical functions, supporting and validating a certain social order and instructing individuals of that order how to conduct their lives.

Mythologies are carved into the stories we tell, the laws we enact, the behaviors we perform ritualistically, and so on. A contemporary medium for shaping mythologies is television—a topic to which we will turn in chapter 11. The situation comedy (sitcom), for instance, is where many modern-day mythologies related to family life are made, developed, and even eventually discarded. Consider, as a case-in-point, the mythological development of TV fatherhood from the 1950s to the late 1990s.

In the 1950s television programs like *Father Knows Best* and *The Adventures of Ozzie and Harriet* sculpted the father figure to fit the mold of the traditional patriarchal family. Most of those early sitcoms painted a rose-tinted picture of the family. The father was in charge, with his wife working behind the scenes to maintain harmony through subservience. This mythology was given a narrative form for people to enjoy on a weekly basis, allowing them to evaluate their own family situations by comparison. There were two notable exceptions to this, *The Honeymooners* and *I Love Lucy*, both of which revolved around strong-willed wives who were, in effect, precursors of later TV feminist characters. But in general the subtext to the 1950s TV sitcom was: *father = godlike know-all and be-all.*

In the 1960s and early 1970s sitcom mythology changed drastically. The TV father was becoming more and more of a ludicrous character. The sitcom that reflected this new subtext most clearly was *All in the Family*. America was divided, ideologically and emotionally, into two camps—those who supported the views and attitudes of the TV father, Archie Bunker, a staunch defender of the Vietnam War, and those who despised them. What was happening inside the Bunker family was apparently happening in families across the continent. American society had entered into a period of emotional turmoil and bitter debate over such controversial issues as the Vietnam War, racism, the role of women in society, and the validity of the patriarchal family. The new subtext that was informing the sitcoms of the late 1960s and early 1970s was *father = a fallen god, an opinionated, ludicrous character*. Throughout the 1970s and 1980s, programs such as *The Mary Tyler Moore Show, Wonder Woman, Rhoda, Maude, The Days and Nights of Molly Dodd, Cagney and Lacey*, and others started focusing more on women, portraying strong, independent women who were attempting to survive, socially and professionally, in a world that was disassembling patriarchal structures.

It is interesting to note that in the midst of that mythological reconfiguration, a program like *The Bill Cosby Show* achieved unexpected success in the 1980s. In hindsight, we can see a number of reasons for the success of that apparent throwback to the patriarchal programs of the 1950s. First and foremost was the fact that Bill Cosby himself was a great comedian who could easily endear himself to a large audience. But, more importantly, the *Cosby Show* was appropriate for the 1980s. Throughout the 1970s, programs like *All in the Family* and *The Jeffersons* were reflexes of a social movement to tear down patriarchal authority. But during the 1980s, with the ascendancy of a new right-wing moralism, the mythology of the family patriarch was making a comeback.

Once more, audiences were searching for TV father figures who were morally strong, but gentle and understanding at the same time. Bill Cosby fit this image perfectly. But there was a difference. Unlike the wife in *Father Knows Best*, Cosby's wife had an assertive role to play in the family. This "new-look" patriarchal family provided reassurance of the strength of traditional values in a world that was, and continues to be, in constant moral doubt and flux.

The total deconstruction of the 1950s mythology of patriarchal fatherhood became apparent in many of the 1980s and 1990s sitcoms. A typical example was *Married...with Children*, a morbid parody of fatherhood and of the nuclear family. The father on this program, Al Bundy, was little more than a physical brute, a reprehensible character who was hardly deserving of the title of *father*. Indeed, as the name of the sitcom suggested, he was merely married and just happened to have children, who were just as shallow and despicable as he was—Bud, his boorish, sex-crazed son, and Kelly, his empty-headed and over-sexed daughter. There was no sugar-coating in that sitcom. *Married...with Children* was implanted on a new parodic subtext: *the father = moron*.

10.4 THE NOVEL

There are many types of narrative. But perhaps the most widely influential one in history, before the advent of cinema, has been the *novel*. Although we read a novel like a text, we recall and interpret it as a sign with a specific meaning. That is why we say "The novel meant..." and then proceed to provide a single interpretation of its meaning. The meaning can, of course, occur on various connotative levels. But all connotations seem to coalesce around a basic core interpretation.

The plots, characters, and settings that well-known novels portray are subsequently diffused throughout the signifying order of culture. Hence, children are sometimes named after characters in novels, real places after places described in novels, and so on. The general meaning of the novel, moreover, is often used as a template for evaluating some real-life event or action in a society. It is amazing indeed to contemplate that a text that is essentially a lie (fiction), is used nevertheless to get at the truth, about people, life, and the universe. This suggests that human representational activity is a way of telling lies in order to grasp truth.

As mentioned above (§10.1), fictional narratives were composed in the ancient world, and to these the term *novel* is sometimes applied. But the novel did not emerge as an autonomous narrative fictional form until the Middle Ages. Actually, for the sake of historical accuracy, many scholars regard the eleventh century *Tale of Genji*, by the Japanese baroness Murasaki Shikibu (978?–1026?), as the first true novel, since it depicts the amorous adventures of a fictional Prince Genji and the staid lives of his descendants. The novel paints a charming and apparently accurate picture of Japanese court life in the Heian period. Among the novel's chief delights are the portraits of the women in Prince Genji's life. These women are individually characterized, with their aristocratic refinements, talents in the arts of music, drawing, and poetry, and love for the beauties of nature. As the work nears its conclusion, the tone becomes more mature and somber, colored by Buddhist insight into the fleeting joys of earthly existence.

Fiction can be said to start in the West with the long verse tale, the prose romance, and the Old French *fabliau* in the medieval period, culminating, as mentioned above (§10.1), with Boccaccio's *Decameron*. Advances were made in Spain during the sixteenth century with the so-called picaresque novel, in which the hero is typically a vagabond who goes through a series of exciting adventures. The classic example is the novel by Spanish writer Miguel de Cervantes Saavedra (1547–1616), *Don Quixote de la Mancha* (Part I, 1605, Part II, 1615), which is considered the first truly great novel of the Western world.

The novel became the dominant and most popular form of narrative art in the eighteenth and nineteenth centuries, as more and more writers started devoting their lives to this art form. Novels became more psychologically real, depicting and often satirizing contemporary life and morals. During this same era, the novel spawned its own genres, including the didactic novel, in which theories of education and politics were expressed, and the Gothic novel, in which the emotion of horror was evoked by depictions of supernatural happenings. The first Gothic novel was *The Castle of Otranto* (1764) by Horace Walpole (1717–1797). But perhaps the most well-known example of the genre is *Frankenstein* (1818) by Mary Wollstonecraft Shelley (1797–1851). One of the most enduring genres of the period is the comedy of manners, which is concerned with the clash between characters from different social backgrounds. The novels of Jane Austen (1775–1817) are considered by many to be the most important of the genre.

Throughout the nineteenth century, and for most of the twentieth, the novel was a powerful medium for probing human nature and human society. Novelists were as popular and well known as media personalities are today. Their critiques of society led to social change; their portrayal of human actions gave the early psychologists insights into how to investigate human character. The French writer Marcel Proust (1871–1922), for instance, explored the nature of memory; the German author Thomas Mann (1875–1955) searched for the roots of psychic angst in social systems; and English authors Virginia Woolf (1882–1941) and James Joyce (1882–1941) plumbed the emotional source of human thoughts and motivations. Since the end of World War II the novels of an increasing number of writers in developing or socially troubled countries have come to the forefront. Many of these portray with vivid realism the clash between classes and races, the search for meaning in a world where materialism reigns supreme, and the desire to reform the world.

Narrative techniques in novels vary from simple first-person storytelling to complex stream-of-consciousness narration, designed to reveal a character's feelings, thoughts, and actions, often following an associative rather than a logical sequence, without commentary by the author. The latter technique is considered by many to be the maximal achievement of the novel form. Not to be confused with interior monologue, it attempts to portray the remote, preconscious state that exists before the mind organizes sensations. The term "stream of consciousness" was first used by William James (1842–1910), the American philosopher and psychologist. Major exponents of the form were American novelist William Faulkner (1897–1962), British writer Virginia Woolf (1882–1941), and Irish writer James Joyce (1882–1941), who perhaps brought the technique to its highest point of development in *Ulysses* (1922) and *Finnegans Wake* (1939). In these novels the inaccessible corners of human memory and the recurrent repertory of feeling and form within the psyche are laid bare before us.

As mentioned previously, cinema has taken over from the novel as the main narrative art form of the contemporary world. But often a novel is the inspiration for a movie script. The conversion of novel to cinematic form is possible because the two tap the same narrative structures. In many ways the movie is a visual novel, with the role of the narrator taken over by the camera, and narrative perspective by the camera's angle.

Functions of the Novel

We have discussed above how narratives create meaning, imparting sense and purpose to human actions and natural events. This is why historical accounts are so believable—they are narratives that examine and interpret actions in ways that only narrative representation can. From myths to novels and comic books, narrative has had both a social and a philosophical function, helping people give expression to their unquenchable search for a purpose to life.

Traditional literary criticism has been dominated, in fact, by the concept of literature as an imitation of life. In the seventeenth and eighteenth centuries, novelists were thought to present realistic accounts of real life, with careful attention to lifelike detail, so as to commemorate historical events, encourage moral living, or inspire piety or patriotism. Others thought, moreover, that narrative art had the function of criticizing society so that it could be reformed. In the nineteenth century, however, a new view of writing emerged, which came to be known as the principle of "art for art's sake." Works of art were thought to have no other purpose than to give human intuitions material form. In the early twentieth century this principle was incorporated by writers such as August Strindberg (1849–1912) and Frank Wedekind (1864–1918) into their narratives.

Several powerful movements, however, came forward shortly thereafter to attack this principle. Twentieth-century Marxist critics, for instance, saw literary works as great only when they were progressive; that is, when they supported the causes of the society in which they were created. Freudian critics, instead, believed that the value of narrative art lay in its therapeutic nature. The conflicts, fantasies, and daydreams of fictional characters, they claimed, are those of ordinary people, and thus the narrative text can be used to provide a means for coming to grips with real-life conflicts, fantasies, and daydreams. The French philosopher and writer Jean-Paul Sartre (1905–1980), on the other hand, saw narrative art as an "escape hatch," so to speak, from inner psychic turmoil, because he saw it as eradicating the guilt from which people ordinarily suffer, thus opening the way for genuine emotional freedom.

Perhaps the most radical view of narrative ever to have been formulated comes from the pen of the French philosopher Jacques Derrida (1930–), who has contended that the traditional, or metaphysical, way of interpreting literary works makes a number of false assumptions about the nature of such texts. A traditional reader believes that the author of a text is the source of its meaning. Derrida has challenged both this belief and the idea that a text has an unchanging, unified meaning. The author's intentions in writing, Derrida has claimed, cannot be unconditionally accepted. There are, in fact, an infinite number of legitimate interpretations of a text.

10.5 THE COMICS

In closing this chapter, a comment upon a modern-day form of narrative, the *comics*, is in order, not only because it has become a target of great interest among cultural semioticians, but also because it exemplifies how narrative can involve the verbal and the nonverbal (visual) modes of representation in tandem. The predecessors of the modern-day comic book are the caricatures or satirical portraits of famous people that became popular in seventeenth century Italy. This art form spread quickly throughout Europe. In the early nineteenth century, caricatures were expanded to include speech balloons, giving birth to the modern comic. The modern form of the comic book came about between 1938 and 1945, the so-called "golden age" of comics.

Comics are narratives told by means of a series of drawings arranged in horizontal lines, strips, or rectangles, called panels, and read like a verbal text from left to right. The term applies especially to comic strips in newspapers but also to comic books. Comics usually depict the adventures of one or more characters in a limited time sequence. Dialogue is represented by words encircled by a line, called a *balloon*, which issues from the mouth or head of the character speaking.

One of the first American works with the essential characteristics of a comic strip was created by Richard Felton Outcault and appeared in the series *Hogan's Alley*, first published on May 5, 1895, in the New York *Sunday World*. The setting was squalid city tenements and backyards filled with dogs and cats, tough-looking characters, and ragamuffins. One of the urchins was a flap-eared, bald-headed, Oriental-looking child with a quizzical, yet shrewd, smile. He was dressed in a long, dirty nightshirt, which Outcault often used as a placard to comment on the cartoon itself. Two other early comics were the *Little Bears* by James Guilford Swinnerton, which first appeared in the San Francisco *Examiner* in 1892, and *The Katzenjammer Kids* by Rudolph Dirks, which first appeared in *The American Humorist* in 1897. Newly formed newspaper syndicates, such as King Features, founded in 1914, made the mass circulation of comics possible. Every small-town newspaper could obtain, for reprinting, templates of the strips from the syndicates, which employed comic-strip artists. Eventually American comic strips were distributed worldwide. *Blondie* by Chic Young became the most widely syndicated comic strip of the mid-twentieth century.

Mutt and Jeff first appeared as *Mr. A. Mutt* in a November 1907 issue of the *San Francisco Chronicle*. The comic strip subsequently was introduced to a wide audience by newly formed newspaper syndicates, and it became the first successful daily comic strip in the United States. To satisfy demand, newspapers published collections of the cartoons, and a 1911 *Mutt and Jeff* collection was one of the first comic books to be published. But the first comic book published independently of any newspaper, containing material specially prepared for it, was *The Funnies*, which ran for 13 issues in 1929. Starting in 1933, a number of comic books, again reprints of well-known newspaper comic strips such as *Joe Palooka* and *Connie*, were published and distributed as premiums with certain merchandise. The first comic book to be sold on newsstands was *Famous Funnies*, which appeared in 1934.

A great impetus was given to the publication of comic books by the phenomenal success in 1938 of *Action Comics*, of which the principal feature was the *Superman* comic strip, later published in *Superman* comic books. Since that time hundreds of comic books have been published, some containing collections of noted comic strips, others consisting of new material. Some deal with contemporary American life; some are condensations of literary classics; still others are adventure stories. Today the comic has become an intrinsic part of the Western signifying order's narrativity and intertextuality. Indeed, nearly all young people between 5 and 17 years of age read comic books regularly, catering to their narrative instinct through this "bimodal" (verbal and nonverbal) narrative medium.

Comics are narratives for the modern world, both reflecting modern life and helping to mold it. Even before the advent of television, they set the style for clothing, coiffure, food, manners, and mores. They have inspired plays, musicals, ballets, motion pictures, radio and television series, popular songs, books, and toys. Modern discourse is permeated with idioms and words created for the comics. For example, the code word for the Allied Forces on D-Day was "Mickey Mouse," and the password for the Norwegian Underground was "The Phantom." Numerous contemporary painters and sculptors have incorporated comics into their art works; motion picture directors have adapted techniques of the comics into their films.

A number of strips have also found a devoted following among intellectuals. *Krazy Kat*, for instance, has been regarded by many as one of the most amusing and imaginative works of narrative art ever produced in America. The art of Charles Schultz (1922–), too, falls into this category. His comic strip *Peanuts*, which was originally titled *Li'l Folks*, debuted in 1950, becoming one of the most popular comic strips in history, appearing in more than 2000 newspapers and translated into more than 24 languages. His characters—Charlie Brown; his sister Sally; his dog Snoopy; his friends Lucy, Linus, Schroeder, Peppermint Patty, and Marcie; and the bird Woodstock—have become icons of pop culture.

The comic book genre is, in sum, extremely well-suited for a generation used to watching television and going to the movies. It is a visually oriented narrative form that fits in well with the populist view of art as a consumable commodity.

11

TELEVISION AND ADVERTISING

*The postmodernists have been fasci-
nated by this whole degraded landscape of schlock and kitsch, of TV series and Reader's Digest culture, of
advertising and motels.*

Jameson (1991: 2)

11.0 PRELIMINARY REMARKS

In this chapter our trek through the domain of culture reaches its destination—the modern world, a world characterized above all else by a reliance on *visual media*, especially television and advertising, for its daily textuality. The focus in the previous chapters was on the nature and type of signs that human beings create, and the codes and sign systems into which these cohere. In this chapter the focus will change somewhat, in that we will be looking more closely at the nature and role of *media* in representation. The *medium* can be defined simply as the physical means by which a sign or text is encoded (put together) and through which it is transmitted (delivered). Before the advent of alphabets (chapter 5, §5.5) the primary media were the oral-auditory and the pictographic ones. With the invention of the alphabet principle, a radical change occurred in human cognitive and cultural life, a change the philosopher Thomas Kuhn (1922–1996) aptly called a "paradigm shift" (1970).

From the Middle Ages to the 1950s, print was the primary medium through which people sought insight, authority, and guidance. As we saw previously (chapter 9, §9.4), McLuhan called the world of print the "Gutenberg Galaxy." But there is no doubt that another paradigm shift has occurred since the middle part of the twentieth century, whereby visual media like the cinema and TV have taken over the role of written texts. Television in particular has instilled its own form of visual literacy that informs, stimulates, and engages more people than at any other time in human history.

Today, scientific research papers on the effects visual media purportedly wreak on individuals and on society at large are proliferating.

Many blame the media for causing virtually everything from obesity to street violence. Are they right? Has television spawned the sordidness that many think now characterizes contemporary society? Are the people who "scream and shout hysterically at rock concerts and later in life at religious revival meetings" the victims of electronic media, as Key (1989: 13) suggests? There is no doubt that TV has had an effect on behavior, but then so has every *social text* of the past—from religious texts to novels. In actual fact, TV is hardly ever innovative or emotionally persuasive. It generates images that reinforce already-forged lifestyle behaviors. To do otherwise would be a commercially risky venture, as the ratings that TV executives ask for regularly confirm.

11.1 TELEVISION

In 1884 the German engineer Paul Nipkow designed a scanning disk that created crude television images. Nipkow's scanner was used from 1923 to 1925 in experimental television systems. Then, in 1926 the Scottish scientist John Logie Baird (1888–1946) perfected the scanning method, and in 1931 the Russian-born engineer Vladimir Zworykin (1889–1982) built the electronic scanning system that became the prototype of the modern TV camera. The first home television receiver was exhibited in Schenectady, New York, in 1928, by American inventor Ernst F. W. Alexanderson. The images were small, poor, and unsteady, but the set was a portent of what was to come.

By the late 1930s, television service was in place in several Western countries. The British Broadcasting Corporation, for example, started a regular service in 1936. By the early 1940s there were 23 television stations operating in the United States. But it was not until the early 1950s that technology had advanced to the point that it became affordable for virtually every American household to own a television set. Immediately thereafter, TV took an emotional stranglehold on society. Television personages became household names, looming larger than life. Actors and announcers became lifestyle trend-setters. People began more and more to plan their daily lives around television programs.

Throughout the 1950s and 1960s television programming developed rapidly into more than an assortment of fact and fiction narratives; it became itself a *social text* for an increasingly larger segment of society. Today, 98% of American households own a television set, and many of them have more than one. People depend on television a large portion of their information, intellectual stimulation, and recreation. Many have become emotionally dependent upon TV, displaying withdrawal-like symptoms if denied access to TV for even a short period of time.

McLuhan (1964) was among the first to decry that electronic media have an impact far greater than that of the material they communicate. He argued that in each culture the medium in which information is recorded and transmitted is decisive in determining the character of that culture. This is why an oral culture is vastly different in social organization and outlook than an alphabetic one. McLuhan also predicted that the worldwide linking of electronic media would create a "global village." And indeed, just as he foresaw, through advances in satellite communications, the world has become an electronic village.

Effects of TV

There are three main psychological effects that TV has had on society at large. These have been called various things by different social scientists. We will refer to them here as the *mythologizing effect*, the *history fabrication effect*, and the *cognitive compression effect*.

The term *mythologizing effect* refers to the fact that television personages are perceived as mythic figures, looming larger than life. Like any type of privileged space—a platform, pulpit, etc. that is designed to impart focus and significance to someone—television creates mythic heroes by simply containing them in its electronic space, where they are seen as suspended in time and space, in a mythic world of their own. To appreciate how emotionally powerful this effect is, the reader should think of how s/he would react to a favorite television personality coming to visit h/er in h/er own home. The reader certainly would not experience that person's presence as s/he would that of any other visitor. S/he would feel the TV personage's presence as constituting an event of momentous proportions, a visitation from an otherworldly being. Media personages are infused with this deified quality by virtue of the fact that they are seen inside the mythical space of the TV or cinematic screen. This is why meeting actors, musical stars, etc. causes great enthusiasm and excitement in many people. Media celebrities are the contemporary equivalents of the graven images of the Bible.

The term *history fabrication effect* refers to the fact that TV literally *fabricates* history by inducing the impression in viewers that some ordinary event—an election campaign, an actor's love affair, a fashion trend, etc.—is a momentous happening. People make up their minds about the guilt or innocence of others by watching news and interview programs; they see certain behaviors as laudable or damnable by tuning into talk shows or docudramas. In a phrase, the events that receive air time are felt to be more significant and historically meaningful to society than those that do not. A riot that gets air time becomes a consequential event; one that does not is ignored. This is why terrorists are seemingly more interested in simply getting on the air than in having their demands satisfied. TV imbues their cause with historical status and, therefore, with significance. Political and social protesters frequently inform the news media of their intentions, and then dramatically stage their demonstrations for the cameras. Sports events like the World Series, the Super Bowl, or the Stanley Cup Playoffs are transformed on television into Herculean struggles of mythic heroes. Events such as the John Kennedy and Lee Harvey Oswald assassinations, the Vietnam War, the Watergate hearings, the Rodney King beating, the O. J. Simpson trial, the Bill Clinton sex scandal, and the like are transformed into portentous and prophetic historical events. They are imbued with the same emotional power that comes from watching the great classical dramas. In a phrase, TV has become the maker of history and its documenter at the same time. People now experience history through TV, and as a result, television is shaping history. The horrific scenes coming out of the Vietnam War that were transmitted into people's homes daily in the late 1960s and early 1970s brought about an end to the war, by mobilizing social protest. Significantly, an MTV flag was hoisted by East German youths over the Berlin Wall as they tore it down in 1989. More people watched the wedding of England's Prince Charles and Lady Diana, and later Diana's funeral, than had ever before in human history simultaneously observed such events.

As mentioned, the *history-making* power of TV has led many to actually stage an event for the cameras. Anderson (1992: 125-130) calls these appropriately "pseudoevents." These are never spontaneous, but planned for the sole purpose of being put on television. Pseudoevents are usually intended to be self-fulfilling prophecies. The American invasion of Grenada on October 25, 1983, and the Gulf War during January and February of 1991 were concomitantly real events and pseudoevents. The actual military operations and conflicts were real events. But the reporting of these wars was orchestrated by a massive public-relations operation. Reporters were censored and kept away from the action so that the news coverage could be stylized and managed more effectively. The idea was to give the viewing public a military and social victory and, therefore, to allow Americans to "feel good about themselves." Pseudoevents constitute theater at its best, because they mesh reality (the real killing and terrorizing of people) with acting, drama, and narrative. As Anderson (1992: 126-127) aptly puts it, the "media take the raw material of experience and fashion it into stories; they retell the stories to us, and we call them reality."

Lastly, the *cognitive compression effect* refers to the fact that TV structures its stories, information, and events in compressed form for time-constrained transmission. This leaves little time for reflection on the topics, implications, ideas, etc. contained in a transmission, and has created a new way of cognizing and recognizing information that has produced both shorter attention spans and a need for constant variety in information content. TV has habituated people to large doses of information, cut up, packaged, and digested beforehand. This has fostered a psychological dependency on information and visual stimulation for their own sake. This is the reason why television is vastly more popular than reading. After work or school in the evenings, it is an arduous task to read a book, since it entails mental effort and thus causes a slowdown in information processing. TV viewing, on the other hand, is very easy. The images do the thinking for the viewer.

Take TV news programs as a case-in-point. The amount of information presented in a short period of time on a news program is torrential. We are able to take it all in superficially because the information is edited and stylized for effortless mass consumption. The camera moves in to select aspects of a situation, to show a face that cares, that is suffering, that is happy, that is angry, and then shifts to the cool handsome face of an anchorman or to the attractive one of an anchorwoman to tell us what it's all about. The news items, the film footage, the commentaries are all fast-paced and brief. They are designed to be visually dramatic snippets of easily digestible information. "Within such a stylistic environment," remarks Stuart Ewen (1988: 265), "the news is beyond comprehension." The facts of the news are subjected to the stylized signature of the specific news program—the same story will be interpreted differently according to who the television journalist is. Thus it is that as "nations and people are daily sorted out into boxes marked 'good guys,' 'villains,' 'victims,' and 'lucky ones,' style becomes the essence, reality becomes the appearance" (Ewen 1988: 265-266).

11.2 TV AS SOCIAL TEXT

Immediately following World War II four companies controlled network television broadcasting in the United States. Two of the companies, the National Broadcasting Company (NBC) and the Columbia Broadcasting System (CBS), had made vast fortunes in radio broadcasting. The remaining two were the American Broadcasting Company (ABC) and the DuMont Television Network; DuMont went out of business in 1955. By the mid-1950s NBC, CBS, and ABC—collectively known as the Big Three—had secured American network television as their exclusive domain. It was not until the mid-1980s that other companies broke their monopoly. At that time, moreover, cable television (television signals transmitted by cable to paying subscribers) ended channel scarcity.

Each network or specialty channel now attempts to attract either a large audience or a specific kind of audience (e.g. movie buffs) through programming, i.e. through the allocation of programs at specific times of the day that will maximize viewership. When looked at globally, programming differences turn out to be matters of detail. Overall, programming patterns are facets of the larger *social text* that TV has become.

A *social text* is an overriding text that informs the entire culture. To see what this means, it is instructive to step back in time with our imaginations to some village in medieval Europe, with no TVs, no novels, no modern-day diversionary accouterments of any kind. What would daily life be like? How would common people organize their day? What *social text* would they likely be living by? It is likely that the daily life schemes of the individuals living in the village would be informed and guided by a Christian social text. Residues of this text are still around today. This is why many people in our society organize significant social activities on religious dates such as Christmas and Easter. In medieval Europe, the Christian text probably regulated one's entire day. In that era, people emphasized going to church regularly during the day and the week, lived by strict moral codes based on the Bible, and listened conscientiously to the dictates of clergymen. The underlying subtext of the medieval Christian social text was that each day brought one closer and closer to one's true destiny—salvation and an afterlife with God. Living according to that text no doubt imparted to many people a feeling of security, emotional shelter, and spiritual meaning.

During the Renaissance, the Enlightenment, and the Industrial Revolution, the Christian social text came to be gradually transformed into a more secular one by society at large. Today, unless someone has joined a religious community or has chosen to live strictly by the dictates of the Bible or some other religious text, the social text by which people live is hardly a religious one. We organize our day around work commitments and social appointments that have hardly anything to do with salvation, and only at those traditional points in the calendar year (Christmas, Easter, etc.) do we reinvest our secular text with its more traditional religious connotations. The secular social text necessitates partitioning the day into "time slots." This is why we depend so heavily upon such devices as clocks, watches, agendas, appointment books, calendars. We would be desperately lost without such things. In this regard, it is relevant to note that in his great 1726 novel *Gulliver's Travels*, Jonathan Swift (1667–1745) satirized the tendency of people to rely on the watch to organize their daily routines—the Lilliputians were baffled by Gulliver's inability to do anything without consulting his watch! Like Gulliver, modern individuals need to know continually what time it is in order to carry on with the normal conduct of their lives.

When television entered the social scene in the 1950s, it became almost instantly the *medium* through which the existing secular social text was delivered to society at large, and through which people thus gleaned information about how to conduct their lives. If the reader were to peruse the daily TV listings and start classifying the programs into morning, noon, and evening slots, s/he would get an idea of what this entails. With cable television and satellite dishes, the range of programming offered would, at first, appear to be a broad and highly varied one. But a closer critical look at the listings will reveal a different story.

Consider morning programming. The listings disclose that most of the programs are information shows (news, weather, sports), children's shows, fitness programs, and (later in the morning) talk and quiz shows. There is very little variation from this menu. One may, of course, subscribe to a cable movie channel or to some special-interest channel to suit one's fancy. But, as ratings research has shown, most people are inclined to watch the regular fare of morning programs. That part of the TV text changes somewhat on weekends, reflecting a different kind of social situation associated with Saturdays and Sundays. But on weekday mornings "Wake up, America" is the overall message of the TV text. As you wake up, "here's what you need to know," blurt out the newscasters. "Get into shape," exclaim the fitness instructors. "Because you're interested, meet people with weird or heart-wrenching stories," bellow the talk show hosts.

In the afternoon the primary type of program is the soap opera, which started on radio as a drama, typically performed as a serial with stock characters and plots of a sentimental nature. This genre was given its name because it was originally sponsored by soap detergent companies. Rather than go out and chitchat or gossip as did medieval people in village squares, people today do virtually the same thing by peering daily into the complicated lives of soap opera personages. The soaps put people on intimate terms with the private lives of make-believe lawyers, doctors, executives, and other glamorous personages. As social mores change, so do the soaps. One reflects the other.

The afternoon is also the time for TV's version of the medieval morality play. Talk shows, interview programs, and the like allow common people to reveal and confess their "sins" in public and, consequently, allow a large viewing audience to participate cathartically in acts of self-revelation and repentance. As Stern and Stern (1992: 123) write, talk shows "are a relief in the sense that it is always nice to see people whose problems are worse than yours." The afternoon is thus a time slot for moral drama, acted out upon a media stage that has replaced the pulpit as the platform on which moral issues are discussed and from which sin is condemned publicly. TV reporters and announcers, like medieval priests, comment morally upon virtually every medical and psychological condition known.

The third part of daily TV programming has traditionally been called "prime time," the period in the evenings, from about 7 PM to 10 PM, when the largest number of people are home to watch TV. The prelude to evening programming is, as it was for the morning component, the news hour. After this, quiz shows and gossip journalism maintain curiosity and interest, until family programming takes over for a couple of hours, with sitcoms, adventure programs, documentaries, movies, and the like. In the 1980s, soap operas were also introduced into this time frame. Prime-time programming meshes fictional narrative with moral and social messages for the entire family. Documentary programs, in particular, showcase real-life events, so that appropriate moral lessons can be learned.

Prime time is followed by "late night" programming—which constitutes a kind of coda to the TV text. There was nothing for medieval people to do past the early evening hours. If they did not go to bed early, then they would talk or pray. But in contemporary America, when the kids are safely in bed, programs allow viewers to indulge in prurient interests or more gossip. Under the cloak of darkness and with "innocent eyes and ears" fast asleep, one can fantasize and talk about virtually anything with social impunity.

TV Culture

Like any social text of the past, TV has become a primary agent for influencing social trends and bringing about social change. By showcasing significant events it often forces the hand of change. Indeed, without it, there probably would have been no civil rights legislation, no Vietnam War protests, no cynical reaction to politics after Watergate. TV programs have become pivotal also in raising consciousness vis-à-vis certain ethical and moral issues. Here's just a sampling of what kinds of issues TV showcased, for instance, over a 25-year period, from the late 1960s to the early 1990s:

1. In 1968 the science fiction series *Star Trek* featured the first interracial kiss in an episode titled *Plato's Stepchildren*.

2. In 1970 the first divorced couple appeared on the sitcom *The Odd Couple*.

3. In 1971 the sitcom *All in the Family* cast the first homosexual characters in prime time.

4. In 1973 the same program dealt with the topic of rape.

5. In 1977 the miniseries *Roots* was among the first to deal forcefully with the enduring problem of racism.

6. In 1991 the first scene of women kissing was aired on an episode of *L.A. Law.*

7. In 1992 an episode of *Seinfeld* dealt with one of the more taboo subjects of Western society at the time, masturbation.

With the advent of satellite transmission technology, TV's influence on cultural change now knows no political boundaries. When asked about the stunning defeat of communism in eastern Europe in the late 1980s, the Polish leader Lech Walesa was reported by the newspapers as saying that it "all came from the television set," implying that television had undermined the stability of the communist world's relatively poor and largely sheltered lifestyle with images of consumer delights seen in Western programs and commercials.

But along with the good comes the not-so-good. Today, we live in a global TV culture. Most people today cannot remember a time without a television set in their homes. There are several billion TV sets around the globe. Spending on television programming has reached hundreds of billions of dollars. As Marshall McLuhan had predicted, by century's end, television had indeed shrunk the world into a "global village." Demographic surveys show that people spend a significant amount of time in front of television sets, that watching TV is bringing about a gradual decline in reading, that the nation-state concept is gradually dissolving as ideas and images cross national boundaries daily through television channels. Television has changed the general shape of world culture, inducing an insatiable craving for entertainment, variety, and visual stimulation in people around the globe. As a consequence we are more apt than previous generations to want to know and do things quickly and without effort. The only real form of immunity against the barrage of TV images that assail us on a daily basis is knowledge of and respect for the history of the TV medium—what it has been and how it has evolved.

What Will Come after TV?

We should emphasize that this emotional dependency on TV is unlikely to be permanent. Nothing in human affairs is. But as we write, it is difficult to foresee what will come forward in the near future to replace TV. Maybe *virtual reality* will trigger the next paradigm shift. *Virtual reality* (VR) is a system of devices that enables users to move and react in a computer-simulated environment, sensing and manipulating virtual objects (objects in computer- or cyberspace) much as they would real objects. Participants have the feeling of being immersed in the simulated world. Virtual worlds are created by mathematical models and computer programs. VR simulations differ from other computer simulations in that they require special interface devices that transmit the sights, sounds, and sensations of the simulated world to the user. These devices also record and send the speech and movements of the participants to the simulation program. In effect, in the VR medium the human subject is interacting inside a world totally madeup, interacting with a pure representation.

To see in the virtual world, the user wears a head-mounted display (HMD) with screens directed at each eye. The HMD contains a position tracker to monitor the location of the user's head and the direction in which the user is looking. Using this information, a computer recalculates images of the virtual world to match the direction in which the user is looking and displays these images on the HMD. Users hear sounds in the virtual world through earphones in the HMD. The haptic interface, which relays the sense of touch and other physical sensations in the virtual world, is, as we write, the least developed feature. Currently, with the use of a glove and position tracker, the user can reach into the virtual world and handle objects but cannot actually feel them.

Living in a simulated world is the ultimate form of *thirdness*, a world of the mind controlling the world of the senses. The VR medium raises some intriguing questions: How will the human species evolve in a VR space? How will society evolve? What kinds of crimes can be committed? And the list could go on and on.

11.3 THE MEDIUM IS THE MESSAGE

The topic of TV raises the larger issue of the effects of media on the signifying order and on *cognitive style* (how people process and understand messages). This can be defined as the ways in which, and the degree to which, the senses are used in processing information. McLuhan (1964) pointed out that human beings are endowed by Nature to process information with all the senses. Our *sense ratios*, as he called them, are equally calibrated at birth. However, in social settings it is unlikely that all senses will operate at the same ratio. One sense or the other is raised or lowered according to the representational codes and media deployed. In an oral culture, the *auditory sense ratio* dominates; in an alphabetic one, the *visual sense ratio* dominates instead. This raising or lowering of a sense ratio is not preclusive. Indeed, in our own culture, a person can have various sense ratios operating in tandem. The ebb of ratios, up and down, in tandem, in opposition, is what defines the *cognitive style* of information processing.

Now, signs and texts can be expressed and transmitted through several media, thus involving different sense ratios according to medium. As a concrete example, consider the word *ball*. If one were to hear this word uttered by someone, h/er auditory sense ratio would be raised in processing the meaning of the word. If, however, the person were to see the word written on a sheet of paper, then h/er visual sense ratio would be raised instead. A visual depiction of the ball together with the utterance of the word *ball* on TV (as is done on children's learning programs) would activate the auditory and visual sense ratios in tandem.

Each medium requires the utilization and, thus, knowledge of one or more type of code—e.g. if the sign or text is transmitted through an auditory medium, then the phonemic code of a language must be known by both the sender and the receiver; if it is written on a piece of paper, then the alphabetic code of the language must be known. The medium thus determines which code is to be deployed in encoding a message and this, in turn, raises or lowers certain sense ratios in the person decoding the message. This sequence thus shapes how a message is processed cognitively. As McLuhan so aptly put it, "the medium is the message":

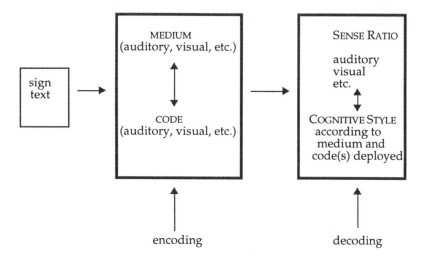

The same sign or text can, of course, be transmitted in more than one medium. So, for instance, a story can be told and listened to as an oral narrative, raising the auditory sense ratio in the decoding process; it can be read as a novel, raising the visual sense ratio; or it can be watched in movie form, raising both sensory ratios in tandem. In this model, *encoding* can be defined simply as the use of a *code* or *codes* to select or create a text according to the medium through which it will be transmitted; and *decoding* can be defined as the process of deciphering the transmitted text on the basis of the medium and code used.

Now, as one type of medium becomes dominant in a society, so too does the sense ratio it entails for encoding and decoding messages. In a tribal oral culture, the auditory sense ratio was high and thus shaped cognitive style. In Western culture, the Gutenberg revolution brought about a shift in cognitive style, by raising the visual sense ratio considerably. Since the advent of TV in the 1950s, the visual sense ratio has been raised even more, making people today highly dependent upon visually encoded forms of information.

11.4 ADVERTISING

Another social text that came to the forefront in the twentieth century to raise the visual sense ratio in cognitive style alongside TV was *advertising*. The contemporary advertising industry was founded at the threshold of the twentieth century on the premise that consumption of a product would increase in proportion to the size of an advertising campaign. Whether or not advertising is as effective as is commonly thought is beside the point of the present discussion. The point we will be focusing on here is that advertising, like TV, is a social text, promoting lifestyle and shaping worldview.

The term *advertising* derives from the medieval Latin verb *advertere* "to direct one's attention to." It designates any type or form of public announcement intended to promote the sale of specific commodities or services. Advertising is to be distinguished from other materials and activities aimed at swaying and influencing opinions, attitudes, and behaviors, such as *propaganda,* the term used in reference to any systematic dissemination of doctrines, views, beliefs reflecting specific interests and ideologies (political, social, philosophical, etc.); *publicity*, the term used in reference to the craft of disseminating any information that concerns a person, group, event, or product through some public medium; and *public relations,* the term commonly used to refer to the activities and techniques deployed by organizations and individuals to establish favorable attitudes towards them among the general public or special groups.

By the mid-twentieth century, advertising had evolved into a form of persuasive social discourse intended to influence how people perceived the buying and consumption of goods. Over the years it became a privileged discourse that replaced, by and large, the more traditional forms of discourse—sermons, political oratory, proverbs, wise sayings, etc.—which in previous centuries had rhetorical force and moral authority. Advertising exalts and inculcates Epicurean values. It envisions human beings as "numerical units" that can be classified into "taste groups," "lifestyle groups," "market segments," etc. and that can, therefore, be manipulated according to the laws of statistics. As Carl Jung (1957: 19-20) warned not too long ago, this view of a human being as a unit in an assemblage, rather than as "something unique and singular which in the last analysis can neither be known nor compared with anything else," is probably the root cause of the pathological forms of anxiety and nervous stress that typically beset people living in modern cultures.

Advertising is designed to create a constant craving for consumption, for the replacement of older things with newer ones. As we pointed out in chapter 9 (§9.5), Roland Barthes (1957) termed this craving "neomania," which he defined as an insatiable appetite for new objects of consumption. Ads and commercials yell out one promise to all: "Buy this or that and you will not be bored, but you will be *happy!*" With a handful of hedonistic themes—happiness, youth, success, status, luxury, fashion, and beauty—the general message of the advertising social text is that solutions to human problems can be found in buying and consuming.

A Historical Sketch

Advertising messages are now spread through numerous and varied media—newspapers, television, direct mail, radio, magazines, business publications, outdoor and transit advertising, window displays, free shopping-news publications, calendars, skywriting by airplanes, and even posters carried by people walking the streets. The messages and images of advertising are everywhere.

But advertising is not an invention of the modern age. It is actually over 3000 years old. A poster found in Thebes dating from 1000 BC is a relic of one of the world's first ads. In large letters it offered a whole gold coin for a slave. Archeologists have found similar kinds of posters throughout ancient societies. Throughout history poster advertising in marketplaces and temples has, in fact, constituted a popular means of disseminating information and of promoting the barter and sale of goods and services.

The dawn of the modern era of advertising occurred in the fifteenth century when the Gutenberg press made the printed word available to masses of people (chapter 9, §9.4). Fliers and posters could be printed easily and posted in public places or inserted in books, pamphlets, newspapers, etc. In the latter part of the seventeenth century, the *London Gazette* became the first newspaper to reserve a section exclusively for advertising. So successful was this venture that by the end of the century new agencies came into being for the specific purpose of creating newspaper ads for merchants and artisans. Advertising spread rapidly throughout the eighteenth century and proliferated to the point that the British writer and lexicographer Samuel Johnson (1709–1784) felt impelled to make the following statement in *The Idler*: "Advertisements are now so numerous that they are very negligently perused, and it is therefore become necessary to gain attention by magnificence of promise and by eloquence sometimes sublime and sometimes pathetic" (quoted in Panati 1984: 168).

The first American advertising agency was started by Philadelphia entrepreneur Volney B. Palmer in 1841, when he decided to sell newspaper space to out-of-town advertisers, charging the papers 25% of their space rates plus postage and stationery costs. By 1849 Palmer had offices in New York, Boston, and Baltimore. Between 1890 and 1920 industrial corporations grew into mammoth structures that transformed the workplace into an integrated economic system of mass production. At that point advertising became a crucial medium not for informing people about the availability and qualities of goods, but for restructuring perceptions of lifestyle that could be associated with the goods. Business and aesthetics had obviously joined forces by the first decades of the century. From the 1920s onwards, advertising agencies sprang up all over, broadening their approaches in attempting to build an unbroken, imagistic bridge between the product and the consumer's consciousness. Everything from product name, design, and packaging to the creation of lifestyle moods came gradually within the purview of the advertising business.

Consumer advertising gave birth to the first agency for recording and analyzing data on advertising effectiveness in 1914 with the establishment of the Audit Bureau of Circulations in the United States, an independent organization founded and supported by newspaper and magazine publishers wishing to obtain circulation statistics and to standardize the ways of presenting them. Then, in 1936 the Advertising Research Foundation was established to conduct research on, and to develop, advertising techniques with the aim of enhancing the authenticity, reliability, efficiency, and usefulness of all advertising and marketing research. Today, the increasing sophistication of statistical information-gathering techniques makes it possible for advertisers to target audiences on the basis of where people live, what income they earn, what educational background they have, etc. in order to determine their susceptibility to, or inclination towards, certain products.

Advertising is thus intertwined with marketing. Marketing agencies conduct extensive surveys to determine the potential acceptance of products or services before they are advertised. If the survey convinces the manufacturer that one of the versions exhibited will attract enough purchasers, a research crew then pretests various sales appeals by showing provisional advertisements to consumers and asking them to indicate their preference. After the one or two best-liked advertisements are identified, the advertiser produces a limited quantity of the new product and introduces it in a test market. On the basis of the outcome the manufacturer can make a decision as to whether a national advertising campaign should be launched.

Techniques

The two main techniques of modern-day advertising and marketing are known as *positioning* and *brand image*. *Positioning* is the targeting of a product at the right people—e.g. the perfume *Drakkar noir* is positioned for a male audience, *Chanel* for a female audience; the marketing of Audis and BMWs is aimed at upper-class or aspiring upscale consumers, the marketing of Dodge vans is aimed at middle-class suburban dwellers; and so on. *Brand image* is the creation of a personality for the product that is meant to appeal to specific consumers. This is done by giving the product a recognizable name, logo, packaging presentation, and pricing.

One way in which advertisers create brand image effectively is through logo design. Take as an example the McDonald's logo. The first thing to note is that people go to fast-food restaurants to be with family or friends, to get a meal quickly, and/or because the atmosphere is congenial. Most people would also admit that the food at a McDonald's or a Wendy's is affordable and that the service is fast and polite. Indeed, many people today probably feel more "at home" at a McDonald's restaurant than in their own households. This is, in fact, the semiotic key to unlocking the meaning that the McDonald's logo is designed to create. The arches constitute a mythic symbol beckoning good people to march through them triumphantly into a paradise of law and order, cleanliness, friendliness, hospitality, hard work, self-discipline, and family values. In a sense, McDonald's is organized and managed like a religion. From the menu to the uniforms, McDonald's exacts and imposes standardization, in the same way that the world's organized religions do. The message created by the arch logo is therefore that, like paradise, McDonald's is a place that will "do it all for you."

A fast food eatery would be inconceivable in a non-industrialized culture, and would have been unimaginable even in ours not so long ago. The popularity of McDonald's and other fast-food restaurants is tied to the socioeconomic need for a two-income household. Fewer and fewer North American families have the time to eat meals together within the household, let alone the energy to prepare elaborate dinners.

And even when they do, it is highly unlikely that they will perceive the eating event as a structured one aimed at preserving family harmony and traditional moral values. In modern-day households, meals are routinely consumed in front of television sets. The home, ironically, has become a place where people now tend to eat apart. Enter McDonald's, to the rescue! Eating at McDonald's is affordable, quick, and cheery; it is a place where the family can eat together, at the same table, with no TV or other distraction. All these connotations are embedded in the symbols that are associated with McDonald's, from its logo to its Ronald McDonald figure.

11.5 THE MESSAGES IN ADS

It was Roland Barthes (1957) who drew the attention of semioticians to the value of studying advertising. Today there is considerable interest in ad analysis. If there is one finding that is of specific relevance to the present discussion, it is that many ads are interpretable at two levels—a surface and an underlying level. The surface level is the actual ad text. The way in which the text is put together, however, is both a reflex of, and a link to, an underlying level: i.e. the surface elements cohere into images that conjure up an array of connotations in the underlying sub-text. The latter is typically evocative of mythic themes (the intertexts). The main intent of advertising, therefore, is to speak indirectly to the unconscious, mythic part of the mind.

The Connotative Sequence

To get a concrete grasp of how ads generate meaning, it is instructive to analyze a lifestyle ad chosen at random from a magazine. For this purpose, we have selected an ad for Marilyn Peach, a sparkling wine, that was found in many European magazines a few years ago. This ad cannot be reproduced here for reasons of copyright. It can only be described verbally. The ad text shows a peach background which appears to match both the color and the taste of the wine. Subtextually, however, the idea that comes to mind is that of the dawn, which, in turn, suggests the Genesis narrative (the dawn of creation, the dawn of life). Several surface level features bear this out—we see a woman's hand holding out a drinking glass of the wine, offering it temptingly to someone; the woman is wearing a bracelet in the form of a snake. Now, in the Book of Genesis the devil came to Eve in the body of a snake to prod her on to tempt Adam. A male partner is probably the one who is being seductively offered the glass. Will he take it? Well, like the Biblical Adam, how can he resist? If one still has doubts about this subtex-

tual meaning, the accompanying French verbal text—*La pêche, le nouveau fruit de la tentation* ("Peach, the new fruit of temptation")—will
undoubtedly dispel them.

Whether or not this ad will induce consumers to buy Marilyn
Peach is open to question. It is certainly not the point of semiotic analysis to determine this. Nor is it the goal of semiotics to criticize makers
of such ads. On the contrary, a semiotician should approach an ad as
s/he would any text. Indeed, the same questions that art and literary
critics ask about a painting or a novel are the ones that a semiotician
asks about an ad. To the semiotician, advertising provides an opportu-
nity to examine how varied aesthetic experiences and classical forms of
expression are realized in a contemporary textual genre.

It should also be pointed out that an interpretation of any advertising text is just that—one possible interpretation. Indeed, disagreement
about what something means is not only unavoidable, but part of the
fun of doing semiotic analysis. Differences of opinion fill the pages of
the semiotic journals and lead, as in other sciences, to a furthering of
knowledge in the field. The point of the above analysis was simply to
illustrate the technique of semiotic analysis itself, not to provide a de-
finitive interpretation of the Marilyn Peach ad. The key to unlocking
the underlying subtext is to consider the surface signifiers in a sequence, just like a comic strip, in order to see where the sequence leads
in the subtext. This technique can be called *connotative sequencing* because each signifier evokes a connotation which then evokes another,
and then another after that, and so on. In the above ad the *connotative
sequence* goes like this:

> the peach background = dawn = dawn of creation = Garden
> of Eden scene = Eve tempting Adam = prodded on by a ser-
> pent (bracelet) = he who drinks the wine will yield to tempta-
> tion (*La pêche, le nouveau fruit de la tentation*)

In most lifestyle ads, the mythic intertext can be wrested from such
connotative sequences, which are often reinforced by the visual and verbal signifiers in the surface text—e.g. by the shape of the product, by
shadows and colors, by the name of the product, etc.

Verbal Techniques

The statement *La pêche, le nouveau fruit de la tentation* is designed to reinforce the connotative sequence. In lifestyle advertising language is both
a reinforcing element in the ad text and a reflex of its subtextual and
intertextual meanings. It is also designed by advertisers as a form of

poetic discourse, in the Jakobsonian sense (chapter 5, §5.6), in order to get a product embedded in the signifying order. There are many verbal techniques that advertisers use to realize these objectives. Some of these are:

- *Jingles and Slogans*: These have the effect of getting a brand name incorporated into daily discourse: *Have a great day at McDonald's; Join the Pepsi Generation;* etc.

- *Use of the Imperative Form*: This creates the effect of advice coming from an unseen authoritative source: *Pump some iron; Trust your senses;* etc.

- *Formulas*: These create the effect of making meaningless statements sound truthful: *Triumph has a bra for the way you are; A Volkswagen is a Volkswagen;* etc.

- *Alliteration*: The repetition of sounds increases the likelihood that a brand name will be remembered: *The Super-free sensation* (alliteration of *s*); *Guinness is good for you* (alliteration of *g*); etc.

- *Absence of language*: Some ads strategically avoid the use of any language whatsoever, suggesting, by implication, that the product speaks for itself.

- *Intentional omission*: This capitalizes on the fact that secretive statements like *Don't tell your friends about...; Do you know what she's wearing?* etc. grab people's attention.

- *Metaphor*: As we saw in chapter 6, this shapes the way in which people come to conceptualize something: e.g. *Come to where the flavor is...Marlboro country.*

- *Metonymy*: This too shapes concept-formation and. thus, evaluation of a product: e.g. *Bring a touch of Paris into your life.*

In television and radio commercials, the *poetic* techniques involve the mode of delivery. The tone of voice, for instance, can be seductive, friendly, cheery, insistent, foreboding, etc. as required by the subtextual theme of the commercial. The sentence structure of ads and commercials is usually informal and colloquial, unless the ad is about some "high-class" product (e.g. a BMW automobile, a Parker pen, etc.), in which case it is normally more elegant and refined. In general, the sentences used in ads are, as we have seen, short imperative phrases—*Pump some iron, Trust your senses*—or aphoristic statements —*Somewhere inside, romance blossoms.* Advertising also borrows discourse styles to suit its purposes: e.g. a TV commercial can take the form of an interview, a testimonial on the part of a celebrity, an official format (*Name:* Mary; *Age:* 15; *Problem:* acne), and so on.

As the foregoing discussion implies, the analyst, the text, the social context, the culture, the product, etc. are all inextricably intertwined in ad interpretation. The connotative sequences that ads generate are psychologically powerful because they are embedded in mythic subtexts, as are many works of art, for that matter. Advertising is not only social discourse, it is also modern art. And, indeed, it has become an artistic genre of its own, with its own prize category at the annual Cannes film festival. Advertising is adaptive, constantly seeking out new forms of expression reflecting fluctuations in social trends and values. Its forms have even been adapted and coopted by mainstream artists and writers. Although some may be inclined to condemn its objectives, as an aesthetic experience virtually everyone enjoys advertising.

11.6 THE EFFECTS OF MEDIA

As mentioned above, media influence cognitive style and thus are critical shapers of cultural worldview. One effect of advertising, for example, has been the juvenilization of Western culture at large —i.e. the emphasis on being, staying, thinking, and looking young at any age. The roots of this phenomenon can be traced to the first decades of the twentieth century, when for the first time in history a single economic system—the one that took shape after the Industrial Revolution of the nineteenth century—was capable of guaranteeing a certain level of affluence to increasingly larger segments of society. With more wealth and leisure time at their disposal, common people became more inclined to live the good life. And with the economic capacity to improve their chances of staying healthier, and thus of living much longer than previous generations, a desire to preserve youth for a much longer period of life started to define the collective state of mind. This desire was nurtured by the messages that bombarded society from radio and print advertising in the early part of the century—messages that became more persuasive and widespread with the advent of television as a social text in the early 1950s. By the 1960s, the desire to be "young" not only meant the desire to stay and look healthier for a longer period of life, but also to act and think differently than "older" people. Being old meant being a part of the corrupt and morally fossilized "establishment," as the consumerist way of life was called by the counterculture dissidents of the era. By the end of the decade, the process of juvenilization had reached a critical mass, on the verge of becoming the defining feature of the mindset of an entire society.

Advertisers tapped into this process astutely and skillfully. Being young and rebellious came to mean having a "cool look"; being anti-establishment and subversive came to mean wearing "hip clothes." "New" and "different" became the two key words of the advertising and marketing lexicon, coaxing people into buying goods, not because they necessarily needed them, but simply because they were "new," "cool," "hip." The underlying subtext of this clever discourse allowed buyers to believe that what they bought transformed them into ersatz revolutionaries without having to pay the social price of true noncon-formity and dissent. As the social critic Ewen (1988: 20) has aptly put it, the business world discovered fortuitously in that era how to incorpo-rate the powerful images of youth protest into "the most constantly available lexicon from which many of us draw the visual grammar of our lives." It was those images that allowed advertisers and marketers to write a new lifestyle grammar with which they could easily build new semantic bridges between the product and the consumer's con-sciousness. This grammar has now systematized the behaviors of neo-mania into the psychological structure of everyday life. This is why the constant craving for new items of consumption is no longer perceived as an aberration, but as part of the search for happiness, success, status, or beauty.

A society bombarded incessantly by advertising images is bound to become more and more susceptible to the effects of extreme forms of objectification (chapter 9, §9.1). Because our consciousness is shaped by the type of stimuli and information to which we are exposed, the bar-rage of images generated by advertisements surreptitiously influence lifestyle and behavior, especially the perception of how many desirable material objects we should own and of how many pleasures we should be feeling.

Junk Food Culture

As an example of the potentially harmful effects media images may have, we will conclude this chapter with a brief commentary on the phenomenon of "junk food." When fast food eateries first appeared in the 1950s—as burger and milkshake "joints"—they were designed to be socializing sites for adolescents. The food served at such places was viewed, correctly, to be junk, injurious to one's health and only to be consumed by young people because their metabolism could ostensibly break it down more quickly and because they could purportedly re-cover from its negative health effects more easily than older people. But in no time whatsoever junk food, promoted by effective advertising campaigns, became an indulgence permissible to anyone of any age, from very young children to seniors. The compulsion to consume junk food has become powerful in contemporary society, inducing dangerous eating habits. The inordinate consumption of junk food is, in fact, one of the main factors contributing to the rise in obesity.

But the negative effects of junk food are hardly just physical. Obesity is at odds with the ultra-slim body images that the media perpetrate as the norm for attractiveness. This disjunction of fact and image has generated culture-based diseases, previously unknown. Anorexia nervosa, fear of gaining weight, leading to excessive weight loss from restricted food intake and excessive exercise, is one of these. Predictably, it occurs chiefly during adolescence, especially in young women, who perceive body image as critical to their sociability among peers. Sufferers may also exhibit bulimia, the practice of eating large quantities of food and then inducing vomiting. No standard therapy for anorexia nervosa exists, nor can exist, given its cultural etiology. Psychotherapy often helps, but many cases of successful recovery show Self-resolution without relapses.

But, as a closing word, the answer to the dilemma of advertising is not to be found in censorship or in any form of state control of media. Even if it were possible in a consumerist culture to control the contents of advertising, it would invariably prove to be counterproductive. Moreover, the ravages of overeating are not a product only of contemporary ad-mediated cultures. They have always been symptomatic of the excess of affluent lifestyles. Scenes of obese aristocrats and emperors abound in history books. The protection against such excesses today is not suppression, but knowledge of how advertising produces messages. Only the latter is effective, because it puts people in a more critical frame of mind for fending off the negative effects that these messages might have.

Part III

A Practical Synthesis

A general semiotics studies the whole of the human signifying activity—languages—and languages are what constitutes human beings as such, that is, as semiotic animals. It studies and describes languages through languages. By studying the human signifying activity it influences its course.

Umberto Eco (1932–)

12

SEMIOTIC ANALYSIS

> *The world, so far from being a solid*
> *matter of fact, is rather a fabric of*
> *conventions, which for obscure rea-*
> *sons it has suited us in the past to*
> *manufacture and support.*
>
> Richards (1936: 41-42)

12.0 PRELIMINARY REMARKS

The purpose of this book has been to illustrate what a semiotic study of culture would entail, what things it would focus on, and how it would envision what culture is. As part of our expository style, we coined the term *Homo culturalis*, explaining h/er appearance on the human evolutionary scene as a successor of several ancestors—*Homo signans*, the maker of signs; *Homo loquens*, the speaker; *Homo metaphoricus*, the maker of concepts; *Homo faber*, the maker of objects, artifacts, and buildings; *Homo mythologicus*, the creator of myths and narratives; and *Homo aestheticus*, the artist, dancer, musician, poet. We then intimated that *Homo culturalis* had given birth to a descendant of h/er own: *Homo technologicus*, the maker of machines and of consumerist culture.

The main idea in using such nomenclature has been to underscore that the human species is a complex one—one that is hardly explainable by facile philosophical or scientific theories. Each human being is a sign-maker, a speaker, a maker of concepts, a maker of objects, a creator of stories, and an artist. These are the creative capacities that define humankind. Access to the nature of humanity is through a study of these capacities, which, as Ernst Cassirer (1944: 25) once remarked, have paradoxically cut off human beings permanently from making any direct contact with reality:

> No longer in a merely physical universe, man lives in a symbolic universe. Language, myth, art, and religion are parts of this universe. They are varied threads which weave the symbolic net, the tangled web of human experience... No longer can man confront reality immediately; he cannot see it, as it were, face to face. Physical reality seems to recede in propor-

tion as man's symbolic activity advances. Instead of dealing with the things themselves man is in a sense constantly conversing with himself. He has so enveloped himself in linguistic forms, in artistic images, in mythical symbols or religious rites that he cannot see or know anything except by the interposition of this artificial medium.

In this final chapter we will tie a few loose analytic strings together. We will start by reviewing what a semiotic approach to culture entails in a succinct way. Then, we will illustrate how to carry out cultural semiotic analysis in specific terms—i.e. in terms of what can be called *macrosemiotic* and *microsemiotic* analysis. Finally, we offer our concluding reflections on the nature of culture, revisiting in a general way several of the more interesting aspects of the question "What is culture?" with which we started off this semiotic trek through the cultural landscape.

12.1 THE SEMIOTIC APPROACH TO CULTURE

The basis for culture, as a system of shared meanings, is what we have called the *signifying order* in this book—the system of signs, the codes into which they cohere, and the texts these codes allow human beings to construct. Although signifying orders now serve the function of making purposeful behavior, knowing, social interaction, and communication fluid and habitual, they came about in the human species, arguably, as reflexes of the ingrained need to find meaning to life. This is perhaps why in all cultures, from tribal to complex technological ones, signifying orders are built from the same blueprint of signifying properties and allow for the same patterns of representation and expression. These are manifest in the bodily schemas, language forms, myths, art works, rituals, performances, artifacts, and other signifying forms and expressions that constitute social life. The primary goal of cultural semiotic analysis is to catalogue and analyze these manifestations in specific social situations.

In so doing, the cultural semiotician is guided by three basic questions: (1) *What* does a certain sign, code, or text mean? (2) *How* does it represent what it means? (3) *Why* does it mean what it means? The semiotician seeks answers to these questions essentially by observing people being themselves in their social ambiances. But, as we have argued throughout this book, the observations of the semiotician are hardly random. They are guided by five specific principles. These can now be summarized as follows:

1. *Interdisciplinarity:* This principle entails that the semiotician should utilize the findings or techniques of any cognate discipline (anthropology, psychology, etc.) that are applicable to the situation at hand (chapter 2, §2.5).

2. *Relativity:* In line with relativistic anthropology (chapter 1, §1.2), this principle asserts that in documenting and explaining signifying orders, the semiotician should keep in mind that signs, codes, and texts have structural effects on individuals (chapter 3, §3.10).

3. *Signification:* This principle asserts that signifying orders are built on the same signifying properties (iconicity, indexicality, etc.) and that these manifest themselves in different ways according to culture where they cohere into a specific system of signification (chapter 3, §3.6).

4. *Dimensionality:* This principle entails that the semiotician should relate the signifying properties identified in a specific situation to the signifying order and to general psychological processes of representation (chapter 3, §3.9).

5. *Interconnectedness:* This principle entails that the semiotician should investigate how meanings are interconnected throughout the signifying order.

The semiotic probe into culture, moreover, does not discriminate between what are known more traditionally as "higher" and "lower" forms of culture, between, say, the fine arts and fast food symbolism. To the semiotician all aspects of social behavior originating in signifying orders are relevant. But h/er focus is not purely that of the social scientist, because, as we have seen in previous chapters, the study of meaning-making is not only a study of communal sense-making. Ultimately it is a study of human *consciousness*—the awareness of one's environment and of one's own existence, sensations, and thoughts.

Throughout history there have been many attempts to study and understand this truly mysterious phenomenon. But, in our opinion, it is the research on semiosis in the last 50 years that has come forward to provide a vital clue to understanding consciousness. In terms of what we have called in this book the *dimensionality principle*, it can be said that human knowing starts out as a *firstness* bodily phenomenon, i.e. as a rudimentary state of consciousness, or *cognizing* that is sensorial, perceptual, and affective in its overall response to the world (chapter 3, §3.1). But this form of knowing is eventually mediated and structured by *semiosis*, which produces a *secondness* form of knowing in the individual, i.e. a reflective state of consciousness that is based on what signs call attention to and on the uses they are put to (*representation*). Finally, the build-up of the signs, codes, and texts learned in a cultural context in the individual's memory system generates a culture-specific way of knowing, i.e. a highly abstract form of consciousness that is shaped by a signifying order. This is, of course, a thirdness form of knowing. In sum, human consciousness can be said to be a concomitant of sensory firstness (= the body), semiosic and representational secondness (= the mind), and communal signifying thirdness based on a signifying order (= culture):

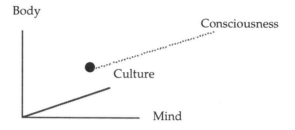

The essence of semiotic method is to show how these three dimensions are immanent in all acts of meaning-making—i.e. in all the forms and expressions that humans continually produce in their discourse, in their arts, in their scientific theories, and in all the other *texts* that make up the fabric of daily life in a culture.

12.2 MACROSEMIOTIC ANALYSIS

As in the social sciences, it is convenient within the field of cultural semiotics to differentiate between a global analysis of the phenomenon of culture and a specific, case-in-point analysis of the manifestations of signification within a cultural setting. The former can be called *macrosemiotic analysis*. This can be defined as the study of the ways in which a signifying order is both implanted in certain meaning structures and produces meanings within them. This implies the study of how specific signifiers are shaped by the interconnectedness that inheres among the diverse codes and texts that make up the signifying order. Macrosemiotic analysis is, in essence, *intercodal* and *intertextual* analysis.

In most of the preceding chapters, we have emphasized the fact that semiotic analysis is really informed people-watching. This implies, in turn, a three-stage methodology. The first stage is observational. This is the stage during which the semiotician compiles data on culture-specific behaviors and texts. As mentioned several times in this book and reiterated above, the analyst is guided by three basic questions in h/er search to understand a specific sign, code, or text, seeking to answer these questions essentially by observing people being themselves in their social ambiances. This allows h/er to observe the particular uses of signifying structures and systems (signs, codes, texts) in specific social situations. The nature of the observation depends on the type of structure or system that is involved: collecting data on bodily schemas, for instance, entails simple ocular observation; compiling information on fictional texts, on the other hand, requires assembling appropriate oral or written materials.

Clearly, this first stage is consistent with general ethnographic methodology, as practiced, for instance, by cultural anthropologists. The emphasis is on the *in loco* observation and description of cultural behaviors, expressions, etc. Only in this way can the semiotician make any intelligent hypotheses as to what an expression or a behavior might mean. In terms of the five principles listed above (§12.1), the observational stage satisfies two at once—namely (1) that the findings or techniques of any cognate discipline (anthropology, linguistics, etc.) that are applicable to the situation at hand should be enlisted (the *interdisciplinarity principle*), and (2) that the structural effects that signs, codes, etc. have on individuals should be documented appropriately (the *relativity principle*).

The second stage of macrosemiotic is simply analysis. After identifying which signifying structures and systems underlie and regulate the observed behaviors and textual practices, the semiotician should then analyze how these reflect tendencies in the signifying order—in line with the third of the five principles of semiotic analysis (the *signification principle*). This will then allow h/er to investigate the dimensionality features of the structures and systems (the *dimensionality principle*). This implies that one of the primary goals of macrosemiotic analysis is determining which minimal meaning elements lie at the constitutive basis of signifying orders. Once these have been identified, then a sign, a code, or a text can be analyzed in dimensionality terms. For the purposes of macrosemiotic analysis, we shall call such minimal meaning elements *macrosignifieds*, since they are signifieds that underlie the specific forms that various signifying structures assume across the signifying order; i.e. a *macrosignified* is a signified that links together signs, codes, and texts throughout the culture.

The third stage in macrosemiotic analysis is synthesis. In line with the *interconnectedness principle*, this entails describing how a macrosignified shapes the signifiers of the verbal and nonverbal codes of the signifying order in a synthetic fashion. The interconnectedness of meanings in a culture is the reason why, from tribes to advanced technological societies, signifying orders impart a sense of wholeness and, thus, of purpose to the activities that people carry out. Macrosignifieds are distributed throughout the network of meaning pathways that define a culture. Michel Foucault (1972) characterized this network as an endless "interrelated fabric" in which the boundaries of meanings are never clear-cut. Every signifier is caught up in a system of references to other signifiers, to codes, and to texts; it is a node within a network of distributed macrosignifieds. As soon as one questions that unity, it loses its self-evidence; it indicates itself. To extract meaning from a sign, code, or text, therefore, one must have knowledge of this network and of the macrosignifieds that constitute it.

The three-stage method of macrosemiotic analysis can be summarized graphically as follows:

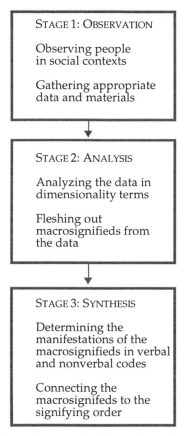

MACROSEMIOTIC ANALYSIS

STAGE 1: OBSERVATION

Observing people
in social contexts

Gathering appropriate
data and materials

STAGE 2: ANALYSIS

Analyzing the data in
dimensionality terms

Fleshing out
macrosignifieds from
the data

STAGE 3: SYNTHESIS

Determining the
manifestations of the
macrosignifieds in verbal
and nonverbal codes

Connecting the
macrosignifeds to the
signifying order

This methodology has, to the best of our knowledge, never been formulated as explicitly as this before in the semiotic literature. However, it is nothing new. It has been implicit in the writings and research orientations of cultural semioticians throughout the last century. It is presented here as a succinct summary of cultural semiotic analytical practices, with the intention of providing future analysts with an explicit methodological framework for conducting research on cultural phenomena.

The "Up-Down" Macrosignified as a Case-in-Point

As a concrete example of what macrosemiotic analysis entails, consider how a single image schema, [verticality], discussed in chapter 6 (§6.2), is diffused throughout the meaning network of one signifying order—the Anglo-American one. Collecting data on this macrosignified (stage 1) consists both in observing people as they talk, posture, gesture, etc. and in collecting samples of appropriate verbal and nonverbal texts. Once the various signifiers (i.e. words, gesticulants, bodily schemas, etc.) that encode this macrosignified have been identified, then it can be analyzed in dimensionality terms (stage 2). On a firstness axis, the up-down schema is probably the result of the bipedal human animal's sensation of looking up and down. As mentioned above, and in other parts of this book, it is at this juncture that semiotics must look to other disciplinary domains—in this case anthropology, biology, historical linguistics, and possibly even sociobiology—to seek probable answers to the question of the origins of this specific macrosignified. At a *secondness* level, the *up-down* macrosignified structures how individuals experience various abstract concepts, as we saw in chapter 6. The analyst can easily document these concepts by interviewing subjects and watching them in socially significant situations. It can then be said that, in *thirdness* terms, the accumulation of these concepts as socially meaningful and useful ones is what renders the *up-down* macrosignified a minimal meaning element in the constitution of codes across the signifying order:

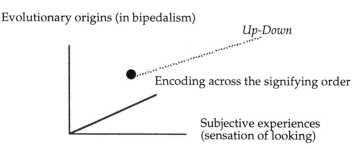

The final task of the cultural semiotician is to document how this macrosignified actually manifests itself across the signifying order (stage 3). Here are just a few of the ways in which it influences the form that various signifiers assume across codes.

In verbal discourse, for instance, it manifests itself in expressions such as: "I'm feeling up"; "They're feeling down"; "I'm working my way up the ladder of success"; "His status has gone down considerably"; etc. These reveal the metaphorical concept *up is better/down is worse*. This same macrosignified is also manifest in religious narratives, where goodness, spirituality, and heaven are portrayed as *up*, and evil, damnation, and hell as *down* in sermons, theological narratives, religious visual representations, the design of churches, etc. In public building design, too, it can be discerned in the fact that the taller office buildings in a modern city are the ones that indicate which institutions (and individuals) hold social and economic power. In musical composition, higher tones are typically employed to convey a sensation of happiness, lower ones of sadness. During speech, the raising of a hand designates notions of amelioration, betterment, growth, etc., whereas the lowering of the hand designates the opposite notions. In bodily representation and perception, this macrosignified shows up in the common viewpoint that *taller is more attractive/shorter is less attractive*. In mathematical and scientific representational practices its influence can be seen, for instance, in the ways in which graphs are designed—lines that are oriented in an upward direction indicate a growth or an increase of some kind, while those that are slanted in a downward direction indicate a decline or decrease.

These are just some of the signifiers that encode the *up-down* macrosignified which, as can be seen, is distributed throughout the pathways that constitute the meaning network of the signifying order. In effect, the extraction of meanings from specific signifiers is dependent upon knowledge of how such a macrosignified is encoded. Such knowledge is normally unconscious in individuals raised and/or living in a culture. The goal of cultural semiotics is to make such knowledge explicit.

This kind of analysis can be extended to the study of the structural or grammatical systems that constitute different codes. But the more specialized, detailed analysis of code structure falls more within the domain of theoretical semiotics (chapter 2, §2.1). For the cultural semiotician, all that is necessary is to determine how macrosignifieds inform the signifying order:

THE *UP -DOWN* MACROSIGNIFIED

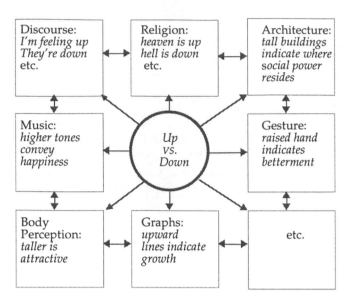

The "Love Is a Sweetness" Macrosignified as Another Case-in-Point

Another example of an image schematic macrosignified is the *love is a sweetness* schema (chapter 6, §6.5). Compiling information on this macrosignified (stage 1) would consist, again, in observing people—in this case as they interact in courtship situations—and in collecting appropriate textual materials (love poetry, romance fiction, etc.). Once the various signifiers that encode this macrosignified have been identified, then it can be analyzed in dimensionality terms (stage 2). On a *firstness* axis, this schema is probably the result of biologally-based sexual experiences resulting from the pleasant sensation that tends to be associated with sexual urges. This is the level of biological *sex* that we described in chapter 4 (§4.2). At a *secondness* level, the *love is a sweetness* macrosignified influences how individuals experience their own *sexuality* (chapter 4, §4.2), and this can easily be documented by interviewing subjects and/or watching them in courtship and love-making situations. In *thirdness* terms, the accumulation of these experiences as communally meaningful in *gender* terms is what leads to the encoding of the *love is a sweetness* macrosignified across the signifying order (chapter 4, §4.2):

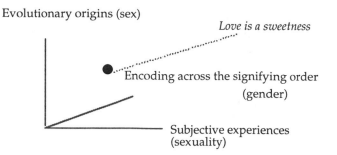

The final task of the analyst is, again, to document how this macrosignified actually manifests itself across the signifying order. Language, for example, reflects the *love is a sweetness* schema in metaphorical expressions such as "She's my sweetheart"; "They're on a permanent honeymoon"; etc. In courtship rituals, it shows up in practices such as the giving of sweets to a loved one at St. Valentine's Day and the eating of a cake at weddings. In the domain of objectification (chapter 9, §9.1), it manifests itself in various symbolized forms—e.g. in the form of logo signifiers (the most well-known one perhaps being the *Baci* line of chocolates by Perugina), in the sweet-smelling scents perfume products are perceived to emit, etc.

THE *LOVE IS A SWEETNESS* MACROSIGNIFIED

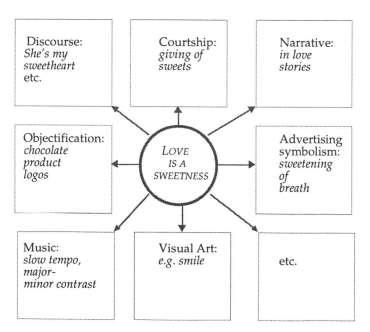

This macrosignified also shows up constantly in love stories (e.g. descriptions of lovers as sweethearts), and in advertising (e.g. scenes of breath being sweetened with candy before kissing). In music, love songs are often composed in a slow tempo and in a major vs. minor contrasting style in order to evoke the contrast between feelings of "sweetness" (associated with the major mode) and those of "bitterness" (associated with the minor mode). In the visual arts, the smile has been similarly used as a signifier to convey the sweetness sentiment associated with the love experience—the *Mona Lisa* (1503–1506) of Leonardo da Vinci being perhaps the most famous use of this signifier.

Other Types of Macrosignifieds

Image schemas are not the only kinds of macrosignifieds that inform the signifying orders of cultures. For analytic purposes, these can be called *image schematic macrosignifieds*. Now, recall from chapter 3 (§3.5) that the word *cat* does not refer to a specific cat, but to the category of animals that we recognize as having the quality "catness," namely a prototypical mental picture marked by distinctive features such as [mammal], [retractile claws], [long tail], etc. This image is extended, by connotation, to encompass other kinds of referents that appear, by association or analogy, to have something in common with it. The relation between denotation and connotation is, thus, really one of interconnectedness, whereby the connotations that are established in social context are due to the use of the prototype (e.g. [mammal], [retractile claws], [long tail], etc.) in verbal and nonverbal ways. Those specific connotations that are then embedded into the signifying order constitute macrosignifeds in the sense described above. This is why, for instance, a devotee of jazz music is referred to as a "cool cat," and why pop culture images emphasize the "catness qualities" of jazz musicians. For analytic purposes such connotations can be called *connotative macrosignifeds*.

Name-giving (chapter 5, §5.4) too is shaped by another type of macrosignified that can be called, for analytic purposes, *onomastic*. In all cultures, *onomastic macrosignifieds* derive from traditions and conventions associated with the kinship and religious spheres. Even in Western culture, where name-giving is a fairly open and untraditional process, it is still shaped by such macrosignifieds. So, a name like *Alexander*, for instance, is hardly given at random; it is assigned to individuals in cultures where it is interconnected historically with the meanings evoked by the name of *Alexander the Great*. In a similar fashion, this is why Biblical names like *Jacob, Sara, Luke, Rebecca, Rachel*, to mention but a few, are still being assigned today.

Finally, *mythic macrosignifieds* can be defined as those that derive from mythic themes, characters, and settings. Thus the mythic theme of *good vs. evil* is a macrosignified that influences, for instance, the perception of sports events, whereby the home team = the *good* and the visiting team = the *bad*, as we saw in chapter 10 (§10.3). As Frye (1981) argued (chapter 1, §1.6), early religious and mythic themes have left their residues in the literary practices and in the everyday discourse of Western society, which defines itself as largely secular. This is because the Bible has provided many of the mythic macrosignifieds that make up the Western signifying order: e.g. the macrosignified of *disgrace is a falling* comes from the story of Adam and Eve, the macrosignified of *life is a journey through the waters* comes from the Noah's Ark story. Political and legal systems, too, are founded on the basis of mythic macrosignifieds—the basis of legal codes and concepts in modern Western cultures, for instance, can be traced to the Biblical Ten Commandments.

The main implication for the study of culture that crystallizes from macrosemiotic analysis is that the meaning of a sign or text is determinable in terms of its interconnectedness to the signifying order. The work in cultural semiotics, therefore, provides a truly fascinating framework for relating what would appear to be disparate and heterogeneous acts of meaning to each other. Indeed, the meaning of a specific sign or text (verbal, visual, gestural, etc.) is determinable in terms of the macrosignified or macrosignifieds that it embodies. Macrosemiotic analysis thus reveals how certain minimal meaning elements provide the "conceptual glue" that keeps the whole system of culture together. This is why signifying orders are powerful shapers of worldview. Because they are understandable in a holistic fashion, they bestow upon everyday actions and expressions an implicit teleological meaning and value—i.e. a certain necessary logic for being as they are.

12.3 MICROSEMIOTIC ANALYSIS

Whereas the goal of macrosemiotic analysis is to describe how basic meaning structures—which we have called *macrosignifieds*—interlink the signs, codes, and texts of the signifying order, the goal of microsemiotic analysis is the reverse—i.e. to describe how these very same structures influence the specific construction of texts. The kinds of data collected in microsemiotic *observation* (stage 1), therefore, are the same as those compiled in macrosemiotic observation. The microsemiotic *analysis* of the data (stage 2) consists in determining how the image schematic, connotative, onomastic, and mythic meanings distributed throughout the signifying order have been projected onto a specific act of text-making. These projections can be called *microsignifieds*. A *mi-*

crosignified can be defined as the specific use of an image schematic, connotative, onomastic, or mythic meaning structure in a text. A *macrosignifed* is a distributed meaning (throughout the signifying order), and a *microsignified* a projected meaning (in the construction of texts). For example, the use of the *up-down* schema in a musical composition can be fleshed out by examining the emotional effects that certain tones have—e.g. Do the higher ones produce feelings of happiness, the lower ones of sadness? It can also be fleshed out by determining the emotional effects of changing mode from major to minor—e.g. Does the raising or lowering of the middle note of the tonic chord by a semitone produce relatively happier or sadder responses respectively? Finally, microsemiotic analysis inheres in determining how these microsignifieds coalesce to produce an interpretation of the text. This constitutes, in fact, the *synthesis* stage of microsemiotic analysis (stage 3), which focuses on what texts mean in specific cultural situations *(text analysis)*:

MICROSEMIOTIC ANALYSIS

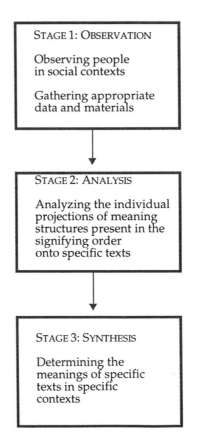

STAGE 1: OBSERVATION

Observing people
in social contexts

Gathering appropriate
data and materials

STAGE 2: ANALYSIS

Analyzing the individual
projections of meaning
structures present in the
signifying order
onto specific texts

STAGE 3: SYNTHESIS

Determining the
meanings of specific
texts in specific
contexts

A Case-in-Point

Microsemiotic analysis is concerned with the message taken from a text. This means identifying the microsignifieds in its make-up in terms of the signifying order from which they were drawn. Consider, for instance, an ad for an *Airoldi* watch that was seen frequently in Italian lifestyle magazines published a number of years ago. This ad cannot be reproduced here for reasons of copyright. It can only be described verbally.

A microsemiotic analysis (stage 2) of this ad is guided by a series of leading questions. The first question—What are the observable microsignifieds of the ad that stand out?—involves establishing the minimal units of meaning that have been projected onto the text by cataloguing its main features. Some of these are as follows:

- An Airoldi watch has apparently been stabbed by a woman's hand holding a dagger.
- The woman's fingernails are painted with nail polish.
- She is wearing a man's ring on her thumb.
- A fingerless leather glove covers the woman's palm.
- A diamond-studded handcuff is discernible on her wrist.

The next question is, What does each one suggest? Answering this question involves showing how certain macrosignifieds have been projected onto the text in terms of the signifiers that make up the text. In the *Airoldi* ad, these are as follows:

- The stabbing suggests some form of violence, perhaps the brutal hunting of human prey.
- The woman's painted fingernails suggest sensuality.
- The man's ring is probably that of her lover or male prey; wearing it on the thumb suggests that it is one of the spoils of the hunt.
- The fingerless leather glove is suggestive of sado-masochistic sensuality.

> • The diamond-studded handcuff reinforces the sado-
>   masochistic imagery of the ad and also implies capture
>   and captivity.

The final question is, How do these microsignifieds (= specific projections of macrosignifieds) coalesce to produce an overall meaning?
According to scholars of mythology, the "huntress" image has a sexual-
erotic meaning in Western culture. The image of a fierce, powerful, and
sexually dangerous female surfaces in all kinds of popular narratives—from ancient myths such as that of Diana to contemporary female movie characters. The mythic macrosignified of the *female-as-
huntress* seems to form a kind of paradigmatic counterpart to the macrosignified of the *female-as-mother.*

The action implied by the ad suggests that the female is stabbing
the center, or heart, of the watch. The watch is thus, by analogy, her
male prey, who cannot escape from the stabbing, as guaranteed by the
handcuff on the woman's wrist, which will not allow the watch to slide
beyond it. The woman has, in effect, caught her man. The hunting act is
final and decisive. The *female-as-huntress* macrosignified, with its sado-
masochistic connotations, is reinforced verbally by the single word *sfi-
dare* "to dare." The ad "dares" female consumers to hunt down and
capture their lovers with sado-masochistic sensuality. In this way they
will neutralize their lovers' potential sexual interests in other women.
As the mythologist Joseph Campbell (1969: 59-60) has observed, the
fear of women has been "for the male no less an impressive imprinting
force than the fears and mysteries of the world of nature itself."

In order to establish the above interpretation of the text as plausible, clearly, the context in which it has been fashioned is a key factor.
Recall from chapter 3 (§3.8), that *context* refers to the real-world conditions—physical, psychological, social, etc.—that ultimately determine
how a text is made or what it means. The interpretation that we fleshed
out of the *Airoldi* ad was made possible by knowledge of the fact that it
was directed towards a female audience, and by knowledge of the macrosignifieds that were available to the text-maker. In a phrase, contextual information provides the semiotician with a frame of reference that
allows h/er to determine which projections of meaning have been utilized in the construction of a specific text. Umberto Eco (1979, 1990) referred to texts as either *closed* or *open.* A *closed text* is one that entails a
singular, or a very limited, interpretive range. A map, for instance, entails a fairly straightforward interpretation of what it means. It is an
example of a closed text. A poem by an enigmatic modern Western
poet, on the other hand, usually evokes different responses and different opinions on the part of readers. It is an example of an *open text.* The

more interpretations a text evokes, the greater seems to be its aesthetic effectiveness. However, as Eco also argues, even open texts are constrained by the signifying order. When asked what an open text means, people will typically provide a pattern of responses that suggests that they are influenced by the macrosignifieds that have been projected onto the text.

The semiotician is well aware that in any culture the primary purpose of open texts is to ask basic questions about the human condition. The more open the text, the more universal the interpretations it seems to evoke; the less open it is, the more constrained the interpretations are by the signifying order from which it was crafted. This raises, of course, fundamental questions that we have addressed in previous chapters. Are there psychic universals that cultural signifying orders translate into specific kinds of signs, codes, texts? Are all signifying orders really communal "Geiger counters" searching for the same pattern of meaning in life? Why does the sapient animal need to search for meaning? Is consciousness a consequence of this search?

12.4 CONCLUDING REFLECTIONS

In chapter 3 (§3.10) we introduced the notion of *structural effects*—i.e. the notion that signifying orders *condition* or *structure* experience, perception, worldview. In colloquial language this is known commonly as "groupthink," a term that nicely captures the idea that in a society individuals tend to think alike. Most of our thoughts and responses are, essentially, culturally conditioned ones. That has been one of the themes woven into this book. Consider pain as an example. The findings of medical practitioners and psychologists (Brand and Yancey 1993) suggest that pain is not experienced in the same way the world over. Pain thresholds are very much set and modified by culture. In North American society, for instance, childbirth is widely regarded as a painful experience. But in other cultures women show virtually no distress during childbirth. As the psychologist Melzack (1972: 223) perceptively remarks:

> Can this mean that all women in our culture are making up their pain? Not at all. It happens to be part of our culture to recognize childbirth as possibly endangering the life of the mother, and young girls learn to fear it in the course of growing up. Books on "natural childbirth" ("childbirth without fear") stress the extent to which fear increases the amount of pain felt during labor and birth and point out how difficult it is to dispel it.

It is instructive to note that the ways in which we talk about pain reveal that one of our strategies for coping with it is to think of the body as if it were a machine:

1.   My pain is *slowing* my body *down*.
2.   My pain is *destroying* my body.
3.   My pain is affecting how my body *works*.
     etc.

These verbal expressions reflect a deeply embedded image schematic macrosignified in Western culture, *the body is a machine*, which in turn predisposes us to experience pain as a malfunction in the machine that can be controlled and thus eliminated. In contrast, speakers of Tagalog, the indigenous language of the Philippines, have no equivalents of the expressions listed above. Their expressions reveal instead that body health is influenced by both spiritual and natural forces. These two different patterns of groupthink produce different responses to pain and disease. People reared in English-speaking cultures are inclined to experience pain as a localized phenomenon, i.e. as a malfunction that can be adjusted or corrected apart from the overall state of well-being of the individual. Tagalog people, on the other hand, are inclined to experience it as intertwined holistically with mental states and ecological forces and, therefore, as treatable in tandem with the overall state of well-being of the person.

But this does not mean that human beings cannot learn from each other, nor that they are incapable of experiencing the world independently of culture. The conundrum of culture, in a phrase, is that it entails groupthink at the same time that it provides the individual with the necessary resources for innovation and creativity. So, on the one side, culture is restrictive in that it imposes upon individuals an already-fixed system of signification that will largely determine how they will come to understand the world around them. On the other side, culture is also liberating because the very same system provides the means by which individuals can seek new meanings on their own. The great artistic, religious, scientific, and philosophical works to which individuals are exposed in cultural contexts open up the mind, stimulate creativity, and engender freedom of thought. As a result, human beings tend to become restless for new meanings, new forms of expression, no matter in what society they live.

The interconnectedness principle, for instance, does not imply that people are prisoners of their signifying order, entangled cognitively in its meaning pathways. On the contrary, the very nature of human signifying orders is such that they allow individuals to think independently and autonomously *if they so desire*. Moreover, the utilization of a signifying order—of its language, its art forms, its narratives, etc.—is constantly subject to the vagaries of the human user. Thus, any act of representation or communication, from a simple greeting to an elaborate artistic performance, is a highly variable subjective act. Human beings are not automaton-like relayers of cultural meanings; they are creative users of these meanings, always searching for new meanings to the very signs they use, no matter how conventionalized these may have become. Signifying orders give historical continuity and stability to the meanings that the genus *Homo* has always been able to make. But these orders are not static; they are dynamic systems responding to the new signs, new art forms, new metaphors that *Homo culturalis* continues to invent. This is why cultures are always in flux, always reacting to new ideas, new needs.

The Life Cycle of Cultures

Because they are dynamic entities, cultures are very much like physical organisms—they are born and they eventually die. The cultures of ancient Sumer, Babylon, Egypt, and Greece, and the Incas and the Maya, to mention but a few, have long since ceased to be, even though the achievements of these cultures have lived on, in different forms and ways, in subsequent cultures. But the signifying orders that gave them life have long since disappeared. This brings us back to emphasizing the distinction between *culture* and *society* (chapter 1, §1.5). Cultures are, essentially, figments of mind; societies are collectivities of people who have come together for specific historical reasons. Indeed, the society that creates a culture does not necessarily disappear when its culture does. Although the ancient Greek culture long ago disappeared, the society that produced it has not and, moreover, the lasting elements of that culture have been absorbed by, or incorporated into, modern-day Greek culture and, indeed, the cultures of every modern-day society.

One of the first to make this very point was the Italian philosopher whose ideas have been enlisted at various points in this book, Giambattista Vico. Vico (in Bergin and Fisch 1984) saw the cultural life cycle as unfolding according to three broad stages. The first stage was one in which natural events in the world were thought to be under the dominion of awesome and frightful gods—hence the emergence of religion, burial rites, the family, and other basic institutions to lay the foundations of a society. He called this primordial phase, appropriately, the "age of the gods." Every culture is born in this "divine age." The primary spheres—kinship and religion—are naturally dominant during this early stage, providing each person with an identity and a vital sense of belonging. The primary form of encoding the culture's signifying order and its history is myth.

In the succeeding "age of heroes," as Vico called it, a dominant class of humans—the "heroes" of the evolving culture—emerges typically to subjugate the common people. These are people with great physical prowess who inspire fear and awe in the common people. The latter typically ascribe divine powers to these "nobles." Again, Vico's theory is remarkably accurate, given that across time, the historical record shows that all cultures have had their legendary heroes, who are purported to have wrested control of the world from the hands of the gods, setting the world on a more "human" course of historical development. During the second stage the primary spheres and the emerging secondary spheres (political, legal, etc.) develop overlapping moral and ethical jurisdictions. The primary form of encoding the culture's changing signifying order and its history is legend—a blend of myth and narrative.

After a period of domination by the heroes, a third stage—the "age of equals," as Vico called it—invariably takes shape in which the common people rise up and win equality; but in the process the culture begins to disintegrate. This is because the third age is one of subtle irony and wit. Language is shallow and does not reflect the passions; it is a language of concepts, method, and logical reasoning devoid of its poetic, mythical functions. The ironic intellect is a destructive one, challenging all forms of moral authority associated with the primary spheres. The secondary spheres assume the reins of social control. But as a consequence, people lose their sense of unity and start retribalizing into small groups. This leads to a demise of the culture as a whole and either to a reversion to one of its earlier stages or to its dissipation. Nevertheless, its main accomplishments are incorporated into emerging signifying orders. The primary form of encoding the culture's changing signifying order and its history is prose narrative history.

The three ages of culture, according to their modes of historical narration, define the dimensionality of a culture:

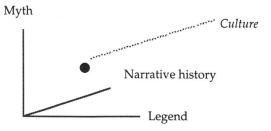

This three-stage life-cycle, according to Vico, is the natural course that human cultures run—a course that is not linear and endlessly progressive, but cyclical. Cultures do not go on forever. But in their "death" they are "reborn" with a more ethical form of human interaction.

The Vichian theory of culture strongly suggests that the evolution of *Homo culturalis* has been shaped by forces that we will never understand. Indeed, for no manifest genetic reason, humanity is constantly reinventing itself in cultural terms as it searches, across time and geography, for a purpose to its existence. This search has led it to invent signifying orders that have set it apart from all other species. It is unlikely that we will ever know what these forces are, for the simple reason that we will have to investigate them with the resources of the very signifying orders that they have made possible. As quantum physicists found out at the start of the twentieth century (chapter 2, §2.6), since theories are formulated with language, it is unlikely that the truth about the universe will ever be known. In quantum theory, the verbal description simply does not seem to fit what the mathematical equations say is going on. The substrate of physical reality appears to obey a logic utterly foreign to verbal concepts. People think of a particle, like a photon or an electron, as occupying space at a certain point in time, and traveling along a specific path. As it turns out, however, a particle does not really exist until it interacts with something, and it travels down not one path but all possible paths at once. Language came about to help people to get around on the earth, not in the mysterious world of subatomic physics.

So, too, with theories of humankind. At best, we can gain some insight into how the mind produces signs. But no theory formulated in language can ever really penetrate the world of mind itself. This is why semiotics wisely limits itself to studying what the mind produces—signs, codes, and texts.

Who is Homo Culturalis?

It is our view that we will, in fact, never really know an answer to the question of *why* culture exists. A more realistic goal is to study *how* it provides the means for making meaning. That has been the modest goal of this book. There is no way to explain the human spirit that is responsible for stimulating in the human species its quest for meaning to life. We can only systematically study language, myths, poetry, and all the other products that *Homo culturalis* has invented throughout the ages and throughout the world to make sense in life. These reveal the structure of h/er mind and the forms of h/er soul. But we will never know who *Homo culturalis* really is. We can, of course, develop religious philosophies, mythical narratives, or scientific theories to explain h/er nature. But these are of our own making. This is because, as Charles Sanders Peirce often pointed out, as a species we are inclined to "think only in signs."

Western people have tended to assume that language is a clear and direct way to know and to communicate knowledge, and thus that a theory of cultural origins couched in language is one that can be tested and either confirmed or rejected empirically. But this assumption is fraught with danger because, as Michel Foucault (1972) argued, the basic ideas that people normally take to be permanent truths about human nature and society change in the course of time, as does the language that frames them. Throughout history, Foucault claimed, people have tried to explain themselves through language in terms of religious ideas (= the *religious resolution*), physical or genetic forces (= the *physicalist resolution*), or mysterious human qualities (= the *humanist resolution*).

The following thought experiment can be used to illustrate Foucault's explication. Picture two married couples who belong to the most highly advanced culture imaginable. Each of the four people has achieved the highest degree of intelligence possible—all are, in fact, Nobel-prize-winning scientists or artists. The four are in a boat in the middle of an ocean. Both of the females are pregnant, and it so happens that they give birth at exactly the same instant to two healthy babies. As soon as the babies see the light of day, the four adults fall overboard and drown. The neonates have thus not had any contact whatsoever with other human beings. Fortuitously, the boat reaches the shore of a nearby island on which no other human being has set foot. The babies are mistaken for cubs by a pack of wolves. The wolves take the human neonates into their care and nurture them as their own kind.

Untouched by human beings and culture, what will these human neonates become and be able to do when they grow up? Will the two grow up to be quadrupeds like their adoptive parents or bipeds like their biological parents? Will they perceive themselves as being qualitatively different from the wolves? Will they start "speaking" to each other?

Typically, the answers people will give to such questions will fall into the three areas described by Foucault:

- Some will argue that the children will be "given," or "infused with," the language faculty and the ability to develop culture by some divine entity who is over them (the *religious resolution*).

- Others will maintain that the children's biological nature will eventually incline them, or their own progeny, to

> speak and develop culture as a result of evolutionary tendencies in the species (the *physicalist resolution*).
>
> * Others still will argue that the children will eventually invent speech and culture on their own for no foreseeable reason other than that it is the human condition (the *humanist resolution*).

As the reader will have figured out after working through this book, we favor the third type of resolution, even though, as mentioned in the opening chapter (§1.2), the physicalist perspective has come to the forefront today in academic circles and in the mindset of many people. But, then, as we have argued in various parts of this book, why do humans continue to crave for biologically useless things as music, paintings, and stories? In our view, theories of human nature drafted from comparisons with animal mechanisms and evolution are specious at best, spurious at worst. How could a purely physicalist definition of culture explain the expressions of spirit that are found in art works and in scientific thinking? Indeed, what kind of evidence would need to be collected to show a causal link between these and genes? Culture is itself a sign, standing for something more fundamental in the human species, a "cosmic signified," so to speak, of which we know virtually nothing.

As a final word, we mention that the human imagination, more than any other human skill or capacity, will continue to be the faculty that will constantly remind us of our enigmatic existential condition. *Homo culturalis* is an ingenious maker of ideas and things because s/he is endowed with *fantasia,* as Vico so aptly put it. This has, in fact, been the thematic thread running through this book. The outer worlds of Nature and Culture have no independent, objective meaning on their own, in the sense that they want to "say something" about themselves. Only reflective humans feel the need to make meaning of Nature, Culture, and themselves. The goal of this book has been to shed some light on why and how we do it, and why we will continue to do so in the future.

Activities and Questions for Discussion

The activities and questions can be taken up in class, or else used as guidelines for self-study to review and elaborate upon each chapter's main ideas and contents.

1 WHAT IS CULTURE?

ACTIVITIES

1. Define the following terms in your own words, using illustrations or cases-in-point to show their meaning:

Age of Enlightenment
archetype
Australopithecus
bilateral kinship
bipedalism
civilization
cognatic kinship
collective unconscious
critical period
Cro-Magnons
cultural sphere
culture
evolutionism
gene
Homo erectus
Homo habilis
Homo sapiens
Homo sapiens sapiens
matrilineal kinship
meme
nation
natural selection
Neanderthal
neoteny
paleontology
parallel kinship
patrilineal kinship
psychoanalysis
race
relativism
Shinto
signifying order
society
sociobiology

super-tribe
tribe
unilateral kinship
Worlds 1, 2, 3

2. Look up a definition of the term *culture* in any contemporary anthropology, sociology, and/or culture theory text. Compare it to the semiotic definition given in this chapter.

3. Summarize the views of both evolutionists and relativists with respect to the *raison d'être* of culture.

4. Can you cite any other manifestations of the trickster archetype, in addition to the ones mentioned in this chapter?

5. List and discuss the evolutionary antecedents to culture.

6. Do you know of any other examples of tribal practices within modern societies that are similar to those of the Palio of Siena?

7. Explain Popper's three Worlds in your own words.

8. List the main spheres of culture, defining each one in your own words.

DISCUSSION

9. Do you think that modern humans could live without culture? Explain your answer.

10. Which theory of culture origins do you find the most persuasive? Why?

11. Do you agree with the sociobiological view that the Self is a physical phenomenon? Explain your answer.

12. Do you agree with the idea that modern-day behaviors reverberate with tribal tendencies? Explain your answer.

13. Why do you think the human species is a *meaning-seeking* species?

14. Do you think that culture shapes human actions and ideas? If so, how is innovation or creativity possible?

2 THE FIELD OF CULTURAL SEMIOTICS

ACTIVITIES

1. Define the following terms in your own words, using illustrations or cases-in-point to show their meaning:

bit
channel
Chinese Room argument
cognitive science
communication
competence
conventional sign
decoding
diachrony
displacement
encoding
environmentalism
evolutionary psychology
feedback
Gestalt psychology
hermeneutics
information content
innatism
langue
medium
morphology
natural sign
noise
parole
phonology
receiver
redundancy
referent
semiology
semiotics
sender
sign
structuralism
symptom
synchrony
syntax
Turing test
Whorfian hypothesis

2. Distinguish between theoretical and cultural semiotics in your own words.

3. What are the three basic questions of semiotic analysis?

4. Analyze each of the following signs using the three basic questions of semiotics.

dog, table, friend, love, democracy

5. Explain the difference between a *concrete* and an *abstract* referent.

6. What is the difference between *semiotics* and *communication science*?

7. Can you devise a logical argument rejecting the Turing test, other than Searle's Chinese Room rebuttal?

8. From what disciplines does cultural semiotics seek insights?

9. List Eco's five criteria for characterizing semiotics as a science. Discuss the validity of each one.

10. List the working axioms of cultural semiotic analysis, discussing their validity or lack thereof.

DISCUSSION

11. Do you think that the ability to produce and comprehend signs is related to some fundamental need in the human species? Could human beings survive without this ability? Explain your answer.

12. Do you agree with the assertion that the ability to lie with language is a powerful one? Explain your answer.

13. Do you think that the human mind is essentially a type of Turing machine? Explain your answer.

14. Do you think that the specific language a person speaks influences how that person views the world? Explain your answer.

3. THE SIGNIFYING ORDER

ACTIVITIES

1. Define the following terms in your own words, using illustrations or cases-in-point to show their meaning:

analogy

annotation
antonymy
argument
code
connotation
context
deixis
denotation
dicisign
firstness
focal color
homonymy
hypoicon
hyponymy
icon
iconicity
index
indexicality
interpretant
legisign
meaning
object
onomatopoeia
paradigmatic structure
primary modeling system
proportionality
qualisign
recognition
referent
representamen
representation
rheme
secondary modeling system
secondness
semantic differential
semiosis
sensory cognizing
sign
signal
signification
signified
signifier
sinsign
structural effect
structural system
structure
symbol
symbolicity
synonymy
syntagmatic structure
tertiary modeling system
text
thirdness

2. Explain *modeling systems theory* in your own words.

3. Summarize Saussure's and Peirce's views of the sign in your own words. Can the two be synthesized into an integrated theory of the sign? How?

4. Explain the difference between *meaning* and *signification* in your own words.

5. Using a vignette of the type used by Hayakawa to define *democracy*, define:

freedom
friendship
love
nation
respect
slavery
totalitarianism

6. Give examples of:
gustatory iconicity
olfactory iconicity
personal deixis
spatial deixis
visual iconicity
vocal iconicity
tactile iconicity
temporal deixis

7. Explain the *dimensionality principle* in your own words.

8. Identify the following signs as icons, indexes, or symbols, or a combination of these:

 ☆ 🐿 ☞ *chat erase Ouch! Wow!* h x s ✔ ✳ ⊘ X⁴ *zap zigzag* ♲ TM 1001 A ∞ ↑ × → *plop* ? $ *

9. Give the denotative meanings first and then several connotative meanings of the following words and pictorial symbols:

blue, cat, car, life, person 👁 𝄞 🌹 🧳 ↑

10. List some connotations of the following color terms. Then discuss any annotations (personal meanings) they might elicit.

black

blue
brown
green
orange
purple
white
yellow

11. Give examples of the paradigmatic, syntagmatic, and analogical properties of:

automobile design
clothing
music
the alphabet
the integers

DISCUSSION

12. Do you think that the signifying order shapes worldview? Explain your answer.

13. Explain the interconnection among *semiosis, representation,* and the *signifying order* in your own words.

14. Do you think that some animals are capable of producing witting signals? Explain your answer.

15. Discuss the debate on color in your own words. Do you think that color is what language says it is? Explain your answer.

4 THE BODY

ACTIVITIES

1. Define the following terms in your own words, using illustrations or cases-in-point to show their meaning:

adaptor
affect display
ballet
clothing
dance
dress
emblem
gender
gesticulant
gesture

haptics
illustrator
interpersonal zone
kinesic code
kinestheme
lovemap
nudity
oculareme
proxeme
proxemic code
regulator
sex
sexuality
sign language
tacteme
tactile code
viseme

2.   Give examples of:

adaptors
affect displays
beat gesticulants
cohesive gesticulants
deictic gesticulants
emblems
iconic gesticulants
iconic gestures
indexical gestures
metaphoric gesticulants
regulators
symbolic gestures

3. Discuss the differences among the notions of *sex, sexuality,* and *gender*.

4. Give examples of how grooming and appearance codes influence how we currently prepare the face for social presentation according to gender and age.

5. What visemes convey the following emotions?

happiness
hate
love

6. Find expressions in addition to those used in this chapter showing how we perceive the face (e.g. *He's just another pretty face*).

7. Summarize in your own words what eye contact patterns are and then give examples (if you know any) of how ours differ from those found in other cultures.

8. Give examples of gestures for:

"good-bye"
"hello"
"stop"
anger
intelligence
love
sureness
surprise
uncertainty

9. Explain the difference between clothing and dress in terms of the *dimensionality principle.*

10. Give a summary of the reasons for, and functions of, *dancing* in the human species.

11. Using the typologies of communication features described in this chapter, compare the following communication systems with human language: bird calls, dog barking, the gestures of many primates.

12. Describe the proxemic patterns involved in shaking hands with the following people:

a friend you haven't seen in a while
a stranger of the opposite sex
a prospective employer
a stranger from a foreign country

13. Describe the tactile patterns, if any, to be employed when interacting with these people in your culture:
a child
a parent
a friend
an acquaintance
a stranger

DISCUSSION

14. Do you think that it will ever be possible to communicate with other species? If so, in what ways?

15. Do you think that gesture is or is not a more rudimentary form of communication than vocal language? Explain your answer.

16. Do you think that the Self is understood primarily as a sign? Explain your answer. How would you define your Self in semiotic terms?

17. Do you see any evolutionary significance in the phenomenon of interpersonal zones? Explain your answer.

18. Do you agree that the face is perceived as a *persona*? Give reasons to support your answer.

19. Do you think that the gender-coded *gazing* pattern whereby the male is the *gazer* and the female the one *looked at* has changed in the last few years? If not, explain why it has not. If so, explain why it has.

20. Do you think that what is obscene is a matter of cultural decisions?

21. Why do you think dancing originated in human life?

5 LANGUAGE

ACTIVITIES

1. Define the following terms in your own words, using illustrations or cases-in-point to show their meaning:

addressee
addresser
aesthesia
alphabet
code
conative
contact
cuneiform writing
discourse
diversification
echoism
emotive
hieroglyphic
holophrase
ideograph
language
literacy
logograph
message
metalingual
name
phatic
phoneme
pictograph
poetry

proto-language
referential
sound symbolism
speech
syllabary
synesthesia
taboo
tag question
Universal grammar
Whorfian hypothesis
word magic
writing

2.   Give examples of:

alliteration
current teen slang
echoic words
lengthening sounds for emphasis
onomatopoeia
sound symbolism in English
sound-modeling
the use of intonation for emphasis

3.   Summarize in your own words the discussion of:

language origin
teenage discourse
the iconic reflex system
the indexical reflex system

4.   Give the meanings of each of the following verbal signs, discussing
how each signifier represents its referent(s):

bang
bow-wow
hi
ouch
ping-pong
slide
slow
try
whack

5. Draw up a list of the main sources of name-giving cited in this chapter, adding any others you may know of.

6. What is the source of your name? Why do you think you were given
that name? What name would you have given yourself? Why?

7. Bring to class your favorite poem, reading it out loud. Then discuss:

what it means
why it means this
what synesthetic and aesthetic effects it produces and how it does this

8. Give examples of your own of each of Jakobson's constituents and functions. Do you think that these categories apply to nonverbal forms of communication? How so?

9. Explain the relationship between vocal speech and writing in your own words.

10. Explain the Whorfian hypothesis in your own words. Give examples that would seem to corroborate it anecdotally. Give examples that would seem to disconfirm it anecdotally.

11. Give a summary in your own words of the social uses of discourse.

DISCUSSION

12. Why do you think vocal language developed in the human species?

13. Why do you think we give names?

14. Do you think that males speak differently than females? If you think that they do, then why is it that they speak differently? Give examples of gender-based differences in discourse.

15. Do you think that communication is a means of presenting a persona? Explain your answer.

16. Why do you think children respond to poetry like that of Dr. Seuss?

17. Do you agree or disagree with the idea that verbal communication is potentially always a dangerous act? Explain your answer.

6 METAPHOR

ACTIVITIES

1. Define the following terms in your own words, using illustrations or cases-in-point to show their meaning:

conceptual metaphor

conceptual metonym
cultural model
ground
image schema
irony
metaphor
metaphorology
metonymy
source domain
synecdoche
target domain
topic
trope
vehicle

2. Give 5-6 examples of each of the following conceptual metaphors and conceptual metonyms (i.e. actual sentences exemplifying the concepts):

life is a stage
justice is blind
hope is breathing
love is a mental disease
friendship is a journey

the part for the whole
the producer for the product
the place for the institution
the institution for the people responsible
the object used for the user

3. Summarize or explain:

the image schematic basis of metaphor
the manifestations of the *face is the person* conceptual metonym in society
the functions of irony in discourse and social interaction
the interconnectedness between metaphor and grammar

4. Give the meanings of each of the following metaphors, discussing how each metaphor creates its meaning, and then identifying the conceptual metaphor that it exemplifies:

My life is a comedy.
Their marriage is a sitcom.
I have lost all hope.
You must weigh all the evidence.
That mistake cost me several hours.

5. Identify the conceptual metaphors that the following utterances reveal about love, giving more examples of your own for each one, and then drawing a cultural model of love:

There were sparks between us.
We are attracted to each other.
My life revolves around her.
I am magnetically drawn toward her.
Theirs is a sick relationship.
Their marriage is dead; it can't be revived.
Their relationship is in good shape.
I'm crazy about her.
I'm constantly raving about her.
He's gone mad over her.
I've lost my head over her.
She cast a spell over me.
The magic is gone.
She has bewitched me.
I'm in a trance over her.

6.   Develop cultural models of:

anger
friendship
happiness
hope
justice
sadness

7. Can you give any examples of mythical residues in common discourse?

8. What is a proverb? Recite any proverbs you know, identifying the kinds of advice they offer.

9. Does the formula *happiness is up/sadness is down* appear in Western social rituals and behaviors? Give examples.

10. Can you give examples of the grammaticalization and lexicalization of conceptual metaphors/metonyms in English?

DISCUSSION

11. Discuss the notion that all abstract thought is metaphorical in its origin. Do you agree? Explain your answer.

12. Do you think that most scientific knowledge is forged by metaphor? Explain your answer.

13. Do you think that metaphor is a symptom of *fantasia*, as Vico called the human imagination? Explain your answer.

14. The following metaphor was uttered by a four-year-old child, in referring to his father's baldness: "My father has a hole in his head." What do you think it reveals about the development of reasoning in children?

15. Why do you think metaphor is so pervasive in ordinary discourse?

7 SPACE

ACTIVITIES

1. Define the following terms in your own words, using illustrations or cases-in-point to show their meaning:

architecteme
architecture
Bauhaus school
map
modernism
postmodernism
shelter
spatial code

2. List various ways in which buildings and places are interconnected with the other codes of the signifying order of a culture.

3. List the various meanings associated with:

the home
the rooms within the home
a sacred space
a mall

4. Describe the semiotic features of maps.

5. Get a map of your region. Does it reflect any culture-specific features or needs? Explain them.

6. Explain the differences among *public, private,* and *sacred* spatial codes.

7. Give a brief summary of the salient points of the history of Western architecture.

9. List the various meanings that are associated with buildings in your city. Explain them in semiotic terms.

10. Give examples of buildings that are considered works of art.

11. Which part of your city do you find to be the most aesthetically pleasing? Why?

12. Do you perceive any survival function in the differentiation between private and public spaces? Explain your answer.

13. What do you think sacred spaces and buildings tell us about the human species?

14. Why do you think people go to malls? Explain your answer.

15. Do you think that someone's personality can be figured out from the type of home s/he lives in? Explain your answer.

16. Do you think that the structure of cities influences people's worldview?

8 ART

ACTIVITIES

1. Define the following terms in your own words, using illustrations or cases-in-point to show their meaning:

aesthetics
art
catharsis
cinema
color signifiers
commedia dell'arte
drama
linear signifiers
music
performance
perspective
photography
pictoreme
postmodern art
shape signifiers
theater
value signifiers

2. Summarize the main theories and perspectives of art.

3. Summarize the discussion of:

cinema
music
photography
the performing arts
visual art

4. Bring to class samples of your favorite type of musical or visual art. Discuss what each sample means.

5. Compare a painting by Vincent van Gogh (1853–1890) with one by Andy Warhol in terms of what each one means and how it delivers its meaning.

6. Now, compare a work by any classical Western composer to any work by a folk or popular music composer in terms of what each one means and how it delivers its meaning.

7. Discuss the influence of Darwinian evolutionary theory on the emergence of the postmodern worldview.

8. Read *Waiting for Godot* or watch a video of the play. Then, discuss the following elements of the play:

its characters
its costumes
its language
its plot
its scenery
its symbols

9. Watch *Koyaanisqatsi*, and *Blade Runner* on video. Then, give your own interpretation of the meaning of each one.

10. Discuss any current movie that you think displays postmodern techniques.

11. Can you find examples of postmodern technique in the musical arts?

DISCUSSION

12. Why do you think art is so intrinsic to human life?

13. Do you agree that cinema is the dominant art form of the contemporary world? Explain your answer.

14. Discuss how one derives meaning from a performance, a musical composition, and a painting.

15. Do you think that people are transformed permanently by great art? Explain your answer.

9 OBJECTS

ACTIVITIES

1. Define the following terms in your own words, using illustrations or cases-in-point to show their meaning:

animism
artifact
artificial intelligence
eating event
fetish
fetishism
food code
gusteme
neomania
object
objectification
pop art
technology

2. Summarize the notion of *objectification* in your own words.

3. Explain why artifacts allow archeologists to reconstruct a culture.

4. Referring to the case of the Cabbage Patch doll craze, discuss any other "toy crazes" that you know of.

5. Explain the difference between *food* and *cuisine* in terms of the *dimensionality principle*.

6. Explain Lévi-Strauss's distinction between "the raw" and "the cooked."

7. In the "Robinson Crusoe" vignette depicted in this chapter, what do you think would happen if the people in the vignette all spoke different languages?

8. List the various ways in which food and eating are interconnected with the other meaning systems of a culture.

9. What do the following food/drink items symbolize in your culture?

apple
banana
bread
grapes
lamb meat
milk
peach
potatoes
wine

10. Describe the table-manner code that applies to each of the following situations:

eating at home
eating at McDonald's
eating at a high-class restaurant
eating at a wedding

11. Discuss the characteristics of Gutenberg's Galaxy and Babbage's Galaxy.

12. Explain and compare the various manifestations of objectification.

13. Discuss what pop art is.

14. Discuss Barthes' notion of neomania. Do you think it describes the consumerist frame of mind accurately?

Discussion

15. Why do you think people are judged on the basis of what they eat?

16. Recall the toys you used to play with. Which ones were your favorites? Explain why, using semiotic reasoning.

17. What do you think the gendering of toys implies? Explain your answer in semiotic terms.

18. Do you think technology has become an extension of the human species? Explain your answer.

19. Why do you think fetishes are so powerful sexually? Explain your answer.

20. Do you think that some of the art produced by pop artists will last beyond the contemporary world? Explain your answer.

10 NARRATIVE

ACTIVITIES

1. Define the following terms in your own words, using illustrations or cases-in-point to show their meaning:

actant
biography
birth and rebirth myth
character
cosmogonic myth
culture hero myth
eschatological myth
fiction
generative trajectory
intertext
myth
mythology
narrative
narrative structure
narratology
narrator
narreme
novel
Othello effect
plot
plot grammar
setting
subtext

2. Give examples of:

ancient works of fiction
the different narrator-induced perspectives
actants
subtexts and intertexts in narratives you are familiar with
residues of myth in modern-day signifying orders

3. Summarize or explain:

why narrative is intrinsic to human life

the origin and growth of fiction
Propp's idea of "plot grammar"
the various views of myth
the various types of myth
the difference between *myth* and *mythology*
the origin and development of the novel

4. Carry out a narratological analysis of the plot, character, and setting of any novel, movie, or TV program. Do you think that these cohere into a single meaning, or levels of connotative meanings?

5. Explain Greimas' concept of *narrative grammar* in your own words. Then take any novel, short story, or comic book and carry out a schematic Greimasian actantial analysis, similar to the one of *Madame Bovary*.

6. Explain the use of myth in psychoanalysis. Do you think this is scientifically legitimate? Explain your answer.

7. Give examples of other mythological rituals, like the football example.

8. Give examples of other mythological concepts, like the one of childhood.

DISCUSSION

9. Why do you think stories are remarkably similar the world over?

10. Do you think that the ways in which we relate our autobiographies are a part of the presentation of Self? Explain your answer.

11. Why do you think the human species has a "narrative instinct"?

12. Why do you think myth has not disappeared from modern-day thinking? Explain your answer.

13. Why do you think mythologies influence social behavior? Discuss the influence on social life that the following mythologies have had:

the mythology of gender
the mythology of adolescence
the mythology of fatherhood
the mythology of motherhood

14. Do you think that art forms other than narrative writing (novel, short story, etc.) and cinema manifest narrative structure? Explain your answer, providing illustrations.

15. Who determines what the meaning(s) of a novel is? Explain your answer.

11 TELEVISION AND ADVERTISING

ACTIVITIES

1. Define the following terms in your own words, using illustrations or cases-in-point to show their meaning:

advertising
alliteration
brand image
cognitive compression effect
cognitive style
connotative sequence
decoding
encoding
history fabrication effect
medium
mythologizing effect
positioning
propaganda
public relations
publicity
sense ratio
television

2. Summarize the history of TV in your own words.

3. Give concrete examples of the *mythologizing, history fabrication,* and *cognitive compression effects.*

4. What is a social text? Give examples of different kinds of social texts.

5. Describe current programs in terms of their meanings and textual functions:

any soap opera
any news and information program
any sitcom
any documentary
any specialty program (sports, movies, etc.)

6. Summarize in your own words the discussion of *sense ratios.*

7. Give an overview of advertising, focusing on its development as social discourse.

8. Describe the two main techniques of lifestyle advertising—*positioning* and *brand image*—with reference to various lifestyle products.

9. Find and bring in an example of each of the following ads, taking each one at random from a magazine. Then analyze each ad semiotically:

a men's perfume ad
a women's perfume ad
a watch ad
a cigarette ad
a men's clothing ad
a women's clothing ad

10. Give examples from current advertising of:

jingles
slogans
the use of the imperative form
formulas
alliteration
intentional omission
the strategic use of tone of voice (in radio or TV commercials)

11. Give examples of the names of the following, discussing their significance:

a perfume
a soft drink
a record label
a luxury car

DISCUSSION

12. Do you agree with McLuhan that the "medium is the message?" Explain your answer.

13. What do you think will replace TV as the next culture-wide social text?

14. If you had the power to transform TV, what would you do and why?

15. Why do you think advertising is so appealing?

16. Do you think that advertising is effective in enhancing desire for a product? Explain your answer.

12 SEMIOTIC ANALYSIS

ACTIVITIES

1. Define the following terms in your own words, using illustrations or cases-in-point to show their meaning:

closed text
consciousness
macrosignified
microsignified
open text

2. Decribe in your own words what a semiotic approach to culture analysis entails.

3. What are the three stages of cultural semiotic analysis? Give a brief account of how you would conduct research on the following cultural phenomena according to this three-stage methodology:

courtship rituals
the meanings of a popular song

4. Carry out a macrosemiotic analysis of the following image schemas inherent in North American culture, giving examples of their interconnectdness across various codes:

life is a journey
love is magic

5. Carry out a microsemiotic analysis of:

any contemporary lifestyle ad
any love poem

6. Explain the *religious, physicalist,* and *humanist* perspectives on human nature in your own words.

7. Summarize in your own words what the signifying order entails in terms of groupthink and individual thinking.

8. Explain the interrelation between the body, the mind, and culture in *dimensionality* terms.

9. After having worked through this manual, how would you define cultural semiotics? Do you think that the semiotic approach to culture is a useful one or not? Explain your answer.

10. How do you think *Homo culturalis* will evolve? Explain your answer.

11. If knowledge is intertwined with representation, will it ever be possible to know the "truth" about the world? Explain your answer.

12. Do you think that representational activities such as art, music, narrative, etc. enhance survivability? Explain your answer.

Biographical Sketches

ARISTOTLE (384–322 BC)
student of the ancient Greek philosopher Plato, Aristotle shared his teacher's reverence for human knowledge, revising many of Plato's ideas by emphasizing methods rooted in observation and experience. Aristotle surveyed and systematized nearly all the existing branches of knowledge and provided the first ordered accounts of biology, psychology, physics, and literary theory. In addition, Aristotle invented the field known as formal logic, pioneered zoology, and addressed virtually every major philosophical problem known during his time.

AUGUSTINE (SAINT) (354–430 AD)
philosopher and religious thinker who was among the first to distinguish clearly between natural and conventional signs and to espouse the view that there is an interpretive component to the whole process of representation.

BARTHES, ROLAND (1915–1980)
French semiotician who claimed that the largely unconscious mythological thinking of human beings manifests itself in all kinds of discourses, spectacles, performances, and symbols.

BENEDICT, RUTH (1887–1948)
American anthropologist, student of Franz Boas, who pioneered ethnological research on Native American tribes during the 1920s and 1930s. Benedict maintained that every culture developed its own particular moral and lifestyle systems that largely determined the choices individuals reared and living in that culture made throughout their lives.

BOAS, FRANZ (1858–1942)
American anthropologist who claimed that culture largely determined the ways in which individuals developed their personalities and their worldviews.

CAMPBELL, JOSEPH (1904–1987)
American writer, editor, and teacher, known for his writings on myth. Influenced by the psychoanalytical ideas of Sigmund Freud and Carl Jung, and the novels of James Joyce and Thomas Mann, he formulated the theory that myths across the world are culture-specific manifestations of the universal need of the human psyche to explain social, cosmological, and spiritual realities.

CASSIRER, ERNST (1874–1945)
German philosopher and educator, whose works dealt mainly with the theory of knowledge, the history of epistemology, and the philosophy of science. He proposed that language and myth spring from the same unconscious creative force, and that the categories of myth underlie human symbols and human actions.

CHOMSKY, NOAM (1928–)
American linguist who claims that the human brain is especially constructed to detect and reproduce language. According to Chomsky, children instinctively apply innate grammatical rules to process the verbal input to which they are exposed.

DARWIN, CHARLES (1809–1882)
British zoologist who formulated the theory of "natural selection," which holds that reproductive success in organisms tends to promote adaptation that is necessary for survival.

DERRIDA, JACQUES (1930–)
French philosopher whose work originated a method of analysis—known as *deconstruction*—that has been applied to literature, linguistics, philosophy, law, and architecture, by which texts are seen to be infinitely interpretable.

DURKHEIM, EMILE (1858–1917)
French sociologist and philosopher who saw remarkable similarities among the world's myths, which he explained as being based in a "collective consciousness" that is a consequence of specific brain functions.

ECO, UMBERTO (1932–)
Italian semiotician and novelist who has provided various theoretical frameworks for the study of signs and who claims that while the interpretation of a text may be influenced primarily by culture, there is, nevertheless, an authorial purpose inherent in the text that cannot be ignored.

ELIADE, MIRCEA (1907–1986)
Romanian-born historian of religions who saw myth as the means by which humans come to a coherent understanding of existence. Although specific myths may over time become trivialized, people have the ability to reexperience their true metaphysical nature.

FOUCAULT, MICHEL (1926–1984)
French semiotician and philosopher who attempted to show that the basic ideas that people normally take to be permanent truths about human nature and society are instead no more than the products of historical processes.

FREUD, SIGMUND (1856–1939)
German psychologist and founder of psychoanalysis who suggested that the moral behavioral patterns that have ensured the survival of the human species are built into human genetic structure. He also formulated the theory of the "unconscious" as a region of the mind that stores wishes, memories, fears, feelings, and ideas that are prevented from expression in conscious awareness. These manifest themselves instead in symbolic and unusual ways, especially in dreams, neurotic syndromes, and artistic texts.

GREIMAS, ALGIRDAS JULIEN (1917–1992)
French semiotician who developed the branch of semiotics known as narratology, i.e. the study of how human beings in different cultures invent remarkably similar stories (myths, tales, etc.) with virtually the same stock of characters, motifs, themes, and actions.

HEGEL, G. F. W. (1770–1831)
German philosopher who argued that reality was filtered largely by acquired mental processes, although there existed a rational logic that governed human actions.

HERDER, JOHANN GOTTFRIED VON (1744–1803)
German philosopher who emphasized the profound differences that existed among individuals who lived in different cultures. His work laid the foundation for the comparative study of civilizations.

HERODOTUS (c. 484–425 BC)
Greek thinker and first historian who spent a large part of his life traveling in Asia, Egypt, and Greece, noting and recording for posterity differences in the dress, food, etiquette, and rituals of the people he encountered. His annotations have come to constitute some of the first analyses of cultural differences.

HIPPOCRATES (c. 460–377 BC)
Greek founder of medical science who established *semeiotics* as the study of symptoms.

HUMBOLDT, WILHELM VON (1767–1835)
Prussian statesman, educational reformer, and philologist who claimed that language reflects the culture and character of its speakers and that the study of language cannot be extricated from a consideration of the cultural system to which it belongs.

JAKOBSON, ROMAN (1896–1982)
Moscow-born linguist and semiotician who carried out most of his work in the United States. Among his contributions to semiotics, linguistics, and communication theory is a widely-used model that identifies the main functions and components of human communication.

JUNG, CARL GUSTAV (1875–1961)
Swiss psychiatrist who believed that the unconscious mind consisted of two interacting dimensions: the personal unconscious, the repressed feelings and thoughts developed during an individual's life, and the collective unconscious, those inherited feelings, thoughts, and memories shared by all humanity. He coined the term *archetype* to refer to the latter. Archetypes manifest themselves as recurring symbols in cultures the world over.

KHALDUN, IBN (1332–1406)
Medieval Algerian scholar who wrote a fascinating treatise on the difference between nomadic and city-dwelling Bedouins. He suggested that the environment in which the two types of Bedouins lived determined their differential behaviors.

LÉVI-STRAUSS, CLAUDE (1908–)
Belgian-born anthropologist based in Paris who sees culture as an external manifestation of the nature of human sign systems.

LOCKE, JOHN (1632–1704)
English philosopher who was among the first to suggest the inclusion of semiotics in philosophical inquiry. In his *Essay Concerning Human Understanding* (1690), Locke defined semiotics as the "doctrine of signs."

LORENZ, KONRAD (1903–1989)
Austrian zoologist who was instrumental in the founding of *ethology*, the study of animals in their natural habitats. He is perhaps best known for his discovery that auditory and visual stimuli from an animal's parents are needed to induce the young to follow the parents, but that any object or human being could elicit the same response by presenting the same stimuli. He called this phenomenon *imprinting*.

MALINOWSKI, BRONISLAW (1884–1942)
founder of the structuralist-functionalist school of anthropology in Britain, Malinowski claimed that each sign, symbol, code, or ritual, even if it might seem strange at first, had structural properties that came about to solve a specific problem and, thus, to serve a specific human function.

MARX, KARL (1818–1883)
German social theorist who claimed that new forms of a society emerged as a consequence of individuals struggling to gain control over the production, use, and ownership of material goods. In Marx's conception of utopia, there is no capitalism and no state, just a working society in which all give according to their means and take according to their needs.

MCLUHAN, MARSHALL (1911–1980)
Canadian communication theorist who argued that electronic technology has transformed the world into a "global village," and that technological innovations are the factors in human evolution.

MEAD, MARGARET (1901–78)
American anthropologist, student of Franz Boas, widely known for her studies of primitive societies and her contributions to cultural anthropology. Mead spent many years studying how culture influences individual personality, maintaining that the specific child-rearing practices of a culture shaped the behavior and temperament of the maturing individual.

MONTAIGNE, MICHEL DE (1533–1592)
French essayist who tried to dispel the pejorative view that had arisen in the sixteenth century vis-à-vis so-called "primitive" cultures, arguing that it was crucial above all else to understand the morality of other peoples on their own terms, not in terms of one's own cultural predispositions and system of ethics.

MORGAN, LEWIS HENRY (1818–1881)
American philosopher who claimed that all cultures, no matter how diverse, developed according to a regular series of predictable stages—from savagery, to barbarism, to civilization.

MORRIS, CHARLES (1901–1979)
American semiotician who conceived of semiosis as a chain of observable phenomena. Morris divided semiotics into the study of (1) relations between a sign and other signs, which he called *syntactics*; (2) relations between signs and their denotative meanings, which he called *semantics*; (3) relations between signs and interpreters, which he called *pragmatics*.

PEIRCE, CHARLES SANDERS (1839–1914)
American logician and mathematician who, along with Ferdinand de Saussure, is considered to be the founder of the modern-day scientific study of signs.

PLATO (c. 428–347 BC)
one of the most famous philosophers of ancient Greece, Plato was the first to use the term *philosophy*, which meant "love of knowledge." Chief among his ideas was the theory of forms, by which he proposed that objects in the physical world merely resemble perfect forms in the ideal world, and that only the perfect forms should be the objective of philosophical inquiry.

POLO, MARCO (c. 1254–1324)
Italian adventurer who was fascinated by the customs of the peoples he met on his travels through China and other parts of Asia. His chronicles of his voyages provided medieval Europeans with a wide range of information about the cultures of the Far East.

RADCLIFFE-BROWN, ALFRED (1881–1955)
British anthropologist who emphasized the social functional aspects of Bronislaw Malinowski's approach to the study of culture.

RICHARDS, I. A. (1893–1979)
English literary critic and educator who emphasized the cognitive importance of metaphor.

ROUSSEAU, JEAN-JACQUES (1712–1778)
French philosopher who linked a life of happiness to the attainment of a state of "natural life" similar to that of indigenous tribes and of children. As a consequence, he advocated the elimination of the corrupting influences of Western civilization.

SAPIR, EDWARD (1884–1939)
American anthropologist and linguist, student of Franz Boas, who investigated how language shaped the minds and behaviors of its users.

SAUSSURE, FERDINAND DE (1857–1913)
Swiss linguist who became a modern-day founder of semiotic theory.

SEBEOK, THOMAS A. (1920–)
leading American semiotician and linguist famous for his work on animal communication and sign theory, and for the establishment of the fields of *zoosemiotics* and *biosemiotics*.

SPENCER, HERBERT (1820–1903)
English philosopher who conceived of societies and cultural institutions as rankable on the exact same scale as living things, from the most simple to the most complex.

TACITUS , CORNELIUS (c. 55–117 AD)
Roman historian who described the character, manners, and geographical distribution of the German tribes he studied.

TURING, ALAN MATHISON (1912–1954)
British mathematician who envisioned a device, referred to as the "Turing machine," that could, in theory, perform any calculation. He also originated the "Turing test," a procedure designed to show that a computer might be judged to be intelligent.

TYLOR, EDWARD B. (1832–1917)
British founder of cultural anthropology who founded the first department of anthropology at Oxford University in 1884. Tylor's studies on the role of religion in cultures, along with his definition of culture, were important early contributions to the field of anthropology.

VICO, GIAMBATTISTA (1688–1744)
Italian philosopher who sought to unravel the origins of culture by analyzing the meanings of the first words. He also proposed a cyclical theory of history, according to which human societies progress through a series of stages from sensory barbarism to civilization and then return to barbarism, but of a reflective kind.

WHORF, BENJAMIN LEE (1897–1941)
American linguist and anthropologist, student of Edward Sapir, who kindled widespread interest among culture theorists in the view that language, thought, and culture are interdependent systems.

WILSON, EDWARD OSBORNE (1929–)
American evolutionary biologist who argues that many human behavioral characteristics (such as heroism, altruism, aggressiveness, and male domi-

nance) should be understood as evolutionary outcomes, and that human behavior is genetically determined.

WUNDT, WILHELM MAX (1832–1920)
German psychologist, generally recognized as the founder of scientific psychology as an autonomous field of study. In 1862, Wundt offered the first academic course in psychology; and in 1879, he established the first laboratory for conducting experimental research in psychology.

Glossary

A

ABDUCTION

term used by CHARLES PEIRCE to designate the form of reasoning whereby a new concept is inferred on the basis of an existing concrete, or already known, concept; abduction is essentially a "hunch" as to what something means or presupposes

ABSTRACT CONCEPT

concept that cannot be demonstrated or observed directly

ACTANT

unit of narration (a hero, an opponent) that surfaces in all kinds of stories

ADDRESSEE

receiver of a message

ADDRESSER

sender of a message

ADVERTISING

any type or form of public communication designed to indicate the availability or to promote the sale of specific commodities or services

AESTHESIA

experience of sensation; in art appreciation it refers to the fact that the senses and feelings are stimulated holistically by art works

AESTHETICS

branch of semiotics that studies the meaning and interpretation of art in general

ALLITERATION

repetition of the initial consonant sounds or clusters of words

ALPHABET

graphic code whereby individual characters stand for individual sounds (or sound combinations)

ALPHABETIC WRITING

writing system consisting of conventional symbols known as characters that can be used singly and in combination to make up the words of a language

ANALOGY

structural relation whereby a form replaces another that is similar in form, function, or use

ANIMISM

philosophical and religious view that objects possess a life force

ANNOTATION   personal meanings associated with a sign

ANTHROPOLOGY   field studying human cultures

ANTHROPOSEMIOSIS   human semiosis

ANTICLIMAX   rhetorical technique by which ideas are sequenced in abruptly diminishing importance, generally for satirical effect

ANTITHESIS   rhetorical technique by which two words, phrases, clauses, or sentences are opposed in meaning in such a way as to give emphasis to contrasting ideas

ANTONYMY   relation by which different words, phrases, sentences, etc. stand in a discernible oppositeness of meaning to each other

APHASIA   partial or total loss of speech due to a disorder in any one of the brain's language centers

APOSTROPHE   rhetorical technique by which an actor turns from the audience, or a writer from h/er readers, to address a person who usually is absent or deceased, an inanimate object, or an abstract idea

ARCHEOLOGY   field studying the material remains of past human cultures, so as to reconstruct the cultures

ARCHETYPE   term coined by psychoanalyst Carl Jung to designate any unconscious image that manifests itself in dreams, myths, art forms, and performances across cultures

ARCHITECTEME   minimal unit of an architectural code (a column, a rood shape, etc.)

ARCHITECTURE   art and science of designing and erecting buildings

ARGUMENT   in Peircean theory, the interpretant of a legisign (symbol)

ART   disciplined expressive activity that provides the people who produce it and the community that observes it with a range of experiences that might be aesthetic, emotional, intellectual, or a combination of these

ARTIFACT   object produced or shaped by human craft, especially a tool, a weapon, or an ornament, that is of archaeological or historical interest

ARTIFACTUAL TRANSMISSION | transmission of messages through artifactual means such as books and letters

ARTIFICIAL INTELLIGENCE | branch of computer science concerned with the development of machines having the ability to perform human mental functions

AUSTRALOPITHECUS | genus of *Homo* discovered at a number of sites in eastern and southern Africa, dating from more than 4 million years ago

AXIOM | statement universally accepted as true, and therefore accepted without proof

B

BALLET | classical dance form characterized by grace and precision of movement and elaborate formal technique

BASIC LEVEL CONCEPT | concept that has a typological (classificatory) function

BAUHAUS SCHOOL | twentieth-century school of architectural design which invented the skyscraper and high-rise apartment building form

BILATERAL KINSHIP SYSTEM | kinship system which assigns membership to kin through both the maternal and paternal lines

BIOSEMIOSIS | semiosis in all living things

BIOSEMIOTICS | branch of semiotics studying semiosis in all life forms

BIPEDALISM | walking upright on two feet

BIRTH AND REBIRTH MYTH | myth informing people about how life can be renewed or about the coming of an ideal society or savior

BRAND IMAGE | creation of a personality for a product through naming, packaging, and pricing

C

CEREBRAL DOMINANCE | theory that posits the left hemisphere of the brain as the dominant one in all the higher mental functions

CHANNEL | physical means by which a signal or message is transmitted

CHARACTER | person portrayed in an artistic piece, such as a drama or novel

CINEMA

visual narrative art form that encompasses the utilization of verbal and nonverbal codes

CIVILIZATION

complex society, or group of societies, whose institutions are grounded in the signifying order of a mainstream culture, but which can encompass more than one culture

CLIMAX

rhetorical technique by which ideas are sequenced in abruptly increasing importance, from the least to the most forcible

CLOSED TEXT

text with a singular or fairly limited range of meaning (e.g. a map)

CLOTHING

apparel to cover the body

CODE

system in which signs are organized and which determines how they relate to each other

COEVOLUTION

sociobiological theory that genes and culture are evolving in tandem

COGNATIC KINSHIP SYSTEM

kinship system which assigns social importance to the relatives of both sexes with little formal distinction between them

COGNITIVE COMPRESSION EFFECT

term used in this book to refer to the fact that TV presents personages, events, and information globally and instantly, leaving little time for reflection on the topics, implications, words, etc. contained in a TV message, thus leading to a state in which information is desired and understood mainly in a compressed form

COGNITIVE SCIENCE

interdisciplinary science studying human consciousness mainly with the techniques of artificial intelligence

COGNITIVE STYLE

particular way in which information and knowledge are processed

COGNIZING STATE

rudimentary state of knowing things through the senses

COMICS

narrative text put together by means of a series of drawings arranged in horizontal lines, strips, or rectangles called panels, and read from left to right

COMMEDIA DELL'ARTE

improvised comedic theater, with stock characters and recurring story-lines adapted to fit the preferences of specific audiences, that arose in sixteenth-century Italy and spread throughout Europe

COMMUNAL KNOWING — knowing that derives from living in a cultural setting

COMMUNICATION — production and exchange of messages and meanings

COMMUNICATION SCIENCE — science studying all the technical aspects of communication.

CONATIVE FUNCTION — effect of a message on the addressee

CONCEIT — elaborate, often extravagant, metaphor or simile that makes an association between things that are normally perceived to be totally dissimilar

CONCEPT — general thought connection or pattern made by the human mind (within cultural contexts) through association, induction, deduction, and/or abduction

CONCEPTUAL METAPHOR — generalized metaphorical formula that defines a specific abstraction

CONCEPTUAL METONYM — generalized metonymical formula that defines a specific abstraction

CONCRETE CONCEPT — concept that is demonstrable and observable in a direct way

CONDITIONED RESPONSE — response that has been elicited by some experimental factor

CONDITIONING — process of causing someone to become accustomed to something

CONNOTATION — extended or secondary meaning of a sign

CONNOTATIVE SEQUENCE — sequence of connotations suggested by a text

CONSCIOUSNESS — awareness of one's environment and one's own existence, sensations, and thoughts

CONTACT — physical channel employed in communication and the psychological connections between addresser and addressee

CONTEXT — environment (physical and social) in which signs are produced and messages generated

CONVENTIONAL SIGN — sign that has no apparent connection to any perceivable feature of its referent

COSMOGONIC MYTH	myth explaining how the world came into being
CRITICAL PERIOD HYPOTHESIS	hypothesis formulated by linguist Eric Lenneberg which claims that there is a fixed period of time, from birth to around puberty, during which the brain organizes its division of labor, especially the localization of language to the language centers of the left hemisphere
CRO-MAGNON	early genus of *Homo sapiens sapiens* who lived in western and southern Europe during the last glacial age
CUISINE	term meant to emphasize the difference between the biological and cultural orders in human life in the area of eating; food pertains to the biological order, cuisine to the cultural order
CULTURAL MODEL	constant juxtaposition of conceptual metaphors that leads to a complex abstract model of a concept
CULTURAL SEMIOTICS	branch of semiotics studying culture
CULTURE	interconnected system of daily living that is held together by the signifying order (signs, codes, texts)
CULTURE HERO MYTH	myth describing beings who discover a cultural artifact or technological process that radically changes the course of history
CUNEIFORM WRITING	writing code consisting of wedge-shaped symbols used in ancient Sumerian, Akkadian, Assyrian, Babylonian, and Persian writing

D

DANCE	art of moving rhythmically, usually to music, using prescribed or improvised steps and gestures
DECODING	process of deciphering the message formed in terms of a specific code
DEDUCTION	reasoning and concept-formation which unfolds by the application of a general concept or line of reasoning to a specific occurrence
DEIXIS	process of locating beings, objects, and events in time, space, or relation to each other

DENOTATION	primary, intensional meaning of a sign
DIACHRONY	study of change in signs and codes over time
DICISIGN	in Peircean theory, interpretant of a sinsign
DIMENSIONALITY PRINCIPLE	term utilized in this book to refer to the fact that all systems of knowledge and representation manifest a three-dimensional pattern of firstness, secondness, and thirdness
DISCOURSE	verbal communication involving an addresser and an addressee
DISPLACEMENT	ability to conjure up the things to which signs refer even though these things might not be physically present for the senses to perceive
DISTANCE	space that people maintain between themselves during socially meaningful contact or interaction
DIVERSIFICATION	formation of languages from one source
DRAMA	verbal performing art that involves actors on a stage or platform with the background support of setting and props
DRESS	system of clothing (e.g. the dress code for weddings)

E

ECHOISM	phonic imitation of sounds heard in the environment
ECONOMIC SPHERE	secondary sphere of culture that emerged to institutionalize and regulate the exchange of goods and services among the members of a collectivity
EDUCATIONAL SPHERE	secondary sphere of culture that emerged to institutionalize and regulate the transmission of culturally relevant knowledge and skills to subsequent generations
EMOTIVE CONNOTATION	connotation that conveys personal perspective
EMOTIVE FUNCTION	addresser's emotional intent in communicating something
ENCODING	process of putting together a message in terms of a specific code

ENTROPY	term referring to anything that is unpredictable in a message or text
ENVIRONMENTALISM	view of human mental functioning and development emphasizing the role of upbringing
ESCHATOLOGICAL MYTH	myth describing the end of the world or the coming of death into the world
ETHNICITY	term used to designate inclusion in a kinship unit or social collectivity on the basis of genetic and/or ancestral links
ETHNOGRAPHY	comparative study of cultures based on field work and observation within the cultures themselves
ETHOLOGY	study of animals in their natural habitats
ETYMOLOGY	study of the origin and evolution of signs
EUPHEMISM	rhetorical technique by which a term or phrase that has coarse, sordid, or other unpleasant associations is replaced by one that is perceived to be more delicate or inoffensive
EVOLUTIONARY PSYCHOLOGY	contemporary school of psychology that sees human behaviors and symbolic phenomena as reflexes of evolution and, thus, as residues of animal mechanisms
EVOLUTIONISM	view that cultures result from evolutionary tendencies that are often capable of replacing physical aspects of evolution completely
EXCLAMATION	rhetorical technique by which a sudden outcry expressing strong emotion, such as fright, grief, or hatred, is interpolated into a text
EXTENSIONAL CONNOTATION	semiosic process by which the intensional meaning of a sign is extended freely to add information, insight, perspective, coloration, etc. to it

F

FASHION	prevailing dress style
FEATURE	something that is marked as being present or absent in the constitution of a sound, word, etc.
FEEDBACK	information, signals, cues issuing from the receiver of a message as detected by the

sender, thus allowing h/er to adjust the message to make it clearer, more meaningful, more effective

FETISH — object that is believed to have magical or spiritual powers, or which can cause sexual arousal

FETISHISM — extreme devotion to objects and desires

FICTION — literary work whose content is produced by the imagination and is not necessarily based on fact

FIRSTNESS — in Peircean theory, the first level of meaning, derived from bodily and sensory processes

FOCAL COLOR — color category that is associated with a universal sequencing of colors

FOUNDATION MYTH — myth recounting the founding of cities

G

GENDER — sexual identity established in cultural terms

GENERAL SEMIOTICS — the general study of signs and sign systems

GESTALT — mental form which is extracted from patterns in sensory perception (e.g. circularity, movement, etc.)

GESTALT PSYCHOLOGY — school of psychology that studies the effects or influence of forms (Gestalten) on perceptual processes

GESTICULANT — gesture unit accompanying speech

GESTICULATION — use of gestures to accompany speech

GESTURE — semiosis and representation by means of the hand, the arms, and, to a lesser extent, the head

GRAMMAR — system of rules that characterize any code

GROUND — meaning of a metaphor

GUSTEME — minimal unit of taste

H

HAPTICS — study of touching patterns during social interaction

HEMISPHERICITY	fact that the human brain has two complementary and cooperative hemispheres
HERMENEUTICS	study and interpretation of texts
HIEROGLYPHIC WRITING	ancient Egyptian system of writing, in which pictorial symbols were used to represent meaning or sounds or a combination of meaning and sound
HISTORY FABRICATION EFFECT	term used in this book to refer to the fact that TV both makes and documents historical events
HOLOPHRASE	one-word utterance produced by infants
HOMO ERECTUS	genus of *Homo* that lived 700,000 to a million years ago and that expanded, at the close of h/er evolution, into the temperate parts of Asia
HOMO HABILIS	genus of *Homo* that lived between 1.5 and 2 million years ago, possessing many traits that linked h/er both with the earlier australopithecines and with later members of the genus *Homo*
HOMO SAPIENS	genus of *Homo* that lived between 200,000 and 300,000 years ago, with a proportionately larger brain than any of h/er hominid ancestors
HOMO SAPIENS SAPIENS	modern humans
HOMONYMY	verbal coincidence by which two or more words with distinct meanings are pronounced and/or spelled in the same way
HYPERBOLE	rhetorical exaggeration for effect
HYPOICON	Peirce's term for an icon that is shaped by cultural convention but which can nonetheless be figured out by those who are not members of the culture
HYPONYMY	semantic relation whereby one concept embraces another
I	
ICON	sign in which the signifier has a direct (nonarbitrary), simulative connection to its signified or referent
ICONICITY	process of representing with iconic signs
IDEOGRAPHIC WRITING	type of writing system in which a character, known as an ideograph, may bear

some resemblance to its referent, but is also in part a symbolic signifier

IMAGE SCHEMA

term used by George Lakoff and Mark Johnson to refer to the recurring structures of, or in, our perceptual interactions, bodily experiences, and cognitive operations that portray locations, movements, shapes, etc. in the mind

INDETERMINACY PRINCIPLE

Heisenberg's notion that observations of natural physical phenomena were indeterminate because of the role played by the observer

INDEX

sign in which the signifier has an existential connection to its signified or referent (i.e. the sign indicates that something "exists" somewhere in time and/or space)

INDEXICALITY

process of representing with indexical signs

INDUCTION

reasoning and concept-formation which unfolds by the extraction of a general pattern from specific facts or instances

INFORMATION

any fact or datum that can be stored and retrieved by humans or machines

INFORMATION CONTENT

amount of information in a message

INNATISM

view of human mental functioning and development emphasizing the role of Nature

INTERCONNECTEDNESS PRINCIPLE

view that all signs, texts, and codes in a culture are connected to each other in signifying ways

INTERDISCIPLINARITY PRINCIPLE

practice in semiotics of referring to the research and findings in other disciplines in order to carry out meaningful research on signifying orders

INTERPRETANT

process of adapting a sign's meaning to personal and social experiences

INTERPRETATION

process of deciphering what a sign or text means

INTERTEXTUALITY

allusion within a text to some other text of which the interpreter would normally have knowledge

IRONY

use of words to express something different from and often opposite to their literal meaning; use of words in a humorous but often sarcastic way

K

KINESICS   study of bodily semiosis

KINESTHEME   minimal unit of significant bodily movement

KINSHIP SPHERE   primary sphere of culture based on a genetic/ancestral system of assigning membership

L

LANGUAGE   verbal semiosis and representation

LANGUE   term used by Saussure to refer to the largely unconscious knowledge that speakers of a language share about what is appropriate in that language

LEGAL SPHERE   secondary sphere of culture that emerged to formalize the ways in which the members of a collectivity must relate to each other

LEGEND   story derived from folk history that differs from myth in that it tells about what has happened in the world since the period of its creation

LEGISIGN   in Peircean theory, a representamen (signifier) that designates something by convention

LEXICAL FIELD   set of lexical items (words) related to each other thematically (weather vocabulary, geometrical terms, etc.)

LINGUISTIC COMPETENCE   term used by Chomsky to designate the innate, often unconscious knowledge that allows people to produce and understand sentences, many of which they have never heard before

LINGUISTIC PERFORMANCE   term used by Chomsky to designate the use of a language in actual situations of speech

LINGUISTIC RELATIVITY HYPOTHESIS claim that language, cognition, and culture are interdependent; also known as the Whorfian hypothesis

LINGUISTICS   field studying language, including its uses in cultures

LITERACY — learned ability to read and write at some level of proficiency; i.e. acquired technical knowledge of how to decode written or printed signs and verbal texts

LITOTES — rhetorical technique involving understatement for enhancing the effect of the ideas expressed

LOCALIZATION THEORY — view that specific mental functions have precise locations in specific areas of the brain

LOGOGRAPHIC WRITING — highly symbolic writing system in which a character, known as a logograph, resembles its referent only in small part

LOVEMAP — mental image of what the ideal mate looks like

M

MACROCODE — characterization of culture as an overarching code providing the signifying resources to know, think, learn, etc.

MACROSEMIOTIC — characterization of the type of semiotic analysis involved in showing how certain meanings are distributed throughout a signifying order

MACROSIGNIFIED — a minimal meaning structure (e.g. *up-down, love is a sweetness,* etc.) that is distributed across the signifying order, shaping the constitution of certain signifiers and texts that make up the various codes of that order

MAP — textual representation of a culturally significant territory or space drawn with a combination of iconic, indexical, and symbolic modes of representation

MATRILINEAL KINSHIP SYSTEM — kinship system that assigns membership to kin through the female kinship line only

MEANING — concept that anything in existence has a design or purpose beyond its mere occurrence

MECHANICAL TRANSMISSION — transmission of messages through such means as radio, television, etc.

MEDIATE — characterization of the influencing effect of signs on cognition

MEDIUM — technical or physical means by which a message is transmitted

MEME	sociobiologist's Richard Dawkins' term for replicating patterns of information (tunes, ideas, clothing fashions, etc.)
MESSAGE	meaning of a text
METALINGUAL FUNCTION	communicative function by which the code being used is identified
METAPHOR	signifying process by which two signifying domains (A, B) are connected (A is B)
METONYMY	signifying process by which an entity is used to refer to another that is related to it
MICROSEMIOTIC	characterization of the type of semiotic analysis involved in showing how specific meanings surface in specific signs and texts
MICROSIGNIFIED	a minimal meaning structure (e.g. *good vs. evil, major vs. minor*, etc.) projected onto a sign or text
MODEL	representational form that has been made (or imagined) to stand for an object, event, feeling, etc. or for classes of objects, events, feelings, etc.
MODELING SYSTEM	species-specific system that generates models
MODERNISM	technique in architecture also known as the Bauhaus school
MORPHEME	smallest meaning-bearing unit or form in a language
MORPHOLOGY	formal structure of signifiers
MUSIC	art form based on the organized movement of sounds (sung or played on an instrument) according to rules of combination and contrast (harmony and melody)
MYTH	story of early cultures that aims to explain the origin of life or of the universe in terms of some metaphysical or deistic entity or entities
MYTH OF THE CULTURE HERO	myth describing the actions and characters of beings who are responsible for the discovery of a particular cultural artifact or technological process
MYTHOLOGIZING EFFECT	term used in this book to refer to the fact that TV imbues its characters with a mythological aura

MYTHOLOGY	use and/or evocation of mythic themes in contemporary behaviors and performances; study of myths

N

NAME	sign that identifies a person or place
NAMING	process by which names are assigned to persons, places, and things
NARRATIVE	something told or written, such as an account, story, tale
NARRATIVE STRUCTURE	universal patterns of plot, character, and setting in storytelling
NARRATIVITY	innate human capacity to produce and comprehend narratives
NARRATOLOGY	branch of semiotics that studies narrativity
NARRATOR	teller of the narrative
NARREME	minimal unit of narrative structure
NATION	territory that some collectivity (tribe, race, society, etc.) has gained, inherited, or acquired, identifying it as its own
NATURAL SELECTION	theory formulated by biologist Charles Darwin, according to which the young of a species that survive to produce the next generation tend to embody favorable natural variations (however slight the advantage may be), passing these variations on genetically
NATURAL SIGN	sign that represents its referent by attempting to imitate in its make-up some perceivable property of the referent
NATURAL TRANSMISSION	transmission of messages naturally (through the air channel, through chemical signals, etc.)
NEANDERTHAL	genus of *Homo*, named after the Neander Valley in Germany where one of the earliest skulls was found, which occupied parts of Europe and the Middle East from 100,000 to about 35,000 to 40,000 years ago, after which it disappears from the fossil record
NEOTENY	prolonged juvenile stage of brain and skull development in relation to the time required to reach sexual maturity

NEUROLINGUISTICS	branch of linguistics studying the relation of language to neural processes
NEURON	nerve cell that is the fundamental unit of the nervous system
NEUROSCIENCE	field studying how the brain processes information, generates mental processes, and underlies all aspects of behavior
NOISE	anything that interferes with the reception of a message
NOSTRATIC	original language of humanity
NOVEL	fictional prose narrative in which characters and situations are depicted within the framework of a plot

O

OBJECT	what a sign refers to
OBJECTIFIABLE	perception of a message as separate from the maker of the message
OBJECTIFICATION	process by which interconnected meanings are projected into the objects of a culture, thus creating the perception that they form an integrated system
OBJECTIVITY	perception of knowledge as independent of knowledge making
OCULAREME	minimal unit of eye signaling or contact
ONOMASTICS	study of names
ONOMATOPOEIA	vocal iconicity
ONTOGENESIS	development of all semiosic abilities during childhood
OPEN TEXT	text with an (in theory) unlimited range of meanings (e.g. a poem)
OPPOSITION	process by which signs are differentiated through a minimal change in their form (signifier)
OTHELLO EFFECT	lying in order to emphasize the truth
OXYMORON	rhetorical technique by which two seemingly contradictory or incongruous words are combined

P

PALEONTOLOGY	field that studies and interprets fossils
PANTOMIME	dramatic representation by means of facial expressions and bodily movements rather than words
PARADIGM	structural relation between signs that keeps them distinct and therefore recognizable
PARADOX	statement that appears contradictory or inconsistent
PARALLEL KINSHIP SYSTEM	kinship system by which both males and females trace their ancestry through their own sex
PARALLELISM	repetition of linguistic patterns
PARAMETER	term used by Chomsky to designate the kinds of constraints imposed by culture on the universal primciples of the speech faculty
PAROLE	term used by Saussure to designate the actual use of language in speech
PATRILINEAL KINSHIP SYSTEM	kinship system which assigns membership to kin through the male kinship line only
PERCEPT	unit of perception; stimulus that has been received and recognized; immediate unit of knowing derived from sensation or feeling
PERFORMANCE	representation and communication of some text, framed in a special way and put on display for an audience
PERSONA	Self that one presents in specific social situations
PERSONIFICATION	rhetorical technique whereby inanimate objects or abstract ideas are portrayed as living beings
PERSPECTIVE	technique of representing three-dimensional objects and depth relationships on a two-dimensional surface
PHATIC FUNCTION	communicative function by which contact between addresser and addressee is established
PHILOLOGY	field that studies written texts to determine their meaning and relevance to a specific stage of a culture

PHONEME	minimal unit of sound in a language that allows its users to differentiate meanings
PHONETICS	description and classification of sounds in language
PHONOLOGY	study of sound systems in language
PHYLOGENESIS	evolution of all semiosic abilities in the human species
PHYSICALISM	view that human cognition and culture are the result of genetic processes
PICTOGRAPHIC WRITING	type of writing system in which a character, known as a pictograph, bears pictorial resemblance to its referent
PICTOREME	minimal unit of visual representation
PLOT	plan of events or main story in a narrative or drama
POETIC FUNCTION	communicative function based on poetic language
POETRY	verbal art based on the acoustic, rhythmic, and imagistic properties of words
POLITICAL SPHERE	secondary sphere of culture that emerged to formalize, through some governing system, the overall organization, goals, and aspirations of a society
POP ART	art form that utilizes themes and images taken from mass technological culture
POP CULTURE	form of culture, characteristic of twentieth-century technological societies, that emphasizes the trivial and the routine in its art and in various other forms of representation
POSITIONING	placing or targeting of a product for the right people
POSTMODERNISM	contemporary state of mind which believes that all knowledge is relative and human-made, and that there is no purpose to life beyond the immediate and the present
PRIMARY MODELING SYSTEM	modeling system based on the sensory properties of the body
PRIMARY SPHERE	the kinship and religious spheres of a culture that precede the advent of other spheres in the history of the culture

PROPAGANDA	any systematic dissemination of doctrines, views, etc. reflecting specific interests and ideologies (political, social, and so on)
PROPORTIONALITY	the meaning of words or forms on the basis of binary features or components which keep them distinct
PROTO-LANGUAGE	mother language of a family of languages
PROXEME	minimal unit of space between persons; minimal unit of bodily orientation
PROXEMICS	branch of semiotics that studies the symbolic structure of the physical space maintained between people in social contexts
PSYCHOANALYSIS	field studying unconscious mental processes
PSYCHOLINGUISTICS	branch of linguistics concerned with such topics as language acquisition by children, speech perception, aphasia, and others that involve psychological aspects of language
PSYCHOLOGY	field studying human thinking, behavior, experience, development, and learning
PUBLIC RELATIONS	activities and techniques used by organizations and individuals to establish favorable attitudes and responses to them on the part of the general public or of special groups
PUBLICITY	craft of disseminating any information that concerns a person, group, event, or product through some form of public media

Q

QUALISIGN	in Peircean theory, the representamen (signifier) that refers to a quality

R

RACE	term designating a collectivity of people who share a greater degree of common genetic ancestry among themselves than they do with the members of other collectivities
RECEIVER	person to whom a message or text is directed
RECOGNIZING STATE	cognitive state whereby a referent is recalled
REDUNDANCY	that which is predictable or conventional in a message or text, thus helping to counter-

act the potential interference effects of noise

REFERENT   what is referred to (any object, being, idea, or event)

REFERENTIAL DOMAIN   specific range of meanings to which signs refer

REFERENTIAL FUNCTION   communicative act in which there is a straightforward connection between the act and what it refers to, or communicative function by which a straightforward transmission is intended

REFLEX SYSTEM   term referring to the conversion of meanings into grammatical forms and categories

RELATIVISM   view that an individual's actions and behaviors are shaped primarily in relation to the culture in which s/he has been raised

RELATIVITY PRINCIPLE   in documenting and explaining signifying orders, principle which asserts that the semiotician should keep in mind that signs, codes, and texts have structural effects on individuals

RELIGIOUS SPHERE   primary sphere of culture anchored in the universal belief of early peoples that there is a supernatural or deistic source to existence

REPRESENTAMEN   in Peircean theory, the physical part of a sign

REPRESENTATION   process by which referents are captured by signs or texts

RHEME   in Peircean theory, the interpretant of a qualisign (icon)

RHETORIC   branch of philosophy and semiotics studying the various verbal techniques used in all kinds of discourses, from common conversation to poetry

RHETORICAL QUESTION   rhetorical technique whereby a question is asked not to gain information, but to assert more emphatically the obvious answer to what is asked

RITUAL   performance, ceremony, set of actions or procedures to symbolize some event that bears great meaning

S

SCHOOL SYSTEM

system of transmission of knowledge set up to guarantee the continuation of a signifying order

SCIENCE

discipline based on the collection of facts and their explanation in some generalizable way

SECONDARY MODELING
SYSTEM

modeling system based on verbal semiosis

SECONDARY SPHERE

cultural sphere that emerges after the primary ones (kinship, religion)

SECONDNESS

in Peircean theory, the second level of meaning, derived from verbal processes

SEMANTIC DIFFERENTIAL

experimental technique developed by Osgood, Suci, and Tannenbaum which aims to assess the emotional connotations or annotations evoked by words

SEMANTICS

study of meaning in language

SEMIOLOGY

Saussure's term for the study of signs, now restricted to the study of verbal signs

SEMIOSIS

comprehension and production of signs

SEMIOTICS

science or doctrine that studies signs and their uses in representation

SENDER

transmitter of a message or text

SENSE RATIO

McLuhan's term for the degree to which a physical sense is used in processing information

SENSORY COGNIZING

knowing an object through the senses

SENSORY KNOWING

initial form of knowing something through the senses

SETTING

place and conditions in which a narrative takes place

SEX

classification of an organism as female or male on the basis of its reproductive organs and functions

SEXUALITY

behavior associated with sex

SHELTER

material covering or structure that can be deployed or built to provide protection from weather changes and security against any predator, invader, or aggressor

SIGN	something that stands for something or someone else in some capacity
SIGN LANGUAGE	language code based on gestures and grammatical rules that share some common points with spoken language
SIGNAL	an emission or movement that naturally or conventionally triggers some reaction on the part of a receiver
SIGNIFICATION	process of generating meaning through the use of signs
SIGNIFICATION PRINCIPLE	principle asserting that signifying orders are built on the same signifying properties (iconicity, indexicality, etc.) and that these manifest themselves in different ways according to culture, where they cohere into a specific system of signification
SIGNIFIED	that part of a sign that is referred to
SIGNIFIER	that part of a sign that does the referring; the physical part of a sign
SIGNIFYING ORDER	interconnection of signs, codes, and texts that makes up a culture
SIMILE	rhetorical technique by which two ideas are compared explicitly with the word *like* or *as*
SINSIGN	in Peircean theory, a representamen (signifier) that draws attention to, or singles out, a particular object in time-space
SOCIAL TEXT	text which underlies a signifying order and thus regulates communal sense-making
SOCIETY	collectivity of individuals who share a mainstream culture
SOCIOBIOLOGY	study of biological evolution in terms of its codependency with social and cultural evolution in all species
SOCIOLINGUISTICS	branch of linguistics studying how language functions in society
SOUND SYMBOLISM	process by which referents are represented through some form of vocal iconicity in speech
SOURCE DOMAIN	class of vehicles that deliver a conceptual metaphor

SPEECH	vocalized or articulated language
STRUCTURAL EFFECT	effect on perception and worldview produced by the specific meanings of signs, texts, and codes
STRUCTURALISM	view that all human signifying systems, including culture, manifest regularity, systematicity, patterning, and predictability, keeping them differentiated
STRUCTURE	any repeatable, systematic, patterned, or predictable aspect of signs, codes, texts
SUBJECTIVE KNOWING	knowing that is specific to an individual, rather than to a group
SUBORDINATE LEVEL	level on which a concept has a detailing function
SUBTEXT	text (message) hidden within a text
SUPERORDINATE LEVEL	level on which a concept has a highly general classificatory function
SYLLABARY	writing system based on characters representing syllables
SYLLABLE	word or part of a word pronounced with a single, uninterrupted sounding of the voice (usually a vowel) and generally one or more sounds of lesser sonority (usually consonants)
SYMBOL	sign that represents a referent through cultural convention
SYMBOLICITY	process of representing with symbolic signs
SYMPTOM	bodily sign that stands for some ailment, physical condition, disease
SYNAPSE	junction point of two neurons, across which a nerve impulse passes
SYNCHRONY	study of signs, codes, texts as they exist at a specific point in time
SYNECDOCHE	signifying process by which a part stands for the whole, the whole for a part, the species for the genus, etc.
SYNESTHESIA	juxtaposition of signs so as to evoke different sense modalities simultaneously
SYNONYMY	relation by which the meanings of different signs overlap

SYNTAGM	structural relation that combines signs in code-specific ways
SYNTAX	syntagmatic structure in language

T

TACTEME	minimal unit of touch
TAG	word, phrase, or clause added to a sentence to emphasize a point, to seek approval, to ascertain some reaction
TARGET DOMAIN	topic of a conceptual metaphor
TECHNOLOGY	system of objects made by humans
TENOR	subject of a metaphor (topic)
TERRITORIALITY	mechanism by which animals seek out territories for survival
TERTIARY MODELING SYSTEM	modeling system based on a signifying order
TEXT	a message put together in terms of a specific code
THEATER	reenactment of some event in nature, in life, in society in some carefully scripted way, involving actors and a spatial location, such as a raised stage, around which an audience can view and/or hear the performance
THEORETICAL SEMIOTICS	study of signs and sign systems; also called *general semiotics*
THIRDNESS	in Peircean theory, the third level of meaning derived from symbolic processes
TONE	vocal or musical sound; pitch or modulation of the voice that expresses a particular meaning or feeling; manner of speaking or writing that shows a certain attitude on the part of the speaker or writer; quality or value of color; relative height of pitch with which a syllable or word is pronounced; any one of the full intervals of a diatonic scale
TOPIC	subject of a metaphor (tenor)
TOPONYM	name referring to a place
TRANSMISSION	physical process of sending messages or texts to a receiver

TRIBE	collectivity of human beings sharing a signifying order, a territory, and a history grounded in the primary spheres
TROPE	figure of speech
TURING MACHINE	computer program
TURING TEST	hypothetical test devised by mathematician Alan Turing to show that one could program a computer in such a way that it would be virtually impossible to discriminate between its answers and those contrived by a human being

U

UNCONSCIOUS	in psychoanalytic theory, a hypothetical region of the mind containing wishes, memories, fears, feelings, and ideas that are prevented from expression in conscious awareness
UNILATERAL KINSHIP SYSTEM	kinship system which assigns membership to kin through either the maternal or the paternal kinship line
UNIVERSAL GRAMMAR	Chomsky's notion that the brain has a set of innate principles that undergird the development of specific languages
UNIVERSAL PRINCIPLES	view that certain features of language are universal, being part of a purported human "language organ"

V

VEHICLE	part of a metaphor to which a tenor is connected
VISEME	minimal unit of visual representation

W

WHORFIAN HYPOTHESIS	view elaborated by Benjamin Lee Whorf that the language one speaks shapes h/er worldview
WRITING	process of representing speech with characters

Z

ZOOSEMIOTICS	branch of semiotics studying semiosis in and across species

Works Cited and General Bibliography

The following bibliography includes both the works cited in the text and more generally the works that have constituted the bibliographical backbone of our exposition of the various topics treated. It thus constitutes a source of reference and a general reading list.

A

Abbott, E. A. (1884). *Flatland: A Romance of Many Dimensions.* London: Seeley.
Abercrombie, N. (1996). *Television and Society.* Cambridge: Polity Press.
Adatto, K. (1993). *Picture Perfect: The Art and Artifice of Public Image Making.* New York: Basic Books.
Aitchison, J. (1983). *The Articulate Mammal: An Introduction to Psycholinguistics.* London: Hutchison.
Aitchison, J. (1996). *The Seeds of Speech: Language Origin and Evolution.* Cambridge: Cambridge University Press.
Allert, B. (1996) (ed.). *Languages of Visuality: Crossings between Science, Art, Politics, and Literature.* Detroit: Wayne State University Press.
Alpher, B. (1987). Feminine as the Unmarked Grammatical Gender: Buffalo Girls Are No Fools. *Australian Journal of Linguistics* 7: 169-187.
Alsted, C., and Larsen, H. H. (1991). Choosing Complexity of Signs in Ads. *Marketing Signs* 10: 1-14.
Alverson, H. (1991). Metaphor and Experience: Looking Over the Notion of Image Schema. In: J. W. Fernandez (ed.), *Beyond Metaphor: The Theory of Tropes in Anthropology,* 94–117. Stanford: Stanford University Press.
Alverson, H. (1994). *Semantics and Experience: Universal Metaphors of Time in English, Mandarin, Hindi, and Sesotho.* Baltimore: Johns Hopkins University Press.
Anderson, J. A. (1983). *The Architecture of Cognition.* Cambridge, Mass.: Harvard University Press.
Anderson, R. C., and Ortony, A. (1975). On Putting Apples into Bottles: A Problem in Polysemy. *Cognitive Psychology* 101: 301-306.
Anderson, W. T. (1992). *Reality Isn't What It Used to Be.* San Francisco: Harper Collins.
Andersson, L., and Trudgill, P. (1990). *Bad Language.* London: Blackwell.
Andren, G. L., Ericsson, L., Ohlsson, R., and Tännsjö, T. (1978). *Rhetoric and Ideology in Advertising.* Stockholm: AB Grafiska.
Andrews, E. (1990). *Markedness Theory.* Durham: Duke University Press.
Andrews, E., and Tobin, Y. (1996) (eds.). *Toward a Calculus of Meaning: Studies in Markedness, Distinctive Features and Deixis.* Amsterdam: John Benjamins.
Appelbaum, D. (1990). *Voice.* Albany: State University of New York Press.
Ardrey, R. (1966). *The Territorial Imperative.* New York: Atheneum.
Argyle, M. (1988). *Bodily Communication.* New York: Methuen.
Aristotle. (1952a). Rhetoric. In: W. D. Ross (ed.), *The Works of Aristotle,* Vol. 11. Oxford: Clarendon Press.

Aristotle. (1952b). *Poetics*. In: W. D. Ross (ed.), *The Works of Aristotle,* Vol. 11. Oxford: Clarendon Press.

Armstrong, D., and Katz, S. H. (1983). Brain Laterality in Signed and Spoken Language: Neural Factors in the Evolution of Linguistic Behavior. In: E. de Grolier (ed.), *Glossogenetics: The Origin and Evolution of Language,* 211–234. Utrecht: Harwood.

Armstrong, D. F., Stokoe, W. C., and Wilcox, S. E. (1995). *Gesture and the Nature of Language.* Cambridge: Cambridge University Press.

Arnheim, R. (1969). *Visual Thinking.* Berkeley: University of California Press.

Arnheim, R. (1986). *New Essays on the Psychology of Art.* Berkeley: University of California Press.

Asch, S. (1950). On the Use of Metaphor in the Description of Persons. In: H. Werner (ed.), *On Expressive Language,* 86–94. Worcester: Clark University Press.

Asch, S. (1958). The Metaphor: A Psychological Inquiry. In: R. Tagiuri and L. Petrullo (eds.), *Person Perception and Interpersonal Behavior,* 28–42. Stanford: Stanford University Press.

Ashley, L. R. N. (1984). *The History of the Short Story.* Washington, D. C.: US Information Agency.

Atwan, R. (1979). *Edsels, Luckies and Frigidaires: Advertising the American Way.* New York: Dell.

Auer, P. (1988). On Deixis and Displacement. *Folia Linguistica* 22: 263-292.

Austin, J. L. (1962). *How to Do Things with Words.* Cambridge, Mass.: Harvard University Press.

Axtell, R. E. (1991). *Gestures.* New York: John Wiley.

B

Bachand, D. (1992). The Art of (in) Advertising: From Poetry to Prophecy. *Marketing Signs* 13: 1-7.

Baigrie, B. S. (1996) (ed.). *Picturing Knowledge: Historical and Philosophical Problems Concerning the Use of Art in Science.* Toronto: University of Toronto Press.

Bal, M. (1985). *Narratology: Introduction to the Theory of the Narrative.* Toronto: University of Toronto Press.

Barbe, K. (1995). *Irony in Context.* Amsterdam: John Benjamins.

Barkow, J. H., Cosmides, L., and Tooby, J. (1992) (eds.). *The Adapted Mind: Evolutionary Psychology and the Generation of Culture.* Oxford: Oxford University Press.

Barlow, H., Blakemore, C., and Weston-Smith, M. (1990) (eds.). *Images and Understanding.* Cambridge: Cambridge University Press.

Barnes, J. A. (1994). *A Pack of Lies: Towards a Sociology of Lying.* Cambridge: Cambridge University Press.

Baron, N. (1992). *Growing Up with Language: How Children Learn to Talk.* Reading, Mass.: Addison-Wesley.

Barrett, W. (1986). *The Death of the Soul: From Descartes to the Computer.* New York: Anchor.

Barthel, D. (1988). *Putting on Appearances: Gender and Advertising.* Philadelphia: Temple University Press.

Barthes, R. (1957). *Mythologies.* Paris: Seuil.

Barthes, R. (1964). *Éléments de sémiologie.* Paris: Seuil.

Barthes, R. (1967). *Système de la mode.* Paris: Seuil.

Barthes, R. (1968). *Elements of Semiology.* London: Cape.

Barthes, R. (1970). *S/Z,* trans. by R. Miller. New York: Hill and Wang.

Barthes, R. (1977). *Image-Music-Text.* London: Fontana.

Basso, K. H. (1976). *Meaning in Anthropology.* Albuquerque: University of New Mexico Press.

Basso, K. H. (1990). *Western Apache Language and Culture: Essays in Linguistic Anthropology.* Tucson: University of Arizona Press.

Battistella, E. L. (1990). *Markedness: The Evaluative Superstructure of Language.* Albany: State University of New York Press.

Bauman, R. (1992). Performance. In: R. Bauman (ed.), *Folklore, Cultural Performances, and Popular Entertainments,* 41-49. Oxford: Oxford University Press.

Bauman, Z. (1992). *Intimations of Postmodernity.* London: Routledge.

Bayles, M. (1994). *Hole in Our Soul: The Loss of Beauty and Meaning in American Popular Music.* New York: Free Press.

Beaken, M. (1996). *The Making of Language.* Edinburgh: Edinburgh University Press.

Bechtel, W. (1988). *Philosophy of Mind: An Overview for Cognitive Science.* Hillsdale, N.J.: Lawrence Erlbaum Associates.

Beer, G. (1983). *Darwin's Plots: Evolutionary Narrative in Darwin, George Eliot and Nineteenth-Century Fiction.* London: Routledge and Kegan Paul.

Bellack, L., and Baker, S. S. (1983). *Reading Faces.* New York: Bantam.

Bénard, J., and Hamm, J-J. (1996) (eds.). *The Book: From Gutenberg to the Microchip.* Ottawa: Legas.

Benedict, H. (1979). Early Lexical Development: Comprehension and Production. *Journal of Child Language* 6: 183-200.

Benedict, R. (1934). *Patterns of Culture.* New York: New American Library.

Bennett, T. J. A. (1988). *Aspects of English Colour Collocations and Idioms.* Heidelberg: Winter.

Berger, A. A. (1996). *Manufacturing Desire: Media, Popular Culture, and Everyday Life.* New Brunswick, N.J.: Transaction Publishers.

Berger, J. (1972). *Ways of Seeing.* Harmondsworth: Penguin.

Bergin, T. G., and Fisch, M. (1984 [1948]). *The New Science of Giambattista Vico.* Ithaca: Cornell University Press.

Berlin, B., and Berlin, E. A. (1975). Aguarana Color Categories. *American Ethnologist* 2: 61–87.

Berlin, B., and Kay, P. (1969). *Basic Color Terms.* Berkeley: University of California Press.

Bettelheim, B. (1989). *The Uses of Enchantment: The Meaning and Importance of Fairy Tales.* New York: Vintage.

Bickerton, D. (1969). Prolegomena to a Linguistic Theory of Metaphor. *Foundations of Language* 5: 34-52.

Bickerton, D. (1981). *The Roots of Language.* Ann Arbor: Karoma Publishers.

Bickerton, D. (1990). *Language and Species.* Chicago: University of Chicago Press.

Bickerton, D. (1995). *Language and Human Behavior.* Seattle: University of Washington Press.

Bierlein, J. F. (1994). *Parallel Myths.* New York: Ballantine.

Billeter, J. F. (1990). *The Chinese Art of Writing.* New York: Rizzoli.

Billow, R. M. (1975). A Cognitive Developmental Study of Metaphor Comprehension. *Developmental Psychology* 11: 415-423.

Birdwhistell, R. (1970). *Kinesics and Context: Essays on Body Motion Communication.* Harmondsworth: Penguin.

Birren, F. (1997). *The Power of Color.* Secaucus, N.J.: Citadel.

Black, M. (1962). *Models and Metaphors.* Ithaca: Cornell University Press.

Bloom, A. (1981). *The Linguistic Shaping of Thought: A Study in the Impact of Language on Thinking in China and the West.* Hillsdale, N.J.: Lawrence Erlbaum Associates.

Bloomfield, L. (1933). *Language.* New York: Holt.

Blumenberg, H. (1985). *Work on Myth.* Cambridge, Mass.: MIT Press.

Boas, F. (1940). *Race, Language, and Culture.* New York: Free Press.

Bonner, J. T. (1980). *The Evolution of Culture in Animals.* Princeton: Princeton University Press.

Boole, G. (1854). *An Investigation of the Laws of Thought.* New York: Dover.

Booth, W. (1979). Metaphor as Rhetoric: The Problem of Evaluation. In: S. Sacks (ed.), *On Metaphor*, 47-70. Chicago: University of Chicago Press.

Bosmajian, H. (1974). *The Language of Oppression*. Washington, D. C.: Public Affairs Press.

Bosmajian, H. (1992). *Metaphor and Reason in Judicial Opinions*. Carbondale: Southern Illinois University Press.

Botha, R. P. (1989). *Challenging Chomsky: The Generative Garden Game*. London: Blackwell.

Bouissac, P. (1973). *La mesure des gestes*. The Hague: Mouton.

Bouissac, P., Herzfeld, M., and Posner, R. (1986) (eds.). *Iconicity: Essays on the Nature of Culture. Festschrift for Thomas A. Sebeok on His 65th Birthday*. Tübingen: Stauffenburg.

Boysson-Bardies, B. de and Vihman, M. M. (1991). Adaptation to Language: Evidence from Babbling and First Words in Four Languages. *Language* 67: 297-319.

Brakel, A. (1983). *Phonological Markedness and Distinctive Features*. Bloomington: Indiana University Press.

Brand, P., and Yancey, P. (1993). *Pain*. New York: Harper Collins.

Bremer, J., and Roodenburg, H. (1991) (eds.). *A Cultural History of Gesture*. Ithaca: Cornell University Press.

Brent, J. (1994). *Charles Sanders Peirce: A Life*. Bloomington: Indiana University Press.

Britton, B. K., and Pellegrini, A. D. (1990) (eds.). *Narrative Thought and Narrative Language*. Hillsdale, N.J.: Lawrence Erlbaum Associates.

Britton, J. (1970). *Language and Learning*. Harmondsworth: Penguin.

Bronowski, J. (1977). *A Sense of the Future*. Cambridge, Mass.: MIT Press.

Bronowski, J. (1978). *The Origins of Knowledge and Imagination*. New Haven: Yale University Press.

Brown, R. L. (1967). *Wilhelm von Humboldt's Conception of Linguistic Relativity*. The Hague: Mouton.

Brown, R. W. (1958). *Words and Things: An Introduction to Language*. New York: The Free Press.

Brown, R. W. (1970). *Psycholinguistics*. New York: The Free Press.

Brown, R. W. (1973). *A First Language*. Cambridge, Mass.: Harvard University Press.

Brown, R. W., Leiter, R. A., and Hildum, D.C. (1957). Metaphors from Music Criticism. *Journal of Abnormal and Social Psychology* 54: 347-352.

Brownell, H. H. (1988). Appreciation of Metaphoric and Connotative Word Meaning by Brain-Damaged Patients. In: C. Chiarello (ed.), *Right Hemisphere Contributions to Lexical Semantics*, 19-32. New York: Academic.

Brownell, H. H., Potter, H. H., and Michelow, D. (1984). Sensitivity to Lexical Denotation and Connotation in Brain-Damaged Patients: A Double Dissociation? *Brain and Language* 22: 253-265.

Brugman, C. M. (1983). *Story of Over*. Bloomington: Indiana Linguistics Club.

Bruner, J. S. (1986). *Actual Minds, Possible Worlds*. Cambridge, Mass.: Harvard University Press.

Bruner, J. S. (1990). *Acts of Meaning*. Cambridge, Mass.: Harvard University Press.

Brunning, J., and Forster, P. (1997) (eds.). *The Rule of Reason: The Philosophy of Charles Sanders Peirce*. Toronto: University of Toronto Press.

Brusatin, M. (1991). *A History of Colors*. Boston: Shambhala.

Buck, C. D. (1949). *A Dictionary of Selected Synonyms in the Principal European Languages*. Chicago: University of Chicago Press.

Bühler, K. (1934). *Sprachtheorie: Die Darstellungsfunktion der Sprache*. Jena: Fischer.

Bühler, K. (1951 [1908]). On Thought Connection. In: D. Rapaport (ed.), *Organization and Pathology of Thought*, 81-92. New York: Columbia University Press.

Burke, K. (1966). *Language as Symbolic Action: Essays on Life, Literature, and Method.* Berkeley: University of California Press.
Bybee, J., Perkins, R., and Pagliuca, W. (1994) (eds.). *The Evolution of Grammar: Tense, Aspect, and Modality in the Languages of the World.* Chicago: University of Chicago Press.

C

Calvin, W. H., and Ojemann, G. A. (1994). *Conversations with Neil's Brain: The Neural Nature of Thought and Language.* New York: Addison-Wesley.
Campbell, J. (1949). *The Hero with a Thousand Faces.* New York: Pantheon.
Campbell, J. (1969). *Primitive Mythology.* Harmondsworth: Penguin.
Candland, D. K. (1993). *Feral Children and Clever Animals.* Oxford: Oxford University Press.
Carlson, M. (1989). *Places of Performance: The Semiotics of Theatre Architecture.* Ithaca: Cornell University Press.
Caron, J. (1992). *An Introduction to Psycholinguistics.* Toronto: University of Toronto Press.
Cartmill, M., Pilbeam, D., and Isaac, G. (1986). One Hundred Years of Paleoanthropology. *American Scientist* 74: 410-420.
Casad, E. H. (1996) (ed.). *Cognitive Linguistics in the Redwoods: The Expansion of a New Paradigm in Linguistics.* Berlin: Mouton de Gruyter.
Cashmore, E. (1994). *And There Was Television.* London: Routledge.
Cassirer, E. A. (1944). *An Essay on Man.* New Haven: Yale University Press.
Cassirer, E. A. (1946). *Language and Myth.* New York: Dover.
Cassirer, E. A. (1957). *The Philosophy of Symbolic Forms.* New Haven: Yale University Press.
Casson, R. W. (1981). Folk Classification: Relativity and Universality. In: R. W. Casson (ed.), *Language, Culture, and Cognition,* 75–89. New York: Macmillan.
Casti, J. L. (1989). *Paradigms Lost.* New York: Avon.
Casti, J. L. (1990). *Searching for Certainty.* New York: Morrow.
Cavalli-Sforza, L., and Cavalli-Sforza, F. (1995). *The Great Human Diasporas: The History of Diversity and Evolution.* Reading, Mass.: Addison-Wesley.
Cavalli-Sforza, L., and Feldman, M. (1981). *Cultural Transmission and Evolution.* Princeton: Princeton University Press.
Chiarello, C. (1988) (ed.). *Right Hemisphere Contributions to Lexical Semantics.* Berlin: Springer.
Chomsky, N. (1957). *Syntactic Structures.* The Hague: Mouton.
Chomsky, N. (1964). Degrees of Grammaticalness. In: J. A. Fodor and J. A. Katz (eds.), *The Structure of Language,* 384-389. Englewood Cliffs, N.J.: Prentice-Hall.
Chomsky, N. (1965). *Aspects of the Theory of Syntax.* Cambridge, Mass.: MIT Press.
Chomsky, N. (1966a). *Topics in the Theory of Grammar.* The Hague: Mouton.
Chomsky, N. (1966b). *Cartesian Linguistics.* New York: Harper and Row.
Chomsky, N. (1975). *Reflections on Language.* New York: Pantheon.
Chomsky, N. (1982). *Some Concepts and Consequences of the Theory of Government and Binding.* Cambridge, Mass.: MIT Press.
Chomsky, N. (1986). *Knowledge of Language: Its Nature, Origin, and Use.* New York: Praeger.
Chomsky, N. (1990). Language and Mind. In: D. H. Mellor (ed.), *Ways of Communicating,* 56–80. Cambridge: Cambridge University Press.
Chomsky, N. (1992). Language and the Cognitive Revolution. *Golem* 2: 3–4.
Chomsky, N. (1995). *The Minimalist Program.* Cambridge, Mass.: MIT Press.
Clark, E. V. (1993). *The Lexicon in Acquisition.* Cambridge: Cambridge University Press.
Clarke, D. S. (1987). *Principles of Semiotic.* London: Routledge and Kegan Paul.

Classen, C. (1991). The Sensory Order of Wild Children. In: D. Howes (ed.), *The Varieties of Sensory Experience*, 47-60. Toronto: University of Toronto Press.

Classen, C. (1993). *Worlds of Sense: Exploring the Senses in History and across Cultures*. London: Routledge.

Classen, C., Howes, D., and Synnott, A. (1994). *Aroma: The Cultural History of Smell*. London: Routledge.

Cleveland, C. E. (1986). Semiotics: Determining What the Advertising Message Means to the Audience. In: J. Olson and K. Sentis (eds.), *Advertising and Consumer Psychology*, Vol. 3, 227-241. New York: Praeger.

Colapietro, V., and Olshewsky, T. (1995). *Peirce's Doctrine of Signs: Theory, Applications, and Connections*. Berlin: Mouton de Gruyter.

Cole, K. C. (1984). *Sympathetic Vibrations*. New York: Bantam.

Colton, H. (1983). *The Gift of Touch*. New York: Putnam.

Connor, K., and Kogan, N. (1980). Topic-Vehicle Relations in Metaphor: The Issue of Asymmetry. In: R. P. Honeck and R. R. Hoffman (eds.), *Cognition and Figurative Language*, 238-308. Hillsdale, N.J.: Lawrence Erlbaum Associates.

Connor, M. K. (1995). *Cool: Understanding Black Manhood in America*. New York: Crown.

Cooley, C. H. (1909). *Social Organization*. New York: Scribner.

Cooper, B. L., and Haney, W. S. (1995). *Rock Music in American Popular Culture*. New York: Harrington Park Press.

Corbett, G. (1991). *Gender*. Cambridge: Cambridge University Press.

Coté, J. E., and Allahar, A. L. (1994). *Generation on Hold: Coming of Age in the Late Twentieth Century*. Toronto: Stoddart.

Coulmas, F. (1989). *The Writing Systems of the World*. Oxford: Blackwell.

Courtenoy, A. E., and Whipple, T. W. (1983). *Sex Stereotyping in Advertising*. Lexington, Mass.: Lexington Books.

Cox, M. (1992). *Children's Drawings*. Harmondsworth: Penguin.

Craig, C. (1986) (ed.). *Noun Classes and Categorization*. Amsterdam: John Benjamins.

Craik, J. (1993). *The Face of Fashion: Cultural Studies in Fashion*. London: Routledge.

Craik, K. (1943). *The Nature of Explanation*. Cambridge: Cambridge University Press.

Crawford, C. (1988). *The Beginnings of Nietzsche's Theory of Language*. Berlin: Mouton de Gruyter.

Crawford, M. (1995). *Talking Difference: On Gender and Language*. Thousand Oaks: Sage.

Crispin Miller, M. (1988). *Boxed In: The Culture of TV*. Evanston: Northwestern University Press.

Crystal, D. (1987). *The Cambridge Encyclopedia of Language*. Cambridge: Cambridge University Press.

Cumming, R., and Porter, T. (1990). *The Colour Eye*. London: BBC.

Curtiss, S. (1977). *Genie: A Psycholinguistic Study of a Modern-day "Wild Child."* New York: Academic.

D

D'Andrade, R. (1995). *The Development of Cognitive Anthropology*. Cambridge: Cambridge University Press.

D'Andrade, R., and Strauss, C. (1992) (eds.). *Human Motives and Cultural Models*. Cambridge: Cambridge University Press.

Dance, F., and Larson, C. (1976). *The Functions of Communication: A Theoretical Approach*. New York: Holt, Rinehart and Winston.

Dane, J. A. (1991). *The Critical Mythology of Irony*. Athens: University of Georgia Press.

Danesi, M. (1976). *La lingua dei Sermoni Subalpini*. Torino: Centro Studi Piemontesi.

Danesi, M. (1987). *Robert A. Hall and American Structuralism*. Lake Bluff, Ill.: Jupiter Press.

Danesi, M. (1989). The Neurological Coordinates of Metaphor. *Communication and Cognition* 22: 73-86.

Danesi, M. (1990). Thinking Is Seeing: Visual Metaphors and the Nature of Abstract Thought. *Semiotica* 80: 221-237.

Danesi, M. (1993). *Vico, Metaphor, and the Origin of Language*. Bloomington: Indiana University Press.

Danesi, M. (1994). *Cool: The Signs and Meanings of Adolescence*. Toronto: University of Toronto Press.

Danesi, M. (1995a). *Giambattista Vico and the Cognitive Science Enterprise*. New York: Peter Lang.

Danesi, M. (1995b). *Interpreting Advertisements: A Semiotic Guide*. Ottawa: Legas.

Danesi, M., and Santeramo, D. (1995). *Deictic Verbal Constructions*. Urbino: Centro Internazionale di Semiotica e di Linguistica.

Daniels, H. (1996) (ed.). *An Introduction to Vygotsky*. London: Routledge.

Daniels, P. T., and Bright, W. (1995) (eds.). *The World's Writing Systems*. Oxford: Oxford University Press.

Danna, S. R. (1992). *Advertising and Popular Culture: Studies in Variety and Versatility*. Bowling Green, Ohio: Bowling Green State University Popular Press.

Darwin, C. (1858). *The Origin of Species*. New York: Collier.

Darwin, C. (1871). *The Descent of Man*. New York: Modern Library.

Darwin, C. (1872). *The Expression of the Emotions in Man and Animals*. London: Murray.

Davidoff, J. (1991). *Cognition through Color*. Cambridge, Mass.: MIT Press.

Davies, R. (1989). *How to Read Faces*. Woolnough: Aquarian.

Davis, F. (1992). *Fashion, Culture, and Identity*. Chicago: University of Chicago Press.

Davis, P. J., and Hersh, R. (1986). *Descartes' Dream: The World According to Mathematics*. Boston: Houghton Mifflin.

Davydov, V. V., and Radzikhovskii, L. A. (1985). Vygotsky's Theory and the Activity Oriented Approach in Psychology. In: J. V. Wertsch (ed.), *Culture, Communication and Cognition: Vygotskian Perspectives*, 59-69. Cambridge: Cambridge University Press.

Dawkins, R. (1976). *The Selfish Gene*. Oxford: Oxford University Press.

Dawkins, R. (1987). *The Blind Watchmaker*. Harlow: Longmans.

Dawkins, R. (1995). *River Out of Eden: A Darwinian View of Life*. New York: Basic.

De Laguna, G. A. (1927). *Speech: Its Function and Development*. Bloomington: Indiana University Press.

De Toro, F. (1995). *Theatre Semiotics: Text and Staging in Modern Theatre*. Toronto: University of Toronto Press.

Deacon, T. W. (1997). *The Symbolic Species: The Co-Evolution of Language and the Brain*. New York: Norton.

Deely, J. (1990). *Basics of Semiotics*. Bloomington: Indiana University Press.

Deely, J. (1994). *New Beginnings: Early Modern Philosophy and Postmodern Thought*. Toronto: University of Toronto Press.

Déjerine, J. (1892). Contribution à l'étude anatomo-pathologique et clinique des différents variétés de cécité verbale. *Comptes Rendus des Sciences de la Société de Biologie* 9: 61-90.

Dennett, D. C. (1991). *Consciousness Explained*. Boston: Little, Brown.

Dennett, D. C. (1995). *Darwin's Dangerous Idea: Evolution and the Meanings of Life*. New York: Simon and Schuster.

Deregowski, J. B. (1972). Pictorial Perception and Culture. *Scientific American* 227: 82-88.

Derrida, J. (1976). *Of Grammatology*, trans. by G. C. Spivak. Baltimore: Johns Hopkins Press.
Descartes, R. (1637). *Essaies philosophiques*. Leyden: L'imprimerie de Ian Maire.
Di Pietro, R. J. (1976). *Language as Human Creation*. Washington, D. C.: Georgetown University Press.
Di Pietro, R. J. (1987). *Strategic Interaction*. Cambridge: Cambridge University Press.
Diamond, A. A. (1959). *The History and Origin of Language*. New York: Philosophical Library.
Dissanayake, E. (1992). *Homo Aestheticus: Where Art Comes from and Why*. New York: Free Press.
Docker, J. (1994). *Postmodernism and Popular Culture: A Cultural History*. Cambridge: Cambridge University Press.
Dondis, D. A. (1986). *A Primer of Visual Literacy*. Cambridge, Mass.: MIT Press.
Douglas, M. (1966). *Purity and Danger*. Harmondsworth: Penguin.
Douglas, M. (1992). *Objects and Objections*. Toronto: Toronto Semiotic Circle.
Douglas, S. J. (1994). *Where the Girls Are: Growing Up Female with the Mass Media*. New York: Times.
Dubin, L. S. (1987). *The History of Beads*. New York: Abrams.
Duchan, J. F., Bruder, G. A., and Hewitt, L. E. (1995) (eds.). *Deixis in Narrative: A Cognitive Science Perspective*. Hillsdale, N.J.: Lawrence Erlbaum Associates.
Dunbar, R. (1997). *Grooming, Gossip, and the Evolution of Language*. Cambridge, Mass.: Harvard University Press.
Dundes, A. (1972). Seeing Is Believing. *Natural History* 81: 9-12.
Dunning, W. V. (1991). *Changing Images of Pictorial Space: A History of Visual Illusion in Painting*. Syracuse: Syracuse University Press.
Dupré, J. (1990). Reflections on Biology and Culture. In: J. J. Sheehan and M. Sosna (eds.), *The Boundaries of Humanity*, 125-131. Berkeley: University of California Press.
Durkheim, E. (1912). *The Elementary Forms of Religious Life*. New York: Collier.
Dyer, G. (1982). *Advertising as Communication*. London: Routledge.

E

Eagleton, T. (1983). *Literary Theory: An Introduction*. Minneapolis: University of Minnesota Press.
Eble, C. (1989). *College Slang 101*. Georgetown, Conn.: Spectacle Lane Press.
Eble, C. (1996). *Slang and Sociability*. Chapel Hill: University of North Carolina Press.
Eccles, J. C. (1989). *Evolution of the Brain: Creation of the Self*. London: Routledge.
Eccles, J. C. (1992). *The Human Psyche*. London: Routledge.
Eckman, F. R. *et al.* (1983) (eds.). *Markedness*. New York: Plenum.
Eco, U. (1976). *A Theory of Semiotics*. Bloomington: Indiana University Press.
Eco, U. (1978). Semiotics: A Discipline or an Interdisciplinary Method. In: A. Sebeok (ed.), *Sight, Sound, and Sense*, 73-88. Bloomington: Indiana University Press.
Eco, U. (1979). *The Role of the Reader: Explorations in the Semiotics of Texts*. Bloomington: Indiana University Press.
Eco, U. (1984). *Semiotics and the Philosophy of Language*. Bloomington: Indiana University Press.
Eco, U. (1990). *The Limits of Interpretation*. Bloomington: Indiana University Press.
Edie, J. M. (1976). *Speaking and Meaning: The Phenomenology of Language*. Bloomington: Indiana University Press.
Eichler, E. *et al.* (1995). *Namensforschung*. Berlin: Mouton de Gruyter.
Ekman, P. (1976). Movements with Precise Meanings. *Journal of Communication* 26: 14-26.

Ekman, P. (1980). The Classes of Nonverbal Behavior. In: W. Raffler-Engel (ed.), *Aspects of Nonverbal Communication*, 89-102. Lisse: Swets and Zeitlinger.

Ekman, P. (1982). Methods for Measuring Facial Action. In: K. R. Scherer and P. Ekman (eds.), *Handbook of Methods in Nonverbal Behavior*, 45-90. Cambridge: Cambridge University Press.

Ekman, P. (1985). *Telling Lies*. New York: Norton.

Ekman, P., and Friesen, W. (1975). *Unmasking the Face*. Englewood Cliffs: Prentice-Hall.

Eliade, M. (1963). *Myth and Reality*. New York: Harper and Row.

Eliade, M. (1972). *A History of Religious Ideas*. Chicago: University of Chicago Press.

Emantian, M. (1995). Metaphor and the Expression of Emotion: The Value of Cross-Cultural Perspectives. *Metaphor and Symbolic Activity* 10: 163-182.

Emmorey, K., and Reilly, J. (1995) (eds.). *Language, Gesture, and Space*. Hillsdale, N.J.: Lawrence Erlbaum Associates.

Engen, T. (1982). *The Perception of Odours*. New York: Academic.

Enninger, W. (1992). Clothing. In: R. Bauman (ed.), *Folklore, Cultural Performances, and Popular Entertainments*, 123-145. Oxford: Oxford University Press.

Espes Brown, J. (1992). Becoming Part of It. In: D. M. Dooling and P. Jordan-Smith (eds.), *I Become Part of It: Sacred Dimensions in Native American Life*, 1-15. New York: Harper Collins.

Everaert, M. *et al.* (1995). *Idioms: Structural and Psychological Perspectives*. Mahwah, N.J.: Lawrence Erlbaum Associates.

Ewen, S. (1976). *Captains of Consciousness*. New York: McGraw-Hill.

Ewen, S. (1988). *All Consuming Images*. New York: Basic Books.

F

Farb, P. (1974). *Word Play*. New York: Bantam.

Fauconnier, G., and Sweetser, E. (1996). *Spaces, Worlds, and Grammar*. Chicago: University of Chicago Press.

Feher, M., Naddaf, R., and Tazi, N. (1989) (eds.). *Fragments for a History of the Human Body*. New York: Zone.

Fernandez, J. W. (1991) (ed.). *Beyond Metaphor: The Theory of Tropes in Anthropology*. Stanford: Stanford University Press.

Fernando, S. H. (1994). *The New Beats: Exploring the Music, Culture, and Attitudes of Hip-Hop*. New York: Anchor.

Fillmore, C. J. (1982). Towards a Descriptive Framework for Spatial Deixis. In: R. J. Jarvella and W. Klein (eds.), *Speech, Place and Action: Studies in Deixis and Related Topics*, 31-59. New York: John Wiley.

Fincher, J. (1976). *Human Intelligence*. New York: G. P. Putnam's Sons.

Fisch, M. H. (1978). Peirce's General Theory of Signs. In: Thomas A. Sebeok (ed.), *Sight, Sound, and Sense*, 31-70. Bloomington: Indiana University Press.

Fischer, J. L. (1961). Art Styles as Cultural Cognitive Maps. *American Anthropologist* 63: 79-93.

Fisher, H. E. (1992). *Anatomy of Love*. New York: Norton.

Fiske, J. (1982). *Introduction to Communication Studies*. London: Routledge.

Fiske, J. (1987). *Television Culture*. London: Methuen.

Fiumara, G. (1995). *The Metaphoric Process: Connections between Language and Life*. London: Routledge.

Flanagan, O. J. (1984). *The Science of the Mind*. Cambridge, Mass.: MIT Press.

Fleming, D. (1996). *Powerplay: Toys as Popular Culture*. Manchester: Manchester University Press.

Fletcher, A. (1991). *Colors of the Mind: Connections on Thinking in Literature*. Cambridge, Mass.: Harvard University Press.

Floch, J. M. (1983). The Semiotics of the Plastic Arts and the Language of Advertising. In: P. Perron (ed.), *Paris School Semiotics: Texts and Documents*, Vol. 1, 67–84. Toronto: Toronto Semiotic Circle.

Fogelin, R. J. (1988). *Figuratively Speaking*. New Haven: Yale University Press.
Forceville, C. (1996). *Pictorial Metaphor in Advertising*. London: Routledge.
Fornäs, J., Lindberg, U., and Senhede, O. (1995). *In Garageland: Rock, Youth and Modernity*. London: Routledge.
Foucault, M. (1972). *The Archeology of Knowledge*, trans. by A. M. Sheridan Smith. New York: Pantheon.
Foucault, M. (1976). *The History of Sexuality*, Vol. 1. London: Allen Lane.
Frege, G. (1879). *Begiffsschrift eine der Aritmetischen nachgebildete Formelsprache des reinen Denkens*. Halle: Nebert.
Freuchen, P. (1961). *Book of the Eskimos*. Greenwich: Fawcett.
Freud, S. (1913). *Totem and Taboo*. New York: Norton.
Fridlund, A. J. (1994). *Human Facial Expression: An Evolutionary View*. New York: Academic.
Friedberg, A. (1993). *Window Shopping: Cinema and the Postmodern*. Berkeley: University of California Press.
Friedrich, P. (1986). *The Language Parallax: Linguistic Relativism and Poetic Indeterminacy*. Austin: University of Texas Press.
Frisch, K. von (1962). Dialects in the Language of Bees. *Scientific American* 207: 79-87.
Frisch, K. von (1967). *The Dance Language and Orientation of Bees*. Cambridge, Mass.: Harvard University Press.
Frutiger, A. (1989). *Signs and Symbols*. New York: Van Nostrand.
Frye, N. (1981). *The Great Code: The Bible and Literature*. Toronto: Academic Press.
Frye, N. (1990). *Words with Power*. Harmondsworth: Penguin.

G

Gallagher, W. (1993). *The Power of Place: How Our Surroundings Shape Our Thoughts, Emotions, and Actions*. New York: Harper Collins.
Gallup, G. G., and Cameron, P. A. (1992). Modality Specific Metaphors: Is Our Mental Machinery Colored by a Visual Bias? *Metaphor and Symbolic Activity* 7: 93-98.
Gamkrelidze, T. V., and Ivanov, V. V. (1984). *Indo-European and the Indo-Europeans: A Reconstruction and Historical Typological Analysis of a Protolanguage and Proto-Culture*. Moscow: Tblisi State University.
Gamkrelidze, T. V., and Ivanov, V. V. (1990). The Early History of Indo-European Languages. *Scientific American* 262/3: 110-116.
Gans, E. (1981). *The Origin of Language: A Formal Theory of Representation*. Berkeley: University of California Press.
Gardner, B. T., and Gardner, R. A. (1975). Evidence for Sentence Constituents in the Early Utterances of Child and Chimpanzee. *Journal of Experimental Psychology* 104: 244-262.
Gardner, H. (1982). *Art, Mind, and Brain: A Cognitive Approach to Creativity*. New York: Basic.
Gardner, H. (1985). *The Mind's New Science: A History of the Cognitive Revolution*. New York: Basic Books.
Gardner, H., Winner, E., Bechofer, R., and Wolf, D. (1978). The Development of Figurative Language. In: K. Nelson (ed.), *Children's Language*, 1-38. New York: Garner Press.
Gardner, R. A., and Gardner, B. T. (1969). Teaching Sign Language to a Chimpanzee. *Science* 165: 664-672.
Garnham, A. (1985). *Psycholinguistics: Central Topics*. London: Methuen.
Gartman, D. (1994). *Auto-Opium: A Social History of American Automobile Design*. London: Routledge.
Garza-Cuarón, B. (1991). *Connotation and Meaning*. Berlin: Mouton de Gruyter.
Gaylin, W. (1990). *On Being and Becoming Human*. London: Penguin.
Geertz, C. (1973). *The Interpretation of Cultures*. New York: Harper Torch.

Gelb, I. J. (1963). *A Study of Writing*. Chicago: University of Chicago Press.
Genette, G. (1988). *Narrative Discourse Revisited*. Ithaca: Cornell University Press.
Gentner, D. (1982). Are Scientific Analogies Metaphors? In: D. S. Miall (ed.), *Metaphor: Problems and Perspectives*, 106-132. Atlantic Highlands, N.J.: Humanities Press.
George, A. (1989) (ed.). *Reflections on Chomsky*. London: Blackwell.
Gibbs, R. W. (1994). *The Poetics of Mind: Figurative Thought, Language, and Understanding*. Cambridge: Cambridge University Press.
Gibson, K. R., and Ingold, T. (1993) (eds.). *Tools, Language and Cognition in Human Evolution*. Cambridge: Cambridge University Press.
Gill, A. (1994). *Rhetoric and Human Understanding*. Prospect Heights, Ill.: Waveland.
Gill, J. H. (1991). *Merleau-Ponty and Metaphor*. Atlantic Highlands, N.J.: Humanities Press.
Ginniken, J. van (1909). *Principes de psychologie linguistique*. Paris: Alcan.
Glucksberg, S. (1988). Language and Thought. In: R. J. Sternberg and E. E. Smith (eds.), *The Psychology of Human Thought*, 214-241. Cambridge: Cambridge University Press.
Glucksberg, S., and Danks, J. H. (1975). *Experimental Psycholinguistics: An Introduction*. New York: John Wiley and Sons.
Goatly, A. (1997). *The Language of Metaphors*. London: Routledge.
Gödel, K. (1931). Über formal unentscheidbare Sätze der Principia Mathematica und verwandter Systeme, Teil I. *Monatshefte für Mathematik und Physik* 38: 173-189.
Goffman, E. (1959). *The Presentation of Self in Everyday Life*. Garden City: Doubleday.
Goffman, E. (1978). Response Cries. *Language* 54: 787-815.
Goffman, E. (1979). *Gender Advertisements*. New York: Harper and Row.
Goldberg, A. E. (ed.) (1996). *Conceptual Structure, Discourse and Language*. Stanford: Center for the Study of Language and Information.
Goldberg, E., and Costa, L. D. (1981). Hemispheric Differences in the Acquisition of Descriptive Systems. *Brain and Language* 14: 144–173.
Goldblatt, D., and Brown, L. B. (1997) (eds.). *Aesthetics: A Reader in the Philosophy of the Arts*. Upper Saddle River: Prentice-Hall.
Goldin-Meadow, S., and Mylander, C. (1990). Beyond the Input Given: The Child's Role in the Acquisition of Language. *Language* 66: 323-355.
Goldman, R., and Papson, R. (1996). *Sign Wars: The Cluttered Landscape of Advertising*. New York: Guilford.
Goldwasser, O. (1995). *From Icon to Metaphor: Studies in the Semiotics of the Hieroglyphs*. Freiburg: Universitätsverlag.
Goode, J. (1992). Food. In: R. Bauman (ed.), *Folklore, Cultural Performances, and Popular Entertainments*, 233-245. Oxford: Oxford University Press.
Goodwin, A. (1992). *Dancing in the Distraction Factory: Music Television and Popular Culture*. Minneapolis: University of Minnesota Press.
Goodwin, C., and Duranti, A. (1992). Rethinking Context: An Introduction. In: A. Duranti and C. Goodwin (eds.), *Rethinking Context: Language as an Interactive Phenomenon*, 1-13. Cambridge: Cambridge University Press.
Goody, J. (1982). *Cooking, Cuisine and Class*. Cambridge: Cambridge University Press.
Goossens, L. *et al.* (1995). *By Word of Mouth: Metaphor, Metonymy and Linguistic Action in a Cognitive Perspective*. Berlin: Mouton de Gruyter.
Gordon, W. T. (1997). *Marshall McLuhan: Escape into Understanding: A Biography*. New York: Basic Books.
Gottdiener, M. (1995). *Postmodern Semiotics: Material Culture and the Forms of Postmodern Life*. London: Blackwell.
Green, K. (1996) (ed.). *New Essays in Deixis, Discourse, Narrative, Literature*. Amsterdam: Rodopi.

Greenberg, J. H. (1966). *Language Universals*. The Hague: Mouton.
Greenberg, J. H. (1987). *Language in the Americas*. Stanford: Stanford University Press.
Greenbie, B. (1981). *Spaces: Dimensions of the Human Landscape*. New Haven: Yale University Press.
Greenwald, T. (1992). *Rock and Roll*. New York: Friedman.
Gregory, B. (1988). *Inventing Reality: Physics as Language*. New York: John Wiley and Sons.
Gregory, R. L. (1970). *The Intelligent Eye*. New York: McGraw-Hill.
Gregory, R. L. (1974). *Concepts and Mechanisms of Perception*. London: Duckworth.
Greimas, A. J. (1987). *On Meaning: Selected Essays in Semiotic Theory*, trans. by P. Perron and F. Collins. Minneapolis: University of Minnesota Press.
Greimas, A. J., and Courtés, J. (1979). *Semiotics and Language*. Bloomington: Indiana University Press.
Grice, H. P. (1975). Logic and Conversation. In: P. Cole and J. Morgan (eds.), *Syntax and Semantics*, Vol. 3, 41-58. New York: Academic.
Griffin, D. R. (1981). *The Question of Animal Consciousness*. New York: Rockefeller University Press.
Griffin, D. R. (1992). *Animal Minds*. Chicago: University of Chicago Press.
Grolier, E. de (1983) (ed.). *Glossogenetics: The Origin and Evolution of Language*. Amsterdam: Harwood Academic Publishers.
Grossberg, L. (1992). *We Gotta Get Out of This Place: Popular Conservatism and Postmodern Culture*. London: Routledge.
Grossman, M. (1988). *Colori e lessico*. Tübingen: Narr.
Gumpel, L. (1984). *Metaphor Reexamined: A Non-Aristotelian Perspective*. Bloomington: Indiana University Press.

H

Haley, M. C. (1989). *The Semeiosis of Poetic Metaphor*. Bloomington: Indiana University Press.
Hall, E. T. (1966). *The Hidden Dimension*. New York: Doubleday.
Hall, E. T. (1973). *The Silent Language*. New York: Anchor.
Hall, K., and Bucholtz, M. (1996). *Gender Articulated: Language and the Socially Constructed Self*. London: Routledge.
Hall, M. B. (1992). *Color and Meaning*. Cambridge: Cambridge University Press.
Hall, S. G. (1904). *Adolescence*. New York: Appleton-Century-Crofts.
Halliday, M. A. K. (1975). *Learning How to Mean: Explorations in the Development of Language*. London: Arnold.
Halliday, M. A. K. (1985). *Introduction to Functional Grammar*. London: Arnold.
Hallyn, F. (1990). *The Poetic Structure of the World: Copernicus and Kepler*. New York: Zone Books.
Hanks, W. F. (1992). The Indexical Ground of Deictic Reference. In: A. Duranti and C. Goodwin (eds.), *Rethinking Context: Language as an Interactive Phenomenon*, 43-76. Cambridge: Cambridge University Press.
Hanson, N. R. (1958). *Patterns of Discovery*. Cambridge: Cambridge University Press.
Haraway, D. (1989). *Primate Visions: Gender, Race and Nature in the World of Modern Science*. London: Routledge.
Hardin, C. L. (1986). *Color for Philosophers*. Indianapolis: Hackett Publishing Company.
Hardin, C. L., and Maffi, L. (1997) (eds.). *Color Categories in Thought and Language*. Cambridge: Cambridge University Press.
Harman, G. (1974) (ed.). *On Noam Chomsky: Critical Essays*. Garden City: Anchor.
Harnad, S. R., Steklis, H. B., and Lancaster, J. (1976) (eds.). *Origins and Evolution of Language and Speech*. New York: New York Academy of Sciences.

Harré, R. (1981). *Great Scientific Experiments*. Oxford: Phaidon Press.

Harris, R. (1986). *The Origin of Writing*. London: Duckworth.

Harris, R. A. (1993). *The Linguistics Wars*. Oxford: Oxford University Press.

Harris, R., Lahey, M., and Marsalek, F. (1980). Metaphors and Images: Rating, Reporting, and Remembering. In: R. P. Honeck and R. R. Hoffman (eds.), *Cognition and Figurative Language*, 201-238. Hillsdale, N.J.: Lawrence Erlbaum Associates.

Harris, R., and Talbot, T. J. (1989). *Landmarks in Linguistic Thought: The Western Tradition from Socrates to Saussure*. London: Routledge.

Harvey, D. (1990). *The Condition of Postmodernity: An Enquiry into the Origins of Cultural Change*. Cambridge: Blackwell.

Harvey, K., and Shalom, C. (1997) (eds.). *Language and Desire: Encoding Sex, Romance, and Intimacy*. London: Routledge.

Haskell, R. E. (1987) (ed.). *Cognition and Symbolic Structures: The Psychology of Metaphoric Transformation*. Norwood, N.J.: Ablex.

Haskell, R. E. (1989). Analogical Transforms: A Cognitive Theory of the Origin and Development of Equivalence Transformations. *Metaphor and Symbolic Activity* 4: 247-277.

Hassan, I. (1987). *The Postmodern Turn: Essays in Postmodern Theory and Culture*. Columbus: Ohio State University Press.

Haste, H. (1993). *The Sexual Metaphor*. Harvard: Harvard University Press.

Hatcher, E. P. (1974). *Visual Metaphors: A Methodological Study in Visual Communication*. Albuquerque: University of New Mexico Press.

Hauser, M. D. (1996). *The Evolution of Communication*. Cambridge, Mass.: MIT Press.

Hausman, C. R. (1989). *Metaphor and Art*. Cambridge: Cambridge University Press.

Hausman, C. R. (1993). *Charles S. Peirce's Evolutionary Philosophy*. Cambridge: Cambridge University Press.

Hawkes, T. (1977). *Structuralism and Semiotics*. Berkeley: University of California Press.

Hayakawa, S. I. (1991). *Language in Thought and Action*, 5th ed. New York: Harcourt Brace Jovanovich.

Heinberg, R. (1989). *Memories and Visions of Paradise*. Los Angeles: J. P. Tarcher.

Heine, B., Claudi, U., and Hünnemeyer, F. (1982). *Grammaticalization: A Conceptual Framework*. Chicago: University of Chicago Press.

Heisenberg, W. (1949). *The Physical Principles of the Quantum Theory*. New York: Dover.

Heisenberg, W. (1962). *Physics and Philosophy: The Revolution of Modern Science*. New York: Harper and Row.

Higginbotham, J. (1992). Semantics in Linguistics: An Outline for an Introduction. *Golem* 2: 7-10.

Hilbert, D. R. (1987). *Color and Color Perception: A Study in Anthropocentric Realism*. Stanford: Center for the Study of Language and Information.

Hinton, J., Nichols, J., and Ohala, J. J. (1994) (eds.). *Sound Symbolism*. Cambridge: Cambridge University Press.

Hobbes, T. (1656 [1839]). *Elements of Philosophy*, Vol. 1. London: Molesworth.

Hockett, C. F. (1960). The Origin of Speech. *Scientific American* 203: 88-96.

Hodge, R., and Kress, G. (1988). *Social Semiotics*. Ithaca: Cornell University Press.

Hoek, K. van (1997). *Anaphora and Conceptual Structure*. Chicago: University of Chicago Press.

Hoffman, R. R. (1983). Recent Research on Metaphor. *Semiotic Inquiry* 3: 35-61.

Hoffman, R. R., and Honeck, R. P. (1987). Proverbs, Pragmatics, and the Ecology of Abstract Categories. In: R. E. Haskell (ed.), *Cognition and Symbolic Structures: The Psychology of Metaphoric Transformation*, 121-140. Norwood, N.J.: Ablex.

Holbrook, M. B., and Hirschman, E. C. (1993). *The Semiotics of Consumption: Interpreting Symbolic Consumer Behavior in Popular Culture and Works of Art.* Berlin: Mouton de Gruyter.

Holland, D., and Quinn, N. (1987) (eds.). *Cultural Models in Language and Thought.* Cambridge: Cambridge University Press.

Hollander, A. (1988). *Seeing through Clothes.* Harmondsworth: Penguin.

Hollander, A. (1994). *Sex and Suits: The Evolution of Modern Dress.* New York: Knopf.

Hollyoak, K. J., and Thagard, P. (1995). *Mental Leaps: Analogy in Creative Thought.* Cambridge, Mass.: MIT Press.

Honeck, R. P., and Hoffman, R. (1980) (eds.). *Cognition and Figurative Language.* Hillsdale, N.J.: Lawrence Erlbaum and Associates.

Howes, D. (1991) (ed.). *The Varieties of Sensory Experience.* Toronto: University of Toronto Press.

Huck, G., and Goldsmith, J. A. (1995). *Ideology and Linguistic Theory: Noam Chomsky and the Deep Structure Debates.* London: Routledge.

Hudson, L. (1972). *The Cult of the Fact.* New York: Harper and Row.

Hudson, R. (1984). *Invitation to Linguistics.* Oxford: Robinson.

Hughes, G. (1991). *Swearing.* London: Blackwell.

Huizinga, J. (1924). *The Waning of the Medieval Ages.* Garden City: Doubleday.

Humboldt, W. von (1836 [1988]). *On Language: The Diversity of Human Language-Structure and Its Influence on the Mental Development of Mankind,* trans. by P. Heath. Cambridge: Cambridge University Press.

Hume, D. (1749 [1902]). *An Enquiry Concerning Human Understanding.* Oxford: Clarendon.

Hunt, H. T. (1989). *The Multiplicity of Dreams: Memory, Imagination, and Consciousness.* New Haven: Yale University Press.

Hunter, K. M. (1991). *Doctor's Stories: The Narrative Structure of Medical Knowledge.* Princeton: Princeton University Press.

Hutcheon, L. (1995). *Irony's Edge: The Theory and Politics of Irony.* London: Routledge.

Hutcheon, L., and Hutcheon, M. (1996). *Opera: Desire, Disease, Death.* Lincoln: University of Nebraska Press.

Hutchison, M. (1990). *The Anatomy of Sex and Power: An Investigation of Mind–Body Politics.* New York: Morrow.

Hyman, S. E. (1962). *The Tangled Bank: Darwin, Marx, Frazer and Freud as Imaginative Writers.* New York: Atheneum.

Hymes, D. (1971). *On Communicative Competence.* Philadelphia: University of Pennsylvania Press.

I

Ingham, P. (1996). *The Language of Gender and Class.* London: Routledge.

Inhelder, B., and Piaget, J. (1958). *The Growth of Logical Thinking from Childhood through Adolescence.* New York: Basic Books.

Innis, R. E. (1994). *Consciousness and the Play of Signs.* Bloomington: Indiana University Press.

J

Jackendoff, R. (1994). *Patterns in the Mind: Language and Human Nature.* New York: Basic Books.

Jackendoff, R. (1997). *The Architecture of the Language Faculty.* Cambridge, Mass.: MIT Press.

Jackson, B. S. (1985). *Semiotics and Legal Theory.* London: Routledge and Kegan Paul.

Jackson, B. S. (1988). *Law, Fact and Narrative Coherence.* Liverpool: Charles.

Jackson, J. B. (1994). *A Sense of Place, A Sense of Time*. New Haven: Yale University Press.

Jackson, J. H. (1878). On Affectives of Speech from Disease of the Brain. *Brain* 1: 304-330.

Jacob, F. (1982). *The Possible and the Actual*. Seattle: University of Washington Press.

Jacobson, M. F., and Mazur, L. A. (1995). *Marketing Madness*. Boulder: Westview.

Jakobson, R. (1942). *Kindersprache, Aphasie und algemeine Lautgesetze*. Uppsala: Almqvist and Wiksell.

Jakobson, R. (1960). Linguistics and Poetics. In: T. A. Sebeok (ed.), *Style and Language*, 34-45. Cambridge, Mass.: MIT Press.

Jakobson, R. (1963 [1957]). *Essais de linguistique générale*. Paris: Editions de Minuit.

Jakobson, R. (1978). *Six Lectures on Sound and Meaning*, trans. by John Mepham. Cambridge, Mass.: MIT Press.

Jakobson, R. (1985). *Selected Writings VII*, S. Rudy (ed.). Berlin: Mouton.

Jameson, F. (1991). *Postmodernism or the Cultural Logic of Late Capitalism*. Durham: Duke University Press.

Jarvella, R. J., and Klein, W. (1982) (eds.). *Speech, Place, and Action: Studies in Deixis and Related Topics*. New York: John Wiley and Sons.

Jaynes, J. (1976). *The Origin of Consciousness in the Breakdown of the Bicameral Mind*. Toronto: University of Toronto Press.

Jenks, C. (1996). *Childhood*. London: Routledge.

Jespersen, O. (1922). *Language: Its Nature, Development and Origin*. London: Allen and Unwin.

Jhally, S. (1987). *The Codes of Advertising*. New York: St. Martin's Press.

Joanette, Y., Goulet, P., and Hannequin, D. (1990). *The Right Hemisphere and Verbal Communication*. New York: Springer.

Johansen, J. D. (1993). *Dialogic Semiosis: An Essay on Signs and Meaning*. Bloomington: Indiana University Press.

Johanson, D., and Edgar, B. (1995). *From Lucy to Language*. New York: Simon and Schuster.

Johnson, M. (1987). *The Body in the Mind: The Bodily Basis of Meaning, Imagination and Reason*. Chicago: University of Chicago Press.

Johnson, M. (1989). Image-Schematic Bases of Meaning. *Semiotic Inquiry* 9: 109-118.

Johnson, M. (1991). The Emergence of Meaning in Bodily Experience. In: B. den Ouden and M. Moen (eds.), *The Presence of Feeling in Thought*, 153–167. New York: Peter Lang.

Johnson-Laird, P. N. (1983). *Mental Models*. Cambridge, Mass.: Harvard University Press.

Johnson-Laird, P. N. (1988). *The Computer and the Mind*. Cambridge, Mass.: Harvard University Press.

Jones, R. (1982). *Physics as Metaphor*. New York: New American Library.

Joos, M. (1967). *The Five Clocks*. New York: Harcourt, Brace and World.

Jung, C. G. (1921). *Psychological Types*. New York: Harcourt.

Jung, C. G. (1956). *Analytical Psychology*. New York: Meridian.

Jung, C. G. (1957). *The Undiscovered Self*. New York: Mentor.

Jung, C. G. (1965). *Memories, Dreams, Reflections*. New York: Vintage.

K

Kant, I. (1790). *Critique of Judgment*. New York: Hafner Press.

Kaplan, J., and Bernays, A. (1996). *The Language of Names: What We Call Ourselves and Why It Matters*. New York: Simon and Schuster.

Kay, P. (1997). *Words and the Grammar of Context*. Cambridge: Cambridge University Press.

Kearney, R. (1991). *Poetics of Imagining: From Husserl to Lyotard.* New York: Harper Collins.

Keesing, R. M. (1981). *Cultural Anthropology.* New York: Holt, Rinehart and Winston.

Kellner, D. (1995). *Media Culture.* London: Routledge.

Kendon, A. (1984). *Sign Languages of Aboriginal Australia: Cultural, Semiotic and Communicative Perspectives.* Cambridge: Cambridge University Press.

Kennedy, J. M. (1984). *Vision and Metaphors.* Toronto: Toronto Semiotic Circle.

Kennedy, J. M. (1993). *Drawing and the Blind: Pictures to Touch.* New Haven: Yale University Press.

Kennedy, J. M., and Domander, R. (1986). Blind People Depicting States and Events in Metaphoric Line Drawings. *Metaphor and Symbolic Activity* 1: 109-126.

Ketner, K. L. (1995). *Peirce and Contemporary Thought.* Fordham: Fordham University Press.

Kevelson, R. (1977). *Inlaws/Outlaws.* Lisse: Peter de Ridder.

Kevelson, R. (1988). *The Law as a System of Signs.* New York: Plenum.

Kevelson, R. (1993). *Peirce's Esthetics of Freedom: Possibility, Complexity, and Emergent Value.* New York: Peter Lang.

Key, W. B. (1972). *Subliminal Seduction.* New York: Signet.

Key, W. B. (1976). *Media Sexploitation.* New York: Signet.

Key, W. B. (1980). *The Clam-Plate Orgy.* New York: Signet.

Key, W. B. (1989). *The Age of Manipulation.* New York: Henry Holt.

Kinder, J. J. (1991). Up and Down: Structure of a Metaphor. In: B. Merry (ed.), *Essays in Honour of Keith Val Sinclair: An Australian Collection of Modern Language Studies,* 283-296. Townsville: James Cook University of North Queensland.

Kitcher, P. (1985). *Vaulting Ambition: Sociobiology and the Quest for Human Nature.* Cambridge, Mass.: MIT Press.

Kittay, E. F. (1987). *Metaphor: Its Cognitive Force and Linguistic Structure.* Oxford: Clarendon Press.

Klein, W. (1982). Local Deixis in Route Directions. In: R. J. Jarvella and W. Klein (eds.), *Speech, Place and Action: Studies in Deixis and Related Topics,* 161-182. New York: John Wiley.

Klein, W. (1994). *Time in Language.* London: Routledge.

Kline, M. (1985). *Mathematics and the Search for Knowledge.* Oxford: Oxford University Press.

Koch, W. A. (1986). *Evolutionary Cultural Semiotics.* Bochum: Brockmeyer.

Koch, W. A. (1989) (ed.). *Geneses of Language.* Bochum: Brockmeyer.

Koch, W. A. (1993). *The Biology of Literature.* Bochum: Brockmeyer.

Koen, F. (1965). An intra-verbal explication of the nature of metaphor. *Journal of Verbal Learning and Verbal Behavior* 4, 129-133.

Köhler, W. (1925). *The Mentality of Apes.* London: Routledge and Kegan Paul.

Konner, M. (1987). On Human Nature: Love among the Robots. *The Sciences* 27: 14-23.

Konner, M. (1991). Human Nature and Culture: Biology and the Residue of Uniqueness. In: J. J. Sheehan and M. Sosna (eds.), *The Boundaries of Humanity,* 103-124. Berkeley: University of California Press.

Kosslyn, S. M. (1980). *Image and Mind.* Cambridge, Mass.: Harvard University Press.

Kosslyn, S. M. (1983). *Ghosts in the Mind's Machine: Creating and Using Images in the Brain.* New York: W. W. Norton.

Kosslyn, S. M. (1994). *Image and Brain.* Cambridge, Mass.: MIT Press.

Kosslyn, S. M., and Koenig, O. (1992). *Wet Mind: The New Cognitive Neuroscience.* New York: The Free Press.

Kövecses, Z. (1986). *Metaphors of Anger, Pride, and Love: A Lexical Approach to the Structure of Concepts.* Amsterdam: Benjamins.

Kövecses, Z. (1988). *The Language of Love: The Semantics of Passion in Conversational English*. London: Associated University Presses.
Kövecses, Z. (1990). *Emotion Concepts*. New York: Springer.
Krampen, M. (1991). *Children's Drawings: Iconic Coding of the Environment*. New York: Plenum.
Kristeva, J. (1989). *Language: The Unknown*. New York: Columbia University Press.
Kroeber, A. L., and Kluckholn, C. (1963). *Culture: A Critical Review of Concepts and Definitions*. New York: Vintage.
Kubey, R., and Csikszentmihalyi, M. (1990). *Television and the Quality of Life*. Hillsdale, N.J.: Lawrence Erlbaum Associates.
Kuhn, T. S. (1970). *The Structure of Scientific Revolutions*. Chicago: University of Chicago Press.

L

Labov, W. (1972). *Language in the Inner City*. Philadelphia: University of Pennsylvania Press.
Laitman, J. T. (1990). Tracing the Origins of Human Speech. In: P. Whitten and D. E. K. Hunter (eds.), *Anthropology: Contemporary Perspectives*, 124-130. Glenview, Ill.: Scott, Foresman and Company.
Lakoff, G. (1987). *Women, Fire and Dangerous Things: What Categories Reveal about the Mind*. Chicago: University of Chicago Press.
Lakoff, G., and Johnson, L. (1980). *Metaphors We Live By*. Chicago: Chicago University Press.
Lakoff, G., and Johnson, M. (1999). *Philosophy in Flesh: The Embodied Mind and Its Challenge to Western Thought*. New York: Basic.
Lakoff, G., and Turner, M. (1989). *More than Cool Reason: A Field Guide to Poetic Metaphor*. Chicago: University of Chicago Press.
Lamb, T., and Bourriau, J. (1995) (eds.). *Colour: Art and Science*. Cambridge: Cambridge University Press.
Landau, T. (1989). *About Faces: The Evolution of the Human Face*. New York: Anchor.
Landesman, C. (1989). *Color and Consciousness: An Essay in Metaphysics*. Philadelphia: Temple University Press.
Landsberg, M. E. (1988) (ed.). *The Genesis of Language: A Different Judgement of Evidence*. Berlin: Mouton.
Langacker, R. W. (1987). *Foundations of Cognitive Grammar*. Stanford: Stanford University Press.
Langacker, R. W. (1990). *Concept, Image, and Symbol: The Cognitive Basis of Grammar*. Berlin: Mouton de Gruyter.
Langer, S. (1948). *Philosophy in a New Key*. Cambridge, Mass.: Harvard University Press.
Langer, S. (1957). *Problems of Art*. New York: Scribner's.
Lashley, K. (1929). *Brain Mechanisms and Intelligence*. Chicago: University of Chicago Press.
Lave, J. (1988). *Cognition in Practice: Mind, Mathematics and Culture in Everyday Life*. Cambridge: Cambridge University Press.
Layton, R. (1991). *The Anthropology of Art*. Cambridge: Cambridge University Press.
Le Guérer, A. (1992). *Scent: The Essential and Mysterious Powers of Smell*. New York: Kodansha.
Leach, E. (1976). *Culture and Communication: The Logic by Which Symbols Are Connected*. Cambridge: Cambridge University Press.
Leakey, R. E., and Lewin, R. (1978). *People of the Lake: Mankind and Its Beginnings*. New York: Avon.
Leary, D. E. (1990) (ed.). *Metaphors in the History of Psychology*. Cambridge: Cambridge University Press.

Leatherdale, W. H. (1974). *The Role of Analogy, Model and Metaphor in Science.* New York: New Holland.

Leder, D. (1990). *The Absent Body.* Chicago: University of Chicago Press.

Lee, P. (1996). *The Whorf Theory Complex: A Critical Reconstruction.* Amsterdam: John Benjamins.

Leeming, D. A. (1990). *The World of Myth: An Anthology.* Oxford: Oxford University Press.

Leiss, W., Kline, S., and Jhally, S. (1990). *Social Communication in Advertising: Persons, Products and Images of Well-Being.* Toronto: Nelson.

Leitch, T. M. (1986). *What Stories Are: Narrative Theory and Interpretation.* University Park: Pennsylvania State University Press.

Lenneberg, E. (1967). *The Biological Foundations of Language.* New York: John Wiley.

Leroy, M. (1997). *Some Girls Do: Why Women Do and Don't Make the First Move.* London: Harper Collins.

Levelt, W. J. M. (1989). *Speaking: From Intention to Articulation.* Cambridge, Mass.: MIT Press.

Levenstein, H. (1993). *Paradox of Plenty: A Social History of Eating in Modern America.* Oxford: Oxford University Press.

Lévi-Strauss, C. (1958). *Structural Anthropology.* New York: Basic Books.

Lévi-Strauss, C. (1962). *La pensée sauvage.* Paris: Plon.

Lévi-Strauss, C. (1964). *The Raw and the Cooked.* London: Cape.

Lévi-Strauss, C. (1978). *Myth and Meaning: Cracking the Code of Culture.* Toronto: University of Toronto Press.

Levin, S. R. (1988). *Metaphoric Worlds.* New Haven: Yale University Press.

Levine, R. (1997). *A Geography of Time: The Temporal Misadventures of a Social Psychologist or How Every Culture Keeps Time Just a Little Bit Differently.* New York: Basic Books.

Lewandowsky, S., Dunn, J. C., and Kirsner, K. (1989) (eds.). *Implicit Memory: Theoretical Issues.* Hillsdale, N.J.: Lawrence Erlbaum Associates.

Lewontin, R. C., Rose, S., and Kamin, L. (1984). *Not in Our Genes: Biology, Ideology, and Human Nature.* New York: Pantheon Books.

Leymore, V. (1975). *Hidden Myth: Structure and Symbolism in Advertising.* London: Heinemann.

Lieberman, P. (1972). *The Speech of Primates.* The Hague: Mouton.

Lieberman, P. (1975). *On the Origins of Language.* New York: MacMillan.

Lieberman, P. (1984). *The Biology and Evolution of Language.* Cambridge, Mass.: Harvard University Press.

Lieberman, P. (1991). *Uniquely Human: The Evolution of Speech, Thought, and Selfless Behavior.* Cambridge, Mass.: Harvard University Press.

Liebert, R. M., and Sprafkin, J. M. (1988). *The Early Window: Effects of Television on Children and Youth.* New York: Pergamon.

Linden, E. (1986). *Silent Partners: The Legacy of the Ape Language Experiments.* New York: Signet.

Liszka, J. J. (1989). *The Semeiotic of Myth: A Critical Study of the Symbol.* Bloomington: Indiana University Press.

Locke, J. (1690). *An Essay Concerning Human Understanding.* London: Collins.

Lodge, D. (1990). Narration with Words. In: H. Barlow, C. Blakemore, and M. Weston–Smith (eds.), *Images and Understanding*, 141–153. Cambridge: Cambridge University Press.

Logan, R. K. (1987). *The Alphabet Effect.* New York: St. Martin's Press.

Longhurst, B. (1995). *Popular Music and Society.* Cambridge: Polity Press.

Lorenz, K. (1952). *King Solomon's Ring.* New York: Crowell.

Lotman, Y. (1991). *Universe of the Mind: A Semiotic Theory of Culture.* Bloomington: Indiana University Press.

Lucente, G. L. (1981). *The Narrative of Realism and Myth.* Baltimore: Johns Hopkins University Press.

Lucy, J. A. (1992). *Language Diversity and Thought: A Reformulation of the Linguistic Relativity Hypothesis.* Cambridge: Cambridge University Press.

Lucy, J. A. (1994). *Grammatical Categories and Cognition: A Case Study of the Linguistic Relativity Hypothesis.* Cambridge: Cambridge University Press.

Lucy, J. A., and Schweder, R. A. (1979). Whorf and His Critics: Linguistic and Nonlinguistic Influences on Color Memory. *American Anthropologist* 81: 581–607.

Lumsden, C. J., and Wilson, E. O. (1983). *Promethean Fire: Reflections on the Origin of Mind.* Cambridge, Mass.: Harvard University Press.

Luria, A. (1947). *Traumatic Aphasia.* The Hague: Mouton.

Lüthi, M. (1970). *Once Upon a Time: On the Nature of Fairy Tales.* Bloomington: Indiana University Press.

Lyle, J. (1990). *Body Language.* London: Hamylin.

Lynch, A. (1996). *Thought Contagion: How Belief Spreads through Society.* New York: Basic Books.

Lyons, J. (1968). *Introduction to Theoretical Linguistics.* Cambridge: Cambridge University Press.

Lyons, J. (1977). *Semantics.* Cambridge: Cambridge University Press.

Lyotard, J-F (1984). *The Postmodern Condition: A Report on Knowledge.* Minneapolis: University of Minnesota Press.

M

MacCannell, D., and MacCannell, J. F. (1982). *The Time of the Sign: A Semiotic Interpretation of Modern Culture.* Bloomington: Indiana University Press.

MacCormac, E. (1976). *Metaphor and Myth in Science and Religion.* Durham, N.C.: Duke University Press.

MacCormac, E. (1985). *A Cognitive Theory of Metaphor.* Cambridge, Mass.: MIT Press.

MacLaury, R. E. (1997). *Color and Cognition in Mesoamerica: Constructing Categories as Vantages.* Austin: University of Texas Press.

Malinowski, B. (1922). *Argonauts of the Western Pacific.* New York: Dutton.

Malinowski, B. (1929). *The Sexual Life of Savages in North-Western Melanesia.* New York: Harcourt, Brace, and World.

Mallery, G. (1972). *Sign Language among North American Indians Compared with That among Other Peoples and Deaf-Mutes.* The Hague: Mouton.

Mallory, J. P. (1989). *In Search of the Indo-Europeans: Language, Archaeology and Myth.* London: Thames and Hudson.

Malotki, E. (1983). *Hopi Time: A Linguistic Analysis of the Temporal Concepts in the Hopi Language.* Berlin: Mouton de Gruyter.

Marcus, G. (1993). *Ranters and Crowd Pleasers: Punk in Pop Music, 1977-1992.* New York: Anchor.

Markel, N. (1997). *Semiotic Psychology: Speech as an Index of Emotions and Attitudes.* New York: Peter Lang.

Marks, L. E., Hammeal, R. J., and Bornstein, M. H. (1987). *Perceiving Similarity and Comprehending Metaphor.* Chicago: Monographs of the Society for Research in Child Development 215.

Marr, D. (1982). *Vision: A Computational Investigation into the Human Representation and Processing of Visual Information.* New York: W. H. Freeman.

Martin, J. H. (1990). *A Computational Model of Metaphor Interpretation.* New York: Academic.

Mathiot, M. (1979) (ed.). *Ethnolinguistics: Boas, Sapir and Whorf Revisited.* The Hague: Mouton.

Matthews, P. H. (1974). *Morphology: An Introduction to the Theory of Word-Structure.* Cambridge: Cambridge University Press.

Maxwell, M. (1991) (ed.). *The Sociobiological Imagination.* Albany: State University of New York Press.

May, R. (1991). *The Cry for Myth.* New York: Norton.

McCracken, G. (1988). *Culture and Consumption*. Bloomington: Indiana University Press.

McCracken, G. (1995). *Big Hair: A Journey into the Transformation of Self*. Toronto: Penguin.

McLuhan, M. (1951). *The Mechanical Bride: Folklore of Industrial Man*. New York: Vanguard.

McLuhan, M. (1962). *The Gutenberg Galaxy*. Toronto: University of Toronto Press.

McLuhan, M. (1964). *Understanding Media*. London: Routledge and Kegan Paul.

McLuhan, M., and McLuhan, E. (1988). *Laws of Media: The New Science*. Toronto: University of Toronto Press.

McNeill, D. (1987). *Psycholinguistics: A New Approach*. New York: Harper and Row.

McNeill, D. (1992). *Hand and Mind: What Gestures Reveal about Thought*. Chicago: University of Chicago Press.

McRobbie, A. (1988). *Zoot Suits and Second-Hand Dresses*. Boston: Unwin Hyman.

Mead, M. (1939). *From the South Seas: Studies of Adolescence and Sex in Primitive Societies*. New York: Morrow.

Mead, M. (1950). *Coming of Age in Samoa*. New York: North American Library.

Megarry, T. (1995). *Society in Prehistory: The Origins of Human Culture*. New York: New York University Press.

Meissner, M., and Philpott, S. B. (1975). The Sign Language of Sawmill Workers in British Columbia. *Sign Language Studies* 9: 291-308.

Melzack, R. (1972). The Perception of Pain. In: R. F. Thompson (ed.), *Physiological Psychology*, 223-231. San Francisco: Freeman.

Melzack, R. (1988). Pain. In: J. Kuper (ed.), *A Lexicon of Psychology, Psychiatry and Psychoanalysis*, 288-291. London: Routledge.

Merrell, F. (1995). *Peirce's Semiotics Now: A Primer*. Toronto: Canadian Scholars' Press.

Merrell, F. (1996). *Signs Grow: Semiosis and Life Processes*. Toronto: University of Toronto Press.

Merrell, F. (1997). *Peirce, Signs, and Meaning*. Toronto: University of Toronto Press.

Metz, C. (1974). *Film Language: A Semiotics of the Cinema*. Chicago: University of Chicago Press.

Miller, A. I. (1987). *Imagery in Scientific Thought*. Cambridge, Mass.: MIT Press.

Miller, G. (1951). *Language and Communication*. New York: McGraw-Hill.

Miller, G. A., and Gildea, P. M. (1991). How Children Learn Words. In: W. S.-Y. Wang, (ed.),*The Emergence of Language: Development and Evolution*, pp. 150-158. New York: W. H. Freeman.

Miller, G. A., and Johnson-Laird, P. N. (1976). *Language and Perception*. Cambridge, Mass.: Harvard University Press.

Miller, J. (1993). *The Passion of Michel Foucault*. New York: Simon and Schuster.

Miller, M. C. (1988). *Boxed In: The Culture of TV*. Evanston: Northwestern University Press.

Miller, R. L. (1968). *The Linguistic Relativity Principle and Humboldtian Ethnolinguistics: A History and Appraisal*. The Hague: Mouton.

Milner, R. (1990). *The Encyclopedia of Evolution: Humanity's Search for Its Origins*. New York: Facts on File.

Mininni, G. (1982). *Psicosemiotica*. Bari: Adriatica.

Minsky, M. (1986). *Society of Mind*. New York: Simon and Schuster.

Mintz, S. W. (1996). *Tasting Food, Tasting Freedom: Excursions into Eating, Culture, and the Past*. Boston: Beacon.

Mitchell, M. (1993). *Analogy-Making as Perception: A Computer Model*. Cambridge, Mass.: MIT Press.

Mitchell, W. J. T. (1986). *Iconology: Image. Text, Ideology*. Chicago: University of Chicago Press.

Mithen, S. (1997). *The Prehistory of the Mind: The Cognitive Origins of Art, Religion and Science*. London: Thames and Hudson.

Mondimore, F. M. (1996). *A Natural History of Homosexuality*. Baltimore: Johns Hopkins University Press.

Money, J. (1986). *Lovemaps: Clinical Concepts of Sexual/Erotic Health and Pathology, Paraphilia, and Gender Identity from Conception to Maturity*. Baltimore: Johns Hopkins University Press.

Montagu, A. (1983). Toolmaking, Hunting, and the Origin of Language. In: B. Bain (ed.), *The Sociogenesis of Language and Human Conduct*, 3-14. New York: Plenum.

Montagu, A. (1986). *Touching: The Human Significance of the Skin*. New York: Harper and Row.

Moog, C. (1990). *Are They Selling Her Lips? Advertising and Identity*. New York: Morrow.

Moore, J. B. (1993). *Skinheads Shaved for Battle: A Cultural History of American Skinheads*. Bowling Green: Bowling Green State University Popular Press.

Morford, J. P., Singleton, J. L., and Goldin-Meadow, S. (1995). The Genesis of Language: How Much Time Is Needed to Generate Arbitrary Symbols in a Sign System? In: K. Emmorey and J. Reilly (eds.), *Language, Gesture, and Space*, pp. 313-332. Hillsdale, N.J.: Lawrence Erlbaum Associates.

Morgan, C. L. (1895). *Introduction to Comparative Psychology*. London: Scott.

Morgan, L. H. (1877). *Ancient Society*. Cleveland: World Publishing.

Morphy, H. (1989) (ed.). *Animals into Art*. London: Unwin Hyman.

Morris, C. W. (1938). *Foundations of the Theory of Signs*. Chicago: Chicago University Press.

Morris, C. W. (1946). *Writings on the General Theory of Signs*. The Hague: Mouton.

Morris, D. (1969). *The Human Zoo*. London: Cape.

Morris, D. (1994). *The Human Animal*. London: BBC Books.

Morris, D. *et al.* (1979). *Gestures: Their Origins and Distributions*. London: Cape.

Müller, F. M. (1861). *Lectures on the Science of Language*. London: Longmans, Green.

Mumford, L. S. (1995). *Love and Ideology in the Afternoon: Soap Opera, Women, and Television Genre*. Bloomington: Indiana University Press.

N

Nadeau, R. L. (1991). *Mind, Machines, and Human Consciousness*. Chicago: Contemporary Books.

Napier, J. (1980). *Hands*. Princeton: Princeton University Press.

Nash, C. (1994). *Narrative in Culture*. London: Routledge.

Neisser, U. (1967). *Cognitive Psychology*. Englewood Cliffs, N.J.: Prentice-Hall.

Nespoulous, J. L., Perron, P., and Lecours, A. R. (1986) (eds.). *The Biological Foundations of Gestures: Motor and Semiotic Aspects*. Hillsdale, N.J.: Lawrence Erlbaum Associates.

Neumann, J. von (1958). *The Computer and the Brain*. New Haven: Yale University Press.

Newcomb, H. (1996) (ed.). *Encyclopedia of Television*. Chicago: Fitzroy Dearborn.

Newell, A. (1991). Metaphors for Mind, Theories of Mind: Should the Humanities Mind? In: J. J. Sheehan and M. Sosna (eds.), *The Boundaries of Humanity*, 158-197. Berkeley: University of California Press.

Newham, P. (1993). *The Singing Cure: An Introduction to Voice Movement Therapy*. Boston: Shambhala.

Newmeyer, F. J. (1986). *Linguistic Theory in America*. Chicago: University of Chicago Press.

Nietzsche, F. (1873 [1979]). *Philosophy and Truth: Selections from Nietzsche's Notebooks of the Early 1870's*. Atlantic Heights, N.J.: Humanities Press.

Noble, W., and Davidson, I. (1996). *Human Evolution, Language and Mind.* Cambridge: Cambridge University Press.
Nochimson, M. (1992). *No End to Her: Soap Opera and the Female Subject.* Berkeley: University of California Press.
Noiré, L. (1917). *The Origin and Philosophy of Language.* Chicago: Open Court.
Noppen, J.-P. van (1985). *Metaphor: A Bibliography of Post-1970 Publications.* Amsterdam: John Benjamins.
Noppen, J.-P. van and Hols, E. (1990). *Metaphor II: A Classified Bibliography of Publications from 1985-1990.* Amsterdam: John Benjamins.
Norman, D. A. (1993). *Things That Make Us Smart: Defending Human Attributes in the Age of the Machine.* Reading, Mass.: Addison-Wesley.
Norris, C. (1991). *Deconstruction: Theory and Practice.* London: Routledge.
Nöth, W. (1990). *Handbook of Semiotics.* Bloomington: Indiana University Press.
Nöth, W. (1994) (ed.). *Origins of Semiosis: Sign Evolution in Nature and Culture.* Berlin: Mouton de Gruyter.
Nuessel, F. (1991). Metaphor and Cognition: A Survey of Recent Publications. *Journal of Literary Semantics* 20: 37-52.
Nuessel, F. (1992). *The Study of Names: A Guide to the Principles and Topics.* Westport: Greenwood.

O

O'Barr, W. M. (1994). *Culture and the Ad.* Boulder: Westview Press.
Ochs, E. (1992). Indexing Gender. In: A. Duranti and C. Goodwin (eds.), *Rethinking Context: Language as an Interactive Phenomenon*, 335-358. Cambridge: Cambridge University Press.
Ogden, C. K., and Richards, I. A. (1923). *The Meaning of Meaning.* London: Routledge and Kegan Paul.
Ong, W. J. (1977). *Interfaces of the Word: Studies in the Evolution of Consciousness and Culture.* Ithaca: Cornell University Press.
Opie, I., and Opie, P. (1959). *The Lore and Language of Schoolchildren.* Frogmore: Paladin.
Ormiston, G. L, and Sassower, R. (1989). *Narrative Experiments: The Discursive Authority of Science and Technology.* Minneapolis: University of Minnesota Press.
Ortony, A. (1979) (ed.). *Metaphor and Thought.* Cambridge: Cambridge University Press.
Ortony, A., Clore, G. L., and Collins, A. (1988). *The Cognitive Structure of Emotions.* Cambridge: Cambridge University Press.
Osgood, C. E., and Sebeok, T. A. (1954) (eds.). *Psycholinguistics: A Survey of Theory and Research Problems.* Bloomington: Indiana University Press.
Osgood, C. E., Suci, G. J., and Tannenbaum, P. H. (1957). *The Measurement of Meaning.* Urbana: University of Illinois Press.
O'Toole, M. (1994). *The Language of Displayed Art.* London: Leicester University Press.

P

Packard, V. (1957). *The Hidden Persuaders.* New York: McKay.
Paget, R. (1930). *Human Speech.* London: Kegan Paul.
Paivio, A., and Begg, I. (1981). *Psychology of Language.* Englewood Cliffs, N.J.: Prentice Hall.
Palek, B. (1991). Semiotics and Cartography. In: T. A. Sebeok and J. Umiker-Sebeok (eds.), *Recent Developments in Theory and History*, 465-491. Berlin: Mouton de Gruyter.
Palmer, G. B. (1996). *Toward a Theory of Cultural Linguistics.* Austin: University of Texas Press.
Palmer, R. (1995). *Rock and Roll: An Unruly History.* New York: Harmony Books.

Panati, C. (1984). *Browser's Book of Beginnings.* Boston: Houghton Mifflin.
Panati, C. (1996). *Sacred Origins of Profound Things.* New York: Penguin.
Parmentier, R. J. (1994). *Signs in Society: Studies in Semiotic Anthropology.* Bloomington: Indiana University Press.
Patterson, F. G. (1978). The Gestures of a Gorilla: Language Acquisition in Another Pongid. *Brain and Language* 5: 72-97.
Patterson, F. G., and Linden, E. (1981). *The Education of Koko.* New York: Holt, Rinehart and Winston.
Pavlov, I. (1902). *The Work of Digestive Glands.* London: Griffin.
Peck, S. R. (1987). *Atlas of Facial Expression.* Oxford: Oxford University Press.
Pedersen, H. (1931). *The Discovery of Language.* Bloomington: Indiana University Press.
Peirce, C. S. (1931-1958). *Collected Papers of Charles Sanders Peirce,* Vols. 1-8, C. Hartshorne and P. Weiss (eds.). Cambridge, Mass.: Harvard University Press.
Penfield, W., and Rasmussen, R. (1950). *The Cerebral Cortex of Man.* New York: Macmillan.
Penfield, W., and Roberts, H. (1959). *Speech and Brain Mechanisms.* Princeton: Princeton University Press.
Penn, J. M. (1972). *Linguistic Relativity Versus Innate Ideas: The Origins of the Sapir-Whorf Hypothesis in German Thought.* The Hague: Mouton.
Penrose, R. (1989). *The Emperor's New Mind.* Cambridge: Cambridge University Press.
Penrose, R. (1994). *Shadows of the Mind: A Search for the Missing Science of Consciousness.* Oxford: Oxford University Press.
Perrine, L. (1971). Four Forms of Metaphor. *College English* 33: 125-138.
Perron, P., and Danesi, M. (1993). *A. J. Greimas and Narrative Cognition.* Toronto: Toronto Semiotic Circle.
Pfeiffer, J. E. (1982). *The Creative Explosion: An Inquiry into the Origins of Art and Religion.* Ithaca: Cornell University Press.
Piaget J. (1969). *The Child's Conception of the World.* Totowa, N.J.: Littlefield, Adams and Co.
Piaget, J., and Inhelder, J. (1969). *The Psychology of the Child.* New York: Basic Books.
Piattelli-Palmarini, M. (1980) (ed.). *Language and Learning: The Debate between Jean Piaget and Noam Chomsky.* Cambridge, Mass.: Harvard University Press.
Piattelli-Palmarini, M. (1994). *Inevitable Illusions: How Mistakes of Reason Rule Our Minds.* New York: John Wiley.
Pinker, S. (1994). *The Language Instinct: How the Mind Creates Language.* New York: William Morrow.
Pinker, S. (1997). *How the Mind Works.* New York: Norton.
Polanyi, L. (1989). *Telling the American Story: A Structural and Cultural Analysis of Conversational Storytelling.* Cambridge, Mass.: MIT Press.
Pollio, H., Barlow, J., Fine, H., and Pollio, M. (1977). *The Poetics of Growth: Figurative Language in Psychology, Psychotherapy, and Education.* Hillsdale, N.J.: Lawrence Erlbaum Associates.
Pollio, H., and Burns, B. (1977). The Anomaly of Anomaly. *Journal of Psycholinguistic Research* 6: 247-260.
Pollio, H., and Smith, M. (1979). Sense and Nonsense in Thinking about Anomaly and Metaphor. *Bulletin of the Psychonomic Society* 13: 323-326.
Popper, K. (1972). *Objective Knowledge: An Evolutionary Approach.* Oxford: Clarendon.
Popper, K. (1976). *The Unending Quest.* Glasgow: Harper Collins.
Popper, K., and Eccles, J. C. (1977). *The Self and the Brain.* Berlin: Springer.
Preble, D., and Preble, S. (1989). *Artforms.* New York: Harper Collins.
Premack, A. J. (1976). *Why Chimps Can Read.* New York: Harper and Row.
Premack, D., and Premack, A. J. (1983). *The Mind of an Ape.* New York: Norton.

Preziosi, D. (1979). *The Semiotics of the Built Environment: An Introduction to Architectonic Analysis*. Bloomington: Indiana University Press.
Prince, G. (1982). *Narratology: The Form and Functioning of Narrative*. Berlin: Mouton.
Proncko, N. H. (1946). Language and Psycholinguistics. *Psychological Bulletin* 43: 189-239.
Propp, V. J. (1928). *Morphology of the Folktale*. Austin: University of Texas Press.

Q

Quain, K. (1992) (ed.). *The Elvis Reader*. New York: St. Martin's Press.
Quinn, N. (1991). The Cultural Basis of Metaphor. In: J. W. Fernandez (ed.), *Beyond Metaphor: The Theory of Tropes in Anthropology*, 56–93. Stanford: Stanford University Press.

R

Radcliffe-Brown, A. R. (1922). *The Andaman Islanders*. Cambridge: Cambridge University Press.
Raffler-Engel, W. von, Wind, J., and Jonker, A. (1989) (eds.). *Studies in Language Origins*. Amsterdam: John Benjamins.
Randazzo, S. (1995). *The Myth Makers*. Chicago: Probus.
Rathje, W., and Murphy, C. (1992). *Rubbish! The Archeology of Garbage*. New York: Harper Collins.
Reed, D. (1994). *Figures of Thought: Mathematics and Mathematical Texts*. London: Routledge.
Renfrew, C. (1988). *Archaeology and Language: The Puzzle of Indo-European Origins*. Cambridge: Cambridge University Press.
Révész, G. (1956). *The Origins and Prehistory of Language*. New York: Philosophical Library.
Reynolds, R. (1992). *Super Heroes: A Modern Mythology*. Jackson: University of Mississippi Press.
Reynolds, S., and Press, J. (1995). *The Sex Revolts: Gender, Rebellion, and Rock 'n' Roll*. Cambridge, Mass.: Harvard University Press.
Richards, B. (1994). *Disciplines of Delight: The Psychoanalysis of Popular Culture*. London: Free Association Books.
Richards, I. A. (1936). *The Philosophy of Rhetoric*. Oxford: Oxford University Press.
Ricoeur, P. (1983). *Time and Narrative*. Chicago: University of Chicago Press.
Ries, J. (1994). *The Origins of Religions*. Grand Rapids: Eerdmans.
Riggins, S. H. (1994) (ed.). *The Socialness of Things: Essays on the Socio-Semiotics of Objects*. Berlin: Mouton de Gruyter.
Robinson, A. (1995). *The Story of Writing*. London: Thames and Hudson.
Robinson, A. H., and Petchenik, B. B. (1976). *The Nature of Maps*. Chicago: University of Chicago Press.
Robinson, P. (1996). *Deceit, Delusion and Detection*. Thousand Oaks, Calif.: Sage.
Rollin, L. (1992). *Cradle and All: A Cultural and Psychoanalytic Study of Nursery Rhymes*. Jackson: University of Mississippi Press.
Roloff, L. S. (1973). *The Perception and Evocation of Literature*. Glenview, Ill.: Scott, Foresman, and Co.
Romaine, S. (1984).*The Language of Children and Adolescence*. Oxford: Blackwell.
Rosch, E. (1973). On the Internal Structure of Perceptual and Semantic Categories. In: T. E. Moore (ed.), *Cognitive Development and Acquisition of Language*, 111-144. New York: Academic.
Rosch, E. (1975). Cognitive Reference Points. *Cognitive Psychology* 7: 532-547.
Rosch, E. (1981). Prototype Classification and Logical Classification: The Two Systems. In: E. Scholnick (ed.), *New Trends in Cognitive Representation: Chal-*

lenges to Piaget's Theory, 73-86. Hillsdale, N.J.: Lawrence Erlbaum Associates.

Rosch, E., and Mervis, C. (1975). Family Resemblances. *Cognitive Psychology* 7: 573-605.

Rousseau, J. J. (1966). *Essay on the Origin of Language*, trans. by J. H. Moran and A. Gode. Chicago: University of Chicago Press.

Royce, A. P. (1977). *The Anthropology of Dance*. Bloomington: Indiana University Press.

Rubinstein, R. P. (1995). *Dress Codes: Meanings and Messages in American Culture*. Boulder: Westview.

Ruesch, J. (1972). *Semiotic Approaches to Human Relations*. The Hague: Mouton.

Ruhlen, M. (1994). *On the Origin of Languages: Studies in Linguistic Taxonomy*. Stanford: Stanford University Press.

Rumbaugh, D. M. (1977). *Language Learning by Chimpanzee: The Lana Project*. New York: Academic.

Rumelhart, D. E., and McClelland, J. (1986) (eds.). *Parallel Distributed Processing*, Vols. 1-2. Cambridge, Mass.: MIT Press.

Russell, B., and Whitehead, A. N. (1913). *Principia Mathematica*. Cambridge: Cambridge University Press.

Ruthroff, H. (1997). *Semantics and the Body: Meaning from Frege to the Postmodern*. Toronto: University of Toronto Press.

Ruwet, N. (1991). *Syntax and Human Experience*. Chicago: University of Chicago Press.

S

Sagan, C., and Druyan, A. (1992). *Shadows of Forgotten Ancestors: A Search for Who We Are*. New York: Random House.

Saint-Martin, F. (1990). *Semiotics of Visual Language*. Bloomington: Indiana University Press.

Sapir, E. (1921). *Language*. New York: Harcourt, Brace, and World.

Saporta, S. (1961) (ed.). *Psycholinguistics: A Book of Readings*. New York: Holt, Rinehart, and Winston.

Sappan, R. (1987). *The Rhetorical-Logical Classification of Semantic Changes*. Braunton: Merlin Books.

Sassienie, P. (1994). *The Comic Book*. Toronto: Smithbooks.

Saussure, F. de (1916). *Cours de linguistique générale*. Paris: Payot.

Savage-Rumbaugh, E. S. (1986). *Ape Language: From Conditioned Response to Symbol*. New York: Columbia University Press.

Savage-Rumbaugh, E. S., Rumbaugh, D. M., and Boysen, S. L. (1978). Symbolic Communication between Two Chimpanzees. *Science* 201: 641-644.

Schank, R. C. (1984). *The Cognitive Computer*. Reading, Mass.: Addison-Wesley.

Schank, R. C. (1991). *The Connoisseur's Guide to the Mind*. New York: Summit.

Schleidt, M. (1980). Personal Odor and Nonverbal Communication. *Ethology and Sociobiology* 1: 225-231.

Schmandt-Besserat, D. (1978). The Earliest Precursor of Writing. *Scientific American* 238: 50-59.

Schmandt-Besserat, D. (1992). *Before Writing*. Austin: University of Texas Press.

Schogt, H. (1988). *Linguistics, Literary Analysis, and Literary Translation*. Toronto: University of Toronto Press.

Scholes, R. (1982). *Semiotics and Interpretation*. New Haven: Yale University Press.

Schrag, R. (1990). *Taming the Wild Tube*. Chapel Hill: University of North Carolina Press.

Schrift, A. D. (1990). *Nietzsche and the Question of Interpretation*. London: Routledge.

Schwartz, R. G., Leonard, L. B., Wilcox, M. J., and Folger, M. K. (1980). Again and Again: Reduplication in Child Phonology. *Journal of Child Language* 7: 75-87.

Scollon, R., and Wong Scollon, S. (1995). *Intercultural Communication: A Discourse Approach*. London: Blackwell.

Scott, W. T. (1991). Law, Semiotics, Coding, and Communication. In: T. A. Sebeok and J. Umiker-Sebeok (eds.), *Recent Developments in Theory and History*, 493-513. Berlin: Mouton.

Scovel, T. (1988). *A Time to Speak: A Psycholinguistic Inquiry into the Critical Period for Human Speech*. Rowley, Mass.: Newbury House.

Sculatti, G. (1982). *Cool: A Hipster's Directory*. London: Vermilion.

Searle, J. R. (1969). *Speech Acts: An Essay in the Philosophy of Language*. Cambridge: Cambridge University Press.

Searle, J. R. (1984). *Minds, Brain, and Science*. Cambridge, Mass.: Harvard University Press.

Searle, J. R. (1992). *The Rediscovery of the Mind*. Cambridge, Mass.: MIT Press.

Sebeok, T. A. (1963). Communication in Animals and Men. *Language* 39: 448-466.

Sebeok, T. A. (1976). *Contributions to the Doctrine of Signs*. Lanham: University Press of America.

Sebeok, T. A. (1979). *The Sign and Its Masters*. Austin: University of Texas Press.

Sebeok, T. A. (1981). *The Play of Musement*. Bloomington: Indiana University Press.

Sebeok, T. A. (1985). Pandora's Box: How and Why to Communicate 10,000 Years into the Future. In: M. Blonsky (ed.), *On Signs*, 448-466. Baltimore: Johns Hopkins University Press.

Sebeok, T. A. (1986). *I Think I Am a Verb: More Contributions to the Doctrine of Signs*. New York: Plenum.

Sebeok, T. A. (1987). In What Sense Is Language a "Primary Modeling System?" In: H. Broms and R. Kaufmann (eds.), *Proceedings of the 25th Symposium of the Tartu–Moscow School of Semiotics*, 67–80. Helsinki: Arator.

Sebeok, T. A. (1990). *Essays in Zoosemiotics*. Toronto: Toronto Semiotic Circle.

Sebeok, T. A. (1991). *A Sign Is Just a Sign*. Bloomington: Indiana University Press.

Sebeok, T. A. (1994). *Signs: An Introduction to Semiotics*. Toronto: University of Toronto Press.

Sebeok, T. A., and Umiker-Sebeok, J. (1994) (eds.). *Advances in Visual Semiotics*. Berlin: Mouton de Gruyter.

Seiter, E. (1995). *Sold Separately: Parents and Children in Consumer Culture*. New Brunswick, N.J.: Rutgers University Press.

Shahar, S. (1992). *Childhood in the Middle Ages*. London: Routledge.

Shannon, C. E. (1948). A Mathematical Theory of Communication. *Bell Systems Technical Journal* 27: 379-423.

Shannon, C. E., and Weaver, W. (1949). *Mathematical Theory of Communication*. Chicago: University of Illinois Press.

Sheehy, G. (1995). *New Passages*. New York: Ballantine.

Shevoroshkin, V. (1989) (ed.). *Reconstructing Languages and Cultures*. Bochum: Brockmeyer.

Shibbles, W. (1971). *Metaphor: An Annotated Bibliography and History*. Whitewater, Wisc.: The Language Press.

Shields, K. (1979). Indo-European Basic Colour Terms. *Canadian Journal of Linguistics* 24: 142-146.

Shields, K. (1994). The Role of Deictic Particles in the Personal Pronoun. *Word* 45: 307-315.

Shuker, R. (1994). *Understanding Popular Culture*. London: Routledge.

Simon, S. (1976). *The Optical Illusion Book*. New York: Morrow.

Simone, R. (1995) (ed.). *Iconicity in Language*. Amsterdam: John Benjamins.

Sinclair, J. (1987). *Images Incorporated: Advertising as Industry and Ideology*. Beckenham: Croom Helm.

Singer, B. (1986). *Advertising and Society*. Toronto: Addison-Wesley.

Singer, M. (1991). *Semiotics of Cities, Selves, and Cultures: Explorations in Semiotic Anthropology*. Berlin: Mouton de Gruyter.

Singleton, J. L., Morford, J. P., and Goldin-Meadow, S. (1993). Once Is Not Enough: Standards of Well-formedness in Manual Communication Created Over Three Different Timespans. *Language* 69: 683-715.

Skinner, B. F. (1938). *The Behavior of Organisms*. New York: Appleton-Century-Crofts.

Skinner, B. F. (1957). *Verbal Behavior*. New York: Appleton-Century-Crofts.

Skomale, S. N., and Polomé, E. C. (1987) (eds.). *Proto-Indo-European: The Archaeology of a Linguistic Problem: Studies in Honor of Marija Gimbutas*. Washington, D.C.: The Institute for the Study of Man.

Skousen, R. (1989). *Analogical Modeling of Language*. Dordrecht: Kluwer.

Small, M. F. (1995). *What's Love Got to Do with It?* New York: Anchor.

Smith, C. G. (1985). *Ancestral Voices: Language and the Evolution of Human Consciousness*. Englewood Cliffs, N.J.: Prentice-Hall.

Smith, J. W. (1977). *The Behavior of Communicating: An Ethological Approach*. Cambridge, Mass.: Harvard University Press.

Solomon, J. (1988). *The Signs of Our Time*. Los Angeles: J. P. Tarcher.

Sontag, S. (1978). *Illness as Metaphor*. New York: Farrar, Straus and Giroux.

Sontag, S. (1989). *AIDS and Its Metaphors*. New York: Farrar, Straus and Giroux.

Sparshott, F. (1995). *A Measured Pace: Toward a Philosophical Understanding of the Arts of Dance*. Toronto: University of Toronto Press.

Sperber, D. (1996). *Explaining Culture: A Naturalistic Approach*. Oxford: Blackwell.

Sperber, D., and Wilson, D. (1986). *Relevance, Communication, and Cognition*. Cambridge, Mass.: Harvard University Press.

Sperry, R. W. (1973). Lateral Specialization of Cerebral Function in the Surgically Separated Hemispheres. In: F. J. McGuigan and R. A. Schooner (eds.), *The Psychophysiology of Thinking*, 209-229. New York: Academic.

Sperry, R. W., Gazzaniga, M. S., and Bogen, J. E. (1969). Interhemispheric Relationships: The Neocortical Commissures; Syndromes of Hemispheric Disconnections. In: P. J. Vinken and G. W. Bryn (eds.), *Handbook of Clinical Neurology*, 273-289. Amsterdam: North Holland.

Spigel, L., and Mann, D. (1992) (eds.). *Private Screenings: Television and the Female Consumer*. Minneapolis: University of Minnesota Press.

Staehlin, W. (1914). Zür Psychologie und Statistike der Metapherm. *Archiv für Gesamte Psychologie* 31: 299-425.

Stahl, S. (1989). *Literary Folkloristics and the Personal Narrative*. Bloomington: Indiana University Press.

Stam, J. (1976). *Inquiries in the Origin of Language: The Fate of a Question*. New York: Harper and Row.

Stamp Dawkins, M. (1993). *The Search for Animal Consciousness*. Oxford: Freeman.

Stark, S. (1997). *Glued to the Set*. New York: Free Press.

States, B. O. (1988). *The Rhetoric of Dreams*. Ithaca: Cornell University Press.

Steele, V. (1995). *Fetish: Fashion, Sex, and Power*. Oxford: Oxford University Press.

Stein, M., and Hollwitz, J. (1994) (eds.). *Psyche and Sports*. Wilmette, Ill.: Chiron Publications.

Stern, J., and Stern, M. (1992). *Encyclopedia of Pop Culture*. New York: Harper.

Sternberg, R. J. (1985). *Beyond IQ: A Triarchic Theory of Human Intelligence*. Cambridge: Cambridge University Press.

Sternberg, R. J. (1990). *Metaphors of Mind: Conceptions of the Nature of Intelligence*. Cambridge: Cambridge University Press.

Sutton-Smith, B. (1986). *Toys as Culture*. New York: Gardner.

Swadesh, M. (1971). *The Origins and Diversification of Language*. Chicago: Aldine-Atherton.
Swain, J. P. (1996). *Musical Languages*. New York: Norton.
Sweetser, E. (1990). *From Etymology to Pragmatics: Metaphorical and Cultural Aspects of Semantic Structure*. Cambridge: Cambridge University Press.
Synnott, A. (1993). *The Body Social: Symbolism, Self and Society.* London: Routledge.

T

Tannen, D. (1989). *Talking Voices*. Cambridge: Cambridge University Press.
Tannen, D. (1990). *You Just Don't Understand: Women and Men in Conversation.* New York: Ballantine.
Tannen, D. (1994). *Gender and Discourse*. Oxford: Oxford University Press.
Taylor, I. (1990). *Psycholinguistics: Learning and Using Language*. Englewood Cliffs: Prentice-Hall.
Taylor, J. R. (1995). *Linguistic Categorization: Prototypes in Linguistic Theory*. Oxford: Oxford University Press.
Terrace, H. S. (1979). *Nim*. New York: Knopf.
Thom, R. (1975). *Structural Stability and Morphogenesis: An Outline of a General Theory of Models*. Reading: W. A. Benjamin.
Thomas, O. (1969). *Metaphors and Related Subjects*. New York: Random House.
Thompson, E. (1995). *Colour Vision: A Study in Cognitive Science and Philosophy of Science*. London: Routledge.
Thorndike, E. L. (1898). *Animal Intelligence*. New York: Psychological Monographs.
Thorpe, W. H. (1961). *Bird-song*. Cambridge: Cambridge University Press.
Tinbergen, N. (1963). On the Aims and Methods of Ethology. *Zeitschrift für Tierpsychologie* 20: 410-433.
Todorov. T. (1977 [1982]). *Theories of the Symbol*. Ithaca: Cornell University Press.
Tolaas, J. (1991). Notes on the Origin of Some Spatialization Metaphors. *Metaphor and Symbolic Activity* 6: 203-218.
Toolan, M. J. (1988). *Narrative: A Critical Linguistic Introduction*. London: Routledge.
Trevarthen, C. (1990) (ed.). *Brain Circuits and Functions of the Mind: Essays in Honor of Roger W. Sperry*. Cambridge: Cambridge University Press.
Trubetzkoy, N. (1968). *Introduction to the Principles of Phonological Description*, trans. by L. A. Muny. The Hague: Martinus Nijhoff.
Tufte, E. R. (1997). *Visual Explanations: Images and Quantities, Evidence and Narrative*. Cheshire: Graphics Press.
Tulving, E. (1972). Episodic and Semantic Memory. In: E. Tulving and W. Donaldson (eds.), *Organization of Memory*, 23-46. New York: Academic.
Turing, A. (1936). On Computable Numbers with an Application to the Entscheidungs Problem. *Proceedings of the London Mathematical Society* 41: 230-265.
Turing, A. (1963). Computing Machinery and Intelligence. In: E. A. Feigenbaum and J. Feldman (eds.), *Computers and Thought*, 123-134. New York: McGraw-Hill.
Turnbull, D. (1989). *Maps Are Territories*. Chicago: University of Chicago Press.
Turner, M. (1991). *Reading Minds: The Study of English in the Age of Cognitive Science*. Princeton: Princeton University Press.
Tylor, E. B. (1865). *Researches into the Early History of Mankind and the Development of Civilization*. London: John Murray.
Tylor, E. B. (1871). *Primitive Culture*. London: Murray.

U

Uexküll, J. von (1909). *Umwelt und Innenwelt der Tierre*. Berlin: Springer.
Umiker-Sebeok, J. (1987) (ed.). *Marketing Signs: New Directions in the Study of Signs for Sale*. Berlin: Mouton.
Umiker-Sebeok, J., Cossette, C., and Bachand, D. (1988). Selected Bibliography on the Semiotics of Marketing. *Semiotic Inquiry* 8: 415-423.
Ungerer, F., and Schmid, H.-J. (1996). *An Introduction to Cognitive Linguistics*. Harlow: Longman.

V

Valentine, T., Brennen, T., and Brédart, S. (1996). *The Cognitive Psychology of Proper Names*. London: Routledge.
Vardar, N. (1992). *Global Advertising: Rhyme or Reason?* London: Chapman.
Varela, F. J., Thompson, E., and Rosch, E. (1991). *The Embodied Mind: Cognitive Science and Human Experience*. Cambridge, Mass.: MIT Press.
Vartanian, A. (1960). *La Mettrie's "L'homme machine": A Study in the Origins of an Idea*. Princeton: Princeton University Press.
Verene, D. P. (1981). *Vico's Science of the Imagination*. Ithaca: Cornell University Press.
Verene, D. P. (1991). *The New Art of Autobiography: An Essay on the Life of Giambattista Vico Written by Himself.* Oxford: Oxford University Press.
Vestergaard, T., and Schrøder, K. (1985). *The Language of Advertising*. London: Blackwell.
Veyne, P. (1988). *Did the Greeks Believe in Their Myths?* Chicago: University of Chicago Press.
Viberg, A. (1983). The Verbs of Perception: A Typological Study. *Linguistics* 21: 123-162.
Vihman, M. M. (1996). *Phonological Development: The Origins of Language in the Child*. London: Blackwell.
Visser, M. (1991). *The Rituals of Dinner*. New York: Harper Collins.
Visser, M. (1994). *The Way We Are*. Toronto: Harper Collins.
Vroon, P., and Amerongen, A. van (1996). *Smell: The Secret Seducer*. New York: Farrar, Straus and Giroux.
Vygotsky, L. S. (1962). *Thought and Language*. Cambridge, Mass.: MIT Press.
Vygotsky, L. S. (1978). *Mind in Society*. Cambridge, Mass.: Harvard University Press.
Vygotsky, L. S. (1984). *Vygotsky's Collected Works,* R. Rieber and A. Carton (eds., and trans.). Cambridge, Mass.: Harvard University Press.

W

Walker, C. B. F. (1987). *Cuneiform*. Berkeley: University of California Press.
Watson, J. B. (1925). *Behaviorism*. New York: Norton.
Watson, J. B. (1929). *Psychology from the Standpoint of a Behaviorist*. Philadelphia: Lippincott.
Watson, L. (1990). *The Nature of Things*. London: Houghton and Stoughton.
Way, E. C. (1991). *Knowledge Representation and Metaphor*. Dordrecht: Kluwer.
Weinstein, E. A. (1964). Affections of speech with lesions of the non-dominant hemisphere. *Research Publications of the Association for Research on Nervous and Mental Disorders* 42, 220-225.
Weissenborn, J., and Klein, W. (1982) (eds.). *Here and There: Cross-Linguistic Studies on Deixis and Demonstration*. Amsterdam: John Benjamins.
Wells, G. (1986). *The Meaning Makers: Children Learning Language and Using Language to Learn*. Portsmouth: Heinemann.

Werner, H., and Kaplan, B. (1963). *Symbol Formation: An Organismic-Developmental Approach to the Psychology of Language and the Expression of Thought*. New York: John Wiley.

Wernick, A. (1991). *Promotional Culture: Advertising, Ideology, and Symbolic Expression*. London: Gage.

Wernicke, C. (1874). *Der aphasische Symptomkomplex*. Breslau: Cohn and Weigart.

Wescott, R. (1980). *Sound and Sense*. Lake Bluff, Ill.: Jupiter Press.

Wescott, R. W. (1974) (ed.). *Language Origins*. Silver Spring, Md.: Linstok Press.

Wescott, R. W. (1978). Visualizing Vision. In: B. Rhandawa and W. Coffman (eds.), *Visual Learning, Thinking, and Communication*, 21-37. New York: Academic.

Westphal, J. (1987). *Color: Some Philosophical Problems from Wittgenstein*. Oxford: Basil Blackwell.

Wheelwright, P. (1954). *The Burning Fountain: A Study in the Language of Symbolism*. Bloomington: Indiana University Press.

Whiteley, S. (1992). *The Space between the Notes: Rock and the Counter-Culture*. London: Routledge.

Whiteside, R. L. (1975). *Face Language*. New York: Pocket.

Whorf, B. L. (1956). *Language, Thought, and Reality*, J. B. Carroll (ed.). Cambridge, Mass.: MIT Press.

Wiener, N. (1949). *Cybernetics, or Control and Communication in the Animal and the Machine*. Cambridge, Mass.: MIT Press.

Wierzbicka, A. (1980). *Lingua Mentalis: The Semantics of Natural Language*. New York: Academic.

Wierzbicka, A. (1990). The Meaning of Color Terms: Semantics, Culture, Cognition. *Cognitive Linguistics* 1: 99–150.

Williamson, J. (1985). *Decoding Advertisements: Ideology and Meaning in Advertising*. London: Marion Boyars.

Willis, R. (1990) (ed.). *Signifying Animals: Human Meaning in the Natural World*. London: Routledge.

Wilson, E. O. (1975). *Sociobiology: The New Synthesis*. Cambridge, Mass.: Harvard University Press.

Wilson, E. O. (1979). *On Human Nature*. New York: Bantam.

Wilson, E. O. (1984). *Biophilia*. Cambridge, Mass.: Harvard University Press.

Wilson, E. O., and Harris, M. (1981). Heredity Versus Culture: A Debate. In: J. Guillemin (ed.), *Anthropological Realities: Reading in the Science of Culture*, 459-467. New Brunswick, N.J.: Transaction Books.

Wilson, F. R. (1998). *The Hand: How Its Use Shapes the Brain, Language, and Human Culture*. New York: Pantheon.

Winner, E. (1982). *Invented Worlds: The Psychology of the Arts*. Cambridge, Mass.: Harvard University Press.

Winner, E. (1988). *The Point of Words: Children's Understanding of Metaphor and Irony*. Cambridge, Mass.: Harvard University Press.

Winograd, T. (1991). Thinking Machines: Can There Be? Are We? In: J. J. Sheehan and M. Sosna (eds.), *The Boundaries of Humanity*, 198-223. Berkeley: University of California Press.

Wittgenstein, L. (1921). *Tractatus Logico–Philosophicus*. London: Routledge and Kegan Paul.

Wittgenstein, L. (1953). *Philosophical Investigations*. New York: Macmillan.

Wolfe, T. (1981). *From Bauhaus to Our House*. New York: Farrar, Strauss and Giroux.

Wundt, W. (1901). *Sprachgeschichte und Sprachpsychologie*. Leipzig: Eugelmann.

Wundt, W. (1973). *The Language of Gestures*. The Hague: Mouton.

Y

Yerkes, R. (1916). *The Mental Life of Monkeys and Apes*. New Haven: Yale University Press.

Yol Jung, H. (1993). *Rethinking Political Theory: Essays in Phenomenology and the Study of Politics*. Athens: Ohio University Press.

Index